DR. RON CH

C000055654

Chasing
JESUS

**FAITH
BUILDERS
WORLD**

Changing the world through Spirit filled books

Chasing Jesus
By Dr. Ron Charles
Copyright © 2013 Faith Builders World
All rights reserved under International Copyright Law.

Published by: Faith Builders World Publishers
PO Box 40,
Knutsford,
Cheshire
WA16 9EB
England
www.faithbuildersworld.com

Manuscript prepared by: Todd Hafer
Design: Lookout Design, Inc.

Unless otherwise noted, Scripture quotations are taken from the King James Version
Author's note: All italicized and all parenthetical material within Scripture quotations are mine.

ISBN hardback book: 978-0-948985-15-7
ISBN softcover book: 978-0-948985-17-1
ISBN epublish book: 978-0-948985-16-4

12 13 14 15 16 17 18   10 9 8 7 6 5 4 3 2 1

AUTHOR'S NOTE:

THIS BOOK IS A WORK OF NON-FICTION. While some names and certain minor details have been changed to protect the privacy of my interview subjects, the events and situations are true.

A few words are in order on the subject of direct quotations from my interviews and readings of various documents. Over the course of 43-plus years of research, I sometimes found myself dealing with time constraints and restrictions on using recording devices or making copies of documents, rare books, and ancient manuscripts. At other times, I found myself simultaneously note-taking and translating. Occasionally, when encountering an unfamiliar language, I relied on the translation abilities of various scholars, museum guides, and others who helped me in my search. In all cases, I have strived to render direct quotations as accurately as possible, reverting to paraphrase whenever doubt arose about the wording of quoted material. That said, many of this book's informal conversations, especially those from early in my research, have been reconstructed from memory, to the best of my ability.

*Many have taken in hand to set forth
in order a declaration of those things
which are most surely believed among us...*

*It seemed good to me also to write
unto you in order that you might know
the certainty of those things...*

TABLE OF CONTENTS:

AUTHOR'S PREFACE

WHEN I FIRST BEGAN to seriously study the life of the historical Jesus, I made a big mistake. I approached Jesus' life using the commonly accepted chronology of events.

This chronology, I reasoned, would take me step by well-ordered step through my search: Jesus was born of the virgin Mary, in winter time, between 4 BC and 2 BC. His birth was witnessed by shepherds and wisemen, who worshipped him at the manger site.

Soon thereafter, Joseph and Mary fled with Jesus to Egypt, because a king named Herod sought to kill him. The family stayed in Egypt for a year or two before returning to Nazareth. When he reached age 12, Jesus went to the Temple in Jerusalem with his parents and astounded the religious officials with his knowledge. At age 30, Jesus was baptized by John the Baptist in the Jordan River. Then he immediately went into the wilderness to be tempted.

Upon his return from the wilderness, Jesus called his first four disciples (Andrew, Peter, James, and John) and began his ministry. Over the course of this ministry, he faced many confrontations with Jewish religious leaders. He also performed many miracles and taught multitudes of people.

His ministry lasted just over three years. On the Sunday before his crucifixion, he was triumphantly welcomed into Jerusalem. The following Thursday, he shared the Last Supper with his disciples. That night he was arrested in a garden where he was praying. He was convicted at a midnight trial. Early on Friday morning, he was condemned to be crucified. By Friday afternoon, he was dead and buried. The following Sunday, he rose from the dead. Fifty days later, he ascended to heaven.

That was the story. One life, presented neatly and orderly.

However, as I plunged deeper into the Gospels, I began to see inconsistencies and chronology problems with the tidy package so many of us have accepted without question or reflection.

The inconsistencies became so numerous and so discomfiting that I was forced to re-evaluate everything. What was historical fact? What was presumption, based on tradition and dogma?

Eventually, satisfied that what I had learned in the biblical Gospels (and was continuing to learn) was factual, I turned my attention to the generally accepted *chronology* of Jesus' life. Was this the source of the inconsistencies? As I researched, I found that the commonly accepted chronology of Jesus' life was grounded in the premise that the Gospels (for the most part) recorded the same events. This premise is sometimes called "The Harmony of the Gospels."

In other words, each important event in Jesus' life was recorded in at least one of the four Gospels: Matthew, Mark, Luke, and John. If two or more Gospels present a similar event, it is assumed that those Gospels cover the *same* event, and any difference in the accounts is the result of the author's interpretation or intended audience.

Today it would be irrational to believe that during a man's lifetime he encountered only one woman with cervical cancer, only one man with a sick daughter, or one military officer with a sick servant. Would we also believe that this man's home region would suffer only one bad storm over the course of three long years? Yet, we are led to believe such things about the life and ministry of Jesus.

Eventually, I became so frustrated with the inconsistencies and the illogical presumptions that I decided to forget tradition, forget everything I assumed to be true. I would start fresh, with no preconceptions or assumptions.

I studied the Gospels in detail. Book by book, chapter by chapter, verse by verse, word by word, and even letter by letter. I realized that each sentence, each word, and each punctuation mark placed in the Gospels was essential. Nothing was incidental or unimportant.

After I finished studying each Gospel, I compared each narrative to the other three. I concluded that, although some of the events in Jesus' ministry were recorded in multiple Gospels, many events were recorded in one Gospel *only*.

After completing this comparative study, I began a comparative study of historical documentation, particularly Roman history and the writings of Christians and non-Christians during the first 10 centuries after Jesus' crucifixion.

I read hundreds of documents about Jesus and reviewed countless chronologies and accounts of his life and ministry. Some were complimentary, proclaiming that Jesus was a great teacher and prophet. Some exalted him to the level of God incarnate. Other accounts were blasphemous, asserting that Jesus was a charlatan, magician, or mystical cult leader.

Some documents confirmed the Gospel accounts of Jesus rising from the dead, ascending to the Father, and serving as humanity's Savior. Other reports acknowledged that Jesus died, but they claimed that he didn't rise from the dead. Instead, his disciples took his body from the tomb and "faked" the resurrection. Other documents claimed that he did not die. But, he survived the crucifixion, recovered from his ordeal, got married (perhaps to Mary Magdalene), had children, and eventually died an old man.

Hundreds of chronologies suggest that Jesus was born anywhere from 25 BC to AD 25, that his mother was anywhere from 12 to 35 years old when he was born, and that he began his ministry anywhere from age 24 to age 40. Some chronologies say his ministry lasted two years. Others say 12 years. He was crucified sometime between AD 2 and AD 25, depending on the source. Some writers claim he was crucified at age 25. Others say 40.

Throughout my years of research, I have maintained that the Gospel records of Jesus are the unassailable truth. Given that the Gospels do not give exact dates (and are sometimes vague about time frames), I chose to disregard all *chronological assumptions* about Jesus' life. Then I resolved to develop a logical chronological timetable. This timetable had to fit within the parameters of Roman history and culture. I realized that my chronology might contradict currently accepted beliefs about Jesus' life. Nonetheless, I felt obliged to find and report the truth.

I don't want to suggest that the hundreds of chronologies (many of them centuries old) are wrong, while mine is right. I am still learning, and as I continue my research, I know I will have to modify my chronology so that it fits more accurately into history's timetable.

I have spent the past 43 years researching and documenting Jesus' life and ministry. This quest will continue until I die. I know I will only be able to explore a small percentage of Jesus' life but I will do as much as I can with the time I have.

In the pages that follow, I offer you a chronicle of Jesus' life, based on both the Gospel records and a variety of extra-biblical sources that confirm the truth of the Gospels.

I will present the information just as I found it. I have not molded facts to make them fit religious tradition or dogma. I found documents that stand in marked contrast to the traditional view of Jesus. This book is not an attempt to change anybody's perception of Jesus. Nor is it an attack on tradition. It's merely the story of an honest search.

I have chosen to use the King James Version of the Bible when quoting Scripture. I don't believe the KJV is more accurate than other versions. I grew up using the King James Version so I am familiar with it and I like its poetic Elizabethan English language. Feel free to look up Scriptures in your favorite version as you read.

ACKNOWLEDGMENTS

I thank Michelle Thomas, Kim Stuckey, Laura Waris, and Dr. Al Pleysier for their proofreading and their suggestions. Without their help, this book would still not be complete.

A very special thanks to my wife, Paula, who spent many weeks and countless nights alone over our past 43 years of marriage—while I traveled the world, researching and collecting information. Moreover, Paula spent seemingly endless hours compiling and writing much of what you will read. She is truly remarkable for putting up with so much so that this book could be published.

INTRODUCTION

❧

A Tale of Two Creeds

TWO GREAT CREEDS, the *Apostles' Creed,* and the *Nicene Creed,* have historically defined and identified the Christian faith, each serving to help Christians stay the course established by Jesus.

The *Apostles' Creed* was created in the second century, probably with the help of Ignatius of Antioch (AD 35 to AD 108), to give Christians clear and consistent answers for those who questioned them about their faith.

Most church-goers recognize the first part of the creed:

THE APOSTLES' CREED:

I believe in God the Father Almighty,
Creator of heaven and earth;
and in Jesus Christ, his only Son, our Lord;
who was conceived by the Holy Spirit,
born of the virgin Mary,
suffered under Pontius Pilate,
was crucified, died, and was buried.
He descended into hell.
On the third day he rose again from the dead,
and ascended into heaven.

It's interesting that this creed moves directly from Jesus' birth to his death. It is silent about his *life*. It could be argued, then, that the *Apostles' Creed* suggests that nothing Jesus said or did while ministering on earth is essential to Christian faith.

The Nicene Creed (adopted in 325 AD) is named after the city of Nicaea. Under the Roman Emperor Constantine's supervision, Christian bishops officially defined the doctrine of Jesus' divinity.

As with the *Apostles' Creed*, it doesn't focus on Jesus' life and teachings.

Like its predecessor, the first half of this creed is the best-known:

THE NICENE CREED:

We believe in one God, the Father, the Almighty,
maker of heaven and earth, of all that is, seen and unseen.
We believe in one Lord, Jesus Christ,
the only Son of God, eternally begotten of the Father,
God from God, Light from Light, true God from true God,
begotten, not made, one in being with the Father;
through him all things were made.
For us and for our salvation he came down from heaven.
By the power of the Holy Spirit he took flesh from
the virgin Mary and became a man.
For our sakes he was crucified under Pontius Pilate;
he suffered, died, and was buried.
On the third day he rose again according to the scriptures.
He ascended into heaven.

Today's Christians disagree about many things, but most agree that the *Apostles' Creed* and the *Nicene Creed* are the foundations of modern Christian doctrine. Yet, according to these creeds, what Jesus did *before* he died is relatively unimportant in living a life pleasing to God. Only Jesus' miraculous birth and sacrificial death seem to matter.

However, the author of John's Gospel wrote, *"And there are also many other things which Jesus did, the which, if they should be written every one, I suppose that even the world itself could not contain the books that should be written. Amen"* (John 21:25). Why would this writer refer to these events in Jesus' life if his birth and death were the only significant events? Why would he say that the deeds and sayings of Jesus during his time on earth could probably not be contained in all the books that existed in the world at the time, (more than a half-million volumes), if the most significant events could comfortably fit into one 20 or 30 page Gospel narrative?

Has the writer of John exaggerated or, have the writers of the classic creeds grossly underestimated the importance of events in Jesus' life?

I believe this Gospel writer is correct. Jesus' words and deeds are of utmost importance to the Christian faith, both then and now. John's Gospel suggests that hundreds of documents could have been written during the first and second centuries after Jesus' death, attesting to the value early Christians placed on his words and deeds.

Imagine someone saying, "All that matters to today's American citizens is that their ancestors declared independence from Britain, and by the 21st century, America was the mightiest nation the world had ever seen. Nothing that happened in between from the Revolutionary War, the emancipation of slaves, the War between the States, World Wars I and II, the stock market crash, the civil-rights movement, Vietnam, the assassination of four presidents and the blight of terrorism, matters to American citizens."

In reality, of course, all of these events provide meaning and context to America's story. The same is true of Jesus' story, but there is a problem with the way his story is told.

Today, most books about Jesus fit into three categories: *scholarly, historical,* and *inspirational.*

Scholars and educators write the scholarly books for their peers, complete with footnotes, commentary, thorough documentation, and so on.

The authors of historical books feel obligated to be honest about the life of Jesus, even if such candid treatment challenges traditional Christian doctrine. They seek to reconstruct Jesus' life using rigorous historical methodology that strips away theory, conjecture, and hearsay, leaving nothing but naked facts. Because Jesus was a real man who lived in a real world and was influenced by real people and events, these authors focus on material that can pass the rigid tests of historical scholarship.

Scholarly books and *historical* books, which are often too academic for the average reader, deal primarily with the fact that Jesus was a loyal 1st-century Jew from the Galilee. He had a Jewish family, Jewish friends, and many Jewish followers. In addition, these books contend that Jesus was a poor, uneducated peasant who became an itinerant teacher. His wisdom was extraordinary for one with a limited education. Further, Jesus displayed a compassion unique among Jews of the era, who lived under Rome's tyrannical oppression.

In the eyes of these authors, Jesus resented Roman oppression and tried to avoid interactions with the Romans. Nevertheless, if Romans approached him (e.g., the centurion in Capernaum), he did not turn them away. Jesus was a loyal Jew, but also a loyal Roman subject whose deeds and sayings were greatly influenced by Roman politics and culture.

Inspirational books are usually written by Christians, for Christians. These authors seek to spiritualize Jesus' deeds and sayings. Generally, these writers care little about confirming the authenticity of the Gospel records. They choose to concentrate on the effect of a particular deed or saying. For example, *Jesus' death cleanses us from sin. His resurrection assures us of eternal life.* Because the Gospels are perceived to be the inerrant Word of God, historical accuracy becomes secondary to spiritual enlightenment. Some inspirational writers denounce scholarly or historical books about Jesus as irrelevant or even heretical.

Authors of inspirational books usually agree that the Gospel narratives say little about the world Jesus lived in. Thus, they tend to apply Jesus' words and deeds to *present-day* circumstances. They assume that Jesus would act today, just as he did in New Testament times.

So, when we evaluate the three types of books about Jesus, we find that they focus on different things.

- The history of Rome and the history of the Jews, including Jesus.
- The spiritual implications of Jesus' life and ministry.
- Jesus' inspirational lessons and their application for today's believer.

Seldom, if ever, does a book address all the above and explore how each influences the others.

With this book, I offer you a fourth choice: A book that seeks to understand why Jesus said what he said and did what he did considering his dual status as a Jew and a Roman subject who was probably educated in Greco-Roman-influenced schools. Later, he worked under the authority of Roman administrators and ministered under the protection of Roman officials. Ultimately, he died as an enemy of Rome. He was punished under Roman law.

The book is not intended to present Jesus in any lesser light than that of deity.

Even though this is a thick book, I can cover only a handful of details about Jesus' life and ministry. With this limitation in mind, I focus on material that can be historically verified beyond *any* doubt.

This book is *historical* because it portrays Jesus' life in Roman Mare Nostrum East (which is now Israel and Syria).

It is *scholarly* because it confirms each Gospel-recorded event with extra-biblical authenticating documentation.

It is *inspirational* because it assumes that the Gospel records of Jesus are the most accurate ones we have. I believe that the Gospel narratives have endured for two millennia because they are the narratives that God knows are the most spiritually beneficial to us today.

In the pages that follow, I will explore Jesus' life by filling in the empty center between his birth and death. I will move beyond a bare-bones historical sketch of Jesus to a fully developed historical epic. I invite you to join me.

CHAPTER 1

My Quest Begins

As I ascend the first flight of stairs leading to a small third-floor auditorium at the University of Texas, I glance at my watch. I am 10 minutes late. The lecture by special guest speaker Dr. Richard Link, professor of Classical Roman History at the University of London, has probably already begun.

I quietly slip into the back of the auditorium, accept a program from the door attendant, and sit in the back row.

Dr. Link is standing behind a lectern. He has not yet begun his lecture, which was titled "Jesus: the Roman Subject."

For as long as I can remember, I've hungered to learn the truth about Jesus. Not what the movies say about him, but the *historical* truth. So, when I had read in the local newspaper that Dr. Link was going to lecture about Jesus, I knew I had to be there.

Dr. Link begins his lecture by asking his small audience to close our eyes and picture a scene.

"Use your imagination," he instructs, "and picture the events as vividly as you can, while I relate a story to you. Keep your eyes closed the entire time. Imagine yourself as an eyewitness to the events of the story. Picture yourself being there. Better yet, imagine yourself as this story's main character: a Roman soldier."

He waits for everyone to close their eyes. Then he begins:

"It is early afternoon on a spring day in the year AD 31. You are a Roman soldier. Not just any soldier. You are a centurion, stationed in the Roman province of Judaea.

Three times each year, the Roman Authority sets aside a day to execute criminals found guilty of sedition. This is one of those days. You have been assigned to maintain order and oversee the execution. The execution is being carried out in the garbage dump of Gehenna, outside the walls of Jerusalem, a city in the state of Judea.

It's an unpleasant but necessary task.

Now, let your imagination run free as we follow the thoughts and actions of the centurion as he oversees the execution.

Dr. Link pauses a few moments before continuing. I sneak a peek and see that his eyes are closed, just like most of us in the audience.

From midday onward, darkness has slowly made its way east from the western horizon," he says. "Now, two hours later, the sky has turned completely dark, a canopy of moist black velvet. People must light torches to see.

As the northeast wind gusts, the flames of the torches flutter and bend. The centurion pulls his scarlet cloak tighter around his neck and turns his back to the squall. He then orders his second in command to increase the number of workers who keep watch over Gehenna's refuse fires, to ensure that the flames will not spread in the wind.

He has never experienced anything like this. Sure, he's endured countless battles with rain, snow, frozen ground, sleepless nights, hunger and thirst, and marching for days on end to help defend the Empire against seemingly insurmountable odds. He's even had to battle at night, with instinct as his only guide, but he's never faced such unpredictable natural forces.

He has seen solar and lunar eclipses, but *this* darkness was caused by neither. This darkness is so unearthly, so mystical. Unless you count sporadic devotion to Mars, the god of war, he is not a believer in any divine entity. He believes in war, in loyalty to Rome. He is dedicated to the Emperor. Little else matters.

The darkness is so thick and heavy that one can feel its weight. The scattered torches provide meager light.

Now the wind begins to blow harder. The centurion wonders how he has ended up in such an intractable region. He has moved up the ranks of legionnaires, accompanying Emperor Tiberius Caesar in his conquests in Gaul and Armenia, until achieving the rank of centurion commander over 100 of the Emperor's finest and bravest.

A battle-hardened veteran, he never imagined he would spend the last years of his military career in Judaea, serving as nursemaid to a cantankerous breed of obnoxious religious separatists, but, here he is. Commanding a guard detail dispatched by Pilate, Procurator of Judaea, which is escorting a group of about 50 prisoners to Gehenna. How degrading! And yet, anything for the good of the empire.

As the wind continues to gust, he studies one broken and bloody mass of torn flesh that was once a man, hanging by iron spikes driven through his wrists. The hanging man is one of a few close enough that he can hear their screams of agony, even over the gale.

The criminals have been crucified in a half-moon arrangement in five rows.

The centurion has taken a position near the middle of the third row, directly in front of one who has been accused, according to the indictment hanging above his head, of claiming to be a king of the Jews.

Here, the centurion must wait for sundown, when he will be allowed to leave this valley of death, reeking of burning garbage, rotting flesh, and bodily waste and consigning the crucified to the dogs, vultures, and other scavengers who hasten the miserable deaths of the criminals by feasting on their bodies.

Watching this man on the cross, the centurion becomes perplexed. He has heard of this "Jesus" over the past few years. But it seemed that Jesus was either doing good deeds or chastising the Jewish religious leaders, who held him in contempt. Because the centurion holds the Jewish religion in low regard, its leaders' negative opinion about Jesus carries little weight.

He has heard stories about Jesus performing miracles, and tales about him controlling the forces of nature. He's heard of Jesus befriending Romans. He has heard that Jesus seemed to support the Jews' submission to Rome. Some stories suggest Jesus is a Roman citizen, by adoption.

Further, many of his teachings are rooted in Roman history, philosophy, and custom. This Jesus was known to cite Roman law as if he had been trained as a Roman lawyer.

Jesus' birth had been acknowledged by Caesar Augustus. Some people claimed he was a direct descendant of the Jewish king David and some kind of god. To the centurion, these claims mean nothing.

Meanwhile, though the sun has been engulfed by the mysterious darkness, the centurion estimates the time to be the ninth hour. Just three more hours and he can leave this valley.

He hopes the time will pass quickly. His thoughts are interrupted when he hears Jesus groan from deep within, a groan marking hope vanishing and being replaced by despair.

He turns to look at Jesus, his flesh hanging in ribbons. He sees Jesus use his waning strength to push against the spikes nailed through his feet so he can exhale just enough of the contaminated air poisoning his body and utter a few words. He cries out in a language unfamiliar to the centurion: *"Eli, Eli, lama, sabach tha-ni?"*

Some on-lookers mock Jesus. A few others say he is asking for something to drink.

Someone dips a sponge into a pot of bitter wine vinegar and approaches Jesus. The centurion stops him, but then studies the bloody mass hanging on the cross. *What difference does it make now?* he thinks. He allows the man to lift the sponge to Jesus' lips, doubting that he will have the strength to drink.

When the compassionate man returns to his place among the crowd, he is jeered. Disgusted, the centurion orders the mockers to leave.

What's wrong with these people? he wonders. *Even when a man is dying, they are not satisfied. They still want to jeer.*

The centurion doesn't understand such disdain. It seems that everyone in Jerusalem hates Jesus. Even the other criminals around him are mocking him! Only a homosexual prostitute (who killed his Roman-citizen lover) defended Jesus. Jesus had turned to this man, who was being crucified next to him, and spoken kind words.

How things have changed, the centurion marvels. While stationed in the Galilee, he heard of Jesus attracting scores of followers. By the

thousands, people gathered around him to hear his message of unconditional love and tolerance. On two occasions, so many people flocked
to Jesus that Roman authorities feared an uprising. They sent military
sorties to keep the peace. But no force was needed. This Jesus seemed to
be able to control a crowd, regardless of its size.

On this day, only a handful showed up to pay their respects. A man,
rumored to be Jesus' brother, and a few women, one of whom is obviously his mother.

Where are the hundreds of friends and followers? The people who
had been *allegedly* healed by Jesus? What about the rest of his family?

As the centurion ponders all this, he hears a stirring coming from
Jesus' cross. He sees Jesus push against the spikes in his feet so that he
can speak again.

Jesus finally succeeds, forcing a groan from his lips. His words are
barely audible over the howling wind. The centurion cannot distinguish
them and once they are spoken Jesus gives a short gasp and lets his head
droop against his chest. He is dead.

Suddenly, the centurion feels a strange jolt, seeming to emanate from
deep in the earth. Or does he? Shaking his head, he dismisses the feeling
as nothing more than imagination.

As he studies Jesus' body, the centurion marvels at the speed of his
death. It usually took a week or more for crucifixion victims to die. Jesus
had died in just over six hours.

He extends his hand to see if he can find a pulse in Jesus' foot, but,
suddenly, the earth beneath him rumbles and shakes. This quake is no
act of the imagination. The ground splits open in many places. Smoke
and heat rise from the fissures. Moments later, huge boulders seem to
be ripped from the surrounding rock cliffs and hurled violently to the
valley below. Lightning streaks from one end of the black sky to the
other, accompanied by thunder crashes so intense that it seems the earth
is being torn in two.

The centurion has witnessed earthquakes and violent storms, but
nothing like this. This all began with the death of a condemned man.

As a child, the centurion had heard myths about nature's forces
reacting to events orchestrated by the gods. Nature mourned over the

death of a mortal. Nature reacted violently over the death of a god-man. Surely these were myths, meant to entertain and inspire, not to be taken literally. Why would nature care what happened to a mortal? Even if nature did care, why would it react like this?

This storm had to be a coincidence.

Unless it wasn't! What if nature *was* reacting to Jesus' death? What if the earth was weeping because a god had just been killed? Killed by Romans under the command of a certain centurion.

Who *was* this Jesus? This man who did good, yet suffered a horrible death? Who attracted thousands of followers, most of whom abandoned him during his most trying moment? Who was this Jew who seemed to be respected more by Romans than by his own countrymen, and yet he suffered death as an enemy of Rome.

So many paradoxes and questions. Jesus was certainly a righteous man, but was he *more* than a man? Could it be that those childhood myths of gods and goddesses were true? Could a god actually give birth to a mortal? Could a man be part-god? Could a son of god be killed? If so, why would a god allow his son to be killed by mere mortals?

As the centurion wrestles with these questions, he realizes that nature's forces are finally beginning to calm. The darkness is fading.

He stands at the foot of Jesus' cross, trying to make sense of everything. Finally, just before sundown, some high-ranking officials approach. They bring orders signed by Pilate, permitting them to remove Jesus' body from the cross so they can bury it.

As they carry the body away, the centurion makes one last walk through the place of execution to ensure all is secure. As he walks, he convinces himself that this man was not only righteous, but that he also must be a god, or at least the son of a god. Probably the son of the Jews' God.

He doesn't sleep much that night, nor for many nights thereafter. He supervised the crucifixion of a divine Jew who was *Roman* in his behavior. Who *was* this divine Roman Jew?"

Dr. Link finishes his story. We all sit silent for several minutes, reflecting on the picture he has painted for us.

Finally, he invites us to open our eyes. "Although this story is my own fabrication," he says, "it could very well be true.

"If we use the Gospels as our primary record, the story follows those narratives very closely. Is there more to Jesus' life than what's recorded in the four Gospels?" Dr. Link asks, before moving on to the remainder of his lecture.

The rest of the lecture centers on the validity of what Jesus said: Did he *really say* what the Gospels have recorded, or did the authors write down what Jesus *probably would have or should have said*, words that were then adopted over the centuries as Jesus' actual words?

After hearing the fascinating opening story, I was excited to hear the rest of Dr. Link's lecture. Maybe I had expected too much. I came away with more questions than answers, more disappointment than contentment.

Although the lecture was not what I expected, it did succeed in sparking a hitherto untapped interest in discovering the historical truth behind the life of Jesus. The truth that authenticated the Gospel records.

So thus began my passionate search for the historical Jesus, a search that has driven me for the past 43 years, taking me to five continents.

Over these years, I have evaluated and examined hundreds of books, documents, manuscripts, and artifacts that support the traditional picture of Jesus' life. Few of these are harmonious with historical fact.

For the most part, these conventional sources seemed to agree on several basic points about Jesus' life. Points that Christianity established as foundational centuries ago, regardless of whether historical fact confirmed them.

Specifically:

- Jesus was a Jew. He had a Jewish father and mother, a Jewish family, and Jewish friends.

- The Jewish people have been one of the most-hated and most-persecuted people throughout world history.

- The events surrounding Jesus' birth are both mysterious and miraculous.

- Jesus was a Galilean Jew who became a teacher. Judean Jews hated Galilean Jews.

- Jesus was also a Roman subject who spent most of his life in Roman occupied Galilee, in the Roman province of Syria.

- No known writings written by Jesus have survived.

- Jesus was totally free from prejudice and bigotry, yet both were instrumental in his death.

- Although Jesus preached love and showed compassion, neither was available to him during the final days of his life.

- Jesus died by crucifixion (one of the most painful of all deaths) as an enemy of Rome and at the hands of Roman officials. This was instigated by Jewish religious officials.

- All those whom Jesus considered his friends and devoted followers abandoned him.

- Jesus' grave was empty when it was investigated three days after his death, fulfilling his prophecy that he would rise from the dead.

- One-third of today's world population honors him and/or claims to follow him.

- The Jesus of first century Galilee seems to be quite different from the Jesus who was interpreted through Christian ideology, theology, art, poetry, and hymnody of the past 2,000 years (i.e. a Jesus totally devoid of Roman influence).

Even though the above statements are fundamental to the Christian faith and are (mostly) harmonious with *doctrinal* truth, they cannot pretend to be *historical* truth. Only substantiated facts can be called genuinely true.

For example, many records of the first century Roman Mare Nostrum East occupation period and its relationship to Jesus' life and ministry omit reference to his Greco-Roman surroundings or how Imperial Rome influenced what he said and did. Jesus was *greatly* influenced by his surroundings.

Jesus was both a loyal Galilean Jew and a loyal Roman subject. He respected, honored, and sought to safeguard the Law of Moses and the rituals and traditions associated with historical Judaism. However, he also respected and honored the Roman authorities, under whose rule he was born. Although many of Jesus' followers were Jewish and his authority to teach in God's name was granted by the Jewish religious hierarchy, he also attracted Roman followers. This motivated him to use Roman history and philosophy to illuminate his teachings. Jesus also used his relationship with Roman officials to enhance his ministry.

The New Testament Gospels insist that Jesus was *more* than just a Jewish rabboni (well-educated teacher) who restricted his ministry to the descendants of Abraham, Moses, and David. Contemporary thinking implies that Jesus ministered primarily to Jewish peasants and rarely interacted with non-Jews. Contemporary Christianity also accepts that the Romans were ultimately responsible for Jesus' death, but beyond this, Rome and Roman culture are seen as having little influence on Jesus' life and ministry.

Nothing could be further from the truth. The Gospels vividly portray Jesus' life as a Roman subject. Dozens of extra-biblical sources support this truth.

Jesus might not have been a Roman citizen by birth, but he was most certainly a loyal and honored (until just before his death) Roman subject, who used that status to enhance his ministry.

For more than a millennium and a half, the four Gospels have been accepted as authentic and undeniable truth by millions. However, these accounts, although separate records that chronicle some separate events, cannot be regarded as four discrete authenticating documents. I believe that they should be regarded as one collective source, one witness to many of the same events.

In order for truth to be established, at least two records must confirm one another. In the case of historical documentation, at least two records from the same time period must confirm one another, or if they are from different time periods, a less ancient document must authenticate a more ancient document. If it is recorded in the Gospels, then a search must be conducted to find a second witness.

CHAPTER 2

❧

I Investigate the Gospels

As I BEGAN MY SEARCH for the historical Jesus, my top priority was to unearth evidence that would either confirm the accepted tradition of who wrote the Gospels or identify the *actual* authors. (I did not evaluate the *Gospel of Thomas,* the subject of much recent scholastic scrutiny, or any other writings that had been formally rejected as part of the biblical canon). Very early in my efforts, I was surprised to discover that the Gospels were probably not written by the people whose names they bear, with the possible exception of Luke.

MARK'S GOSPEL

The Gospel According to St. Mark, perhaps the earliest of the four Gospels, was my starting point. (Incidentally, Mark is the text from which the authors of Matthew and Luke probably gleaned most of their information.)

I found out that the earliest fragments of Mark, written predominantly in Greek—with some passages penned in a Greek/Syriac/Chaldean combination date to perhaps as early as AD 60, but most certainly to

AD 75. These fragments were found near Luxor, Egypt in 1961. This Gospel is not only the first of the four, but it also seems to be the most chronologically accurate.

It's important to note that, contrary to popular belief, John Mark, a colleague of the apostle Paul, did not write this Gospel.

Let me explain. In AD 130, Papias, the Bishop of Hierapolis, claimed that a John Mark of Canatha had written the Gospel in AD 60, using information he had received from James, Jesus' brother, as well as from the apostles Peter and Barnabas.

At the University of Texas, I found evidence that James, the afore-mentioned brother of Jesus, is the most likely author of Mark's Gospel. James was the first acknowledged leader of a sect of Nazarenes known as "Christians."

According to anthropologist Dr. Mary Thudeaux, a guest lecturer for one of the university's Western Civilization courses, less than 15 years after Jesus' death and resurrection, James sought to create a permanent record of Jesus' ministry. He hoped to use this record to encourage the newly established Nazarene convert groups, many of whom were former Jews scattered throughout Judaea.

According to Dr. Thudeaux's extensive research (her doctorate was in Middle Eastern anthropology), James wrote using his personal knowl-edge of Jesus, and he included additional information provided by the apostle Andrew. The result was a "rough outline" of Jesus' ministry. This draft was then distributed to Nazarene groups scattered throughout Judaea with a promise from James that he would send a more detailed record once he had finished writing it.

James entrusted the delivery of his early draft to a young Greek associate named Mark (or possibly John Mark of Canatha). This draft became known as *A Record of the Service of Jesus the Christ as Written by James, a disciple whom Jesus loved, and Delivered by Mark, a Brother and Fellow-Laborer.*

Tragically, before James could complete his comprehensive account, he was martyred. Hence, the only accurate and authentic *eyewitness* account of Jesus' ministry by a credible source is this "rough outline draft," written by Jesus' brother and delivered by a young Greek named Mark.

Within ten years of James's death, this document had become known as *The Gospel of Jesus, Written by James, Delivered by Mark*. After another decade or so, the title had morphed to *The Gospel of Jesus Delivered by Mark*. This evolved into *The Gospel Delivered by Mark* and finally, by the end of the second century, *The Gospel According to Mark*.

Unfortunately, by this time at least one-fourth of James' original content had been lost. So, although Mark was the first Gospel written, it is not, nor was it intended to be, a detailed record of Jesus' ministry. It was intended to provide enough content about Jesus' ministry to "tide over" the Nazarene groups until James could complete a detailed record.

Nevertheless, this Gospel became the primary source for two of the other three Gospels. (It can be argued convincingly that the authors of Matthew and Luke used another common source sometimes called "Q" as well.)

MATTHEW'S GOSPEL

Next, I investigated *The Gospel According to St. Matthew*. This Gospel seems to have originated around the same time that the Roman general Titus laid siege to Jerusalem (AD 70) and destroyed the Jewish Temple. Matthew might have been the second Gospel written. The earliest Greek/Latin fragments of *Matthew*, dating from as early as AD 140, were discovered in Romania in 1940 and are housed at the Middle Eastern Museum in Vienna. Although the author of this Gospel is traditionally believed to be Matthew, the former tax collector and apostle of Jesus, this authorship theory wasn't even offered until the mid-second century, when Cedus, Bishop of Berea, claimed that an angel appeared and told him of Matthew's authorship.

A more likely scenario is that Matthew was written by a late first century or early second century Jewish convert to Christianity, perhaps an early church leader. (Two early Saxon texts now housed at England's Sunderland University claim that Isador, a second century disciple of Justin Martyr, is the author).

In any case, whoever wrote this Gospel possessed remarkable knowledge of first century BC and first century AD Jewish history, manners, and customs. Further, although the author didn't place the events of Jesus' life in chronological order, he did preserve the primary teachings, character, and purposes of his ministry. Because Christians of this era were being martyred by the hundreds, the author probably felt that a permanent record of Jesus' ministry should be preserved, just in case all his followers were exterminated. Thus, some biblical historians believe that Matthew's Gospel was the one generally read to assemblies of early Christians.

LUKE'S GOSPEL

Next, I investigated *The Gospel According to St. Luke.* I discovered that this Gospel was probably the third to be written, though it could have been the second. The earliest fragments of this Gospel, written in Greek, date to about AD 150. In 1897, these fragments were discovered in an almost-inaccessible cave in Egypt. Another fragment of Luke's Gospel, dating from AD 180, was found in Bulgaria, near the Macedonian border, in 1932. It is housed in the Rylands Library Museum in Manchester, England.

The Gospel According to St. Luke was probably written about 20 to 30 years after the apostle Paul's death (circa AD 67), but because the exact year Paul was martyred is unknown, we can't pinpoint the time of this Gospel's creation.

Tradition holds that Luke, a physician and companion of Paul, wrote this Gospel, as well as The Acts of the Apostles (the fifth book of the New Testament). However, my research leads me to believe that if Luke wrote this Gospel, he had help from at least one of his disciples. Evidence suggests that a disciple named Cedes of Antioch compiled Luke's information from personal interviews. Moreover, I believe that Luke also gleaned information from earlier writings by the apostle Andrew (and, possibly, the apostle Philip).

"Luke" never gives himself credit for writing the Gospel bearing his name, even though he had an excellent opportunity in the introduction, where the author dedicates his writings to "His Excellency Theophilus" and notes that his Gospel is just one of many accounts of the life of Jesus. However, evidence that directly *refutes* Luke's authorship is scarce. So

I have tentatively chosen to accept Luke as at least a key contributor to this Gospel.

JOHN'S GOSPEL

This brings us to the fourth and final Gospel to have been written: The *Gospel According to St. John*. The earliest fragments of this Gospel, discovered in Egypt in 1935, are referred to as the Papyrus Bodmer II. Historians once dated these Greek-language fragments to AD 115. Then, in 1965, papryologists at the University of Hamburg determined that the fragments had not been written before the mid-third century and probably as late as the fifth century. Today these fragments are on display at Israel's Library of Magdalene College.

My research on this Gospel led me to writings of theologians who believe that the John Rylands papyrus (circa AD 125) contains passages that seem to correspond to passages from John's Gospel. However, while I do not claim to be an expert in the comparative languages of ancient manuscripts, it seems to me that the form of writing used by the author of the Rylands papyrus is more similar to Mark's Gospel than to John's.

In researching John's Gospel, I also discovered that, until the time of the Fourth Council of Bishops (or Council of the Lateran) circa AD 1215, Christians believed that the apostle John had been killed, along with his brother, James, by Herod Agrippa in AD 44. If this is true, John, obviously, could not have written this Gospel.

After the 1215 council, another theory emerged: John was boiled in oil in AD 95, during the widespread persecution of Christians under Domitian. John somehow survived this ordeal, only to be exiled to the Isle of Patmos, a first century Roman penal colony in the Aegean Sea. The council supposed that he either died of natural causes on Patmos at about age 100 or after serving his time on Patmos he moved to Ephesus and died of natural causes there at age 100 or 104 (circa 115 AD). I could find no hard evidence to support either speculation.

At the council, John was credited with authorship of the *Gospel According to John, The Revelation,* and the three *Epistles of John.* But throughout the Middle Ages, controversy raged over who actually wrote these New Testament books. Since the sixteenth century, many

Protestants have contended that John was killed by Herod Agrippa and that the writings in question were penned by three separate authors. These Protestants have cited sources like John Foxe, who wrote (in 1563): "Without a doubt, both James and John were beheaded by Herod Agrippa in AD 44."

However, the Catholic Church has held to the belief that John authored all five works.

To further complicate matters, a fourth-century Gnostic manuscript titled *The Fourth Gospel* claims that *The Gospel According to John* and *The Revelation* were written in the mid-second century by John Presbyter, a supposed contemporary of early Christians like Polycarp, Ignatius, and Papias. However, some historians question John Presbyter's very existence.

An eighth century Coptic manuscript found near Cairo in the late nineteenth century and titled *The Gospels of the Canon* claims that James (Jesus' brother) wrote the *Gospel According to Mark, The Epistle to the Hebrews*, and the final 17 chapters of *The Revelation*. (This corroborates Dr. Thudeaux's research on Mark.) This manuscript credits the *Gospel According to John* to a second century bishop named John of Illyricum. John of Illyricum claimed to have read the personal records of James, Jesus' brother. Much of his account was based on those records.

Meanwhile, Empress Eudoxia, wife of Arcadius (Emperor of the Roman East), claimed that John Chrysostom, bishop of Constantinople from AD 398 to 403, authored *The Gospel According to John* and John's three epistles as well as the first quarter of *The Revelation*.

As you might imagine, my early investigation into the Gospels' authorship led me to conclude "who wrote what" is a mystery that might never be solved.

Undaunted, I dove headlong into dissecting the Gospels' content to learn how Greco-Roman culture and society influenced Jesus.

I also committed to investigating extra-biblical texts that could confirm the authenticity of the Gospel accounts.

CHAPTER 3

✦

My Two Golden Nuggets

ALTHOUGH I COULD SPEND the rest of my life studying the Gospels, I eventually became sufficiently confident in my knowledge of these four books that I could begin exploring research beyond the Gospel records. For this I began with the premise that the Gospels' account of Jesus' life and ministry was unimpeachable truth and that all other sources should be compared against the high Gospel standard.

As this phase of my search unfolded, I discovered two golden nuggets of truth, which have proven vital to my work.

The first golden nugget came as advice from a man named Francis LeBeaux from Boulogue, France.

I was dead tired when I arrived in Boulogue late in the afternoon one March day. I wanted to rent a room someplace, *anyplace*, and go to sleep. I stopped at the first accommodation I found, a small waterfront inn called Jean's.

Jean's seemed to be more a pub than an inn, but it offered four upstairs rooms available for rent.

The building's main floor was one big open room, furnished with three long, wooden tables, each with bench seats made of split logs. I guessed this furniture was at least 200 years old. A huge roaring fireplace provided heat. The assortment of pots and kettles hanging in or near the fireplace told me that meals were cooked over the fire as well. (I would soon learn that the inn had no kitchen or bar. All the food and the thick, strong coffee was cooked over the fire.)

Jean's other beverages were heavy ale, cheap wine, and watered-down rum, which were stored in huge wooden barrels lining the room's back wall.

Wooden stairs led from the dining area to a balcony, from which one could access the four rental rooms.

Entering my room, I found my bedframe to be hand-hewn wood, topped with a goose-down mattress and a centuries-old handmade quilt.

The room offered no electricity or running water. A couple of candles and a coal oil lamp provided my only light. There was no shower, but the owner supplied each room with fresh drinking water daily, as well as a bucket of hot bathing water and an ample supply of towels. My cost for these accommodations: five dollars a night. This fee included supper and the privilege of listening to exciting tales of pirates, smugglers, highwaymen, and swashbuckling adventurers, all told by the inn's owner, the aforementioned Francis LeBeaux.

On this day, I was the only overnight guest, although a few dining and drinking patrons came and went throughout the night.

After settling into my room, I accepted Francis's invitation to have supper before turning in for the night. My dining choices included venison stew, roasted game bird (it looked like partridge or pheasant), and fish soup, as well as bread and a drink.

I sat at one of the tables with three other men and enjoyed some of the venison stew and roasted bird. I washed down my meal with a big mug of black coffee. I was about half-finished when one of the men asked Francis to "tell us a story or two."

As Francis spun tales of pirates and smugglers, he painted a picture so vivid that I half-expected a band of pirates to stumble through the door, pieces of eight in hand, demanding pots of rum. Although I was dead tired, I quickly became transfixed as I listened to Francis. After story No. 2, the three men bid us goodnight, leaving me and Francis alone. I craved sleep, but Francis was so interesting and amiable that I could not break away. We spent another two hours talking before he encouraged me to call it a night. During our conversation, Francis told me that the inn had been built in 1680 and that his family had run it continuously since then.

Francis was a big man, standing well over six feet and weighing at least 250 pounds. He looked to be in his mid-50s, with a gray-streaked beard and hair that almost reached his shoulders. He possessed a thunderous voice. He seemed incapable of whispering. He told me he had never married. "Never had dee time fo dee women," he explained.

As the night's only rental guest, I was treated like royalty. Thus, I decided to extend my stay. Francis served as my tour guide as we walked all over the little town. Those three days were some of the most intriguing I have ever experienced.

On the second night, as we sat eating roasted pork, I told Francis about my search for the historical Jesus. Francis was not a religious man; he hadn't seen the inside of a church since childhood. Still, he was interested in my quest. I spent almost the entire evening telling him about my efforts and acquainting him with the real, personal Jesus, not the untouchable and impersonal catechism Jesus that he was introduced to as a child.

NUGGET NO.1

During this conversation, Francis offered me that first golden nugget of truth. I asked him where he thought I should concentrate my research. He told me to focus on the small towns, the libraries, and the cathedrals that were *not* typical tourist attractions. He said that much of the information I sought could be found in Europe, but it wasn't made accessible to tourists, nor would it ever be.

He asserted "the church" tried to ensure that only documents and manuscripts supporting traditional teaching and beliefs are available to the public. He assured me that other documents were "out there," but not on display. He urged me to investigate French cities like Reims, Nancy,

Orleans, and Avignon and similar towns in other European countries. He advised me to avoid the big cities like Paris, London, Berlin, Madrid, and Vienna. "Wheen yo researcher," Francis said, gently patting my cheek, "yo must go to plass whir touris is not, or not so much."

The day I left the inn, Francis bear-hugged me when I told him good-bye. Then he walked away so I wouldn't see his tears. I knew I had made a friend for life.

N U G G E T   N O .   2

The second golden nugget revealed itself soon after my visit with Francis. However, this nugget wasn't advice; it was a discovery. A discovery that at one time there existed hundreds of extra-biblical writings about Jesus' life. Some of these manuscripts dated from Christianity's earliest days.

Many of these records had been lost, but perhaps they could be found. As with the first nugget, I had Francis to thank. He had advised me to visit St. Anne's Cathedral in Reims and see what treasures it might hold. I was eager to see what I might discover.

Upon arriving in Reims, I checked into a small hostel just two blocks from the cathedral.

St. Anne's was once part of the thirteenth century Monastery of St. Anne. The monastery was abandoned in the eighteenth century, and most of its buildings had been torn down. Somehow the church had survived.

Stepping into the centuries-old building, I was filled with wonder at how much care had been invested in its preservation. The massive main cathedral, with an altar as its centerpiece, was beautiful. After spending several awe-filled moments in the cathedral, I followed signs to the manuscript library, which was the lone remaining original building from the 13th century.

The library was much smaller than I had anticipated, but it was large enough to hold a rather impressive collection of letters, ancient bound volumes, and loose pages from various manuscripts.

Two men seated at an oval desk glanced at me when I entered. Neither offered to assist me, but they both put a forefinger to their lips, signaling me to do whatever I would be doing *quietly*. They needn't have bothered.

Prominent signs, in French, German, and English, warned: SILENCE—NO TALKING PERMITTED.

The documents on display were propped up on stands or placed under glass. A brief description, in French and English, accompanied each text. I spent two full hours walking from one display to the next and studying the descriptions. Then I got down to my serious, detailed research.

The library had a microfiche and film file, as well as an old-school card catalog. I chose to go "modern."

EXTRA-BIBLICAL AND NON-CHRISTIAN RECORDS

After reviewing the film file for an hour or so, I learned that the library housed many texts about Jesus, but most of them were suspect in that they differed sharply from the Gospels. I did discover a few manuscripts that seemed both intriguing and historically reliable, like a certain 200-plus-page hieotike Latin text. (Hieotike is a high-quality parchment.) The notes that accompanied this bound volume informed me that it was the sole survivor of a three-volume set written by Alphonsus Liguori of Naples, who served as bishop of St. Agatha from 1762 to 1775. Liguori had titled his series *Testimonies of the Death and Resurrection of The Light.* Only volume 1 had survived to the twentieth century.

Liguori founded the Order of the Redemptorists in November of 1732, which brought him a bit of local notability, but when he published a book titled *Moral Theology* in 1748, he earned international prestige. Liguori prided himself in being a well-educated writer. He traveled all over Europe and the Middle East, researching and collecting data from hundreds of documents and manuscripts. However, the object of his research was often a mystery. During his frequent travels, his Order fell into conflict. This plunged him into a deep depression. In 1775, Pope Pius VI relieved the bishop of his duties, allowing him to retire (to a small, cell-like room) to try and recover.

Thus, Liguori began a secluded retirement, with his massive research as his primary companion. His only visitor was his trusted aid, Francesco Alfredo, who had worked with the bishop for 20 years.

For 12 years, Liguori toiled over his three-volume *Testimonies*, until, one day, Alfredo visited the cell and found the bishop dead. A few days later, Francesco was found dead in the same cell, raising suspicion that the despondent aide had committed suicide.

The hundreds of pages of *Testimonies*, found among Liguori's belongings, were sent to Paris to be bound. For some reason, this binding project took four years. The *Testimonies of the Death and Resurrection of The Light* were assembled into three volumes in the summer of 1792, just in time for the French Revolution.

The Revolution, as you might remember from a history class, brought riots in the streets. Shops and government buildings were ransacked and burned. Warehouses were plundered. Churches and religious institutions were pillaged and destroyed. One of the victims of these riots was the prestigious book bindery Rigaud le Grand, where Liguori's writings had been sent, and where they had remained. This was because the Abbot of St. Agatha (who had ordered the writings to be bound) hadn't paid his bill, so when the bindery was destroyed, only one volume of Liguori's work (and a book by Rousseau) survived. As the bindery was being attacked, shop owner Michael Prouse grabbed these books as he fled the shop and sprinted for his life. Later, Prouse handed the books to the monks of St. Anne's for safekeeping. He never returned to reclaim them.

As I began reading Liguori's work, I knew that if its contents were half as fascinating as the story *behind* the manuscript, I was in for a treat.

Liguori begins *Testimonies* by describing how he and Francesco Alfredo traveled all over Europe and the Middle East, collecting valuable documentation. He focused on early Christian writings, while Alfredo concentrated on Jewish documents, including the early Talmuds.

Next, Liguori explains his near-obsession with discovering documents, especially those from non-Christian writers, confirming the life, death, and resurrection of Jesus.

Liguori claims that because of Jesus' worldwide fame, there should be many non-Christian records about him including court records, letters, histories, legislative records, testimonials, and so on.

He further reasons that the first century AD Roman Empire was filled with debaters, historians, and various writers. He also cites the meticulously kept Roman court records. Wouldn't they contain information about Jesus' alleged crimes, trial, and execution?

Moreover, the Jews of Jesus' time were among the educated elite of the Roman Empire. Like the Romans, they kept careful records of their life and times. Some of these writings had been preserved in places like Jerusalem's great library of the Sanhedrin. Tragically, this building was burned by the Romans.

Furthermore, it is common knowledge that Jewish leaders of the first five centuries systematically erased references to Jesus from their records, histories and legislative reports.

If this news weren't bad enough, more documents were destroyed when the great libraries at Alexandria, Jerusalem, Rome, Ephesus, Antioch, and Constantinople were ransacked and burned. Pope Gregory IX had cartloads full of Talmuds and Jewish writings burned. When Rome destroyed Jerusalem, anything and everything of material worth and educational value was confiscated.

Despite all this, Liguori believed that, somehow, some extra-biblical, non-Christian records about Jesus had survived.

For example, he wondered about the fate of the library of Serenus Samnaticus. In the third century, Samnaticus amassed a huge library of first, second and third century Christian writings. (It's possible that he possessed the actual court documents from Jesus' trial before Pilate, and Pilate's report of the trial.) When he died in AD 236, Samnaticus left 62,000 volumes (of an estimated 80,000 volumes) to his student M. Antonius Africanus. The remaining 18,000 volumes were reportedly given to a teacher who had tutored Samnaticus's children. Unfortunately, both sets of records vanished.

Liguori spends pages pondering the fate of various collections. Then he concludes with a list of "knowns." This list became the focus of his and Alfredo's search.

To establish a link between Gospel and extra-Gospel records, I decided to use this list of "knowns" for myself. Here is that list, as delineated by Liguori: "It is known that:

1. The Jewish rabboni (and Pharisee doctor) Pseudonymanus Joseph ben Gorion compiled the works of Philo in

AD 150, and he also compiled the legal records of the Sanhedrin from the time of Herod the Great until the sacking of Jerusalem in AD 70. These documents could have included records of Jesus' ministry and certainly of his trial and execution.

2. Another Jewish rabbi, Ekaba, compiled the writings of Josephus in the second century. He was given the responsibility (by the Jewish Council of Rabbonis) of deleting any mention of Jesus, his teachings, his actions, and his ministry from official records of the Jewish State. Ekaba and his students destroyed more than 1,000 manuscripts and documents, Christian and non-Christian alike, which mentioned Jesus.

3. About 2,000 Coptic Christian manuscripts have been found—dating from the first century to the tenth century.

4. At least 3,000 documents and manuscripts, written in the Iranian, Arabic, and Semitic languages, were discovered in AD 953. Most of them dealt with various Christian doctrines, as well as the history of Christianity from the first century to the seventh century. This history includes Jesus' life and ministry.

5. Lucian of Syria, one of the most respected ancient historians, testified of Jesus' existence and affirmed the existence of documented evidence of Jesus' life and influence. In a letter written in 170 AD, Lucian described Jesus as: *'...the man who had been fixed to a stake in Judaea; ... as one still worshipped for having introduced a new code of morals into life...as that first lawgiver of theirs (the Christians)...and who made them believe that they are all brothers, and....(they have) worshipped the crucified man who is their teacher, and have begun to live according to his laws...of which so much has been written of him and his wisdom...by his brothers (and) by our own chroniclers that surely his appeal and his effect will not soon be subdued.'*

6. Many other historians wrote dozens of volumes about the life, ministry, trial, death, and resurrection of Jesus, and about his influence and the spread of the religious

philosophy bearing his name. Among these historians was Quadratus, who wrote a defense of Christianity to Emperor Hadrian in the early second century. Other histories were written by Justin Martyr, Tertullian, Vincentius, Cilens the First, Origen (who wrote eight massive volumes on the subject), Duranzo, Rabbi Akiba, Celsus, Aretas (the king of Arabia), and Arcadius (the eldest son of Theodosius the Great), who became Rome's emperor in AD 395.

7. It was known that in year 748 of the Empire (year 330 of the Christian era), Constantine moved his seat of government from Rome to Constantinople, taking with him all the original volumes of Christian literature known to him. The *original* writings of the Scriptures and *original* first century commentaries on the Scriptures were rewritten on hieotike and were bound between solid gold plates into 50 massive (about 3 feet by 4 feet and 2 feet thick) volumes, called the *Imperial Volumes of Constantine*.

8. Constantine left copies in Rome's library of all the Jewish Talmuds and Sanhedrin records including those taken from Jerusalem(probably about 30,000 manuscripts and scrolls), along with copies of another 40,000 documents, manuscripts, and volumes covering a variety of subjects by hundreds of writers. The originals were taken to Constantinople. The Visigoths destroyed the library of Rome in 410, with King Alaric personally torching the building. Before the library was burned, approximately 42,000 works were saved and hidden in various basilicas constructed by Constantine. Over the next twelve centuries, all of these basilicas, except St. Peter's, were ransacked and robbed repeatedly. Many of the pillaged documents ended up at St. Peter's, where they are still housed today.

9. The Latin historian Justin said that he had *personally* inspected and studied several Roman judicial and senatorial documents, including several of Pilate's reports of Jesus' trial, Caiaphas's report to Pilate (concerning Jesus), and the Sanhedrin's report to Pilate about the trial."

Later in his book, Liguori notes that it is an unimpeachable fact that Roman Emperor Constantine transferred to Constantinople all the original scrolls and documents that had been accepted as inspired Scripture (by the first three centuries' leaders of Christianity). There, he had the Scriptures compiled and bound into 50 volumes and placed in the newly constructed educational library for public view. Some historians have claimed that the volumes were so large that it took two men to open one of them. Upon completion of this project, Constantine inspected the volumes. As he approved each one, he dated it and placed his name and official seal upon it.

These volumes were written on hieotike in large bold Latin characters. The leaves were bound between thick gold plates, and each front plate bore a sculptured figure of a man hanging on a cross, with the inscription *Jesus, Son of God, crucified for the sins of the world.*

In a letter discovered by Francesco Alfredo, Constantine commissions Eusebius (a bishop and a historian) to make 50 copies of the 50 volumes. These 50 copies were to be distributed to Christian churches in and around Constantinople. They would not be as large as the originals, about 2.5 feet square, and would be written on parchment and bound between cedar boards.

The following is a quote from Constantine's letter:
"Victor Constantine Maximus Augustus to Eusebius:
It happens through the favoring of God our Savior that great numbers have united themselves to the most holy church in this city, which is called by my name. It seems, therefore, highly requisite, since the city is rapidly advancing in prosperity, that the number of churches should also be increased. I have thought it expedient to your Prudence to order 50 copies of each of the bound sacred Scriptures, the provisions and use of which you know to be most needful for the instruction of the churches, to be written on prepared parchment, in a legible manner by transcribes thoroughly practiced in their art. The procurator of the diocese has also received instructions by letter from our Clemency to be careful to furnish all things necessary for the preparation of such copies, and it will be for you to take special care that they be completed with as little delay as possible."

According to Liguori,

"Whether Eusebius completed his task is a mystery, but we do know from the testimony of Jerome in AD 416 that at least six sets of the copied Scriptures were completed and distributed to churches in Constantinople, but because both Eusebius and Constantine had adopted Aryanism as official doctrine, the Church did not recognize the 'Scriptures of Constantine' as authorized. It was not until Jerome completed the Latin version of the Scriptures in AD 414 that the Church recognized his translation as the authorized translation of the Scriptures."

As I studied Liguori's words, it became obvious to me that a wealth of information lurked out there somewhere, information that would further confirm the truth of the Gospels. Yes, many ancient documents and manuscripts had been lost or destroyed over the centuries, but dozens (perhaps even hundreds) more were waiting to be discovered! I resolved to find as many as I possibly could.

CHAPTER 4

❧ ❧

The War Zone of Jesus' Youth

AT THIS POINT IN MY RESEARCH, I understood that the Gospels weren't intended to be chronological accounts of Jesus' life and ministry. Instead, they were written to emphasize Jesus' teachings and his relationship with God the Father and with his fellow humans. I also discovered that beyond the commonly acknowledged "missing years" in Jesus' life (from age 12 to 30), there were missing days, weeks, and months right in the middle of his active ministry.

Thus, I decided to create my own chronological record of Jesus' life, which would serve as a road map for my search.

Of course, it would be futile to launch this search without a clear picture of the political, social, and religious Roman world into which Jesus was born, and in which he lived and ministered.

HASMONEAN STATE TO ROMAN PROVINCE

Half a century before the region where Jesus lived became a Roman Province, it was a Hasmonean State. The word Palestine used today to describe a geographical area of ethnic Jewish occupation (generally inclusive of the region of Roman Syria, Judaea, Phoenicia and the region of the Sinai), was not used about this distinct area until the seventeenth century. The word Palestine comes from the Latin. *Palestina,* and was the name given to the entire region of the eastern Mediterranean by the Roman Emperor Hadrian in 135 AD. This followed his suppression of a Jewish rebellion led by the self-proclaimed messiah Bar Cochba. The name Palestine was never used to identify Judaea, the Galilee or any area within the region until after 135 AD.

Within the Jewish State of Palestine, the Sadducee sect was *the* dominant religious power, and the Sanhedrin committee of elders (controlled by the Sadducees) was *the* dominant judicial body.

The era's most renowned Hasmonean (member of a priestly family of Jewish leaders) was John Hyrcanus, who ruled over the state from 134 to 104 BC. Hyrcanus was consumed by the notion that he was chosen by God to restore the ancient Davidic kingdom. Claiming that God had given him a vision to conquer what would become known as Palestine, Hyrcanus set out to exterminate all foreign cults and religious sects from "God's chosen land."

Driven by his religious fundamentalism, Hyrcanus and an army of mercenaries destroyed the Samaritan temple in BC 130. Later (circa BC 109-108), he destroyed the city of Samaria itself. He then turned his attention to the Greek city of Scythopolis. He burned the city and massacred its inhabitants, simply for being Greek. This slaughter was quickly followed by his conquest of the Idumaea province.

John Hyrcanus's son, Alexander Jannaeus (who served as High Priest and Governor from 104 to 76 BC), adopted his father's expansionist policy. He invaded the Greek-dominated Decapolis, as well as other cities. Many of Alexander's subjects thought he was crazy, as he massacred all who opposed him or refused to convert to the Hasmonean form of Judaism.

Eventually, Jannaeus's cruelty led to a revolt by the Jewish people and a civil-war. This war lasted six years and cost the lives of more than 50,000 Jews before it ended in victory for Governor Jannaeus.

Upon the Governor's death in 76 BC, his widow, Alexandra Salome, assumed his reign. When she died in 67 BC, rebellion flared again, and her two sons, Aristobulus II and Hyrcanus II, found themselves opposing one another. For the next four years, both sides killed thousands of Jews as the populace aligned itself with one side or the other of Salome's rivaling sons.

Knowing that more civil war would result in thousands more deaths, Hyrcanus II appealed for military help from Pompey the Great, the newly appointed Consular of Rome's eastern-Asian territories. Antipater, the most able and most powerful Idumaen chief-minister of Hyrcanus, negotiated the agreement with Pompey on Hyrcanus' behalf. A deal was struck. In exchange for Pompey's military assistance, Hyrcanus II guaranteed that upon the defeat of Aristobolus all Hasmonean-controlled lands would become subject to Rome. Pompey, in turn, agreed to make Hyrcanus II a vassal King/High Priest of Judea. And that both Antipater's family and any other notable Idumaen families recommended by Antipater would be able to flourish unmolested under Roman protection.

In 63 BC, after mercilessly crushing Aristobolus and his forces, which cost the lives of 12,000 Jews, Pompey marched triumphantly into Jerusalem. As pledged, he installed Hyrcanus II as vassal King/High Priest. On the day Pompey entered Jerusalem, all Hasmonean-controlled lands became subject to Rome, ending the last independent Jewish State for more than 2000 years.

A simmering rivalry soon developed between the brothers Aristobulus II and Hyrcanus II, a rivalry that would intensify over the next 16 years. Hyrcanus II sought to build power by developing a strong relationship with his Judean subjects; his younger brother focused on developing strong relationships with Rome. Around 50 or 49 BC, one of Hyrcanus II's high-ranking officials, Antipater the Idumaean, named his son Herod Governor of the Galilee. (This Herod would later be a key figure in Jesus' early life.)

By 47 BC, Aristobulus II had become so politically influential that he convinced Gaius Julius Caesar (dictator of the Roman Republic) to dissolve the office of vassal King and bring Judea under direct Roman rule—through the office of Procurator. Hence, Hyrcanus II was removed from the office of vassal King, although he retained the position of High Priest. Aristobulus II was appointed the first Roman Procurator of Judea.

Meanwhile, Herod (who would one day be known as Herod the Great), a lifelong friend of the Roman consul Mark Antony, was building a reputation as a brilliant politician. In 43 BC, he was appointed Tetrarch of the Galilee.

Herod was also a borderline-insane barbarian. Flavius Josephus, the Roman/Jewish historian, wrote that (Herod)"...was no King but the most cruel tyrant who ever ascended the throne. He murdered a vast number of people, and the lot of those he left alive was so miserable that the dead might count themselves fortunate. He not only tortured his subjects singly but ill-treated whole communities. Within a few years, the Jews suffered more misery under Herod than had their forefathers at any other time. In 35 years, hardly a day passed without someone being sentenced to death."

In 40 BC, turmoil again rocked Judea. Antigonus, a nephew of Hyrcanus II, seized Jerusalem. He removed Hyrcanus II from his position as High Priest. Soon, Hyrcanus II was found dead in his prison chamber.

When Antigonus marched his mercenary army north to invade the Galilee, Herod fled to the safety of Rome. There, he appealed to the Roman Senate for help. They responded by making him King of Judea, with the formal title of *rex socius et amicus populi Romani,* or allied king and friend of the Roman people.

In 37 BC, Herod returned to Judea with a Roman army. Combined with his own troops, he commanded 30,000 infantry and 6,000 cavalry. He retook Jerusalem and mercilessly crushed the rebels, massacring thousands. Afterwards, Herod received a new title: *King of all the Jews.* He ruled Judea until his death in AD 4.

Throughout his reign, Herod remained Rome's most loyal and most reliable provincial authority.

Herod the Great was ruling in Judea when Jesus was born.

Herod never forgave the Hasmoneans for their role in the 40 BC revolt. Thus, he waged an unrelenting 40-year war against them, killing hundreds and confiscating their possessions. By 20 BC, the Hasmoneans were nearly extinct.

Herod also forcibly separated the Jewish political state from its religion. His first act upon assuming power (in 37 BC) was to execute 46 members of the Sanhedrin, effectively stripping it of its political powers.

For the rest of Herod's reign, the Sanhedrin was nothing more than a religious court, separated from political and secular matters.

Only after Herod's death did the Sanhedrin began to regain political influence by exploiting their friendship and cooperation with Roman authorities. (Remember this fact when we come to Jesus' arrest and trial, later in the book.)

As you can see, no one could accuse Herod the Great of being compassionate, but he was an effective politician.

Herod was the best friend Rome had in the East. Through his grand Greco-Roman-style construction projects, he created a strong physical presence, which reflected Roman authority. He built stadiums, circuses, and hippodromes in Sidon, Damascus, Tyre, Antioch, Caesarea Maritima, Samaria, Jerusalem, and Scythopolis. He built seaports, fortresses, roads, cities, palaces, the wondrously magnificent Jewish Temple, as well as equally magnificent temples dedicated to Zeus, Apollo, Bacchus, Venus, Mars, and other deities. He also built canals, waterways, dams, schools, and dozens of fine amphitheaters.

Through Herod's liberal education policy (education was free and mandatory through age 17 for all male subjects and through age 14 for all female subjects), he made his subjects the most educated in the Roman Empire. In the second century, Phinehas the Rabbi recorded that at the time of Herod's death, illiteracy among Jewish men did not exist in the Roman Empire, and that only very old Jewish women could neither read nor write.

However, all this achievement carried a heavy price. During one 12-year period (25 to 13 BC), Herod taxed his subjects mercilessly by doubling their tax load annually. This led to unrest among the people, and Herod's reaction was quick and savage. He killed hundreds, if not thousands, in each of those 12 years. Herod's ruthless treatment of his subjects became so well-known that he caught the attention of Emperor Caesar Augustus (great-nephew of Gaius Julius Caesar), who once declared, "It is better to be Herod's dog than his subject."

The years following Herod's death continued to be horrifying for the people of Judea and the Galilee. Archelaus, Herod's son and heir, proved to be as ruthless as his father. Eventually (in April of

AD 6), a delegation of Judean Jews went to Rome to lodge a protest with Emperor Augustus against Archelaus. They demanded Jewish self-rule.

Augustus, a longtime proponent of local self-rule, gave the Judean delegation a confusing response. He revoked Archelaus's authority and exiled him to Gaul, but he flatly denied the Jews the right of self-rule. Instead, he incorporated Archelaus's three former domains into a single Senatorial protectorate province called Judaea, consisting of three states: Judea, Samaria, and Idumaea. This new province would be administered by a Roman Procurator.

FIRST ROMAN PROCURATOR OF JUDAEA

The appointment of a Roman Procurator in Judaea caused a violent revolt in Jerusalem (in February of AD 7, when Jesus was 13 years old). Enraged Jerusalem nationals took out their wrath on Sabinus, the Roman Procurator. Fearing for his life, Sabinus sought refuge in Herod's palace in Jerusalem. The rebels surrounded the palace and threatened to burn it to the ground. Then, leaving a contingent at the palace, the rebels turned their attention to Roman citizens and authorities living in Jerusalem. They imprisoned Romans, confiscated their property, and burned their homes and businesses.

Simultaneously, a revolt broke out in the Galilee, led by a man known as Judas of Gamala.

Upon receiving word that procurator Sabinus was under siege and that Judas of Gamala had started a rebellion in the Galilee, Quirinus, the Governor of Syria, dispatched troops to Jerusalem. He invaded the Galilee himself.

Quirinus overwhelmed the rebel-held city of Sepphoris, burning it to the ground. Then he tortured and dismembered Judas of Gamala (in a ghastly two-day display) and crucified the other rebels. Next, Quirinus turned his forces south, to help rescue Sabinus.

On August 19 of AD 7, Quirinus's troops joined the other forces and marched into Jerusalem. He overwhelmed the rebels who had laid siege to Herod's palace, rescuing Sabinus in the process. He then unleashed terror on the city. He executed 5,000 people by archery firing squad.

Two thousand more were crucified. Another 800 were beheaded, pulled apart, trampled by horses, or killed in battle.

After this suppression, an eerie calm reigned in Judaea and the Galilee until the first year of the procuratorship of a man named Pontius Pilate in AD 26.

And this brings us back to Jesus.

According to one account of the above events, "This rebellion and inexorable cessation by Quirinus doubtless made a tremendous impression upon the 13 and 14 year-old Jesus."

Indeed, can you imagine what was going on in Jesus' mind during this time? One of the most memorable events in his life up to that point had taken place only months before the upheaval began. In April of AD 6, he had become a Jewish *Son of the Law*. With the magnitude of that event still fresh on his mind, he found himself caught in the middle of a violent insurrection. Sepphoris, just five miles north of Jesus' home, was left in ashes. Most of its people were killed or enslaved. The governor's army marched right through Jesus' hometown en route to laying siege to the holy city of Jerusalem. Jesus' world would never be the same.

It took Jerusalem seven years to recover from Quirinus's punishment. In AD 10, the Procurator Ambivius convinced new ruler Herod Antipas (son of Herod the Great and brother of Archelaus) to rebuild Sepphoris and to use its enslaved former residents as laborers.

TIBERIUS APPOINTED SECOND EMPEROR OF ROMAN EMPIRE

In April of AD 13, Emperor Augustus appointed Tiberius Julius Caesar as his successor and the second Emperor of the Roman Empire. (Some people confuse Tiberius Julius Caesar with Gaius Julius Caesar. It might be helpful to remember that Tiberius became Emperor some 57 years *after* Gaius Julius Caesar was assassinated by Marcus Brutus and others.)

In AD 14, the Roman Senate sought to deify Augustus before his death. Augustus responded by consulting "the Sybil (prophetess) of Janus" to determine if someone mightier than he had been born, or would be born.

If the Sybil said no, then he would agree to be deified. If the Sybil said yes, he would not agree to deification, because someone else would be more deserving. As the legend goes, when Augustus questioned the Sybil, the prophetess replied, "*A heavenly child, who will be known as the Son of the Living God, has been born of a spotless virgin, in your Eastern provinces. He is mightier than you and mightier than any who will ever be born.*"

Thus, one of Augustus's last acts was to erect an altar on Capitol Hill, dedicated to "The Son of the Living God."

On August 18 of AD 14, Augustus died at age 76. Jesus was 21 years old.

Ruins of Tiberias. Roman construction dating from the time of Jesus is on the right. The remainder of the ruins dates back to the Crusades era—Israel.

CHAPTER 5

The Dream That Changed the World

AD 17

AFTER EMPEROR AUGUSTUS'S DEATH, five significant events took place in quick succession, which shaped Tiberius's career and influenced Rome's politics for centuries.

The Senate proclaimed Tiberius to be the new Emperor. (He was known formally as Tiberius Julius Caesar Augustus.)

Agrippa Postumus (adopted son of the deceased Augustus) was executed. (Some years earlier, Agrippa had been disinherited and exiled by Augustus because of his degenerate ethics.)

Tiberius proclaimed that the power to elect officials would be transferred from Rome's citizens to the Roman Senate.

The Senate decreed the deification of the deceased Augustus. Soon, Augustus's own chronicle of his reign was displayed on two bronze plates at the front of the Mausoleum Augusti. This marked the beginning of *mandatory* emperor worship. Refusal to worship was a crime.

The legions in Pannonia (a Roman province in what is now central Europe) revolted, and Tiberius sent his adopted son, Germanicus, to squash the revolt.

A Landmark Year in Tiberius's Reign.

On the night of March 13, Tiberius had a dream in which a man calling himself Genius told him about the birth of *The Theophus.*

I should note here that for years I had heard various stories about Tiberius's Theophus dream and its connection to Jesus but I had never uncovered credible documentation of this dream.

Then, I traveled to Greece.

There, I visited the library of St. Stephen's monastery. The brothers (monks) at the monastery had translated every document in the library into Italian, French, Greek, and English and had written background history for everything.

As I perused the library, I found a large three-leaf manuscript, written in French on three 12-by-32-inch sheets of the finest parchment. These pages were bound between two pieces of cedar, held together with brass clasps. Obviously, the pages were once part of a larger text.

As I read this manuscript and its background information, my assumptions about Tiberius's famous dream were confirmed. This document was a fourteenth century French copy of a German document (written by Gothard, an eleventh century Abbot of a Bavarian monastery). The original German document had disappeared during Napoleon's purge of Bavaria.

The French translation was discovered in Auch, France, in 1610, during the renovation of an old monastery. Two days after the discovery of this translation, a monk from Auch, acting on what he deemed to be divine direction, stabbed King Henry IV to death. (This monk apparently believed that the discovery of the manuscript was God's cue to murder the king.)

When Henry's supporters discovered the motive behind the monk's actions, they were furious. For the next three months they rode throughout southern France searching all monasteries, convents and churches on a search and destroy mission targeting all religious manuscripts, documents, and relics. Word of this campaign spread rapidly, so most of the treasured ancient manuscripts were hidden until the rage had passed. However, the manuscript that caused all the problems, the one that I held in my hands, did not escape. Of this volume's 40-plus pages, only three survived.

Here is why: At the Auch monastery, Henry's supporters seized the bound volume and started ripping its pages from the binding and throwing them into a fire. The monastery's Abbot managed to rescue three leaves from the flames. Then he dashed into the church for safety. Henry's henchmen didn't bother to pursue him. After all, they had most of the manuscript along with dozens of other confiscated documents to destroy.

However, the Abbot continued to fear for his life, so he fled to Greece's Meteora monastic community, bringing the salvaged pages with him.

As I continued to study the Meteora monks' historical records, I learned that the pages I held in my hands were once part of a large three-volume collection detailing the rise and fall of Jesus' popularity in Rome.

Fortunately for me, the French monk who translated the collection had used both sides of large parchment sheets and he wrote in very small letters. So my three pages contained a wealth of information.

My pages focused on the famous life-changing dream of Emperor Tiberius.

In the dream, a man wearing royal garb appears to Tiberius, who sits on his sentencing chair. Tiberius rises and, uncharacteristically, bows to his visitor. The man tells Tiberius not to bow before him, as he is a mere messenger representing the *I am*. The messenger introduces himself as Genius. He proclaims that during the reign of Augustus Caesar, a man known as *The Theophus* was born of a simple virgin maiden, in the eastern province of Augustus's domain. (The title *The Theophus*, by the way, means "King and Emperor forever.")

Genius goes on to tell Tiberius that The Theophus' kingdom will be eternal, encompassing the earth. Further, this being will perform miracles, signs, and wonders. Even nature will obey him. Further, he will demonstrate great insight and wisdom. Genius then warns Tiberius that he shouldn't accept worship directed to him (Tiberius).

When Tiberius woke from this dream, he was bewildered, but he was also convinced that the dream's message was true. He became determined (some might say *obsessed*) to find The Theophus.

Tiberius became so fixated on his search that he offered automatic and irrevocable Roman citizenship to every resident of the state or province in which The Theophus was found.

Tiberius also proclaimed that he would not tolerate any form of personal exaltation or worship.

Tiberius sent personally chosen ambassadors from Rome to every eastern province in the Roman world to interview and appoint trustworthy representatives to search for any sign that The Theophus lived in a given region or that he had been born in that region.

As you might guess, this campaign led to a host of alleged "Theophus sightings." Claims poured into Rome. All claims were dutifully investigated by the appointed ambassadors. By the time Jesus' ministry began, these ambassadors were buried in a two-year backlog of various sightings and claims, each waiting to be confirmed or debunked.

The Abbot Gothard claimed that Herod Antipas' followers proved themselves relentless in their search for The Theophus, knowing their efforts would be richly rewarded by Tiberius, with political privileges, tax benefits, citizenship, and prestige. During Tiberius's reign, these Herodians enjoyed the highest level of influence and respect.

I stopped reading and sat for a few minutes, trying to process what I had just learned. If this information was true, it explained the Herodians involvement in Jesus' ministry.

I had been taught that the Herodians joined with the Pharisees and Sadducees in their enmity toward Jesus. They were complicit in efforts to trap Jesus into doing or saying something politically seditious or religiously blasphemous.

However, if the Herodians were assisting Tiberius, I needed to re-evaluate why these people sought Jesus and why Herod Antipas (when he questioned Jesus before his crucifixion) hoped Jesus would perform a miracle for him.

Perhaps the Herodians were *not* trying to trap Jesus. Instead, they were trying to gather intelligence central to Tiberius's Theophus. Without a doubt, Jesus would have been regarded as a possible Theophus.

This perspective made sense to me. After all, the Herodians were not religious. They could accurately be called agnostic. Why would they join forces with the Sadducees and Pharisees? The answer was obvious. They didn't. They merely used the Sadducees and Pharisees to provoke Jesus and force a reaction from him so that they could observe his character and temperament. The true Theophus would react to any snare with patience. He would respond to deviousness with wisdom.

Armed with this new insight, I plunged back into the Gothard manuscript.

VALLEUS PATERCULUS

According to official documents from the Senate of Rome, a prominent Roman citizen named Valleus Paterculus was central to Tiberius's Theophus investigation. Paterculus was a well-respected Roman historian who was 19 years old when Jesus was born. Paterculus had been a close friend of Augustus Caesar, who promoted him repeatedly until he became one of the most influential men in Rome. Some time between the age of 35 and 40, Paterculus retired to his villa to write his *Historia Romania*.

Paterculus was to have an influence that transcended politics or literature. I'll explain how. After his Theophus dream, Tiberius commissioned 130 Ambassadors to investigate sightings or actions of The Theophus. If one of these Ambassadors felt he had discovered something important, a *Chief Ambassador* would be dispatched for further investigation. This Chief Ambassador would then report his findings to Tiberius, who would either dismiss the report or resend his Chief Ambassador along with four Roman Senators, a Magistrate from the Roman Treasury, and a top Military Magistrate for more research. This research would include interrogations of any Theophus candidate.

At this point, if the Chief Ambassador determined that the subject in question *was* The Theophus, he had the authority to announce the news to the world. The cash rewards promised by Tiberius would be distributed, and the lucky residents of the region would be exempted from taxes and military service.

Tiberius' choice for the vitally important role of Chief Ambassador was the recently retired Valleus Paterculus.

Within three years of Tiberius' dream, Paterculus and his team of Ambassadors were, arguably, the most powerful group of men in the world. Tiberius gave this "Theophus Commission of Ambassadors" unprecedented power and vast financial resources to carry out their task.

With this fact, I came to the end of Gothard's manuscript.

As I considered what I had just read, I understood how Tiberius' obsession with The Theophus influenced how Roman authorities treated Jesus.

MURIAS OF THEOPHUS

The next step on my "Theophus" search was a visit to the Musee Historique Lorraine in Nancy, France.

I began my visit to this museum by strolling through its collections of Greek and Roman artifacts. In the Roman sector, I discovered a statue unlike any of the hundreds I had seen before. It was a statue of a beautiful bare-breasted woman holding a bird in one hand. With the other hand, she cupped one of her breasts. The sculpture was titled *A Muria of Theophus*. The caption below the title read, *A tribute to the members of the Murias of Theophus as appointed by Tiberius first century AD.*

I was astounded. Here was that name *Theophus* again.

As I studied the sculpture's every detail, a 20-something woman approached me. I had been running my hand across the statue's marble arms, and she reprimanded me, politely: "Please don't touch the works of art."

I hastily apologized, then asked, "Can you tell me about this statue?"

"Although the sculpture's creator is unknown," she told me, "we know that it dates back to the first-century reign of Tiberius Caesar. It depicts a religious movement that sprung from a dream of Tiberius, which evolved into a cult religion called The Murias of Theophus."

I nodded, and she continued: "In the first century, a member of the Murias confronted Jesus. This incident is recorded in St. Luke's Gospel, chapter 11:27-28." Then, to my surprise, she quoted the Scripture.

LUKE 11:27-28

[27] And it came to pass, as he spake these things, a certain woman of the company (Murias) lifted up her voice, and said unto him, Blessed is the womb that bare thee, and the paps which thou hast sucked.

[28] But he said, Yea rather, blessed are they that hear the word of God, and keep it.

I asked her if she knew anything more about the Murias cult.

She confessed that she knew only a little. The cult fizzled out, she told me, after Tiberius' death.

"Contrary to his request," she said, "Tiberius *was* deified. His successor Caligula, third emperor of the Roman Empire, claimed that Tiberius actually fulfilled his own dream. Caligula officially proclaimed that Tiberius was The Theophus.

"After this proclamation," my young friend continued, "the cult died out. The fervent searches for the Theophus were abandoned. Within 100 years of Tiberius's death, the cult was pretty much forgotten.

"Consequently, all that is known about *The Murias of Theophus* comes from a few historical texts from that period, a few first-century Senate reports, a handful of state treasury records, and a few lines from a few biographies."

She must have seen my disappointment, because she quickly added, "But I will tell you everything else I know about the cult."

We sat down on a wooden bench near the sculpture, and she began to explain *The Murias of Theophus*. What follows is a paraphrase of that explanation:

After Tiberius had his dream, his wife, Livia, claimed she had been visited by the Roman goddess Juno, who told her that she (Juno) was the mother of The Theophus and that Livia was to organize a *murias* (a myriad or a group of 10,000 devoted prophetesses) who would be led by Juno's spirit. They would roam throughout the eastern empire, searching for The Theophus.

The theologian Athanasius tells us that on March 20 of AD 22, these 10,000 roaming prophetesses left Rome. Legend holds that Juno gave them special insight so that they would be able to recognize The Theophus when they found him. By AD 30, The Murias of Theophus cult center had been moved from Rome to the Temple of Juno in Caesarea Philippi. By then, the original spirit of the mission had deteriorated into nothing short of roaming religious prostitution.

The standard method of operation used by members of *The Murias of Theophus* group confirms the biblical account in Luke 11.

When a Murias prophetess approached a man of her choosing, she would say in a voice loud enough for all to hear, "Blessed is the womb that conceived thee and the paps which nourished thee." This pronouncement signified that Juno had recognized the chosen man as a possible Theophus candidate. The prophetess commanded the chosen man to repeat after her, 'Blessed is the fruit of the queen of heaven'

It was claimed these prophetesses were Juno in human form and that through a sexual encounter Juno would recognize her son. As her son, The Theophus would not be able to bring the sexual encounter to completeness because his seed would naturally reject the potential impregnation of his own spirit mother.

If the man completed the sexual union, he would give the prophetess a monetary contribution. Three-quarters of the contribution was delivered to the Temple of Juno in Caesarea Philippi and the remaining one-quarter was allowed to be used by the prophetess. If the man did not complete the sexual union then this action was perceived to be a sign that the man may qualify as a candidate for The Theophus. The man was then encouraged to accompany the prophetess to the Temple of Juno in Caesarea Philippi. There he would go through a three-day ordeal of numerous sexual encounters with the three Most High Priestesses of Juno. If he successfully endured these encounters without a climactic ending, he was chosen as a Theophus candidate and was given his reward in gold.

From a social viewpoint it was a great honor for any man to be chosen by a member of The Murias of Theophus. He could qualify to receive gold equal to 13 years' wages of an average tradesman. That was enough to catapult any man's economic status from one of poverty or mediocrity to that of extreme wealth.

While much of her story was disturbing, it did help explain why Jesus on occasions abruptly left one region to travel to another and so often warned people he healed not to tell anyone. I had been taught all my life it was because it was not yet time for Jesus to reveal who he really was. If it was well known that Jesus was being examined as a possible candidate for The Theophus, then previously unexplained, unjustified, and illogical actions can now be logically explained and justified. It could explain why the Pharisees were so antagonistic, the Sadducees were so cynical, the scribes were so sarcastic, and the Romans so accommodating throughout his ministry until the last few weeks of his life.

CHAPTER 6

Life Under the Rule of Herod the "Great"

NOW THAT WE HAVE a broad summary of the Roman political and religious scene, it's time to explore the state of Judea's *specific* political climate in the years leading up to Jesus' birth.

Enter a book titled *The Life of Herod the Great,* published in 1876 by Elbert Conway, a professor of biblical history at Edinburgh University. I found a copy of this book in the library of England's Lancaster University.

Conway notes that Gaius Julius Caesar's assassination in 44 BC triggered a Roman civil war. When Herod's politically powerful father, Antipater, died a year later, Herod became Judea's unofficial ruler. Herod managed Judea and the Galilee so well that he was eventually named official Tetrarch of Judea.

KING OF THE JEWS APPOINTED

Civil war again erupted in western Rome near the end of 40 BC. Taking advantage of the instability, the Parthians invaded Roman Syria (which included Judea) a year later. Because of the civil war, Rome could not afford to send troops to confront this invasion. Thus, the Roman

Senate granted the title *King of the Jews* to Herod, giving him authority to defend Judea and the Galilee against the Parthian invasion.

At first, according to Conway, Herod's defensive effort went badly. The Parthians captured Jerusalem and installed a Hasmonean named Antigonus as Judea's ruler. Herod fled to Rome. However, he returned with Roman troops and battled for three years to retake Jerusalem. He spent another year driving the Parthians out of the Galilee and Syria. The victory cemented Herod the Great's status as *King of the Jews*, a title he would hold until his death in 4 BC, while Jesus was still a toddler.

Throughout his reign, Herod remained a friend and ally of Rome, but he was hated by his subjects in Judea.

He was feared even among his own family. During his 32-year reign, he had two of his wives and three of his sons killed. More than 400 of Herod's family members were killed, upon his orders.

Herod the Great lacked morals. He was capable of extreme brutality, but he was also devious. Aware of his disfavor among the religious community and his Judean subjects, Herod tried to appease them by launching grandiose building projects, as we saw back in Chapter 4.

By the time of Jesus' birth, Herod the Great had become Judea's most powerful homegrown political figure in more than eight centuries.

Herod's status placed Emperor Augustus (who succeeded Gaius Julius Caesar) in a quandary. Augustus despised Herod for his senseless cruelty, yet he couldn't ignore the king's political skills. The Judean area comprised the crossroads of Roman trade routes, and a skilled administrator for the region was essential. Hence, Augustus chose to look the other way when it came to Herod.

A grave that has been identified as belonging to
the House of Herod. Tradition says that Herod Antipas
was buried here—Israel.

CHAPTER 7

Religion During the Days of Jesus

NOW IT IS TIME to move from the political to the religious. What was religious life like in Jesus' time? I found a great resource on this topic at the Rococo Library in Mannheim, Germany—in the form of a Latin manuscript written in 372 by Pope Damasus I.

Like most of this library's ancient documents, Damasus' work had been translated into German, French, Spanish, and English. According to the accompanying historical information, the manuscript was a school lesson written by the Pope for his new secretary, Jerome (who later became St. Jerome). The seven surviving manuscript leaves were part of a 60-leaf text explaining the prevailing religions and philosophies of Jesus' day and how those influences were still very much alive in the fourth century.

This manuscript captivated me. According to Pope Damasus, the religious climate of Jesus' day was as diverse as it is in today's United States. Some of Jesus' teachings and parables were influenced by other religions, especially religions observed by the Romans.

In Damasus's introduction, he states his intention to focus on religions other than Judaism.

He goes on to say that the Greco/Roman Hellenistic social system was a hodgepodge of religious beliefs and philosophies. Judaism was dominant in Judea, but elsewhere one could find the influence of other belief systems. Here are just a few:

1. *Greek Hellenic and Roman cults.* These included worship and ritual observances associated with Greek and Roman mythological gods. Apart from Judea and Jerusalem, these Greek and Roman religions were dominant in Judaea.

2. *Emperor worship.* This was the deification of the Roman Emperor. Emperor worship didn't become an official religion until after Augustus's death, but during Jesus' ministry such worship was common.

3. *Astrology.* By the second century BC, this pseudo-science (imported from Babylon) was widespread in the Greco-Roman world.

4. Zoroastrianism. Imported from Persia, Zoroastrianism was probably the No. 1 religion in the Galilee and in the Decapolis from 2 BC until 3 AD. Eudemos Zoroastrian philosophy, which is a philosophy rooted in the mystical ascension to God dogma of the religion, had its greatest influence with the higher educated of Syria. This philosophy, along with Cynicism, was taught in all public education institutions in the Galilee (Eudemos Zoroastrianism teaching was compulsory up to age 17, while Cynicism was optional, but strongly recommended).

5. *The Mystery Religions.* By the first century AD, Syria was home to at least 60 mystery cults. Imported from Egypt and Babylon, these cults popped up throughout the Greco-Roman world in the 300-year period between the first century BC and second century AD.

According to Damasus, religious worship during this era was separate from everyday life. Philosophy on the other hand *was life.* It guided how a person lived daily. Four of these philosophies had their roots in the early Platonism of the Greeks:

1. *Epicureanism.* This school of thought was dedicated to the pursuit of happiness. It taught that people could do things to improve their standing in life. Epicureanism was an extremely optimistic philosophy.

2. *Stoicism.* The Stoics believed that a controlling Reason-Fate dominated all of nature. They taught that the human soul was divine, but imprisoned in an evil physical body. One could achieve liberty from the body by living in harmony with "the Universal Mind" and nature.

3. *Cynicism.* This philosophy was championed by Diogenes of Athens. Its core doctrine: Humanity could save itself. Diogenes espoused simplicity and virtue and encouraged people to meet death with courage, because a better life lay ahead. The apostle Paul was greatly influenced by Cynicism.

4. *Skepticism.* This philosophy claimed that knowledge was a fallacy. Certainty was impossible. This most pessimistic of philosophies was highly influential among the Herodians.

Damasus also explores a few other influential religions of Jesus' time. I will summarize the most relevant of these for you:

1. *Hinduism.* One of the world's oldest religions, Hinduism came from India. According to Damasus, Hinduism had a huge following in upper Syria and Persia during the days of Jesus.

2. Hinduism gave birth to *Buddhism.* (Buddhism began in India about 500 years before Jesus' birth.) Its founder was Siddhartha Gautama, born in 560 BC. About 200 years after his death, Siddhartha (or Buddha) began to be worshipped as a god, contrary to his teachings.

3. *Confucianism.* More ethical system than religion, Confucianism was founded by Chiu King, circa 520 BC. Around 200 BC, Chiu's followers deified him. (As with Buddhism, this deification was contrary to its founder's

teaching.) Confucianism was taught in every school of higher education in the Roman Empire. Thus, it spawned thousands of disciples. Jesus was probably well-versed in Confucianism.

Damasus concludes this analysis by saying,

"All of these religious and philosophical influences were active in the Galilee during the time of Jesus' life and ministry. To speculate that Jesus was not acquainted with them or that his thinking was not influenced by them would be illogical and presumptuous. Jesus had been taught most of these religious ideas and philosophies as part of his compulsory education in schools in Egypt and in the Galilee.

Our question should not be whether he was acquainted with or influenced by these religions and philosophies, but rather how was Jesus able to garner conceptual truth out of each, and then combine and use those truths in a way that was not only the absolute truth, but was truth pleasing to God the Father, and beneficial to the people to whom he was ministering.

In essence, Jesus was the ideal master discerner of truth and the faultless artisan of compilation of that truth. Quintessentially, Jesus' teachings were neither a compilation of religious ideas nor a conglomeration of heathen religious philosophies and ethics. Rather, they were an acquisition of absolute truth as instructed and directed by the Holy Spirit."

These insights from Damasus prepare us for our next destination, an understanding of the *social order* of Jesus' day.

SOCIAL ORDER

At The German National Museum in Nuremberg, I found an 1809 manuscript written by Vincent Strambi, Bishop of Macerata and Tolentino. Bishop Strambi was banished by Napoleon for refusing to swear an oath of allegiance. He fled to the northern Italian/Austrian border and stayed there until Napoleon was defeated at Waterloo.

Like the Damasus manuscript (and so many others I discovered), Strambi's was only partial. Seven pages of 50 had survived.

In these pages, Strambi describes the various social orders found in Judaea and the Galilee at the time of Jesus' ministry.

He first concentrates on the province of Judaea. The following is a paraphrase of his insights:

At the time of Jesus' ministry, Judaea was divided socially rather than culturally or nationally. The population was roughly 20 to 30 percent Jewish, and almost 85 percent of this Jewish segment lived in the state of Judea.

The categories of the population in Judaea were divided along social and political ranks and orders.

- *The aristocracy:* the upper classes with money and official power.

- *The patricians:* the second level of wealth and political authority.

- *The esquirian:* "earned" authority.

- *The middle class:* small and formed the backbone of Judean society.

- *The proletariat:* the commoners, majority of the free Judean population

- *The plebeians:* lowest level of commoners. It was the second largest free Judaean population group.

- *Slaves:* by far the largest social group in the Roman Empire, but second to the proletariat in the province of Judaea.

Although these Judean Jews identified with traditional Jewish ancestry, it is doubtful that even 1 percent of those professing Judaism could trace their ancestry back to a pure Hebrew bloodline. Most had a mixed-race heritage, which technically (according to the Old Testament) would have disqualified them as pure Hebrew/Jews.

The remainder of Judaea's population comprised at least 30 other groups. However, because of the strong presence of Jews in Judea, many non-Jews adopted Jewish lifestyle and mannerisms. Moreover, the Jewish religious community was given so much freedom by the Roman authorities that Jews attempted to proselytize non-Jews. Apparently, they were somewhat successful. More than 75 percent of the non-Roman population identified with Judaism or with Jewish customs, manners, rituals, celebrations, and observances.

In other regions, however, (e.g., Idumaea and Samaria) Judaism was not honored. At best, it was tolerated.

Next, Strambi turns his attention to the Galilee. Judea's Jewish population viewed the Galilee and its residents with little respect. They referred to the Galilee as *Galil-ha-goyim*. Translation: *Galilee, the land of the heathen and the uneducated.*

In the Galilee, about 99 percent of the population was from a lineage other than Jewish. They were Syrian, Greek, Persian, Babylonian, Phoenician, Assyrian, Egyptian, and others.

Again, as he did with Judaea, Strambi aligned the population of the Galilee along social strata.

- *The aristocracy:* As it was in Judaea, these were the upper classes with money and official power.

- *The particians:* They were the second level of wealth and political authority.

- *The esquirian:* As in Judaea, it was the level of authority and wealth that was earned.

- *The middle class:* This group in the Galilee was larger than the middle class in Judaea.

- *The proletariat:* the commoners.

- *The plebeians:* the lowest level of commoners.

- *The slaves:* The third largest population group in the Galilee.

It's also noteworthy that Galilean Jews were far more liberal in their religious views and observances than their Judean counterparts.

So despised were the Galilean Jews by Judea's religious leaders that it was almost impossible for a Galilean to become a rabbi. If a Galilean Jewish student managed to ascend the religious education ladder to the level of rabbi or Rabban (master teacher), it was regarded as an historic event.

Although Galilean Jews were more religiously liberal than Judean Jews, they were far *less* liberal when it came to politics. Thus, they were less cooperative with Roman authorities. At the time of Jesus' ministry, Galilee was a hotbed of anti-Roman sentiment, which sometimes expressed itself violently.

Because the Galilee was so volatile politically, entire legions of Roman soldiers were permanently stationed there. The presence of Roman soldiers was a constant in Jesus' life.

This is not to say that a Galilean Jew was automatically an enemy of Rome. If someone cooperated with Roman authorities and stayed out of political trouble, he could live a quiet and productive life. Also if he befriended local Romans and attempted to make peace, as Jesus did, he could rise to a high level of influence in Roman-occupied Galilee.

Strambi emphasizes that even though the Galilee was subject to Roman rule, it was socially and culturally *Greek*. Greek was *the* official language of all the countries, territories, and provinces of the Mare Nostrum area, as well as the official language of the eastern Roman Empire. Moreover, Greek culture, philosophy, religion, architecture, morality, art, education, and so on were the order of the day.

This last surviving page of Strambi's work addresses the distinctive dress styles that characterized Judaea and the Galilee.

Again, I will paraphrase Strambi:

In Judea (especially Jerusalem), dress and general appearance reflected Jewish tradition and custom. For men, that meant unshaven faces, uncut hair and long robes that also served as a head covering (head covering was compulsory).

It was customary for women to have long hanging hair, veiled faces, covered heads, a long (ankle length) heavy linen or wool undergarment, a long wool outer robe, and sandals. The remainder of the Jews in Judaea, except for those in the state of Judea, dressed more like Galileans. In other words, they dressed *Greek*.

For Galilean men, sporting a Greek appearance meant short hair and a clean-shaven face. (Or perhaps a short and well-trimmed beard.) For most of the year, these men wore a short-sleeved linen or light wool body garment, adding a longer, course-woven woolen outer robe in winter. Footwear consisted of lace-up sandals. Normally there was no head covering.

Their female counterparts wore their hair short or gathered it on top of their heads. A married woman wore a short (knee-length) sleeveless or short-sleeved dress-like linen garment called a *stola*, along with brief-style silk or linen undergarments. In winter, they added a long linen or wool outer robe.

Joseph and Mary, Jesus, and most of his disciples would have dressed in this Galilean/Greek fashion. They would have culturally and socially been Greek with Greek customs and manners, and they would have spoken Greek in their everyday conversation. When he was growing up, the only time Jesus would have spoken Hebrew was when he went to the Temple (if even then), and the only time he would have spoken Aramaic (if at all) was when he went to Jerusalem.

At home, Mary, Joseph, and their children would have spoken Greek, as long as they lived in the Galilee. However, after Joseph's death (circa early AD 30), the family moved to Jerusalem and probably switched to Aramaic as their everyday language.

With this bit of information, the Strambi manuscript ends, as does this chapter.

The Dome of the Rock, built over the ancient site of the Jewish Temple of worship in Jerusalem. It is the second most holy site for Muslims—Israel.

CHAPTER 8

❧

John: A Son in Old Age

Now, with a rather full political, religious, and social backdrop established, it is time to focus on Jesus *himself*. Let's begin our exploration with a pair of angelic visits.

In the first chapter of Luke's Gospel, the angel Gabriel appears to the priest Zacharias, announcing that his wife, Elizabeth, will have a son. He is to be named John. (Eventually he will be known as John the Baptist.)

History indicates that Zacharias, of Levite ancestry (from the house of Aaron through the line of Abijah, Nehemiah 12:17), was an ordinary priest whose primary duty was Temple service.

According to Shillel, a priest serving in Hebron at the time of Herod the Great, there were more than 24,000 priests. Although priests like Zacharias were allowed to perform religious duties twice during a year, the honor of performing Temple duties was given to an ordinary priest only once in a lifetime. The privilege of burning incense was determined by drawing lots. It was during this singular opportunity that Gabriel appears to Zacharias. In Luke 1:8-9 we read:

LUKE 1:8-9

[8] And it came to pass, that while he executed the priest's office before God in the order of his course,

[9] According to the custom of the priest's office, his lot was to burn incense when he went into the temple of the Lord.

It's vital to note that we are talking about a very old priest here. Zacharias had waited a lifetime for this privilege, which was the highlight of his career.

This old man Zacharias and his wife Elizabeth were childless. According to Jewish tradition, childlessness to a woman, like sterility to a man, was viewed as a curse from God, perhaps caused by some secret sin. When Gabriel appears and tells Zacharias that his prayer has been answered, it is safe to conclude that the priest's prayer was for a child.

Gabriel announces that Elizabeth, though well past childbearing years, will have a son, who is to be called *John*. John is a Greek name (Ioannes) that means *loved* or *favored*.

GABRIEL TALKS WITH MARY

Some six months after Elizabeth conceives, Gabriel returns. This visitation (Matthew 1:18-23 and Luke 1:26-38), involves another "birth announcement." Its subject is Jesus.

Before I continue further, I want to give a little background concerning the first chapter of Luke. Luke is the primary source of information on the birth of John and Mary's visit to Elizabeth. Luke, the physician, typically wrote in Greek or Latin. Unusually Luke 1:5-47, and Luke 1:56-80 were written in Aramaic.

According to a third century Arab/Christian tradition, the difference in the language used by Luke was because these portions of chapter one are a record of Luke's personal interview with Mary, the mother of Jesus. The interview was conducted some 25 years after the death and resurrection of Jesus, probably in Jerusalem.

Mary answered Luke's questions in the language of the hearth, the Aramaic language used by most Jerusalem Jewish commoners of that day. Few Galileans spoke this language. Luke wrote as Mary had spoken to him, in the language she chose to speak, Aramaic, rather than her native Galilean Greek dialect.

Luke reverts to the Greek language in Luke 1:48-55 as he gives his own personal tribute and praise to Mary, much of it imitating the Song of Hannah in the Old Testament. Then in Luke 1:56-80 he again picks up his interview with Mary and writes in the Aramaic language as Mary spoke to him.

I found a most-fascinating resource on the annunciation (and the issue of Mary's virginity) at Emory University's Candler School of Theology in Atlanta, in the form a book by Rev. Charles Chauncy. (Chauncy pastored the First Church of Boston from 1727-1787.)

In his *Seasonable Thoughts on the State of Religion in New England* (published in 1743), Chauncy explores the espousal of Joseph and Mary. Early in the book, he paints a picture of Joseph and Mary, quoting from Isaiah and the Gospels of Matthew and Luke:

MATTHEW 1:18, 23

[18] Now the birth of Jesus Christ was on this wise: When as his mother Mary was espoused to Joseph, before they came together, she was found with child of the Holy Ghost.

[23] Behold, a virgin shall be with child, and shall bring forth a son, and they shall call his name Emmanuel, which being interpreted is, God with us.

LUKE 1:26-27, 31-32, 34-35

[26] And in the sixth month the angel Gabriel was sent from God unto a city of Galilee, named Nazareth,

[27] To a virgin espoused to a man whose name was Joseph, of the house of David; and the virgin's name was Mary.

[31] And, behold, thou shalt conceive in thy womb, and bring forth a son, and shalt call his name JESUS.

[32] He shall be great, and shall be called the Son of the Highest: and the Lord God shall give unto him the throne of his father David:

[34] Then said Mary unto the angel, How shall this be, seeing I know not a man?

[35] And the angel answered and said unto her, The Holy Ghost shall come upon thee, and the power of the Highest shall overshadow thee: therefore also that holy thing which shall be born of thee shall be called the Son of God.

ISAIAH 7:14

¹⁴ Therefore the Lord himself shall give you a sign; Behold, a virgin shall conceive, and bear a son, and shall call his name Immanuel.

Chauncy follows these Scriptures with commentary, which I will paraphrase for you.

Traditional interpretation of Matthew 1:18 states that this Scripture *implies* Mary's virginity by indicating she is with child *"before they came together."* The Greek word for this phrase is *sunelthein*. However, this word has two meanings. The first is "before living together." The other is "come together physically." Hence, this Scripture isn't a definitive statement of Mary's virginity.

The same can be said of Matthew 1:23 and Luke 1:27, often cited as proof texts of Mary's virginity. In each of these references, the Greek word used for "virgin" is *parthenos*, meaning "an unmarried maiden, a maid of marrying age, or a young girl."

Chauncy then evaluates Isaiah 7:14, a foundational verse for the virgin birth of Jesus. Here, Isaiah prophesies, "Behold a virgin shall conceive." The Hebrew word used for virgin here is *almah*, or "a young woman, or a woman of childbearing age." This word, Chauncy notes, was typically used about empires, kingdoms, races of people, social systems, or nations. *Almah* is used 30 times in the Old Testament. Only twice does it refer to a young woman and specifically an unmarried young woman.

Chauncy claims that the translators of the Greek Septuagint, when translating Isaiah 7:14-16, correctly translated the Hebrew *ha-almah* to the Greek word *pathenos* (which the King James renders *virgin*), meaning "a young girl just into puberty," but when the Greek text was translated *back* into Hebrew and then into Latin, the translators incorrectly used the word *patanos*, instead of pathenos. Patanos means "a virgin, a woman who has never had sexual relations."

Because of this error, the translators used the Hebrew word *betulah* (meaning "virgin"), instead of *almah*.

By the time the King James translation was completed in the early 1600s, Mary's virginity had become a foundational rock upon which the Roman Catholic Church stood. Hence, to challenge the accepted meaning of the Isaiah Scripture would be heresy.

So, Chauncy summarizes, it seems that only one Scripture (Luke 1:34) makes a definitive statement about the virgin birth. (Of course, even one Scripture is enough!)

In this Scripture, Mary questions Gabriel, who has delivered amazing news to her. She asks how she could bear a child, since "I *know not a man?* The key Greek word here is *gignosko* (*cognoscere*, in Latin). Both words were used to describe a woman who has had no physical relations with a man. A detailed definition of the Greek word means "to produce a child through marriage relationships." The Latin word means "sexual relations."

Consequently, (in the Greek) Mary is saying, "*I cannot produce a child; I am not married.*" In Latin, she is saying, "*I have not had sexual relations.*"

After making this key point, Chauncy describes the annunciation.

According to the Luke setting, the angel Gabriel appeared to Mary in the city of Nazareth, but it does not say where she was at the time. Speculation has ranged from when she was sleeping in her house to shopping in the market.

However, an eleventh century Latin manuscript I discovered in London, reputed to be a copy of some of St. Ignatius's second century writings, claims that as Mary approached a fountain in Nazareth, to fill her water pitcher, Gabriel appeared to her.

An Arabic manuscript written by a scribe named Abid of Damascus in the eighth century says that Mary was impregnated by the spirit of God while she slept and that when she awoke an angel ate bread with her. The angel told her that she had conceived during the night and that the fruit of her womb would be the son of the Most High.

Concerning Mary's virginity and the virgin birth of Jesus, I found significant information at Queen's College Cambridge. I read literally dozens of book segments, manuscripts, and documents that ranged from the early Talmuds to the first and second century Christian writers, and from early Arabic traditions to Gnostic spiritualist writings.

What I discovered was that the controversy concerning the virgin birth had been ongoing from the time of Jesus' earthly life up to the present day.

After studying numerous documents, I concluded that about half of what I had read at Queen's College supported the virgin birth of Jesus. The other half either flatly rejected the virgin birth or tried to explain it away.

The authors of the documents supporting the virgin birth generally did not go into detail about why they believed in it. It appeared they accepted the virgin birth as a matter of principle.

The documents that rejected the virgin birth usually seemed to have attached to their rejection a justification, and an alternate theory of what they claimed was the truth about Jesus' birth. In these non-virgin-birth hypotheses, there seemed to be a common thread of quasi-logic. The one thread of "logic" that all seemed to share was that Mary, a young girl, probably age twelve, thirteen, or fourteen, had sexual relations before she was married and became pregnant.

Chauncy reasons, of course if a person begins his search for the truth about the virgin birth with a pre-determined conclusion of unbelief, then chances are he will eventually find some documentation someplace to justify his conclusion.

At this point, Chauncy posits a series of theological arguments that did not add much to his case. So, I skipped ahead and picked up again with his retelling of some of the myths associated with Mary's conception.

Chauncy cites several stories, both eye-opening and disturbing to anyone who cherishes the traditional biblical accounts of Jesus' birth, but it is important to realize how many alternate theories about Jesus' conception were floating around during the first centuries of Christianity.

Central to the *true* account of Jesus' birth, of course, is Mary and her angelic visit. Let's get back to this event and its ramifications.

After Mary had received the visit from Gabriel, she left her home in Nazareth in the Galilee and traveled to Judea to visit Elizabeth.

LUKE 1:39-41
[39] And Mary arose in those days, and went into the hill country with haste, into a city of Juda;
[40] And entered into the house of Zacharias, and saluted Elisabeth.

[41] And it came to pass, that, when Elisabeth heard the salutation of Mary, the babe leaped in her womb; and Elisabeth was filled with the Holy Ghost:

During my years of research, I found a truly enlightening document describing this event while I was exploring the British Library in London. The document was a thirteenth century Old English commentary on a ninth century Latin book titled *Protevangelium of James* compiled by a man who identified himself as Richard of Tadcaster.

I will paraphrase Richard's commentary for you here:

After Gabriel's visit, Mary hurriedly left her home to visit her cousin Elizabeth, who was pregnant with John. If tradition is correct, Mary was pregnant at this time, meaning that Jesus was probably conceived in July or August of 8 BC.

The Gospels say that Joseph and Mary had three other sons: Joses or Joseph, Judas, and Simon, as well as an unspecified number of daughters. According to the *Protevangelium of James*, Mary had ten sons and four daughters. Along with Jesus, Joses, Judas, and Simon, she also had Judas Thomas, Jonas, Judah, Enos, and Levi James. The daughters' names were Miriam, Melkha, Eskha, and Ruth.

Richard of Tadcaster writes that of these, Mary's second son, James, was born in Egypt, or in Nazareth immediately before they fled to Egypt. The other sons, (except for Judas Thomas) and daughters were born in the Galilee, Edom, or Moab.

As for Elizabeth's son, for centuries the Roman Church depicted John the Baptist as a religious "wild man," growing up as a hermit in the desert. According to Luke, Mary went to visit Elizabeth *in a city* in Judah. This would indicate that John grew up in a city and, when he reached a certain age, left home to live in the wilderness. Thus, John's social background for the first 25 years of his life was urban, not nomadic.

Meanwhile, Luke records nothing about Mary's long journey (about 80 miles) to Elizabeth's home. This trek could have taken up to 10 days. Luke is also silent about Joseph's reaction to the trip. Instead, Luke immediately takes us to Elizabeth's home and focuses on the women's meeting.

Luke says that Elizabeth was filled with the Holy Ghost the moment she heard Mary's greeting. In Luke 1:15, the angel tells Zacharias that John would be filled with the Holy Ghost *"from his mother's womb."* In other words, John would be filled because his mother was filled.

In Luke 1:41, the angel's promise to Zacharias comes true. Elizabeth is filled with the Holy Ghost, which in turn fills the unborn babe. Elizabeth immediately cringes because of the birth contractions, but the pain gives way to joy, as she greets *the mother of my Lord.*

Richard notes that the word used for 'mother' here is a neologism, a combination of two words from two languages: *Eloah-theos.* The first part of this word, *Eloah,* is Hebrew. It is a Hebrew form for God, meaning *God, the Divine One.* The second part of the word, *Theos,* is the Greek word for God, meaning *Deity, the Supreme God.*

Mary, who was probably 12 or 13, was astonished by Elizabeth's emotional eruption. She obviously didn't know how to respond, but she wanted to say *something.* Mary's timid and perhaps somewhat fearful response to Elizabeth's praise/salutation is recorded in Luke only:

LUKE 1:46-47
[46] And Mary said, My soul doth magnify the Lord,
[47] And my spirit hath rejoiced in God my Saviour.

The next portion of Luke's record is Luke's poetic hymn of tribute. These *ARE NOT* the words of the young Mary. The hymn is strictly a testimonial by Luke. There is *no* evidence that the hymn represents Elizabeth's tribute to Mary, or that Mary composed the words herself.

Luke then states that Mary stayed with Elizabeth until the birth of John, probably either in October or November of 8 BC. Then Mary, four months pregnant, returned to Nazareth.

Luke's Gospel chooses to remain silent about Mary's return to Nazareth, the implied controversy (Matthew 1:19) between her and Joseph and the people of Nazareth, and the next five months of her pregnancy. Luke doesn't pick up the story of Jesus again until right before his birth.

And this brings us to the subject of our next chapter.

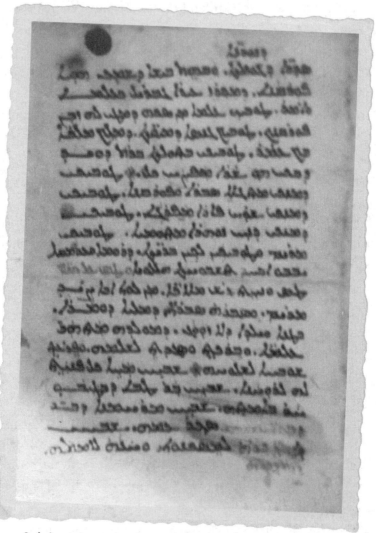

Original Syriac manuscript describing Gabriel's
announcement to Mary that she will birth a son.
It was written by Eusebius of Caesarea
in about the year AD 330—Armenia.

CHAPTER 9

༄

The Nativity: A Fresh Look at an Old Story

THROUGHOUT CHRISTIANITY'S HISTORY, much has been written and taught about Joseph and Mary. They might be the most famous married couple in world history. This is unusual, given the scant historical material written about them.

Thus, I was delighted to find *The Carpenter's Mentor* at Georgia Tech University.

This book was published in France in 1661, by special order of Louis XIV. Author Count Berini Comeaux delivers something far different from the typical storybook account of Jesus' parents. He breathes life into the mysterious Joseph and explores his relationship with Jesus and Mary, and he removes Mary from her divine pedestal to explore her humanity.

According to Comeaux, Joseph (*Pappos* in Hebrew) was indeed a carpenter. The Aramaic word for carpenter means *architect and builder in stone and metal.* The Greek word for carpenter means *designer of stone buildings.*

Arabic tradition says that Joseph was a stone carpenter/architect. Indeed, by most accounts, Joseph was a stonemason. Regardless of the medium, Joseph was a master builder. According to Comeaux, Joseph and his family built a successful construction business in Nazareth, and they were probably wealthier than the average Galilean Jewish family.

An Interview with Mary and Joseph

Comeaux writes extensively about a scroll found in 1652 in Constantinople. This sheepskin scroll contained a record of two interviews with Joseph and Mary. The interviews were, allegedly, conducted by Gamaliel the Elder (who would become a leading 1st-century Sanhedrin authority. Gamaliel's father was Simeon who prophesied over the infant Jesus in Luke 2:25; and his grandfather was Hillel the great teacher. Gamaliel later became St Paul's teacher). Gamaliel was sent by the Sanhedrin in Jerusalem. The interviews were titled *Talmuds of the Jews Interrogation of Joseph and Mary in Regard to Herod's Child in Bethlehem, Whom He Feared Would Be King.*

According to the scroll itself, Gamaliel (who is mentioned in the New Testament book of Acts) conducted the first interview in Mecca, in the land of Ammon or Moab. (Considering his estimate of Mary's age, this interview occurred circa 15 AD). The second interview took place about four years later in Nazareth.

In the interviews, Joseph and Mary say that after Jesus' birth in Bethlehem, they returned to Nazareth. Then, fearing Herod, they left Nazareth and fled to Moab, then to Egypt.

Later, they settled again in Moab, in the city of Mecca. There they lived for 18 years, before returning to Nazareth.

Joseph describes himself as a stone worker who learned the trade from his father. He had worked in the family business in Nazareth before marrying Mary.

According to Gamaliel, Joseph was about 40 to 45 years old, very tall, with hair that was once auburn, but had turned mostly gray. Gamaliel noted that Joseph was a simple talker, whose yes was yes and whose no was no. However, Gamaliel sensed that Joseph and Mary didn't communicate well with one another.

According to the interview, Joseph had eight children, seven who looked very much like him. The oldest, Jesus, closely resembled his mother.

Joseph seemed ambivalent about Jesus. He acknowledged that his eldest was a good worker with the acumen and professionalism to carry on the family business. However, until very recently, Jesus had not shown much interest in assuming this responsibility.

Discussing the vision of the angel Gabriel, Joseph described it as a "strong thought in the mind," rather than a true vision. Somehow, Joseph sensed that, through God's spirit, Mary was pregnant and that he was to marry her and raise the child Jesus as his own. When Jesus reached adulthood, he would bring God's kingdom to the people.

Joseph confessed that he sometimes questioned whether this "strong thought" was a divine message, or just his imagination. Nonetheless, because of his devotion to Mary, he married her.

Count Comeaux then turns his attention to Gamaliel's interview with Mary. The word *mary* (in Egyptian) meant rebellious or one apt to rebel. At the time of Mary's birth, a rebellious daughter was often referred to as a mary. *Mary* might not have been the birth name of Jesus' mother. Perhaps it was a nickname describing her character as a child.

The Gospels say nothing about Mary's childhood and almost nothing about her life before Jesus' birth. Luke tells us only "*she was a virgin, that she was full of grace* (or beautiful and pleasing to look upon), *and that she was espoused to Joseph.*"

As noted earlier, Gamaliel's scroll includes two interviews with Mary. Gamaliel notes that at the time of the first interview, she appeared to be about 35 years old. She had a cheerful, happy, and somewhat mischievous spirit, and she was fair to look upon despite having birthed eight children.

Gamaliel further describes Mary as *rather fleshy, with dark brown eyes and dark brown hair.*

Describing Mary's life after leaving Egypt, Gamaliel's scroll notes: "Leaving her mother in Egypt, Mary was brought by her father to Judea in the days of Augustus. Her father arranged her espousal to Joseph, the son of a wealthy builder of stone buildings and homes in the Galilee. Later her uncle, Joseph of Arimathea, who was also her adoptive father, arranged the marriage of her and Joseph.

"She (Mary) said that she was very young, 12 years old, and frightened when the angel told her she would conceive and birth a son. Naturally, she thought that the son would be from Joseph. Again the angel appeared and told her that she would conceive by the Holy Ghost and that the son will save his people and reign over kingdoms.

"She did not believe the visions until she began to swell. She left her home to visit friends. While she was away, her father was then put away by the authorities, and her uncle arranged for her adoption. Upon her return, she told Joseph about the pregnancy. He decided to put her away for tax purposes. Soon after, Joseph said that a strange, frightening thought made him change his mind and he decided he must marry her.

Later in the scroll, Gamaliel observes: Mary does not have a good relationship with all of her children. Three seem to side with her in disputes that often occur between her and Joseph, although Jesus, the eldest son, usually chooses not to take sides. She says of Jesus that he was a thoughtful child who caused very few problems. He was thoughtful to the point of carelessness at times. He is not close to any of his brothers and sisters, except Miriam, the second-oldest daughter, and at times James, the second-oldest son."

In Gamaliel's second interview with Mary, she told him: "Jesus is always kind to women, which is not the character for most men, but he has little interest in those women of his own heritage, although I know there is a young woman of Egyptian heritage in Bethany and another in Scythopolis that he is fond of. I suspect that he will marry the young woman from Bethany, if that occasion presents itself."

When asked about the angel's prediction that Jesus would reign, Gamaliel says that "Mary laughed, noting that Jesus had taken his rightful position as elder brother and accepted his responsibility as a provider, along with his father, for the family. She questions whether Jesus will be able to rule his own family, much less a kingdom."

Gamaliel observes that like most Galileans, Mary and Joseph care little about the Jewish nation or the Roman oppression. They both seem to be self-seekers, interested in nothing concerning our plight. It seems that Jesus' teacher was a former rabboni whose name was Massalian, of Egyptian estate, who had become a priest and who now lives in Bethany. Massalian says that Jesus was an excellent student, thoughtful and pious, and dedicated to the true purpose of God's dealing with man. He, at times, grew impatient with Jesus because of his obsession with details and because of his desire to apply the Law to daily life without the benefit of an interpreter. He said Jesus is interested in a young woman in the village and plans to marry her.

Comeaux's book also contains a history of the fascinating interview scrolls. How the scrolls got to Constantinople is a mystery. However, local tradition holds that more than 300 Gamaliel-penned scrolls, including those recording his interviews with Joseph and Mary, were housed with hundreds of other scrolls, manuscripts, and parchments at Jerusalem's library of the Sanhedrin.

When the Roman Emperor Titus laid siege to Jerusalem in 70 AD, he destroyed this library. While the library was burning, 13 priests risked their lives to save as many documents as possible. Nine of the priests perished, but the four who survived rescued more than 60 scrolls, books, parchments, and manuscripts. Ten of Gamaliel's scrolls escaped the flames. The four priests brought all the material to Judea for safekeeping.

In Judea, a priest named Daniel of Herodium took possession of the Gamaliel scrolls and brought them to Apollonia, where he hid them. There they remained hidden until the first crusade. Then, in 1097, Raymond, Count of Toulouse, discovered the scrolls when his army pillaged the city. Raymond confiscated the scrolls and brought them to the Holy Land.

An entire book could be written about the survival of these scrolls over the next three and a half centuries, but suffice it to say that these documents survived revolutions, sieges, kidnapping, and simple neglect.

More than once, the scrolls seemed to be lost forever. Eventually, they resurfaced in 1463, when they were discovered in an underground salt cavern near Damascus by a Turkish salt trader. He took the scrolls to

Constantinople, hoping to sell them, at a high price, to Muhammad II, the Ottoman Turk who had conquered Constantinople. As the trader tried to enter Constantinople through the ancient Golden Gate, Muhammad's authorities discovered the scrolls, confiscated them, and presented them to Muhammad, who placed them in an underground vault in the church of St. Irene. There the scrolls rested until the construction of the Topkapi Palace forced the removal of many religious treasures housed within St. Irene. Among these treasures were the Gamaliel scrolls. The scrolls were then placed in one of the hundreds of small cave vaults in the lower chambers of Constantinople's Hagia Sophia cathedral. There they remained, forgotten *again*, until their rediscovery in 1652.

Reading the text of Gamaliel's scrolls caused me to wonder again about the alleged scandal surrounding Mary's pregnancy.

SCANDALS

Contrary to the picture painted by movies and TV and even some sermons, the Gospels do not suggest a scandal. There is a brief mention of Joseph contemplating putting Mary away privately to spare her from being a public example (Matthew 1:19), but this intention had little to do with scandal or controversy.

While researching at Baylor University, I found a rare book titled *Scandals*, written by Herman Bavinck in 1884. Only 100 copies were printed.

Bavinck begins his book with the alleged scandal of Joseph and Mary. He quotes Matthew 1:19.

MATTHEW 1:19

[19] Then Joseph her husband, being a just man, and not willing to make her a public example, was minded to put her away privily.

Bavinck then explains what prompted Joseph's contemplation:

By the time Mary returned to Nazareth (probably in November of 8 BC), she was already four or five months pregnant. The baby had begun to show. Her return was, presumably, met with mixed emotions from Joseph, and from Mary's father. They would have been delighted to see her after a long separation, but they would have been shocked and disturbed to discover that this 12-year-old espoused wife and beloved daughter had returned to them *pregnant.*

How did Joseph respond when Mary tried to explain that she was still a virgin and that God was responsible for her conception?

The public scandal over Mary's pregnancy, which tradition depicts, may not have happened. If these circumstances had occurred in the state of Judea, then most definitely a vicious and perhaps even violent scandal would have developed immediately. In the Greek-culture dominated and Romanized Galilee, where situations of this nature were not unusual, Mary's condition may not have caused even a stir.

Matthew 1:19 does suggest that Joseph was concerned enough about *something* that he seriously contemplated nullifying the espousal contract. If he was relatively unconcerned about a public scandal, what was troubling him?

ROMAN MARRIAGE TAX

Bavinck explains: At this time in the Galilee, although the Romans had very lackadaisical laws relative to marriage, there were strict laws concerning taxation. The Roman law of marriage taxation was strictly enforced, to the point of imprisonment.

Within 10 days after a marriage, the new husband had to report the marriage to the local Roman tax authority and pay a nuptial tax. If the tax was not paid within 10 days, it was doubled daily until it was paid in full. If the tax was not paid after 30 days, the husband was imprisoned.

With the birth of the first, third, and fifth child, another tax was levied. This was a successor tax, which had to be paid within the first year of a child's birth. If not paid on time, the tax was doubled every 30 days until paid. If it was not paid by the child's second birthday, the father was imprisoned. The mother and her children would then be sold as domestic servants.

In the case of an espousal followed by marriage, the espousal tax had to be paid within two years after espousal documents were registered. After marriage, the nuptial tax was due, but the married couple could deduct from that tax the amount already paid for espousal tax. (Indeed, tax laws were cumbersome, even 2,000 years ago!)

If a woman pledged to be married became pregnant before the wedding, the espousal tax, the full nuptial tax, and the successor tax were due before the sixth month of pregnancy. If these taxes were not paid on time, the man would be imprisoned and the woman sentenced to servanthood.

If the pregnant woman was neither pledged nor espoused, then the Roman government levied no tax. Instead, she was made a ward of the local government. She remained a ward until the child's birth. Then she could either be responsible for her own livelihood or return to her family.

One of the ways Galileans circumvented this "triple tax" was to put the pregnant woman *away privately*. The Romans didn't closely track the marriages of Galilean Jews. They let the Jews police themselves. Marriage records received an official review only once every 90 days. If a Jewish man had a pregnant woman on his hands, and he enjoyed a good relationship with local authorities, he could get his registration documents altered or nullified (for a small fee) before the Romans official review. The local Galilean authorities called this process *putting her away, privately*. This practice allowed a man to avoid taxes and extricate himself from marriage responsibilities. As a result, many children were born illegitimate.

This raises a big question: Did Joseph *want* to extricate himself from marriage to Mary?

The Bible states "*Joseph was an honest and just man,*" so it seems likely that instead of "*putting Mary away privately,*" he might have contemplated subjecting Mary to the *ordeal of innocence*. If Joseph was an uncompromisingly dedicated orthodox Jew then this ritual of the ordeal of innocence would have been demanded by the local Jewish religious leaders.

The ordeal of innocence began with a woman's being asked if she was guilty of promiscuity. (Under Mosaic law, promiscuity was punishable by stoning. However, under Rome's law, stoning and all forms of capital punishment were not allowed for infractions of religious laws or principles.)

Still, promiscuity was punishable, if the punishment was non-fatal and delivered by Roman authorities. A promiscuous woman could be subject to any or all of the following:

- Marring: the cutting off of one's nose, right ear, right hand, or right breast or possibly all four.

- Being abandoned to the streets, condemned to live as a beggar.

- Being exiled.

According to Bavinck, few Galilean women faced these punishments. Most likely, the guilty woman was simply offered a bill of divorce and given a token fine of less than one day's wages. This relieved the man of any support responsibility and allowed the woman to move on with her life as an independent single mother.

If the accused woman maintained her innocence, she faced the *trial of the bitter water that causeth the curse* at the hands of a priest sent from the Temple in Jerusalem.

This *trial* required that the woman be brought to a local synagogue to stand before a priest, who poured blessed water into a pottery vessel and mixed into it a handful of dust from the synagogue floor. He then pronounced ritual incantations and curses over the mixture.

Next, he turned to the woman and said, "If no man has lain with thee, and if thou hast not gone aside to uncleanness with another instead of thy espoused husband, be thou free from this bitter water that causeth the curse. But if thou hast gone aside to another instead of thy betrothed, the Lord make thee a curse among thy people, when the Lord doth make thy thigh to rot, and thy belly to swell, and this water that causeth the curse shall go into thy bowels, to make thy belly to swell, and thy thigh to rot." (Numbers 5:11-31)

The priest recorded these words on a parchment, and then erased them by plunging the parchment into the bitter water. At this point, the woman drank the water. If she was indeed an adulteress, the water was supposed to perform an abortive function, which would prove fatal to the woman. If she suffered no ill effects, she was held guiltless and was free to return to her family or her husband, *if* he still wanted her.

JOSEPH AND THE ANGEL

Now, we don't know what prompted the angel to appear to Joseph. We don't know what this carpenter was contemplating, but whatever it was, he didn't follow through.

Bavinck quotes Matthew 1 beginning at verse 20:

MATTHEW 1:20-25

20 But while he thought on these things, behold, the angel of the LORD appeared unto him in a dream, saying, Joseph, thou son of David, fear not to take unto thee Mary thy wife: for that which is conceived in her is of the Holy Ghost.

21 And she shall bring forth a son, and thou shalt call his name JESUS: for he shall save his people from their sins.

22 Now all this was done, that it might be fulfilled which was spoken of the Lord by the prophet, saying,

23 Behold, a virgin shall be with child, and shall bring forth a son, and they shall call his name Emmanuel, which being interpreted is, God with us.

24 Then Joseph being raised from sleep did as the angel of the Lord had bidden him, and took unto him his wife:

25 And knew her not till she had brought forth her firstborn son: and he called his name JESUS.

Bavinck notes: It is not known how long after Mary's return from visiting Elizabeth that Joseph had his dream, but I speculate that the angel appeared to him within a month or two after her return to Nazareth.

Bavinck points out that while church doctrine insists that the married Mary and Joseph had no sexual relations until after Jesus' birth, he could not find facts to confirm this. He contends that whether Joseph had sexual relations with Mary or not, something frightened him to the point that he feared having any, or any further relations with her.

This being the case, the angel appears and instructs Joseph to be unafraid to *"take Mary your wife"* and/or be unafraid to have sexual relations with her. So, following angelic prompting, Joseph renews relations with Mary. They go to Bethlehem, where Mary's son is born. Joseph names him Jesus.

At first glance, Matthew's account of the angelic visit seems straightforward. An angel appears to Joseph in a dream, telling him to take Mary as his wife. Joseph obeys. A baby is born.

Closer investigation of the text reveals confusion, especially in verses 19, 20, and 24. None of these verses indicates that Joseph was commanded to marry Mary. Verses 19 and 20 imply that Mary was *already* his wife. He feared "*taking her*" and having sexual relations with her while she was pregnant. Verse 24 implies the same thing.

In 1589, a theory emerged, stating that because Joseph and Mary were espoused, it was permitted for each of them to claim to be husband or wife, and be recognized as such. According to the theory, *this* is the reason the words "husband" and "wife" are used in the biblical reference to Joseph and Mary even though they were not married.

Nothing in Jewish, Greek, or Roman history describes such a practice, and the opposite was usually true in Roman-ruled countries. In the Galilee, for example, it was not permitted, for tax reasons, for a person to claim to be a husband or wife, unless legally married. One can assume that Rome followed this policy in all countries it controlled.

Bavinck concludes, then, that Mary, a 12-or 13-year-old virgin, conceived Jesus by the Holy Ghost. She immediately left home to visit Elizabeth. She stayed with Elizabeth until after John's birth. Mary returned home and was adopted by her uncle. Joseph married Mary, thus subjecting himself to the Roman triple tax. Then, for some reason, he became frightened and determined to avoid sexual relations with Mary. The angel appeared to him and told him to be unafraid to have relations with her. The couple went to Bethlehem, where Jesus was born.

ESPOUSAL CONTRACT

Bavinck adds that espousal was a serious commitment for Jews of this era. Specific laws governed age, procedure, and the espousal ceremony. Since the days of Ezra, the lawful espousal age for a Jewish man was 17. If the man was beyond age 19, espousal or engagement was *not necessary*. Between the ages of 17 and 19, espousal was *mandatory*.

Consequently, if Joseph was a devout Jew, and if he was espoused to Mary, we can conclude that he was at least 17 years old, but not over 19.

A woman became eligible for betrothal upon reaching puberty, signified by her first menstrual cycle. (This usually occurred around age 12 or 13.) Immediately after her seven days of ritual cleansing, she became eligible for marriage. Then, her father, oldest brother, or oldest surviving male relative went to the synagogue and registered her as being eligible for marriage. Any man seeking a wife could then negotiate with the young lady's father (or appropriate relative) to marry her. If the young man was between 17 and 19, he had to submit to a period of espousal. If he was over 19, he could negotiate for marriage.

The young lady's name remained on the register of young ladies eligible for espousal or marriage for two years. If she was not espoused or married within two years, her name was removed for one year. After this time, she could be registered again, for another 18 months *only*. If she was not espoused or married during the 18-month period, she would be proclaimed by the local synagogue leader as 'not fit for marriage.' Fortunately, most young Jewish ladies never faced this curse.

For most Jewish young ladies in the Galilee, the future husband was chosen well in advance of puberty. There are examples of husbands being committed to a family as early as a girl's sixth birthday. Betrothal negotiations often began the day a girl completed her first seven days of purification.

So, most likely, Mary was no older than 13 when she became espoused to Joseph.

The custom of the Jewish people, when negotiating to secure a bride for a son, illustrates just how serious betrothal really was to them. Even though, as noted earlier, espousal was not necessary if the man was over 19, it was still required that the would-be-bride present a dowry to the groom-to-be's family, and that the man, regardless of age, sign a betrothal covenant.

Betrothal was not a simple promise between a man and a woman that they pledge to marry. It was a legal contract, signed in the local synagogue, witnessed by the synagogue president, an elder of the village council, and an elder from each family of the couple. The document was then permanently filed in the local synagogue. The betrothal contract was so binding that if the future husband died before the marriage, the future wife would have the full status of a widow.

THE TAX CENSUS

Now, let's turn our attention to another important chapter in the story of Jesus' birth: the tax census and Joseph and Mary's journey to Bethlehem. (There was a village called Bethlehem in the Galilee, located about seven miles from Nazareth, but overwhelming evidence indicates that the Bethlehem to which Joseph and Mary traveled was located in Judea).

This tax census has faced extreme scrutiny over the past 100 years. Some theologians and historians claim that it never happened. Others insist it did. Because I began with the belief that Luke's record of the tax census is true, I disregarded any resources that argued against the historical fact of a tax census at the time of Jesus' birth. I focused, instead, on resources that confirm the Gospel account.

I discovered a significant resource at Magdalene College library. Magdalene College may house the *only* known authentic record of the official tax and census during the time of Jesus' birth. This record appears in an untitled manuscript fragment, labeled simply *MSCL125*.

According to its accompanying background information, this fragment is all that survived of a letter written by Epiphanius, Bishop of Pavia, in the year 490. The letter was sent to Clotilda, who became the wife of Clovis, King of the Salian Franks. In previous correspondence, Clotilda had asked Epiphanius how the census that caused the Virgin to travel to Bethlehem was conducted, given that at least three civil authorities ruled the area when Jesus was born. Epiphanius, claiming to have relied on legal documents once housed at Emperor Alexander Severus' private library, gives an answer that attempts to reconcile the seemingly conflicting historical accounts from the era.

Epiphanius begins his answer to Clotilda by quoting a portion of Luke's Gospel:

LUKE 2:1-5
[1] And it came to pass in those days, that there went out a decree from Caesar Augustus that all the world should be taxed.
[2] (And this taxing was first made when Cyrenius was governor of Syria.)
[3] And all went to be taxed, every one into his own city.

⁴ And Joseph also went up from Galilee, out of the city of Nazareth, into Judaea, unto the city of David, which is called Bethlehem; (because he was of the... lineage of David:)

⁵ To be taxed with Mary his espoused wife, being great with child.

Epiphanius notes that Rome's financial health was fragile at the time. The empire had endured a long civil war (after Gaius Julius Caesar's murder in 44 BC), as well as the Pannonia revolt. Thus, Augustus decreed in 9 BC that, on top of the customary 14-year census, there would be another special tax census throughout the empire. This census would apply to every non-Roman male subject. Augustus further proclaimed that every woman (both Roman and non-Roman) who was or would become with-child had to pay the tax. In other words, every woman who was pregnant when her region was taxed had to pay a tax on her unborn child. The tax was to be paid at the town of either her husband's or father's birth.

Epiphanius goes on to say that the Roman consul Publius Sulpicius Quirinus ordered a tax-census in 7 BC. At the same time, Herod the Great demanded that each Jewish-descendant male age 15 to 60 register between March and June of that year and be taxed in his birth city.

Next, Epiphanius summarizes the sequence of events that led to Joseph's being taxed as a result of this special tax-census.

1. Augustus decrees that a special tax census will accompany the routine 14-year census. This tax census demanded that all non-Roman males between the ages of 15 and 60 pay a special census tax at the time of their routine registration. Each woman with child at the time the region was taxed (over the next three years) would pay a tax on that child.

2. By 7 BC, it was Syria's turn to be taxed. Quirinus delegated the tax's implementation to four Tetrarchs who governed Syria's four regions.

3. Herod the Great was King of the Jews and the Tetrarch of Judaea. He chose to implement the tax census in his region by demanding that each non-Roman citizen Jewish male age 15 to 60 register at the city of his birth, and that each non-Jewish non-Roman citizen male register at an appointed city.

4. Herod divided his Tetrarchy into 15 taxing districts with each district given a specific 7 day time limit to complete its registration process. All 15 districts would complete the taxation within the four month period (March to June) decreed by Herod.

Epiphanius says that these rules forced Joseph to wait for the official census bidding of his district before traveling to his birth city to register himself and Mary's unborn child.

Each district had only seven days to complete its registration. Bethlehem was about a 4 or 5 day journey from Nazareth so Joseph was obliged to leave for Bethlehem immediately upon receiving his registration orders.

The district comprising Nazareth probably received its registration orders in April of 7 BC. (Because her unborn child would be taxed, Mary was required to accompany Joseph.) Unfortunately, the registration deadline overlapped with Mary's due date. As the duo drew closer to Bethlehem, it became clear that this strange city, far from friends and family, would be their child's birthplace.

BETHLEHEM

Bethlehem, the traditional birthplace of King David, was about six miles south of Jerusalem. As they approached this city, Joseph and Mary would have realized that accommodation space would be extremely limited. So they probably sought refuge in a northern suburban area of Bethlehem. The lack of accommodation space was caused by the tax census, and by the housing demand created by pilgrims traveling to Jerusalem to observe Passover. (In 7 BC, the Passover celebration would have begun on April 12 and ended on April 18.)

With this information, Epiphanius's manuscript abruptly ends. To my dismay, the historians who wrote the manuscript's supplementary material declined to speculate on what the remainder might have said. Still, this bishop's words provided much-needed clarity regarding a confusing series of seemingly unrelated tax censuses decreed by three separate authorities.

The Gospels don't provide much detail about Joseph's registration, but Luke's account suggests that Joseph and Mary arrived in Bethlehem a day or two before Jesus was born. This would have given Joseph enough time to register and pay the tax before Mary gave birth:

LUKE 2:6
⁶ And so it was, that, while they were there, the days were accomplished that she should be delivered.

While researching at Rice University in Houston, Texas, I found another intriguing document relating to Jesus' birth, a document that compelled me to reevaluate some commonly held assumptions about the event.

The document was a sermon written by Marcel LeRue Dimireaux, a French Catholic priest who fled France during the days of Napoleon's rise to power. He settled in Prussia. There, Dimireaux renounced Catholicism and joined a splinter group of Protestant reformists who called themselves *Purstrictists*. They sought to purge Christianity of all traditions, dogmas, and doctrines that they felt hindered a pure interpretation of Scripture.

According to Dimireaux, Bethlehem was a major source of room and board during Passover because of its proximity to Jerusalem. Given that Joseph and Mary would have arrived in Bethlehem during the height of this holy season, it's not surprising "there was no room at the inn."

Dimireaux goes on to explain *the inn* was likely to be a fenced enclosure designed especially for travellers. It comprised small houses containing guest rooms. Guests' animals were kept in the courtyard area of the enclosure, which included a wood or stone building filled with feed such as straw and corn husks. (Some inns had no such building, just a large pit.)

Whether building or pit, this food source for animals was called a *manger*. It wasn't unusual for an inn to allow travelers to spend the night in the manger, either free of charge or for a reduced fee.

As to the celebrated date of Jesus' birth, Dimireaux notes that the December 25th date comes from a merging of the celebration of the pagan "sun god" and Christianity. Long after Jesus' death and resurrection, an edict from Emperor Constantine (AD 272-337), proclaimed December 25, the birthdate of the sun god, to be Jesus' birthday too. By the time Theodosius II made Christianity Rome's official religion in 395 AD, December 25 was officially recognized by the western Christian church as Jesus' birthday.

Offering his opinion, Dimireaux states that I am not a legalist when it comes to dates and times. I celebrate Jesus' birth on December 25 because it commemorates his birth and because it is the date recognized and celebrated by our society, even though I know without a doubt that he was born sometime during April.

SANCTIFIED SHEPHERDS

This brings us to another major part of Jesus' birth story: the shepherds' visit to the birth site. This event is recorded in Luke 2:8-18.

LUKE 2:8-18

8 And there were in the same country shepherds abiding in the field, keeping watch over their flock by night.

9 And, lo, the angel of the Lord came upon them, and the glory of the Lord shone round about them: and they were sore afraid.

10 And the angel said unto them, Fear not: for, behold, I bring you good tidings of great joy, which shall be to all people.

11 For unto you is born this day in the city of David a Saviour, which is Christ the Lord.

12 And this shall be a sign unto you; Ye shall find the babe wrapped in swaddling clothes, lying in a manger.

13 And suddenly there was with the angel a multitude of the heavenly host praising God, and saying,

14 Glory to God in the highest, and on earth peace, good will toward men.

15 And it came to pass, as the angels were gone away from them into heaven, the shepherds said one to another, Let us now go even unto Bethlehem, and see this thing which is come to pass, which the Lord hath made known unto us.

16 And they came with haste, and found Mary, and Joseph, and the babe lying in a manger.

17 And when they had seen it, they made known abroad the saying which was told them concerning this child.

18 And all they that heard it wondered at those things which were told them

by the shepherds.

At the University of Istanbul in Turkey, I discovered a manuscript that deepened my understanding of these shepherds. The manuscript was one of two that University of Istanbul archaeologists discovered hidden deep in the underground vaults of the St. Saviour Chora church. The manuscript was (apparently) written in the first half of the fifteenth century by a Regimold of Iconium, and it featured a compilation of what Regimold believed to be the most accurate extra-biblical records of the shepherds' visit to Jesus.

Regimold states the angel's appearing to the shepherds provides two key clues about when Jesus was born.

In Judea, flocks of sheep were allowed to graze from mid-spring until early fall. So the presence of shepherds and their sheep in a field is consistent with the timing of the censuses and Passover.

Moreover, the area known as the *Hills of Ramat*, just north of Bethlehem, featured lush, rolling hills. Many years before Jesus' birth, the High Priest in Jerusalem had sanctified the area and placed it under his jurisdiction. The temple priests used the hills as a grazing area for sheep used as Passover sacrifice animals. Hundreds of sheep were sacrificed in various ceremonies, but only seven Passover lambs were sacrificed for the sins of the world. (Only a lamb born during Passover could qualify for this honor.)

According to Regimold, the shepherds in Luke were "Sanctified Shepherds of the seed of Jacob," chosen by the High Priest to care for the sanctified Passover sheep. This was a rare honor. Only 12 sanctified shepherds were chosen each year. These shepherds were required to have been born into a sanctified shepherd family (a family that had served in this capacity for at least three generations). Groups of seven sheep were each attended by a sanctified shepherd, a Levite, and an elder rabbi from the line of Zadok. The shepherd would care for the sheep, the Levite would see to the sheep's ritualistic cleanliness, and the *presbyteroi* would choose the sheep to be sacrificed. Once a sanctified shepherd had served this Passover role, he was ineligible to serve again.

Given all this, it seems amazing that these shepherds would forsake a once-in-a-lifetime honor to search for a newborn. We have no idea how long the shepherds searched the crowded city of Bethlehem, but it is likely it took them most of the night to find Jesus.

When they located Joseph, Mary, and Jesus, the three were probably resting in a large dugout manger in the inn's courtyard, along with many other guests. After the shepherds confirmed the truth of the angel's message, they departed and began to proclaim the news.

It's significant that Luke does not report that these shepherds bowed before Jesus or worshiped him in any way. (The tradition of the shepherds' worshipping at the manger dates back to the days of St. Jerome, who introduced this notion.)

It's worth noting here that the angel's appearing to the shepherds was certainly unprecedented. However, the shepherds might not have obeyed the angel, had he not proclaimed that the newborn babe was a "Savior" and that he was "Christ the Lord."

At this time in Jewish life, there was great anticipation for the imminent arrival of two great Jewish deliverers:

- A religious leader and Savior called Messias.

- A social and political leader, a Christ, called Messiah.

The Jews looked to someone who would free them from their sins and someone *else* who would free them from political oppression and re-establish the kingdom of David. No one expected a *single* deliverer, especially not an infant deliverer.

Exploring this expectation, Regimold points to an important discovery in 1379. Venetian explorers, searching a cave on the island of Corfu (near Greece's western coast) discovered a first-century goatskin scroll containing seven letters written by the great rabbi Hillel the Third. The letters were addressed to a rabbi named Josh ha Rushi. In the tenth century, an Islamic scribe translated these letters into Arabic and titled his work *The Hillel Letters Regarding God's Providence to the Jews*. The letters were then hidden and forgotten for hundreds of years.

The seventh of these letters was extremely long and dealt with, among other things, the anticipation of the two deliverers.

Hillel writes,

"Not only was the expectation of a remarkable personage universally prevalent among the Jews at the time of the birth of Jesus, called by his followers, The Christ...there was at the time a Messianic phraseology derived from the writings of the prophets which embodied and expressed all their anticipation. There was to be a Messiah, there was to be a new dispensation, and there was to be an anointed prophet of sacrifice, a Messias. No one knew precisely how each was to appear, or how it would be. The one whom we call Messias was thought to be a religious reformer, and the new state of things to be a condition of higher religious perfection.

The universal expectation among the Jews seems to have been that he was to be a prophet like Moses, but greater, who will save us from sin. Another was Messiah, a great personage whose coming was shortly expected as a king greater than any who had sat upon the Jewish throne. It was this expectation that followed the Galilean, Jesus, through his itinerancy and even after his death and supposed resurrection (so claimed by his followers.)"

After quoting from Hillel's letter, Regimold continues with his treatise, which I will paraphrase for you:

When the angel announced that the Savior (both *Messiah* and *Messias*) had been born in Bethlehem, the holy men watching the sanctified sheep were at once confused, shocked, amazed, afraid, anxious, delighted, and bewildered. Could the angel *really* mean that both *Messias* and *Messiah* had been born? Whatever the case, they had to go to Bethlehem.

After finding the babe with his mother and earthly father, they spread the news about what the angel had said. Then they returned to the *Hills of Ramat* to prepare for Passover.

Regimold notes that for centuries the only sources, beyond the Bible, that mentioned the shepherds' visit to the manger were obviously embellished fabrications. They were written to secure Mary's exalted position of Blessed Virgin.

Then (in 1224) numerous scrolls, titled *The Senatorial Courts of Tiberius Caesar, and by the Sanhedrin in Jerusalem,* were discovered—in a centuries-old underground vault among the burial catacombs of Janina.

One of these scrolls contained four separate manuscripts. Two of these dealt with Jesus' birth and the shepherds search for him. One manuscript was titled *Jonathan, the son of Heziel, interview with sanctified shepherds of Ramat.* The other was titled *Letters of Melker, Priest of the Synagogue at Bethlehem. Sanhedrim, 88B, by R. Jose, order No. 2.*

The *Jonathan* manuscript contains an interview conducted by a chief scribe named Jonathan with three of the sanctified shepherds who were watching over the sanctified Passover sheep the night Jesus was born. The shepherds told Jonathan,

> "It was the third watch of the night when we were awakened by a bright light as bright as the light of day. All at once the night seemed to be filled with human voices saying, 'Glory! Glory! Glory to the Most High God! Happy art thou Bethlehem, for God hath fulfilled His promise to the fathers; for in thy chambers is born the King that shall rule in righteousness! The Savior, which is Christ the Lord!'
>
> Their shouting would rise up in the heavens, and then would sink down in mellow strains, and roll along at the foot of the mountains, and die away in the most soft and musical manner; then it would begin again high up in the heavens and descend in sweet and melodious strains, the light would seem to burst forth high in the heavens, and then descend in softer rays and light up the hills and valleys, making everything more visible than the light of the sun.
>
> They (the shepherds) said that it shone around the whole city and some of the people were frantic until the priest Melker came out to the people clapping his hands in joy and addressed them, saying that this thing was of God and was a fulfillment of prophecy. They went into the city and found a young mother with her newborn baby and her husband resting in a feeding closure for animals. We felt in our hearts that this babe may be the cause of such joyous praise."

The second manuscript was a letter the priest Melker (noted in the shepherds' interview above), wrote to the Sanhedrin in Jerusalem. In the letter, Melker states:

> "The night that the heavens shone like the sun of day, 18 guardians of the sanctified Passover sheep approached me in the streets, asking me where the child lay who caused such a commotion in the heavens. I told them to search the city until they had found a child

that had been born that night. They returned to me near daybreak, saying that they had found the baby to the north of the city, near Ramat, and related to me a story, which the very young mother had told them concerning an angel who had appeared to her, saying that the child was a gift from God. That he would rule his people. Afterwards, some returned to the flocks, while the others spread the news of their discovery throughout the hill country. After some eight days, I sent for the mother, to have the babe circumcised. She repeated the same story to me. I am informed that she could have been tried by law because she could not give a better evidence of her virtue than to claim her child was gifted from God, but that she and her husband had residence in the Galilee, where such stories and claims give no rise for question. If she lived in Judea, she could have been stoned according to the Law, although I must admit that I can think of no other case that such apparent divine manifestations, manifestations to which I was witness, were seen on the occasion of the birth of her son. In the past, I have examined at least 20 different young women who claimed to be virgin and who claimed to be with child, of the spirit of God. None had accompaniment of such manifestations as was witnessed that night in Bethlehem. Had not she fled back to the Galilee with her husband, a stonemason's master in Nazareth, no doubt she would have been presumed innocent even in Judea and Jerusalem."

Evaluating these manuscripts Regimold confesses, "It cannot be proven without a doubt that these were authentic records. I believe there is certainly more validity to them than in the hundreds of other embellishments (excluding the Gospel accounts) that materialized during the first thousand years after Jesus' birth."

And with that, Regimold's record of the shepherds' visit to Jesus' birth site concludes.

CIRCUMCISION AND NAMING

Because of the Gospel records, we know that after Jesus was born, Joseph and Mary stayed at least eight more days in the Bethlehem area. Eight days after his birth, Jesus was taken to the local priest and was circumcised and named.

Mary was commanded by the angel to name her son, Jesus, a Greek name which identified him with a barbarian people, rather than with the Jews. Matthew 1:21, says that this son of Mary will save his people, or the people of his lineage, from their sins. The word save in the Greek is *sodzo;* it usually implied salvation from sin, sickness, or spiritual conflict through personal sacrifice.

Jesus is a Greek name that until the fourth century AD had a Greek definition. The name meant *eternal, eternity, or for eternity.* This seems to correspond with what the angel said when he told Mary that her son would (in the future) be called Emanuel. The word Emanuel is a Persian word that was borrowed by the Greeks, and came to mean *God eternal* or *God with us for eternity.* Alexander the Great was praised as Emanuel after his conquest of Persia's Emperor Darius. It was not until the fourth century, that St. Basil declared that the name *Emanuel* meant salvation or God who is with us. This is now the commonly accepted definition for the meaning of the name, Emmanuel.

> LUKE 2:21
> [21] And when eight days were accomplished for the circumcising of the child, his name was called JESUS, which was so named of the angel before he was conceived in the womb.

> LUKE 1:35
> [35] And the angel answered and said unto her, The Holy Ghost shall come upon thee, and the power of the Highest shall overshadow thee: therefore also that holy thing which shall be born of thee shall be called the Son of God.

It is interesting that the term *Son of God* (above) is translated in Greek as *huios theos.* It means, *a man, the offspring of a man of a Godhead.* It refers to a god beginning his human life.

The term *Son of the Highest* in Greek is *huios hupsistos.* It was first used by Chaldean magi in Babylonia and then by Zoroastrian priests in Persia to describe their god who had been selected by the eternal Supreme God of all gods in all the universes (they taught that there were four universes), to come to Earth and to be born a man and rule the people of Earth.

In a letter to the Magnesians, St. Ignatius (Bishop of Antioch) writes that this sonship referred to Jesus' humanity, not his deity: "As God, He had no beginning. As a man, he did. In the realm of heaven, God had no son, for sonship is human and refers only to Jesus' humanity. Only on earth was Jesus the Son of God, a man without sin, in whom God could reside."

PURIFICATION CEREMONY

According to the Law of Moses (Leviticus 12), a new mother was considered unclean, just as with her menstrual cycle, for seven days after childbirth if she had birthed a boy, 14 days for a girl. After the seven-day period, she still had to remain isolated, not touching any holy thing and was not allowed to enter the Temple for an additional 33 days, if she had given birth to a son (66 days for a daughter). She had to undertake her own purification ritual by offering the appropriate sacrifice: a lamb as a burnt offering and a young pigeon or turtle dove as a sin offering. In case of poverty or if she was not from a direct Hebrew bloodline, a turtle dove or a young pigeon could be substituted for the lamb as a burnt offering. Considering Mary presented the least expensive offering, it was either because she was not of pure Hebrew blood (which would be the case if her mother or grandmother were Egyptian), she and Joseph were poor (unlikely if Joseph was a master stonemason), or they did not bring enough money with them to buy a lamb.

Along with the purification ritual for the mother, the father of the male child was required (Exodus 13:11-16; Leviticus 12:2-8) to redeem the child from the Lord, in what was called the Redemption Ceremony. According to Numbers 18:15-16, the first-born son was sacred and had to be redeemed from the Lord for five shekels (about 20 days' wages for a common laborer) payable to the presiding priest.

On the day that Joseph and Mary brought Jesus to the Temple to be presented to the Lord, the Holy Spirit led Simeon to the Temple. Luke 2:27 implies that Simeon met them upon their arrival at the Temple.

The Holy Spirit had promised Simeon, a devout and just man, that he would not see death until he had seen the Lord's Christ. He immediately recognized the baby as Messias, God's anointed prophet of sacrifice and the religious reformer he had been waiting to see.

Simeon took the baby from the parents and held him in his arms. He then prophesied that this Jesus would be a light to the Gentiles and would be a glory to the Jews.

Joseph and Mary were totally taken aback by the words of Simeon, who then blessed them individually.

They were then joined by an elderly prophetess, Anna. Anna recognised the babe as the Messiah, a king who would be greater than David and who would bring social and political reform. Anna spoke about him to all who were looking forward to the redemption of Jerusalem.

After concluding their ritual duties in Jerusalem, Joseph and Mary took the infant Jesus and returned to their home in Nazareth, in the Galilee. By this time it was probably near the latter part of May or early June of the year 7 BC.

Nothing more is recorded in the Gospels for two years concerning Jesus life. However, I discovered a manuscript at the University of Toledo in Ohio that helped me understand what was happening in the area that is now known as Palestine, during that two-year Gospel silence.

WORLD PEACE

The manuscript was a thirteenth century French copy of an earlier Latin manuscript written in about the year 400 by a Roman Senator by the name of Pammachius. Pammachius had married the daughter of St. Paula and was a devoted friend of St. Jerome. He and St. Fabiola founded a hospice for pilgrims at Porto. The manuscript was an explanatory commentary addressed to Jerome, clarifying the political state of Herod's kingdom immediately following Jesus' birth, before Joseph and Mary fled to Egypt.

This is a paraphrase of Pammachius' words:

Joseph, Mary and the babe Jesus return to the Galilee from Bethlehem and Jerusalem after the birth of Jesus. Following the Passover celebration of that year (7 BC), Herod the Great decreed the initiation of a great four-month long summer celebration and feast to commemorate the declaration of world peace by Caesar Augustus. From Panias to

Idumaea and from Peraea to the Mediterranean, Herod proclaimed a kingdom-wide celebration. For four months, beginning with the first signs of summer (probably in May or June) his subjects were relieved of their kingdom tax burden (this did not include taxes paid to Rome; it applied only to taxes that were paid to Herod), and every night, in every principal city of his kingdom, from sundown to sunup, free food, wine, and entertainment were provided for whomever chose to accept it. This four-month celebration was followed by another one of Herod's famed grandiose building surges, which spread to all corners of his kingdom. During this period of massive construction, 100 percent of all able-bodied Jewish workers were employed. It is the first and only time that this occurred in the history of the Jewish people. Note that these projects were not constructed by slave labor. All workers were paid employees of Herod.

Because of the four-month long celebration and the enormous construction efforts of Herod that followed, comparative peace and prosperity reigned throughout his kingdom. During that entire two-year period, in every city, town, and village in every area and region of Herod's kingdom, there was peace and prosperity.

Then came the ambassadors to Judea—representing the kingdoms of the East, and peace and prosperity were no more to be.

CHAPTER 10

Mary: The Mother of God

BEFORE WE LEAVE THE EARLY DAYS of Jesus' life and explore his "mystery years," I want to explain how many of our traditions regarding Jesus and the Virgin Mary have developed.

Let me take you to a mid morning Swissair flight from Zurich to Cairo.

Because my coach-class seat was broken, I was moved to first class next to a distinguished-looking gentleman named Dr. Richard Hawkinson. He introduced himself as a Professor of Cultural Anthropology at the University of Toronto.

As you might guess, our conversation quickly turned to my search for the historical Jesus. Dr. Hawkinson told me he was non-religious, but, still, he was fascinated by my search.

For more than three hours, we discussed Christian doctrines, dogmas, and theories. Despite his "non-religious claim," he had a commanding knowledge of the Bible and Christianity.

At one point, he told me, "I want to be real honest with you. Some Christian traditions and dogmas were introduced in a calculated effort to destroy what you as Christian believers now perceive as truth."

I found this statement bracing (and rather difficult to comprehend). I asked him to elaborate.

He responded (and I will paraphrase): What you must do in your research is address and confront three fundamental quasi-theological tenets that have led to an array of false dogmas and doctrines. For centuries, these falsehoods have been used to enslave millions. Here is what you must confront: (1) The virgin birth of Jesus. (2) The divine mother and incarnate son. (3) Mary, the mother of God.

If you don't address these, you cannot hope to build a rational justification for believing what you profess, and you will have no grounds for projecting your beliefs to others. Although we do not have time to discuss all three tenets, we can cover one, at least partially."

Let's look at the virgin birth. If you will recall your traditional Old Testament ideology, God promised, way back in Eden, that the *head* of the serpent (historically known as a manifestation of Satan) would be crushed by the 'seed of woman,'a woman's offspring.

It is now assumed by most 'mystics' and ideological historians that the Luciferian hierarchy could not and would not allow the miraculous arrival of the obliterator of their system. Hence, the Luciferian hierarchy launched a two-front assault to neutralize God's vengeance strategy. One front would concentrate on the denial of a virgin-born redeemer. The second would concentrate on the widespread *acceptance* of a virgin-birthed redeemer. On one hand, the virgin birth would be mocked and ridiculed. On the other, the virgin birth would become a foundational mainstay of Christian doctrine, but also of virtually every religion in the world.

Let's look at the denial tactic first, if a person denies the virgin birth of a redeemer, Jesus, in this case, then he must deny three foundational Christian beliefs.

1. The first is the belief in divine conception.

2. The second is the belief in virgin conception and birth.

3. The third is that the Bible is the unerring Word of God.

The Luciferian power structure has been phenomenally successful in portraying to the intellectual world the utter impossibility of a virgin birth and the ridiculousness of accepting this notion as fact.

Let me quickly cover the attack on Jesus' virgin birth. This attack centers on divine conception being at the root of many religions and belief systems. Thus, by the time the *true* virgin birth occurred, it was rejected by the Jews as just another myth.

For example, in western mythology, the Greek hero Perseus is the son of the virgin Diana and the god Zeus. Hercules is the son of Alcmene, a mortal woman (sometimes depicted as a virgin) and Zeus. Aeneas was the son of the goddess Aphrodite and a mortal man. More examples of a virgin birth can be identified in the mythological religious foundations of cultures throughout the world: from the Aztecs and the Mayans to the Eskimos. From Japan, Australia, and Korea to South America and Africa.

Unfortunately, just as Dr. Hawkinson began explaining his second tenet, the plane rolled to a stop at our gate. He said he was sorry he could not elaborate more on his theory. So was I.

VIRGIN DIVINE MOTHER AND INCARNATE SON

In Cairo, I spent about two weeks doing research and visiting tourist sites, but I found little documentation relevant to my search. So, I decided to fly to Damascus, Syria, home of the Damascus Museum.

The Damascus Museum is located next to the beautiful Taqiah Mosque in the western part of the city.

The museum was built by the French in the 1920s, and it has become world renowned for its ancient Babylonian, Assyrian, and Persian artifacts and exhibits, as well as its extensive Islamic history section. Additionally, the museum displays artifacts from virtually every civilization and culture to occupy the Tigris-Euphrates Rivers area from the seventh millennium BC to the sixth century AD.

To my great surprise and delight, I found a virtual gold mine of manuscripts and tablets relating to the 'virgin divine mother and incarnate son' issue, which Dr. Hawkinson had raised. Because the museum had translated most of the ancient manuscripts and cuneiform tablets into Arabic, French, and English, I had no problem reading them and their accompanying information.

Most of the manuscripts and tablets I read were ancient Babylonian, Sumerian, Akkadian, Assyrian, Hindu, Seminite, and Roman works, dealing with a variety of subjects: history, mythology, religion, politics, and more. I spent a week studying in the manuscript library and another three days doing research in the Islamic history sector.

I began to understand how effectively the divine mother and incarnate son Luciferian assault has been conducted through the ages. I also began to piece together a picture of how this assault evolved and how it was designed to work.

By reading Babylonian, Akkadian, and Sumerian tablets and their commentaries, I discovered that, upon the death of Babel's King Nimrod (circa 4599 BC), the divine mother and incarnate son myth emerged, thanks to the efforts of Semiramis, Nimrod's queen. By 4550 BC, this doctrine was firmly entrenched in Babylonian religious lore. Fifty years later, the myth had become the foundation of Babylon's entire religious system.

From Babylon, the doctrine spread rapidly, until, by 4000 BC, it had penetrated every religious system in the world.

By studying many Assyrian and Seminite tablets, I discovered that in Egypt the divine mother and incarnate son became known as Isis and Osiris. In India, they were called Isi and Iswara. In Asia, they were called Cybele and Deoius. In early Rome, they were known as Fortuna and Jupiter-puer. In Greece, they were known as Ceres (or Irene) and Plutus. In China, they were known as Shing Moo and her holy child.

As the centuries rolled by, the names of mother and children, their representation, their duties and powers, and their purposes changed to conform to evolving cultures.

Thus, Semiramis evolved from mother/wife queen, to divine mother, to a mother-goddess who derived her glory, power, and deity from her son.

The son portion of the legend evolved as well. Ninus, the son of a virgin mother, evolved into Tammuz, the son who was sacrificed. Then he evolved into Kronos, the son who became a god. From Kronos, he evolved into Phoroneus, the mighty deliverer. Phoroneus became Zero (or Zeroastes), the only seed of woman who can emancipate. Next, he became Ben-Almet-Ishaa, the redeeming son of the virgin of salvation. Finally, by 280 BC, this personage became El-Bar, the son of god, the crusher of the serpent.

This kind of human-to-deity evolution took place in Greece, Rome, Asia Minor, China, India, Mexico, early Europe, South America, North America, Egypt, Africa, the Mesopotamian cultures, Canaan, Australia, Indo-China, and Japan. For this reason, amazing similarities can be found in virtually all gods and goddesses, regardless of race, culture, social system, nation, kingdom, or time in history.

Thus, by the time of Jesus, the divine mother/incarnate son doctrine was deeply entrenched in many pagan and religious systems. The thought of such doctrine penetrating Orthodox Judaism was a sacrilege.

By researching in the Islamic-history sector of the museum, I discovered information I needed to assemble the final pieces of the Luciferian picture-puzzle. I learned how the divine mother and incarnate son deception is alive and working its influence *today.*

One part of the museum dealt with Islam's history, but it also included a wealth of information relative to Islam's relationship to the Jews, the Pope, and Christianity. (Those relationships have fluctuated from mutual respect and admiration to extreme animosity.)

In most early first and second century Christian writings, Mary was given little, if any, consideration in doctrine or ritual observance. She was honored as the mother of Jesus. Beyond that, she was not regarded as anyone special. For the first three centuries after Jesus' birth, the church took little interest in Mary's life, whether she had children besides Jesus, what happened to her after Jesus' death and resurrection, and so on.

According to the museum's information, Mary did not become a "perpetual virgin" until John Chrysostom proposed the idea in AD 399. He said that Mary must be "called a virgin *ante partum, in partu, post partum,*" and hence, *perpetual virgin.*

It was also during the fourth century that Constantine I prepared the way for Christianity to become the official state religion, thus ensuring that Mary would ascend to the pedestal of deity. As it turned out, after obtaining official recognition from Constantine I, Christianity absorbed as equals the whole mass of pagans who had never been converted. So, to accommodate the new "pagan-Christians," the state recognized, approved, and brought into the new state religion of Christianity many pagan doctrines and rituals.

MOTHER-GODDESS

One doctrine the new Christians demanded was that of the mother-goddess.

In the Roman world the goddess cult given the most devotion was that of the Great Mother of Phrygia. This was followed by the cult of Isis, and the cult of the Phoenician goddess Astarte. Soon, Mary was elevated to the level of these goddesses. Many statues of Isis and the Mother of Phrygia were transformed into statues of Mary. Many epithets formerly assigned to Isis and Astarte, such as Redemptress, Savior, and Virgin Mother, became epithets of Mary.

The idea of Mary's perpetual virginity became an official observance of the Catholic church in AD 575 by proclamation of Pope Benedict I. Pope Pelagius II, in AD 583, again proclaimed the "fact" of Mary's perpetual virginity and issued a Papal Bull declaring the obligation to "defend the doctrine by force of arms," if needed.

By AD 599, "defending the doctrine by force of arms" had evolved into an offensive tool to justify Gregory I's demand to "bring all infidels under the protection of The Virgin, even if an infidel had to forfeit his life to ensure his salvation."

In AD 675, the Tolentino Council confirmed this dogma as an official, fundamental Church doctrine.

Oddly, as Mary evolved into the "perpetual virgin" and the "virgin mother," Joseph became characterized as an impotent old man, while Jesus' brothers and sisters became depicted as either his cousins or his stepbrothers and stepsisters from a former marriage of Joseph's. They were distanced from Mary.

Another pagan trait that made its way into church doctrine was the "Mother of God" notion.

Mary's evolution to "Mother of God" began at the first Council of Nicaea in AD 325. Council members stated that because Jesus was the Son of God, then he must also be God. Council participants further argued that Jesus was part of the Holy Trinity and, effectively, God on Earth. Hence, through Council proclamation, Jesus became God.

The Council's intention might have been to bring honor and praise to Jesus, but in so doing they created a problem regarding Mary. Namely, could the mother of Jesus (*christotokos*), who was God the Son and a member of the Holy Trinity, be the mother of God (*theos-theotokos*)? In other words, if Jesus was truly God, how could God owe His origin to a woman *unless* that woman was divine too?

This argument (seemingly) was settled by proclamation at the Council of Ephesus in AD 431. Mary was proclaimed to be *Deipara* or "The Divine Virgin, The Mother of God." From that time on, "Mary, Mother of God," began to occupy the divine pedestal previously reserved only for God the Father, God the Son, and God the Holy Spirit.

The Council of Ephesus proclamation was rapidly adopted as doctrine throughout the Christian world. Hence, the western Roman Empire built churches in Mary's name and dedicated them in her honor.

Meanwhile, new and/or expanded attributes were ascribed to Mary, attributes previously ascribed to pagan goddesses like Isis, Ceres, Minerva, and Venus. These traits included the powers of regeneration, redemption, and spiritual mediation. Thus came the dogma that through Mary, humanity's redemption and salvation were assured.

Temples once dedicated to goddesses were rededicated to the worship of Mary.

The Rise of Islam

One of the most surprising discoveries that I made was the honor and praise that the Muslims had given first century Orthodox Judaism and the first and second century Christians, for their efforts in neutralizing the deceptive and blasphemous doctrine of the divine mother of God. The early Muslims acknowledged with pride that the 4,600-year-old Babylonian doctrine of divine mother and incarnate child had been stopped temporarily as a result of the dogged immovability of Orthodox Judaism of the first century, coupled with the first and second century early church evangelists' spread of the Gospel.

Over the next century, the "Mother of God" doctrine was steadily propagated. During the papacy of Gregory I (AD 590 to AD 604), the doctrine was pushed dogmatically and militantly upon the "peoples whose faith in The Virgin is lacking in guidance or absent in practice."

Gregory had declared in AD 599, "Every man, every woman, and every child will, under penalty of death, give The Blessed Virgin her rightful place in their lives."

In the West, most people accepted Gregory's edict and adopted the Mary, Mother of God doctrine as canon. However in the East, especially in the Arabian Peninsula, an uneasy undercurrent rolled. Eventually, a violent rebellion against Gregory's "forced blasphemy" resulted in the creation of a new religious philosophy. This philosophy spread rapidly, and, for more than 1,000 years, it threatened Christianity's existence. This philosophy was the religion of Islam.

Upon learning this new information, I sat in amazement. According to what I had just read, the creation of the Islamic religion had been totally preventable. Had the third and fourth century Christians merely followed Jesus' simple instructions, and the example set by their predecessors regarding individual, faith-based, personal conversion, rather than trying to forcibly convert the whole world, the Islamic religion might have not been born?

After taking some time to contemplate the significance of this conclusion, I continued reading and taking notes.

So effective were the efforts of the early Christian evangelists, that by AD 550 the Arabic world led by a group of monotheist converts known as Banifs had not only embraced the Jewish-based and Christian-inspired doctrine of monotheism, but had adopted the fundamental truths of the Christian doctrine as proclaimed by the early Christian evangelists. The truths adopted by the Arabic tribes and taught by the Banifs were:

1. There is only one true God.

2. The one true God chose the descendants of Abraham to be the recipients of His principles, His plan, and His purpose.

3. A segment of Abraham's descendants, the Hebrews or Jews, rejected God's love, principles, and standards.

4. This segment, the Hebrews or Jews, were in turn sent a divine messenger in the form of a man, born of a virgin: the prophet Jesus, the son from God.

5. This messenger, the prophet Jesus, the son from God, lived a life of perfection on Earth and gave his life as a sacrifice for the Hebrews.

6. The Hebrews rejected that perfect sacrifice of God.

7. In turn, God raised Jesus from the dead and established him as the perfect sacrifice for all of mankind.

8. God then exalted him to the position of My precious sacrifice My Son. His position as Son is everlasting and eternal.

I want to point out real quick, before I continue with my notes on the creation of Islam, that the last statement, point number eight, was included in the very earliest versions of The Imrans, the traditional third sura of The Koran, but began to be omitted from The Imrans in versions of The Koran by the late seventh century.

I then continue with my notes.

During the past 100 years from AD 500, the banifs had successfully guided the Arabic tribes through the troubled waters of paganism and the worship of multiple gods and goddesses, into the refreshing calm of the Jewish-based, Christian inspired doctrine of monotheism, and the worship of the one and only true God.

I learned that at the time of Gregory I's papacy, Arabia was on its way to becoming an eastern stronghold of Christianity. Then came Gregory's "declaration of blasphemy," as it was called by Caliph al-Ma'mun some years later.

Because the Arabic tribes were new converts to monotheism, Gregory viewed them as "infidels at heart." They were unworthy of occupying the same level of esteem as inceptive Christians or Jewish converts to Christianity. Hence, the Arab tribes were grouped with all other "infidels and barbarians," becoming primary targets for "forced observance."

At first, the Banifs, the unofficial religious leaders of Arab tribes, did not realize that Arabs were infidels in Gregory's eyes, infidels who must be forced to worship Mary. When they realized what was happening, the Banifs sought to keep Gregory's edict from the Arabic people. They did not succeed. By the year AD 601, the Banifs made public Gregory's proclamation which sent shock waves from one end of Arabia to the other.

The unrest convinced the Banifs that they had to take a stand or face open rebellion from the Arab people.

Rebellion came. The rallying cry of the Arabs was, "How could Allah, the One God, God Supreme, be born of a woman?"

In AD 602, Gregory learned that Arabic tribes had taken a stand against him. He became furious. He responded by issuing an avalanche of edicts and decrees directed specifically at the Arabs and their religious leaders.

Gregory claimed to speak for God Himself. He insisted that every word he spoke or wrote was God speaking. Thus, every word must be obeyed without question, under penalty of death.

Among Gregory's dozens of papal proclamations, a few severely alienated the Arabic people. For example:

1. Mary, the mother of Jesus, was, is, and always will be a virgin.

2. Mary was sinless throughout her life, and she, too, was born of a virgin.

3. Mary ascended into heaven bodily, upon her death.

4. Through Mary, humanity has the assurance of redemption and salvation.

5. Mary "The Queen of Heaven" is humanity's mediator before God.

The more arrogant and insistent Gregory became, the more defiantly the Arabs stood in defense of monotheism. To them, Gregory's decrees were steadily becoming less Christian and increasingly pro-Mary.

Gregory sent armies far and wide to enforce obedience. Throughout the 'pagan' world people submitted, but not in Arabia. There, Gregory's ruthlessness had the opposite effect. With each new papal proclamation, the Banif-inspired Arabs became increasingly anti-Mary, and anti-Pope.

It's important to note that, at first, the Arabs were not *anti-Chris-tian*. They affirmed Christian truths and doctrines. They accepted that Jesus was God's son, who was sacrificed. Historical evidence shows that the Arabs considered the Christianity of the first three centuries to be *the* true religious doctrine.

However, because the Pope claimed to be the singular spokesman for Christianity, the Arabic tribes developed an anti-Christian sentiment. They did not despise, hate, or resent Christians or Christianity. They despised the Pope and his blasphemous Mother of God doctrine.

In AD 604, the Banifs countered Gregory's assault by issuing their own standards of worship, doctrine, and tenets of faith. They began preaching these new tenets throughout Arabia.

This should have opened the eyes of the Catholic Church and its leadership. It did not. After Gregory I, six popes (Sabinianus (604-606), Boniface III (607), Boniface IV (608-615), Deusdedit (615-618), Boniface V (619-625), and Honorius I (625-638) continued to proclaim and enforce the controversial Marian edicts.

By AD 608, the Arab people, having been vigorously evangelized and instructed by the Banifs, adopted a new religious philosophy. Islam had as its principal elements both Jewish and Christian doctrines, yet it was unique in that it rejected all the supplemental elements of Judaism and Christianity added by decree over the course of seven centuries.

As I continued to study the evolution of Islam, it became obvious to me that Pope Gregory I and his forced exaltation of Mary were instrumental in the founding and rapid spread of Islam. Moreover, this Pope contributed to the death of millions of Muslims, Jews, and Christians in the so-called Holy Wars.

The irony and tragedy is that Islam and Christianity are so similar. The main difference is the position of Jesus. Christians accept Jesus as Son of God and Redeemer. Muslims accept Jesus as God's prophet and God's perfect sacrifice, hence "a son of God, redeemer." However, followers of both religions have been manipulated and told that they are *very* different. These manufactured differences have created politically motivated "Holy Wars." Millions of lives have been lost.

By using the Mother of God dogma as its keystone doctrine, the post-fourth-century Catholic leadership literally re-wrote the Scriptures to incorporate Mary's newly attained virtues.

Elevating Mary to divinity led to denying any sin in her, including original sin. True to form, Sixtus IV (in 1476) proposed that the doctrine of Mary's sinlessness be added as an article of faith.

IMMACULATE CONCEPTION

In 1546, at the Council of Trent, an official proclamation was issued. Mary was immune from all sin, even venial sin. Thus, the doctrine of the *Immaculate Conception* was birthed.

In 1854, Mary's long journey from humble maiden to sinless virgin was complete when Pius IX made Mary's sinlessness an official article of the Church.

After Pius IX's proclamation, the next logical steps were to confirm Mary's deification and her bodily ascension into heaven.

In 1950, Pius XII declared that upon Mary's death, she was assumed into heaven *bodily*. This was followed in 1954 with the announcement of the endowing of the Feast of Mary the Queen, which celebrates her inferred deity.

The Mother Queen was now a goddess. As such, she was given the ability to mediate and to forgive sin. In 1958, at the Mariological Congress of Lourdes, Mary was granted the ability to mediate and forgive sin. This was reconfirmed in 1964 by Paul VI. Thus, Mary, over the course of 1500 years, evolved from simple earthly mother of Jesus into humanity's primary mediator and redeemer.

Thus, the Luciferian neutralization of the truth by infiltration and deception has worked to perfection. Today, doubt and confusion about Jesus, his birth, his life, and his ministry are the norm, not the exception.

The pyramid of Khafra (foreground) and
the Great Pyramid of Cheops (behind)—Egypt.

CHAPTER 11

∿

An Invasion from the East

THE NEXT MAJOR GOSPEL-RECORDED EVENT in Jesus' life occurred about two years after Joseph took his wife and infant son back to Nazareth. During the two years after Jesus' birth (while Joseph and family lived in Nazareth), Joseph gained quite a reputation as one of the Galilee's greatest master stonemasons. Thanks to Herod the Great's massive building efforts, Joseph's construction business was booming.

During this time of prosperity in Herod's kingdom, the Magi arrived from the East. They showed up in Jerusalem, uninvited, and demanded to see the recently born King of the Jews.

Every year, Christmas nativity scenes depict three wise men, gifts in hand, bowing before the manger and worshipping the newborn King.

This is tradition, not truth, as you'll soon see.

Many years ago, I visited a beautiful church library in Augsburg, Germany: the library of the twin Catholic/Protestant churches of St. Ulrich and St. Afra.

There, I discovered a document proving the wise men did not arrive in Herod's kingdom until two years *after* Jesus was born.

This document was a journal of sorts, a collection of personal notes written by the Swiss theologian Karl Barth, some time after 1932. Barth never published any of this material, nor had anyone else.

In these writings, Barth commented on a variety of subjects, including the specter of Adolph Hitler's rise to power. Barth, fearing his notes would fall into Nazi hands, gave them to his brother (who lived in Innsbruck, Austria).

When it became apparent that Hitler would take control of Austria, the bound volume of Barth's notes was taken to the churches of St. Ulrich and St. Afra and hidden in a vault. After the war, Barth donated the volume to the church library.

As I scanned Barth's hand-written words, I was amazed at his depth of theological understanding and reasoning.

Although he had much to say about the "mad-man Hitler and his party of demons," he did not dwell on this.

He focused most of his attention on various theological disputes and analyses, and on the history of Christian thought and doctrine.

Among his writings on Christian dogma and tradition, I found pages and pages about the wisemen and their role in the nativity story.

Barth begins his discussion of this topic by noting that Herod's kingdom enjoyed relative peace during the two years following Jesus' birth, but by 5 BC things changed.

Barth quotes Matthew 2, beginning with verse one.

MATTHEW 2:1-23

[1] Now when Jesus was born in Bethlehem of Judaea in the days of Herod the king, behold, there came wise men from the east to Jerusalem,

[2] Saying, Where is he that is born King of the Jews? for we have seen his star in the east, and are come to worship him.

[3] When Herod the king had heard these things, he was troubled, and all Jerusalem with him.

[4] And when he had gathered all the chief priests and scribes of the people together, he demanded of them where Christ should be born.

[5] And they said unto him, In Bethlehem of Judaea: for thus it is written by the prophet,

[6] And thou Bethlehem, in the land of Juda, art not the least among the princes of Juda: for out of thee shall come a Governor, that shall rule my people Israel.

⁷ Then Herod, when he had privily called the wise men, enquired of them diligently what time the star appeared.

⁸ And he sent them to Bethlehem, and said, Go and search diligently for the young child; and when ye have found him, bring me word again, that I may come and worship him also.

⁹ When they had heard the king, they departed; and, lo, the star, which they saw in the east, went before them, till it came and stood over where the young child was.

¹⁰ When they saw the star, they rejoiced with exceeding great joy.

¹¹ And when they were come into the house, they saw the young child with Mary his mother, and fell down, and worshipped him: and when they had opened their treasures, they presented unto him gifts; gold, and frankincense and myrrh.

¹² And being warned of God in a dream that they should not return to Herod, they departed into their own country another way.

¹³ And when they were departed, behold, the angel of the Lord appeareth to Joseph in a dream, saying, Arise, and take the young child and his mother, and flee into Egypt, and be thou there until I bring thee word: for Herod will seek the young child to destroy him.

¹⁴ When he arose, he took the young child and his mother by night, and departed into Egypt:

¹⁵ And was there until the death of Herod: that it might be fulfilled which was spoken of the Lord by the prophet, saying, Out of Egypt have I called my son.

¹⁶ Then Herod, when he saw that he was mocked of the wise men, was exceeding wroth, and sent forth, and slew all the children that were in Bethlehem, and in all the coasts thereof, from two years old and under, according to the time which he had diligently inquired of the wise men.

¹⁷ Then was fulfilled that which was spoken by Jeremiah the prophet, saying,

¹⁸ In Rama was there a voice heard, lamentation, and weeping, and great mourning, Rachel weeping for her children, and would not be comforted, because they are not.

¹⁹ But when Herod was dead, behold, an angel of the Lord appeareth in a dream to Joseph in Egypt,

²⁰ Saying, Arise, and take the young child and his mother, and go into the land of Israel: for they are dead which sought the young child's life.

²¹ And he arose, and took the young child and his mother, and came into the land of Israel.

²² But when he heard that Archelaus did reign in Judaea in the room of his father Herod, he was afraid to go thither: notwithstanding, being warned of God in a dream, he turned aside into the parts of Galilee:

²³ And he came and dwelt in a city called Nazareth: that it might be fulfilled which was spoken by the prophets, He shall be called a Nazarene.

Next, Barth provides a summary of this passage, observing that two years *after* Jesus' birth, the wisemen suddenly appeared in Jerusalem, demanding to see the newborn king.

Herod was in Jerusalem at this time (possibly because of Passover), rather than at his capital/governmental seat in Caesarea Maritima.

Along the way, Barth raises some age-old questions: "*Who were these wisemen? Where did they come from? Why were they in Jerusalem?*"

Addressing these questions, Barth notes that these visitors were not kings. That particular Christian tradition was based on a late thirteenth century misinterpretation of Psalms 72:10 & 15. The word wisemen is a Greek form of the word magi, the source for our word magician.

Magi is a general term. It can refer to astronomers, interpreters, teachers, physicians, Zoroastrian priests, scientists, astrologers, court historians, royal counselors, administrators, or governors. Magi were also official ambassadors, representing their kings in foreign countries.

In short, magi were sent by their rulers to a foreign country, with the full power to speak and act on a ruler's behalf. They weren't mere emissaries. They were acting *rulers* of their country.

The Bible does not say how many individual magi left their country or kingdom in search of the young child, but we can assume that a variety of magi, representing several empires, traveled to Jerusalem.

Why?

A brief historical recap will help us answer this question. At this time in history, Daniel, the captive Jew who rose to prominence in Nebuchadnezzar's Babylon, was known as the most respected of all Chaldean magi. Within 300 years of his death, Daniel had been exalted to the position of deity.

All Eastern kingdoms and empires afforded Daniel great honor, and they believed his writings to be divine. The disciples and priests of

Zoroaster and the Chaldean magi believed that Daniel's writings prophesied that a savior and world leader would arise in the region of Roman Syria (or Judea).

Daniel wrote hundreds of scientific, social, philosophical, and prophetic documents while in the court of Babylon and Persia. The document that probably excited the New Testament magi the most is recorded as Daniel 7:13 & 14:

DANIEL 7:13-14

[13] I saw in the night visions (stars and constellations), and, behold, one like the Son of man came with the clouds of heaven, and came to the Ancient of days, and they brought him near before him.

[14] And there was given him dominion, and glory, and a kingdom, that all people, nations, and languages, should serve him: his dominion is an everlasting dominion, which shall not pass away, and his kingdom that which shall not be destroyed.

Now, Persian history claims Zoroaster was a student of Daniel, and that Daniel had revealed to him that when a new star appeared in the constellation Coma, it would be a sign that the King of kings had been born in the area of Jerusalem. So, through their system of interpretation, the magi who arrived in Jerusalem had concluded that this prophetic writing would be fulfilled during the declared Pax Romana of Emperor Augustus. In 7 BC Augustus declared universal peace. As royal counselors and confidants of their respective rulers, the magi persuaded their rulers that to ensure the continuation of their monarchies and to guarantee friendship with the *future all-powerful world ruler*, it was necessary for the magi to embark on an important mission. They must find the newly born king and shower him with allegiance and honor.

Barth writes that he found ancient documentation indicating that the magi succeeded in convincing the various Eastern rulers that it was vital to show this allegiance.

At this point, Barth makes an interesting digression:

"Before I get back to the historical documentation that I discovered confirming the main purpose of the magi's visit," he writes, "I first want to cover some of the documentation which deals with this pandemonium in the heavens that so electrified these magi. It excited them so much that they traveled thousands of miles in search of the cause and meaning of such a tumult.

"According to the medieval astronomer Johannes Kepler, a conjunction of Saturn and Jupiter in the constellation Pisces took place in April of 7 BC.

"An acquaintance of mine, the German astronomer Dr. P. Schnabel confirmed the find by Kepler. The conjunction of Saturn and Jupiter did take place in April 7 BC.

"The Italian astronomer Ricciotti says that three comets would have been seen over Judea in the spring of 7 BC. Also, seven combined eclipses of the sun and moon would have been visible from Judea during the year 7 BC.

"Vespiani, the second-century Roman astronomer, said, 'Mercury, Venus, Mars, Jupiter, and Saturn aligned with the earth in the constellation of Pisces during the Passover of the Jews in the year that Jesus was born."

Barth then makes a personal comment,

"If any of these reports are true, (and why shouldn't they be? For what motivation would these astronomers have in deceiving or falsifying their own research reports?) is it any wonder that the wisemen of the East set out to search for the one whose birth was responsible for such a heavenly display, which had been, until that time, unprecedented?'"

The 4th-century Arabic astronomer Agobid would have agreed with Barth. He wrote, "At the time of the birth of the prophet Jesus, over the city of Jerusalem could be seen, for 30 consecutive days, brilliant comets streaking across the sky."

Let's go back even further in time: Pherialious, a 2nd-century Greco-Roman historian and astronomer, wrote, "The tumult in the heavens, with comets, alignments, eclipses, and conjunctions that accompanied the birth of the one whom the sect of Christians call Christ surely must indicate that his was truly a miraculous birth; even the heavens testify of him."

With this historical corroboration in place, let's now return to Barth and his review of the magi's travels. I will paraphrase his thoughts below:

The Matthew account does not say how many magi came to Judea. Considering the gifts mentioned in the Matthew account, western Christian tradition maintains that there were three. Eastern Christian tradition says 12. Other writings claim even higher numbers. Who is right?

There were some well-respected non-Christian, non-Jewish historians who lived during the time of Jesus' birth and life (or immediately thereafter) who accurately recorded events related to the magi's visit. Their writings can be considered authoritative and non-biased. Su-Ma-Chen, the Chinese/Persian historian, accompanied the magi caravan and wrote as an eyewitness. Others who wrote about the event include Barborus, the Parthian historian; Hue-Lo, the Greek/Chinese historian who was living in Jerusalem when the magi arrived; Tacitus, the Roman historian; and Sueronius, the Latin historian.

Su-Ma-Chen wrote that he accompanied a caravan of 100 ambassadors, along with servants, officers, and military escorts sent by the kings of the Empire of Parthia, the nine kings of the Kushan Empires, the Han Empire of China, the kingdom of the Babylonians and of the Arabs, and the kingdom of Persia to Roman Syria—all in search of the new King of the Jews born in Judea.

Barborus wrote that a great caravan of camels, ambassadors, and astronomers, sent by 13 kings of the East during the days of Publius Quirinus, passed continually through the Ester Gate in Damascus from sunup to midday, as they journeyed to Jerusalem to seek an allegiance with and to give homage to the newborn emperor.

Hue-Lo wrote that there was only one time in history that the great empires of the East united under a single purpose: This was when the new king was born in Syria at the time of the tumult in the heavens, during the time of the *Pax Romana*.

A CAMEL TRAIN OF 800 CAMELS

Tacitus recorded that when Quirinus was governor of Syria a caravan of more than 800 laden camels arrived from an eastern confederacy of 13 kingdoms, uninvited, in Jerusalem to search for a king they claimed was born in Judea, whose birth had been announced by the tumult of the stars.

After this historical over view, Barth continues with his own observations. I will now quote him directly.

"It seems obvious to me that as per these dependable and trustworthy historians the rulers of the great kingdoms of the East united to give their allegiance to the great world emperor. They had sent their ambassadors (court magi) to Roman Judea to search for a new emperor. It took them more than two years, from the time they first witnessed the tumult in the heavens until they arrived in Judea. Having invaded the Roman Empire, uninvited (considered an act of war), they felt it necessary to follow diplomatic protocol and to present themselves to Roman officials. Hence, they arrived in Caesarea Maritima, the governmental seat of Judea. Discovering that Herod was in Jerusalem, they journeyed to Jerusalem and presented themselves. Both Herod and the entire city of Jerusalem *were terrified*. Representatives delineating the rulers of the greatest empires of the East, whose combined kingdoms, land areas, populations, and military forces were many times greater than that of the Roman Empire, had traveled for more than two years and more than 2,000 miles to invade the Roman Empire with a caravan of as many as 1,000 camels. There were more than 100 ambassadors representing at least 13 Eastern kingdoms and empires. They were accompanied by a large military escort and by their needed servants, physicians, technicians, and caretakers and by state officials and ministers, and by court historians and scribes. They demanded that Herod take them to see the King of the Jews. It's certainly not surprising to me that Herod was terrified, and all of Jerusalem with him."

Barth continues,

"Herod was in a volatile situation. If he did not play his cards right, his life would be considered worthless from four different directions:

- If it was true that a new king had been born, who even the empires of the East knew as *King of the Jews*, why didn't Herod report it to Rome? Hence—*TREASON*.

- The invasion by the eastern confederacy was without warning, and Herod was not ready. He would have to answer to Augustus for allowing this invasion. Hence—*TREASON*.

- Herod's domain could be the battlefield for the greatest war ever, a war between the greatest confederation of eastern powers and the greatly feared Roman Empire.

Why had not Herod notified Rome that such a battle was developing? Hence—*TREASON*.

- If a new king was born in Judea who would become the king of the Jews, why had Herod allowed this king to live? What if an alliance was solidified between this new king and the eastern confederacy? It would, in essence, relinquish the entire area to the confederacy. Hence—*TREASON*."

Barth's conclusion is clear:

"Herod was trapped. He had to do something, fast. To give himself breathing room, he asked the Sanhedrin if such an event was anticipated. The Sanhedrin confirmed that a world ruler was expected to be born in Bethlehem.

"Herod felt that he had to eliminate this threat to his throne and to Rome, preferably before the representatives of the eastern confederacy formed an alliance with the new king. He sent the magi to Bethlehem and asked them to return to him immediately upon discovering the babe's location, so that he could 'go and pay homage to him also.'

"Herod's true intent was, most likely, to eliminate the babe, either by death, exile, or kidnapping and preferably without the magi knowing about it.

"According to Matthew, the magi left Jerusalem, heading south to Bethlehem. However, as they traveled, they again saw one of the heavenly signs: a star in the sky north of them. They turned north to follow it.

"They followed the star until, over the city of Nazareth, it seemed to stand still, then disappear.

"Then the magi probably left their huge caravan outside the city and found the house where Joseph, Mary, and the two-year old Jesus lived. Inside the house, the magi presented the toddler with gifts. Ancient historians have identified these as the three Gifts of Ramses intended to solidify a political allegiance between the new king and the eastern confederation. These gifts were given to Ramses, the Great, Xerxes, Alexander the Great, Hannibal, Tigleth-Pilser, Cyrus the Great, and Antripitus as expressions of allegiance. The gifts were gold (to acknowledge the recipient's royal position as king), frankincense (to acknowledge the recipient's position as the highest of priestly orders), and myrrh (to acknowledge the recipient's deity or his god/man position).

"The Gospel of Matthew says that after presenting their gifts, the magi were warned by God to avoid returning to Herod. So they and their immense caravans returned to their native countries, leaving directly from Nazareth.

"After the magi's departure, an angel appeared to Joseph in a dream and told him that Herod wanted to kill Jesus. The angel told Joseph to take his family and flee to Mary's ancestral home, Egypt. There they would stay until it was safe to return.

"When Herod learned that the magi had returned home without reporting to him, he became furious."

It should be noted that the magi had probably been gone for days or even weeks before Herod was told of their departure. No one wanted to deliver the bad news, as it was widely known that Herod, in a fit of rage, might "kill the messenger." Literally.

Eventually, the news reached Herod. He also probably learned that the magi had made an alliance with the child-king, sealed by the immutable Gifts of Ramses, the most honored and universally recognized of all diplomatic signs of allegiance between powers. This alliance, Herod knew, would dissolve his kingdom and place his realm under someone else's jurisdiction.

Even the whole Roman Empire was no match for this new confederacy, so Herod dare not attack the returning caravan. However, he would not let this insult go unavenged.

SLAUGHTER OF THE INNOCENT

Thinking the child-king was still in Bethlehem, Herod turned his wrath on male children, ages two years and below, in the area surrounding Bethlehem.

This slaughter was to occur during September and October of 5 BC.

The historian Livy recorded that over a period of 50 days, Herod killed one male child below the age of two every day, in the region of Bethlehem and Jerusalem.

Sueronius wrote that Herod's slaughter of the infants was not restricted to Bethlehem, nor only to Jewish babies. His crime reached beyond Bethlehem to include Hebron, Herodium, Juttah, Ramah, Bethany, and Emmaus. It involved not only the destruction of 11 Jewish infants, but many Greek, Syrian, Egyptian, Idumaen, and Arabian infants as well. Even infants in Herod's court were not immune to the butchery.

Ignatius of Antioch wrote that when Augustus learned of Herod's slaughter, he kicked over an image of Mercury and cried out, "It is better to be Herod's ass than to be his son or subject."

One of Barth's source documents for his account was a manuscript that he had studied while on an investigative visit to the Vatican library in 1922, shortly after Mussolini became premier of Italy. The scroll was discovered in 1660 in an underground vault of the Vatican I library. It was a copy of a much more ancient manuscript that was titled *Herod Antipater's Defense Before the Roman Senate in Regard to His Conduct at Bethlehem.* The original manuscript was alleged to have been the actual records of Herod's defense before the Roman Senate and Augustus

The following is Barth's transcription of Herod's first-person defense:

HEROD'S DEFENSE

"My guards told me that a large caravan of over 1,000 camels and an armed escort of one thousand infantrymen from an allied association of all the eastern empires beyond the Euphrates had entered Jerusalem and had caused the whole city to fear destruction. Their kings' representatives appeared at my gate, at least twenty or more sent by their emperors. They were in search of a babe who they say had been born king of the Jews. I told them that I ruled the Jews under Caesar Augustus. They said that the babe would rule after me. I sent them away and told them that I would send for them in three days after I investigated.

The excitement in the city had grown until it was intense and I sensed a rebellion of fear. I felt that if left to itself, nothing would be able to control it. I called the Hillel court, which read out of the Law and the prophecies of the Jews that a king was to be born of a virgin in Bethlehem. Out of the writings of Daniel, the respected Chaldean magician, whom they of the East call divine, they read that his kingdom would be worldwide and that it would last forever. They also said that the spectacle witnessed in the heavens signaled the birth of the new king.

"Although this spectacle was nothing but a phenomenon of nature, it did not better the condition I was in. A man will contend for a false faith stronger than he will for a true one. The truth defends itself, but a falsehood must be defended by its adherents: first, to prove it to themselves, and secondly that they may appear to be right. But the fact is, this case is as follows: The Roman taxation was cutting off the support of the priests, and they were hurtful under it. Again, the double taxing, that is, the tithes to the priests and the tax to the Romans, although my own taxes had been excused for almost two years, was bearing heavily on the common people.

"It had already become a proverb with the children of Bethlehem and Jerusalem that if the Jews had a new king, (then) neither Caesar nor Herod would reign any more, and that (the Jews) would have to pay no more taxes to keep up the Roman government. So I saw an insurrection brewing fast and nothing but a most bloody war as the consequence. In my honest judgment, it was best to pluck the undeveloped flower in its bud, lest it should grow and strengthen and shed its deadly poison over the empire and ruin it. I have no malice toward infants. I took no delight in listening to the cries of mothers. No! I saw nothing but an insurrection and a bloody war were our doom, and in this the overthrow and downfall of our nation."

As his words above suggest, the last few years of Herod's life were a nightmare for his subjects in Judea, and for his family. He was always suspicious and accused almost everyone, including his two eldest sons, of treason. During the last year of Herod's life (4 BC), he was stricken with several serious illnesses: intestinal cancer, ulcers, swelling of the legs, respiratory problems, bone cancer, and (probably) a brain tumor. He suffered more during his last year than in the previous 69.

Knowing that Herod's illnesses were incurable, two Jerusalem rabboni, Judas ben Sariphaeus and Mattathias ben Margalit, seized the opportunity to incite a revolt. Though bedridden, Herod still managed to squash the rebellion. He had the two rabboni burned alive and he had 40 of their accomplices strangled.

He then disposed of the High Priest, whom he accused of knowing about the plot. The priest was tied to a stake with a corpse. The man died as the corpse decayed. Herod would die a week later.

THREAT OF WORLD WAR

It should be noted that the last year of Herod's life saw an event that would forever change Judea's social and political climate. On January 18 of 4 BC, Caesar Augustus received an emissary at his court in Rome. The emissary had been sent by a coalition of 13 kings who were in the process of mobilizing an army of more than 500,000 on the great plain between the Chouspus River and the Tigris River.

The emissary informed Augustus that the coalition intended to invade the Roman Empire's eastern border within the year. He went on to say that he had been given the authority to declare war on Rome. The reason for the impending war: The news that Herod had killed the "new king" spoken of by the divine Bel-tesh-Azzar (aka Daniel).

Augustus was beside himself when he learned the coalition's intent. According to Irenaeus (a second century historian and religious leader), Augustus replied that Herod was a madman whose butchery was carried out without the approval of Augustus or the Roman Senate. Augustus added that he had not received confirmation that the child in question was among Herod's victims. Augustus explained that Herod was dying. He was mentally incapable of governing his kingdom. Thus, the emperor declared that he would issue a proclamation dissolving and re-districting Herod's kingdom. He went on to promise that if the coalition would refrain from attacking, he would investigate the killing and that Rome would not seek expansion into territories beyond the Euphrates River. To sweeten the deal, Augustus offered 10 years of duty-free trade with the coalition.

There is no official record of the coalition's response, but we do know that the coalition did not invade Rome. If that had happened, a world war would have erupted. Thus, it is safe to assume that Augustus's response pacified the coalition.

On February 4 of 4 BC (40 days before Herod's death), Augustus decreed that in 100 days (or upon Herod's demise, whichever came first), Herod's kingdom would be divided among three to five successors. Herod was tasked with choosing the successors. However, when a month passed with no decision, Augustus threatened to place Herod's entire kingdom under Roman procuratorship.

Two days later, the lame-duck king finally got moving. Because he had executed Antipater and banished Herod, Herod the Great named his next three sons as heirs. Archelaus was given the region comprising Judah and Idumes. Herod Philip received Iturea, Trachonitus, Gaulanitis, Auranitis, and Batanea. Herod Antipas was given the Galilee and Peraea, which he ruled until AD 39, eight years after Jesus' death.

Meanwhile, after Herod's death, Matthew 2:21-23 tells us that Joseph was instructed in a dream to leave Egypt and return to the Palestine region.

MATTHEW 2:21-23
²¹ And he arose, and took the young child and his mother, and came into the land of Israel.
²² But when he heard that Archelaus did reign in Judaea in the room of his father Herod, he was afraid to go thither: notwithstanding, being warned of God in a dream, he turned aside into the parts of Galilee:
²³ And he came and dwelt in a city called Nazareth: that it might be fulfilled which was spoken by the prophets, He shall be called a Nazarene.

We don't know how long after the angel's instructions that Joseph and the family left Egypt. A second century Cappadocia account I discovered while researching at Egypt's Cairo University says that Joseph made quite an impressive name for himself as a master stonemason in Egypt, circa 4 BC. So, when the angel appeared to him, he would have been hesitant to close down his thriving business and return to his homeland.

However, when Augustus levied a tax on all new and future heavy-construction projects in February of AD 4 (eight years after the angel's appearance), Joseph would have certainly realized it was time to go. He and his family arrived in Nazareth in September of AD 4. Jesus would have been about eleven years old.

Dr. Ron Charles with close friend and colleague
Dr. Al Pleysier visiting Moses' Rock in the Sinai
during one of Dr. Charles' summer tours.

CHAPTER 12

꒰ ꒱

Jesus: A Son of the Law

ON THIS NEXT STEP IN OUR JOURNEY, we encounter Jesus as a teenager. A notable event in his life took place in April of AD 6 when he was 13 years old. Jesus became a *Son of the Law* (Luke 2: 41-52).

On the eve of entering his teen years, Jesus travels to Jerusalem with his parents to participate in the *Son of the Law* ceremony, which is celebrated during the Passover of one's thirteenth year. (Jesus turned thirteen near the end of Passover.)

While I was visiting a friend in Sur, Lebanon, I found an ancient document related to this event.

Deogratias, Bishop of Carthage from AD 436 to 452, wrote the manuscript in Latin, addressing it to one Genesius of Clermont.

Apparently, Genesius had contacted Deogratias, seeking his opinion on several questions about Jesus' life and ministry.

This manuscript contained Deogratias' responses.

The manuscript includes the biblical account (Luke 2:41-52) of the ceremony in Jerusalem, when Jesus became a *Son of the Law*:

LUKE 2:41-52

⁴¹ Now his parents went to Jerusalem every year at the feast of the passover.

⁴² And when he was twelve years old, they went up to Jerusalem after the custom of the feast.

⁴³ And when they had fulfilled the days, as they returned, the child Jesus tarried behind in Jerusalem; and Joseph and his mother knew not of it.

⁴⁴ But they, supposing him to have been in the company, went a day's journey; and they sought him among their kinsfolk and acquaintance.

⁴⁵ And when they found him not, they turned back again to Jerusalem, seeking him.

⁴⁶ And it came to pass, that after three days they found him in the temple, sitting in the midst of the doctors, both hearing them, and asking them questions.

⁴⁷ And all that heard him were astonished at his understanding and answers.

⁴⁸ And when they saw him, they were amazed: and his mother said unto him, Son, why hast thou thus dealt with us? behold, thy father and I have sought thee sorrowing.

⁴⁹ And he said unto them, How is it that ye sought me? wist ye not that I must be about my Father's business?

⁵⁰ And they understood not the saying which he spake unto them.

⁵¹ And he went down with them, and came to Nazareth, and was subject unto them: but his mother kept all these sayings in her heart.

⁵² And Jesus increased in wisdom and stature, and in favour with God and man.

Deogratias offers many insights on the *Son of the Law* ceremony. He says that it was common for Jewish men and women to come to Jerusalem from all over the world to commemorate the annual celebration of Passover. However, as children were not allowed to participate, Jesus would have not been able to take part until he had completed the *Son of the Law* (Bar Mitzvah) ceremony.

The *Son of the Law* ceremony was performed in the Temple in Jerusalem. Ever since the days of Ezra, the ceremony had signified a young man leaving childhood and entering manhood. (It's interesting that since the time of Ezra, an Orthodox Jewish mother suckled her first-born son every Sabbath until he was 13 and had been invested as a *Son of the Law*. However Galilean Jewish mothers like Mary eschewed this tradition.)

At this time in Jerusalem (AD 6), a typical Passover celebration would draw more than three million Jewish celebrants. This did not include the hundreds of merchants and vendors, the non-Jewish sightseers, the Roman authorities, the Roman military, and so on. For a young man, his first real Passover in Jerusalem was momentous.

During his first Passover as a *Son of the Law* candidate, one was allowed to participate in three observances: Pesach, the day the Passover lamb was killed; the holy convocation, the most solemn period of the Passover; and Matsoth, the day of the sheave offering celebrating the first harvest.

On Matsoth, Joseph paid five shekels in redemption money, marking the beginning of Jesus' *Bar Mitzvah/Son of the Law* ceremony.

On the day following his ceremony, Jesus (a new *Son of the Law)* was allowed to attend teachings featuring the most prestigious rabbonis and Rabbans. These teachings were presented beneath the arcades of the Temple. During this time, Jesus would be allowed to remain in the Temple (all day and all night if he wanted to) for the rest of Passover.

Luke implies that Jesus spent the remainder of his celebration discussing and asking questions of the rabbonis and Rabbans, whom Luke calls "doctors of the law"

This raises a question for Deogratias: How was it that a 13-year-old boy was allowed to question this prestigious group of teachers?

One theory that has been voiced for at least 100 years is that Luke's record contends that Jesus was allowed to attend the teaching meetings of the Sanhedrin, who traditionally met in the Temple compound during Passover. Again, how did he manage to spend up to five days with the teaching Sanhedrin, given that their meetings were closed to all who were not members?

Meanwhile, Luke's Gospel tells us that Joseph and Mary began their journey home, thinking Jesus was somewhere in the returning caravan, probably with other relatives. The caravan traveled for a day, covering as few as 8 miles, but perhaps as many as 30. At camp that first night, Joseph and Mary discovered Jesus was missing. They immediately returned to Jerusalem, where it took three days to locate their son.

If Jesus was allowed to stay in the Temple compound during this time, he would have eaten and slept there. If *not*, where would a lone 13-year-old boy sleep and eat in a city overflowing with more than three million people?

JOSEPH OF ARIMATHEA

Enter Joseph of Arimathea.

The Bible says little about this man. We know he was a wealthy (and secret) disciple of Jesus and that he claimed the Lord's crucified body from Pilate and buried it in his own tomb. He was a member of the Sanhedrin who disagreed with the decision to crucify Jesus.

LUKE 23:50-51

[50] And, behold, there was a man named Joseph, a counsellor; and he was a good man, and a just:

[51] (The same had not consented to the counsel and deed of them;) he was of Arimathaea, a city of the Jews: who also himself waited for the kingdom of God.

According to the Jerusalem Talmuds and *The Roman Senatorial Annals and Chronologies*, Joseph of Arimathea, a Roman citizen by conferance, was the younger adopted brother of Mary's father. Thus, Joseph of Arimathea was Mary's uncle and Jesus' grand-uncle. (First century Christian tradition says that Joseph of Arimathea was adopted by Mary's father as a small boy of eight or nine, after he was orphaned. Both his parents and his older brother and sister were killed in a ship wreck.)

First-century Christian tradition holds that Mary's father was imprisoned or killed while Mary was pregnant with Jesus. So Joseph of Arimathea stepped in and legally adopted Mary. Under Roman law, when he adopted Mary, he also adopted her unborn child. This means that when Jesus was born, he became the adopted son/grandson of Joseph of Arimathea. Thus, Mary and Jesus were legal Jewish Roman citizens, Jewish by birth, Roman by adoption. Joseph had a natural daughter, Anna, whom Mary called consobrina or blood-cousin.

The aforementioned Talmuds and *Roman Senatorial Annals and Chronologies* refer to Joseph of Arimathea as *Joseph de Marmore*. This was a Roman title of honor given to a Jew of royal bloodline who had proven himself loyal to Rome and been granted Roman citizenship. This honor conferred Roman citizenship on all of Joseph's children, heirs, and direct descendants.

According to early church tradition, Joseph was one of the richest Romans—and *the* wealthiest Jew—in all Syria.

This brings us to another brief digression from young Jesus' Passover saga.

Deogratias points out that Joseph's status might explain why he was able to claim Jesus' body after death. (According to Roman and Jewish law, only the next of kin could claim and bury a victim of capital punishment.)

If Joseph was a Roman Senator and the Imperial Minister of Mines and Mining for Rome, he would have direct access to Pontius Pilate. Incidentally, Joseph was far more significant than Pilate in the eyes of Roman authorities.

Of course, this sparks an important question, which Deogratias phrases eloquently:

"If Joseph of Arimathea was a Roman Senator and if he was as powerful as stated, why did he not stop the crucifixion of Jesus?"

Deogratias then answers his own question. During Tiberius' reign, the prefect Sejanus moved his guard to the outskirts of Rome and encamped there, refusing to withdraw until all of his demands for social equality had been met. Meanwhile, various accusations and counter accusations of treason and disloyalty flew back and forth between Sejanus and Tiberius, resulting in the death of thousands through executions and suicide. This turmoil continued until Sejanus' execution in October of AD 31.

Deogratias adds that, in the midst of this crisis, Tiberius became so incensed that he withdrew from Rome and retired to the island of Capri. (Tiberius governed from Capri, via courier, until his death in AD 37. See Chapter 15.)

During this crisis, Jesus was crucified. So fragile was the Roman government that every accusation and suspicion of treason was treated seriously. Thus, verdicts of high treason could only be appealed to, and overturned by, the emperor.

However, during Tiberius's self-isolation, he would accept visits only from the Theophus commission.

Thus, more than 9,000 allegations of high treason against Rome were brought to Sejanus, including the one against Jesus. Every one of the accused was found guilty and sentenced. Jesus was one of about 4,900 people who faced the death penalty. So, even if Joseph had protested Jesus' sentence, it would have done no good. Tiberius refused to hear *any* appeals, even one from someone as influential as Joseph of Arimathea.

With this aside complete, Deogratias returns to Jesus' Passover adventure and its connection to Joseph of Arimathea. He states that Joseph of Arimathea's status probably influenced the Sanhedrin Doctors of the Law to entertain questions and debate from the teenage Jesus. It is possible that while in Jerusalem, Mary, Joseph, and Jesus stayed with Uncle Joseph at his Jerusalem residence.

Moreover, the caravan's first stop on the return trip from Jerusalem could have been Arimathea, some 18 miles north of Jerusalem. So, it's reasonable to assume that Jesus' parents gave him permission to accompany Uncle Joseph on this leg of the trip.

Of course, when the caravan stopped and Jesus wasn't with his uncle or anyone else, Mary and Joseph quickly returned to Jerusalem. There, they found Jesus, debating in the Temple. They scolded him. He replied that he was merely doing his father's business. In other words, Deogratias explains, Jesus told his earthly father and mother that he was now a Son of the Law. He was doing *this* father's business (the Law's business), which was to debate, comment on, and teach the Law.

If Deogratias is correct, Jesus was not referring to his *heavenly Father's* business. He is not suggesting (yet) that he is the Son of the Heavenly Father.

EDUCATION IN GALILEE

At this point in the document, Deogratias departs from Jesus' specific story and explores the educational life of a Jewish boy growing up in the Galilee. Now, a summary of curricula doesn't make for the most scintillating reading, but to understand Jesus better, it's important to take a quick look at what his education was like. As we explore Deogratias's summary, which I will paraphrase for you, let's imagine Jesus going through this rigorous process.

In the Galilee, the Jewish population was a tiny minority. Educational requirements reflected this fact. The Galilee was extremely cosmopolitan, with no dominant ethnic group or race.

Education was under the *direct control* of the Roman authorities, and because the Galilee was so diverse, Rome allowed only limited ethnic education up to age 12 and only *if* that education didn't interfere with the Roman agenda. Thus, education about Jewish culture was optional. When such classes were allowed, they were taught by Roman approved Jewish tutors, usually for the first two hours of the school day. The remaining six hours were devoted to compulsory classes supervised by Roman officials. After age 12, no ethnic education was permitted.

In the Galilee, education began at age five and was compulsory for boys up to age 17.

For a Jewish child in the Galilee, the two-hour optional segment of the day was conducted either at the local Jewish synagogue or another approved location. Children like Jesus were taught the Law, the Shema, the Psalms, the prophets, Jewish history, Jewish philosophy, Jewish manners and customs, Jewish ethics, laws of sacrifice, the origins of Judaism, and limited portions of what became the Talmuds. This was far less than the Jewish education available to a Jewish student in Judea. Thus, Judean Jews considered Galilean Jews "unlearned" in Jewish ways and customs.

This is why religious leaders in Jerusalem called Jesus' Galilean apostles unlearned (See Acts 4:13). These leaders weren't saying Jesus' apostles were *uneducated*. Rather, they were saying that Peter and John had not been trained in the rabbinic schools, nor did they hold official positions in recognised religious circles. The Romans insisted that Galileans receive the best education possible. The accusation was that Galileans didn't understand "Jewish ways" as well as their Judean counterparts did.

The compulsory Roman education that Jesus endured included etiquette; music; the art of war; all forms of mathematics; poetry; gymnastics; wrestling; track and field; geography; the Greek language; Latin, Greek and Roman culture; Greek and Roman manners and customs; Greek and Roman philosophy; cultural philosophy; world history; Roman history; Roman law and government; Roman diplomacy; Persian history; world religions; world philosophies; economics; trade and merchandising; architecture; engineering and construction; art; agriculture and animal husbandry; speech and oratory; writing and communication; the history of religion and philosophy; and the history of ancient civilizations. (Parents, share this information with your kids next time they complain about their schooling.)

The teacher-to-student ratio was usually one-to-four.

Upon completion of this education, the 17-year-old graduate named Jesus would have enjoyed several options: He could choose a job and start working. He could continue his education at one of the Roman universities scattered throughout the Empire. He could attend a Roman political school to train for a political career. He could attend a Roman military school. He could attend a Roman trade school. He could *try* to train for the priesthood. (The odds of a Galilean being approved for priesthood education were less than one in a million.)

Then there was the teaching profession or rabbinical training. Galilean students pursuing either of these two options received special consideration. Because the Rabbinate schools were all located in Judea, it was impractical for a student in the Galilee to travel all that way. Thus, Roman authorities demanded that Rabbinate schools each accept 10 Galilean students annually. These Galilean students did not have to go to Judea for their training. Instead, they studied, *for eight years*, under Judean Rabbinate-school-appointed tutors who set up residences in the Galilee. Each tutor invited no more than two students per year to live and learn at his residence.

In AD 11, when Jesus was 17-18 years old, nine of these tutors lived in the Galilee and trained Galilean rabbi students.

Upon completion of his rabbi training, at age 25, a Galilean student had to submit to five years of understudy, the same period required in Judea.

Each year's top rabbi student from the Galilee had the opportunity to advance to either rabboni training or scribe training. Here again, Roman authorities intervened. They demanded that if a top student decided to pursue rabboni training, an approved Rabban or a Roman-approved Sanhedrin member was obligated to establish a residence in the Galilee and tutor this student.

If the top student chose to follow the path of a scribe, the Sanhedrin was obligated to establish a Galilean residence for a *soferim*, who could personally tutor the young scribe-to-be. Joseph of Arimathea could have been the Sanhedrin/Roman appointed soferim to the Galilee at the time of Jesus' educational training.

Interference by the Roman authorities into the religious education of rabbis and scribes was a major point of dissension between the Roman authorities and the Judean religious leaders, and between the Judean rabbis, rabbonis, and scribes and their Galilean counterparts.

Considering all of this it is obvious that Jesus' education was far more Greco-Roman than Jewish.

Deogratias went on to say the reason Jesus was a stranger to his own people was because he and his mother, Mary, had lived with their uncle Joseph of Arimathea, for 12 years (from Jesus' age 17 to age 29), in both Judaea and Britain. During that time it is presumed that Jesus traveled with him on his many trips to and from Britain.

Joseph was The Minister of Mines and Mining for the Roman Empire. He owned or controlled virtually all metals shipping trade between Syria and Europe and traveled on behalf of the Roman Empire anywhere mines were being worked to buy and sell ore and minerals. Joseph was the Roman Senator representing Britain, so a great deal of time was spent in England.

Jesus spent time traveling with Joseph, making him a virtual stranger to the Galilee. That would explain why most of the Jews had questions about who he was. Even his cousin John the Baptist did not recognize him (John 1:31) Jesus was required to pay the Stranger and Wanderers

Tax recorded in Matthew (17:24-27). Bartholomew, the Nathanael, who lived close to Nazareth, had no idea who Jesus was. Jesus was known by very few in his home town, which could explain why a 12-year-old boy could so astound the great Professors of the Law in Jerusalem, and yet have nothing more recorded about him until he is nearly 30 years of age. If he had remained in Judaea or the Galilee area, surely something would have been written about this boy phenomenon. Jesus at age 30 was more a resident of Britain than he was a resident Galilean. The traditions of Glastonbury say that he and Mary, his mother, had built a home on the south end of Lake Glastonbury, near the home of Joseph, and had lived there for some time on two different occasions. At the completion of the second stay, they left Britain to return to the Galilee when Jesus was around 29 years old.

Glastonbury is located within the region of the Silurian Kingdom, the center of Druidic worship. Roman Senatorial records show that the Roman Senate appointed Arviragus king of Britain. He allotted to the Roman Senator Joseph, said by the infidels to be of Arimathea in provincial Judaea, 12 hides (just over 1900 acres) of land in Joseph's Senatorial provincial district of Glastonbury. This gift was given to Joseph in the name of the Roman Senate as compensation to Joseph for the wrongful death of his adoptive son, known to his followers as "the Christ" during the reign of Tiberius. It was on this land that Joseph built a church.

With this information, Deogratias's manuscript ends.

This manuscript helped me see the young Jesus' adventure in Jerusalem in a new light. After Jesus became a Son of the Law at age 13, Luke 2:51-52 tells us that he returned to Nazareth with his father and mother and remained subject to them. During that time, he grew in stature and increased in wisdom and favor with God and man. Beyond that, the Gospels say no more about his life until his baptism in AD 23 when he was 30 years old.

Because of this silence, many writers have felt it necessary to "fill in the gaps" with what they presume was happening in Jesus' life. In my many years of research, I have read literally hundreds of stories about these "hidden" years: Legends detailing Jesus' travels to the New World and preaching to American Indians. His search for truth with priests,

Indian gurus, Buddhist monks, and Nepalese holy men. His studying Confucianism in the royal courts of China. Let's not forget his many miracles, ranging from making water come out of rocks to stretching wood to turning trees into soldiers.

Yet, in this horde of stories, I found nothing that would add value to what is recorded in Luke. Perhaps Jesus' life for the next 17 years was not unusual, not miraculous. It was a typical life of a typical young man who went to school, became a rabbi (and then a rabboni), and learned a trade by helping his father in a stonemasonry construction business.

I like what Henry James says in his book *Including Christ*:

"Contrary to popular portrayal, I do not believe that Jesus lived his life in virtual solitude, walking slowly over the hills of the Galilee with perhaps a lamb in his arms meditating and contemplating the things of God and the future of mankind. I think he was far more normal than that.

"I think that if he did live in the Galilee he fitted in well with the typical Galilean. I think he worked hard in his father's stonemasonry business, building public buildings; places of worship, including Jewish synagogues; Roman baths; amphitheaters; residences; and anything else his father's business was contracted to construct.

"I think that he had friends and that he communicated with his family and relatives, including his Uncle Zebedee and his cousins, James and John, whom he called the sons of thunder. He probably met and conversed with people he would later minister to or even heal.

"I think that he was a normal young man who had a normal childhood. He had relatives, some of whom were very close to him, and some with whom he had a less than enthusiastic desire to become close. He had chores and duties. He attended school. He went to work. He played sports and games. He had friends, some were very close. He may have even had a girlfriend. He probably had to be disciplined by his parents and, like all children, he learned by his mistakes. He may have felt that his life was more than the norm and that there truly was something special about him and his relationship with God.

"Concerning Jesus and the Son of God issue, whether or not Jesus knew as a boy that he was destined to be man's Savior, I do not think Jesus knew any of this while he was growing up. While he might have suspected that there was something different about him, especially if his mother told him about the strange events that surrounded his birth and his early childhood (the Bible seems to imply that she did not tell him, she instead kept all those things to herself), I do not think that he concluded that he was of divine nature, was commissioned to be the Savior of the world, or was the long-awaited Messiah/Messias until after his baptism, in AD 23, and his wilderness experience immediately thereafter.

"I think Jesus grew up like a typical Galilean of his day, no more, no less.

"It was not until after he had submitted himself to the mission to which he was appointed by his Father that he came into the full realization of his divinity and his mission.

"From the time of his baptism until the launching of his ministry (in AD 26), Jesus had three years to try to comprehend his mission. Early in AD 23, Sejanus was rapidly becoming the most influential political figure in Rome. At the same time in the Galilee, temporarily insulated from the political turmoil in Rome, Jesus began preparing for a jaunt to the Jordan River.

"This trip would signal his embarkation upon a pilgrimage that would culminate in the redemption of man, and in his own death and resurrection."

Ruins of the walls of Herod's Temple in Jerusalem are in the background. Ruins of a Byzantine wall are in the middle, and ruins from the crusades era are in the foreground—Israel.

The Wailing or Western Wall in Jerusalem. This is all that remains of Herod's Temple—Israel.

CHAPTER 13

✿

Jesus' Baptism and Beyond

AD 23

IN AD 23, JOHN THE BAPTIST was rapidly climbing the stairway of popularity. He was Judea's first big-name "evangelist-prophet" in more than 500 years. Thousands of people flocked to the desert regions near the Jordan River to hear John preach and to be baptized. Billy Graham called the atmosphere "a cross between a medieval carnival, an evangelist crusade, and a Great Awakening camp meeting. It was new and refreshing and exciting."

Like other reclusive desert dwellers of his day, John wore a loin garment made of camel leather and ate the standard diet of locusts and wild honey.

He preached that repentance was the only key for entering God's kingdom. This teaching contradicted the Pharisees belief that entrance was based on a person being chosen by God. (Of course, the Pharisees believed that they had been chosen *first*.)

John also preached that public baptism was necessary to show true repentance. (The Pharisees taught that baptism was a sign confirming one's becoming a believer in the Jewish religion.)

Enter the 30-year-old Jesus, another person seeking to be baptized by John.

Like most of the events of Jesus' life, I discovered a multitude of legends, stories, and myths associated with this baptism, but they all seemed shallow or contrived or mystical. They seemed out-of-step with the Gospels. The Gospel records are so pure and direct.

Indeed, as I read the many strange and mystical stories about John the Baptist and Jesus, I wondered if I would *ever* find anything genuine that would match the simplicity of the Gospels.

BAPTISM RITUALS

Finally, in 1991 (22 years into my search), I found what I was looking for, in, of all places, Albania's National Library.

The library is located behind the Palace of Culture in downtown Tirana. There, I discovered a book written in 1603 by the French bishop Francis of Sales. Titled *Baptism and Sanctification,* it had been translated into English and German. It answered so many of my questions about Jesus' baptism.

Francis asserts that the message John the Baptist proclaimed had been taught and practiced for decades in the Hasid Hakamin communities. However, it was something the average citizen in Judaea and the Galilee had *never* heard. This is one reason thousands of people traveled to hear him.

Francis states:

> "John might not have known Jesus personally when he baptized him. If the two were cousins by blood, they might have been acquainted. If Jesus' mother and Elizabeth were just casual friends, their sons might not have crossed paths.
>
> "Whatever the case, the fact that John continued to preach and baptize for six years after he baptized Jesus implies that he didn't fully understand who Jesus was (as the Messias or the Messiah)."

Discussing the details of Jesus' baptism, Francis says:

"Jesus demanded that John use a unique ritual, one that recalled the days of the Old Testament prophet Ezra, rather than his usual method.

"In Ezra's day, baptism for priesthood candidates included one's being buried in the ground, to signify the death and burial of the old self and its ways. Then the candidate was exhumed, signifying his being raised into a new way of life. As you might guess, some candidates died after being buried too long. I could find no record of a standard "burial time," but I learned that is was common for candidates to be unconscious when they were retrieved from the ground.

"By the time of the Maccabean revolt (168-165 BC), the practice of ground burial had been replaced by 'burying in water'. The candidate was held under water until he passed out. This signified the death and the burial of the old self. The candidate was then raised out of the water and revived, to signify being raised into a new life of dedication to God.

"In 7 BC, Caesar Augustus outlawed all forms of 'initiation by baptism' for non-Romans of all religions under Rome's authority, including Judaism's 'suffering of baptism.' Violators could be imprisoned. However, for Roman citizens wishing to follow a given religion's ritual requirements, the ban did not apply. Thus, a non-Roman could not participate in the Jewish suffering of baptism, but a Roman citizen could."

So, at the time of Jesus' baptism, the ritual he requested of John had been illegal for non-Romans for 30 years.

Of course, this doesn't prove Jesus was a Roman citizen, but it does strongly suggest this was the case. At the very least, Jesus had a strong connection with Roman authorities.

Before Augustus's decree, there were as many as 200 different variations of the practice of baptism. Three were most common:

- The suffering of baptism used by the Jews (which we have just explored).

- Being buried in sand for one full day and night, leaving only the head exposed.

- The "trial by fire and water" practiced by many Greek, Babylonian, and Syrian sects. In this initiation, the inductee was set on fire, then thrown into water and held under until he passed out.

After Augustus's decree, the only type of Jewish baptism allowed for non-Romans was "purification of the spirit." This consisted of a quick, total immersion in water, or a partial covering of the person by sand, or the dipping of the upper part of one's body into water with the person drinking some of that water while submerged.

It is generally accepted that Jesus was baptized by John in the Jordan River. (Jordan, incidentally, is an old Sumerian name meaning "piss" or "piss drain." The Jordan River had served as a sewage disposal channel for centuries and was, at the time of Jesus' baptism, badly polluted.)

Now, Luke reports that Herod arrested John before Jesus' baptism. If this is true, then we have no record of who baptized Jesus. One commonly accepted explanation is that Luke's record is incomplete. That is, part of Luke's account of this event was lost or destroyed. Thus, Matthew and John's accounts are more accurate.

Another traditional explanation is that John submitted to Jesus' request and inaugurated him into the ministry with the "suffering of baptism ritual." Then, later on, Jesus was re-baptized (by Rome-approved methodology) after John's imprisonment. Thus, Jesus was baptized as a Roman and as a Jewish religious leader.

In any case, after his baptism, Jesus was led into the wilderness for another step in his rabboni training in self-discipline and spiritual awareness. Typically, rabboni training with a private Rabban (Rabban is a title of honor for presidents, both present and former, of the Sanhedrin) lasted five years. Two years into this training, the rabboni hopeful was initiated by baptism, followed by an isolated wilderness challenge of extended fasting and prayer—coupled with physical, emotional, psychological, and spiritual temptation. The duration of this isolation was determined by the Rabban but usually not less than 10 days, but no more than 50.

I discovered an excellent account of Jesus' wilderness experience in a book titled *The Cost of Leadership*, while researching at the Palace du Palais' historical reference archives in Avignon, France. (The walled city of Avignon was the seat of the papacy during the Church's period of schism in the 14th century. The Palace du Palais is the former papal residence.)

FASTING

The Cost of Leadership was written by Hans von Dohnaniy, the brother-in-law of Dietrich Bonhoeffer, the great anti-Nazi theologian (executed by the Nazis in 1945).

Below, I will paraphrase von Dohnaniy:

Immediately after Jesus' baptism, the Gospel of Mark says that Jesus was driven by the Holy Ghost into a harsh and desolate wilderness to be tested. Most theological historians agree that this was probably the wilderness surrounding the Dead Sea. The Gospels of Mark and Luke say that Jesus fasted 40 days and nights, and was continually tested. Matthew 4 says that Jesus was tested *after* the 40 days.

Thus, we can conclude that Jesus fasted for *at least* 40 days, during which time he was continually tested in many ways.

His testing included the temptation to (1) turn stone into bread, (2) bow down and worship the tempter, and (3) seek protection from angels. How many times these three temptations tormented Jesus is unknown. What is known is that these three were presented during the 40 days of fasting and at least once afterwards.

Von Dohnaniy claims it is common knowledge that if a person is healthy, and if he drinks a lot of fluids and expends minimal energy he should be able to endure a 40-day fast. Jesus' situation may have been different. He had just concluded the taxing ordeal of the suffering of baptism. This would have left his body severely weakened. Then he was forced into the hot, dry desert.

During a normal fast, a person usually loses his desire for food after about five days.

After 10 days, all solids are eliminated from the body, meaning that one's perspiration and other secretions are drastically reduced.

By day 15, spiritual sensitivity is greatly increased and the person becomes in-tune with his body, mind, and spirit.

By day 20, the person will have eliminated most bodily toxins, making his breath very sweet. Day 20 also marks the date on which he must increase fluid intake or suffer from hallucinations.

On days 40 through 45, hunger returns with extreme agony and starvation begins to set in.

There is much speculation about the events surrounding Jesus' wilderness experience. The most commonly accepted belief, taught by the Catholic Church and then adopted by non-Catholics, is that Jesus was tempted by Satan, in an attempt to undermine his holy mission.

In his book *Reflections on the Nature of the Mind*, Alfred Glastonbury (nineteenth century English theologian turned mystic), claims that Jesus' temptations were brought on by hallucination. Jesus faced internal conflict over the mission he had been called to. His spiritual self wanted to answer the call; his emotional self did not.

Conversely, eighteenth century historian Raymond Billsbugh asserts that Jesus was not tested by a spiritual evil force (Satan) but by an evil human, a renegade religious hermit or even his own Rabban.

Now, let's return to von Dohnaniy. As he discusses the three specific temptations, Von Dohnaniy contends that the chronological differences between the Matthew and Luke records are of little import. It's reasonable that Jesus faced the same temptations more than once during such a long ordeal.

The first temptation concerns the human craving for food and Jesus' miraculous abilities as the Son of God. Jesus overcame this temptation by quoting Deuteronomy 8:3:

DEUTERONOMY 8:3
[3]... that he might make thee know that man doth not live by bread only, but by every word that proceedeth out of the mouth of the LORD doth man live.

The second temptation sees Jesus being taken to a high mountain, where he is shown (apparently in a split-second) all the world's kingdoms and their glories, past, present, and future. This temptation attacked human vanity and the desire for power.

Again, Jesus overcomes a temptation by quoting Deuteronomy.

DEUTERONOMY 6:13
¹³ Thou shalt fear the LORD thy God, and serve him, and shalt swear by his name.

In the final temptation, Jesus is taken to the holy city (which Luke identifies as Jerusalem) and invited to stand on a temple's pinnacle. Then he is ordered to cast himself down—because God can send angels to protect him. Jesus responds by saying, "Thou shalt not tempt the Lord thy God" (Luke 4:12).

DEUTERONOMY 6:16
¹⁶ Ye shall not tempt the LORD your God...

Meanwhile, von Dohnaniy observes, after this time of temptation, the Gospels record nothing about Jesus' life for the next three years except reporting that "he increased in the power of the Spirit" (Luke 4:14) "and in wisdom and stature and in favor with both God and men"(Luke 2:52).

What did Jesus do during this time? Perhaps he lived in Nazareth and helped his father with the construction business. Perhaps he returned to school. Some writers claim that he became one of John the Baptist's disciples.

There is also the possibility that he traveled to far lands in his quest for knowledge.

This notion is supported by von Dohnaniy, who quotes a first century Roman named Lucius, a Senator under Claudius, who penned a letter stating:

"They (the Jews) are a people totally void of honor and pride. None must be allowed to inhabit the same region as Romans. All but one has shown reason why they should not be eradicated from the earth. This one I received while on the imperial business of Tiberius. A one Jesus, the son by adoption of our Briton provincial Senator called Joseph, who served by appointment of Augustus as Imperial Minister of Mines, who [Jesus] was accused of treason and crucified for such offense by Procurator Pontius Pilate, although I have found no cause for such means, but for the sake of the honor of Caesar, must be of necessity, who was contracted to build the Acreopolisium circus in Scythopolis. With talent that can only be compared to the greatest of that of Athena and Egypt, he built the circus in two years that to others of his trade and race would have finished in five. So pleased was Coporius (the administrative governor of the Decapolis) that a feast in honor of its completion was ordered. This stone-mason, Jesus, was to be celebrated. He refused the honor, instead was content to feast with the workers of his employ. I could have demanded his honor, but chose to tribute instead his desire for no glory. Upon which time, through my persuasion, this stonemason, Jesus, accompanied me to Rome, where he lived in the home of his adopted father, Josephius Maximus and learned the ways of Rome and was taught in the histories of the world by the Senate historians and philosophers of my own choosing. Had he not returned to his home region, the Galilee at the time of the appointment of Pontius Pilate, he would have become a Senator for the Empire. Such a loss is to our regret and to the shame of the Jews. For he and he alone is, of all of his race, worthy of life sustained."

Of course, no discussion of the three lost years between Jesus' wilderness experience and the beginning of his ministry should exclude the training required of one seeking to become a rabboni, training alluded to in Lucius' letter above. It's logical to assume that the five years of mandatory rabboni training included these three silent years.

TRAINING FOR THE PRIESTHOOD

I found a source that addresses this training while studying at the library of Jerusalem's Albright Institute.

There I discovered a book written in 1836 by Jacob Lowpinski, a rabbi who later became a Christian. Titled *Rabbonis in Training,* the book describes the educational requirements and expectations of a rabbi seeking to advance to the position of Rabboni.

The book's third chapter is titled *Jesus' probable training.* Lowpinski introduces the chapter by saying that some of Jesus' rabboni training occurred during the so-called silent years between his baptism and wilderness experience.

Lowpinski then traces the educational requirements necessary for becoming a rabboni. The requirements lead him to important conclusions about Jesus.

He notes that if a young student wanted to be a rabbi, he had to enroll in one of the two Rabbinate schools (the school of Hillel or the school of Shammi). For the next eight years, the student would live at school while learning about the Law and the Scriptures, the Mishan, the Midrash, the Torah, The Talmuds, Greek and Roman history, government regulations, Greek philosophy, and world religions.

After eight years, the student would graduate, as a rabbi. However, he would then serve as an understudy to a local rabbi for five years before earning his independence.

Lowpinski also points out that the *top* graduate from Rabbinate school had a choice of beginning training to become a rabboni or a scribe (a lawyer specializing in the Jewish Law).

If this elite grad chose the rabboni route, he had to submit to *another* five years of individual training by a Rabban. This training included extended travel to the world centers of civilization. At some point during this training, the rabbi was expected to submit to the ordeal of baptism and to a time of fasting lasting from 10 to 50 days.

After the five years, the student faced an interrogation before the entire Sanhedrin. If he survived this grilling, he earned the title of *Rabboni*, bestowed by the High Priest. After becoming a Rabboni, the student could choose to become a Rabban by submitting to *another* 12 years of training under the direct tutoring of the Rabboah of Innan, the top-ranking Rabban authority.

If Jesus followed the traditional path of rabboni training, Lowpinski contends, he was trained by a personal Rabban. Two years into this training, Jesus would have submitted to the ordeal of the baptism. In Jesus' case, the period of isolation and fasting lasted for at least 40 days.

During this time, he also endured his ordeal of temptation. Next, he would have returned to the Rabban and submitted to another three years of training, which included travel to Egypt, Parthia, Rome, Greece, Persia, Syria, and (perhaps) India. In each place, Jesus would have studied the culture, traditions, history, and religious philosophies all courtesy of his Rabban and various native teachers.

I paused for a moment to consider Lowpinski's words. If he was right, Jesus' baptism and subsequent fast and wilderness experience were part of his rabboni training, and that would shed a different light on *why* Jesus needed to be baptized. He wasn't setting an example for future Christians to follow. He was simply following a mandatory part of his rabboni training.

Now, let's return to my paraphrase of *Rabbonis in Training.*

Lowpinski confirms that Jesus followed the typical rabboni training, citing as proof a letter written in the second century by a Jewish doctor named Ekaba. In the letter, Ekaba quotes a first century Rabban named Hillel the Eminent, who states,

> "Afterward, Jesus returned from his retirement and fasting and to mature his rabboni training. His Rabban felt it was time for him and Jesus to sojourn in the eastern lands, to learn from the philosophers of Zoroaster, the magi of Chaldea, the rhijas of Arabia, and the shaman of the Indias."

Based on this letter and his other research, Lowpinski concludes,

> "To me, it seems quite obvious that the reason for the three years of silence was that Jesus was in the midst of his five years of rabboni training. He began that training two years before his baptism and time of isolation, and it continued for three years after his baptism and wilderness experience. Then, upon completing that rabboni training, Jesus again appeared on the scene, as a Rabboni, authorized by the High Priest."

As we'll soon see, the Rabboni Jesus was unique among all who held that prestigious title.

The Jordan River just south of the southern
outlet of the Sea of Galilee—Israel.

The probable wilderness where Jesus was tempted.
It is located near the Dead Sea—Israel.

CHAPTER 14

꒰ ꒱

Jesus' First Year of Ministry

AD 26

IN THE SPRING OF AD 26 (the year Pontius Pilate became Procurator of Judaea), Jesus completed his rabboni training. (According to the chronology I developed, he was 33 at the time.)

After completing this training and becoming a High Priest-accredited rabboni, Jesus left his home in the Galilee for Bethabara, where John the Baptist was preaching and baptizing.

JOHN 1:29
[29] The next day John seeth Jesus coming unto him, and saith, Behold the Lamb of God...

The "Lamb of God" pronouncement was followed by Jesus calling his first disciple, Philip, a Greek from the city of Bethsaida.

While researching at UCLA, I found an intriguing resource detailing John's pronouncement and Philip's calling.

I spent hours studying in the library's rare books and documents section before discovering an extraordinary resource, a book titled *The Calling*. This rare leather-bound volume was written by historical theologian Fredrick Shelley in 1822 and published in 1851 by Shelley's grandson (after the author's death). UCLA boasted one of the 30 known copies of the book.

In *The Calling*, Shelley describes how 40 great leaders (including Jesus, Buddha, Zoroaster, and Plato) called their first disciples. He claims to have gleaned his information from ancient sources, but he does not identify these sources, leaving one to speculate on their credibility.

Shelley begins his section on Jesus by stating that John the Baptist preached that repentance and public baptism were vital to entering God's kingdom.

According to John 1:28, Jesus left the Galilee to see John the Baptist. The next verse implies that John did not immediately recognize Jesus. This is logical, as John would have not seen Jesus since baptizing him three years earlier.

However, Jesus returns to the same place one day later, and this time John does recognize him, as evidenced by the proclamation, "Behold the Lamb of God which taketh away the sin of the world." (John 1:36)

Yet another day later, Jesus returns to where John is baptizing.

JOHN 1:35-36
35 Again the next day after John stood, and two of his disciples;
36 And looking upon Jesus as he walked, he saith, Behold the Lamb of God!

Apparently, Jesus spends some time in the area, then, at about 4 p.m., he decides to leave. Two of John's disciples follow him. Aware that he is being followed, Jesus turns around and asks the two men what they want. They respond by asking, "Where do you live?" (or "Where are you staying?") Jesus tells them to follow him and they'll find out. Apparently they stay with Jesus for the rest of the day.

Later that evening, one of Jesus' new companions, a man named Andrew, finds his brother, Simon Peter, and tells him that he has found *Messias* (or the Christ).

When Andrew introduces Simon Peter to Jesus, Jesus responds by telling this brother that though his name is *Simon*, meaning a reed, he was going to be called *Cephas*, an Aramaic word referring to a chip of granite rock.

Following this introduction, Simon and Jesus become friends. However, Jesus does not immediately call Simon to be his disciple.

The next day, Jesus returns to the Galilee. There, he finds Philip and invites him to, *"Deute poiso mou"* (come after me). This was a typical invitation from a Galilean rabboni to a potential disciple. What is quite atypical is that Jesus' first disciple wasn't a religious leader or a Jew; he was Greek.

We don't know if Philip joined Jesus immediately. John 1:45 implies that Philip did not. Instead, he went looking for a friend, a Nathanael, whom he found meditating under a fig tree.

A *Nathanael*, by the way, was a rabbi who was in the middle of training for the priesthood. The word is a title, not a proper name.

Priesthood legend says that a Nathanael chosen by God to become the High Priest would recognize the Messiah and would be given a vision confirming his priestly calling. This vision would occur while the Nathanael was meditating under a fig tree, called the "tree of meditation." The vision would feature Jacob's ladder and angels ascending and descending it.

This vision would signify that the Nathanael had been selected by God to recognize the Messiah and to represent the Jewish people to the Messiah. This ritual had been observed by hundreds of Nathanaels for 300 years.

When Philip found his friend the Nathanael, he told him that the one Moses and the prophets had written about had been found. His name: Jesus of Nazareth.

The Nathanael responded by quoting a familiar saying: "Can anything good come out of *Nazareth*?"

This jab at Nazareth had historical basis. During the days of the kings of Israel, limestone was quarried from the region's sheer cliffs. Quarrying ceased during the Assyrian and Babylonian conquests, but it resumed during the time of Alexander the Great's various building projects.

A tower (or *nazarat*) was built on top of one of the cliffs, overlooking the Great Plain. From this nazarat, one could oversee the quarrying efforts. Eventually, a small community developed near the tower. Most of the community's inhabitants were quarriers, so it became known as "the house of the tower" or *Nazaratha*. The term was later shortened to *Nazareth*.

After Alexander's death, the quarrying shrunk dramatically. To survive, Nazareth allowed surrounding communities to use its abandoned quarry pits for the discarding of animal carcasses, for a fee, of course. Thus, Nazareth became known as a carcass disposal site.

Within 200 years, Nazareth became *the* major refuse/disposal site for the Galilee, Judea, Samaria, and Syria. About 75 percent of Nazareth's population worked at the disposal areas. There was money in garbage. Some historians claim that a Nazareth resident could earn more in one day than most workers from nearby towns could make in a week. This good living came with baggage. Foul baggage. Nazareth became *the* joke of Syria. *Nazareth* was derogatory slang for anything despicable, dirty, or diseased.

Nazareth provided a vital service that people needed, but those people hated what Nazareth represented. It was a garbage dump, a breeding ground for a variety of diseases that attacked the body and the mind.

With this background in mind, think of what must have been running through the Nathanael's mind when he encountered Jesus of Nazareth.

When Jesus meets the Nathanael, he speaks first and calls Philip's friend an "Israelite indeed, one with no guile." This term identified an Israelite who was outspoken, yet honest.

The Nathanael responds, asking Jesus how he could know this about him. Jesus answers that even before Philip found the Nathanael under the fig tree, he (Jesus) had seen him.

This is enough to convince the Nathanael that Jesus is the Son of God, despite his being from Nazareth.

This Nathanael is not mentioned again in Scripture unless he is, as some believe, the disciple Bartholomew. John 21:2 speaks of a Nathanael from Cana in Galilee, who might have been Philip's friend. I believe it's more likely that Bartholomew (the Nathanael from John 21), didn't join the disciples until after Jesus' death.

I should note that Shelley seems to disagree with me. He writes, "I will assume as fact that the Nathanael from John's Gospel was named Bartholomew and that he was called to be Jesus' second disciple. Both he and Philip followed Jesus from that time forward."

A Confrontation in a Synagogue

On a Sabbath sometime after their arrival in Nazareth, Jesus and his two disciples go to one of the local synagogues, where Jesus stands and addresses the worship participants.

While researching at the University of Leipzig's School of Theology library, I came across some enlightening manuscripts. One of them addresses this event in the Nazareth synagogue.

In 1523, Jacques LeFèvre, a historian serving at a university in Paris, wrote an account of a Sabbath-day confrontation between Jesus and his synagogue audience. Unfortunately, only two pages remain of LeFevre's 34 page work, which was itself a French translation of a Latin manuscript written in 789. Paulus Diaconus, a court historian for Charlemagne, titled his work *Christos de Admonito*, which he bound between gold-plated cedar boards and presented to Charlemagne as a Christmas gift. *Christos de Admonito* was a collection of historically accurate stories from Jesus' life in Nazareth.

Luke 4:16-30, covers the events in question. I won't relay the entire text here—just enough to set the stage for you:

LUKE 4:16-30

[16] And he came to Nazareth..and..went into the synagogue on the sabbath day, and stood up for to read.

[17] And there was delivered unto him the book of the prophet Esaias. And when he had opened the book, he found the place where it was written,

[18] The Spirit of the Lord is upon me...

[20] And he closed the book...and sat down.

[21] And he began to say unto them, This day is this scripture fulfilled in your ears.

[22] And they said, Is not this Joseph's son?

23 And he said ...Ye will surely say unto me this proverb, Physician, heal thyself: whatsoever we have heard done in Capernaum, do also here...

24 And he said, Verily I say unto you, No prophet is accepted in his own country.

28 And all they in the synagogue...were filled with wrath,

I will now paraphrase LeFëvre's translation of Diaconus's eighth century work.

Because of Jesus' rabboni position, he was allowed to actively participate in Sabbath ceremonies. Apparently, he had been participating in these ceremonies since returning to Nazareth.

On the Sabbath in question, the ceremony progressed smoothly, until Jesus spoke.

Typically, a Sabbath ceremony began with the congregation (men and women were separated) standing in the sanctuary and chanting psalms. Then, an elder, wrapped in his prayer shawl, read from the Ten Commandments. This was followed by the pronouncement of the *Shema* (the prayer of Hebrew monotheism). When the prayer was complete, the elder chanted the *berakoth* (benedictions). After each benediction, the congregation responded by saying in unison, "Amen." This portion of the service ended with the *Bareku*, one of Judaism's oldest prayers, as the elder and the congregation spoke in turn.

After this, the *shammash* (the sacristan of the synagogue) removed a parchment scroll from the *aron* (an ark or wooden chest) and found the passage for the day's oral reading. The sacristan then waited for a rabboni to volunteer to read from the parchment. The readings were to be presented in order, from one Sabbath to the next, as prescribed by the High Priest in Jerusalem. Thus, all synagogues read the same passage on any given Sabbath. It would take about 12 years to finish reading the entire scroll.

After reading, the rabboni would sit and comment on the text addressing questions from the congregation. When this process was complete, the congregation was dismissed.

On this Sabbath, Jesus volunteers to read. The scroll is opened to the scheduled passage, but instead of reading this passage, Jesus chooses something else. A 750-year-old Messianic prophecy uttered by Isaiah and which we identify as Isaiah 61:1-2.

ISAIAH 61:1-2

¹ The Spirit of the Lord GOD is upon me; because the LORD hath anointed me to preach good tidings unto the meek; he hath sent me to bind up the brokenhearted, to proclaim liberty to the captives, and the opening of the prison to them that are bound;

² To proclaim the acceptable year of the LORD, and the day of vengeance of our God; to comfort all that mourn;

After Jesus reads, he rolls up the scroll and hands it to the *shammash*. Then he sits and prepares to offer commentary.

The people are surprised and confused that Jesus has read a text out of order. This behavior could be perceived as an act of defiance, and the resulting penalty could have seen Jesus banned for life from synagogue rituals and ceremonies.

The congregation hasn't seen anything yet. Jesus tells his audience that the 750-year-old prophecy has just been fulfilled, right before their eyes, by a young man who is the son of the carpenter, a carpenter most of them know. Imagine the impact.

The people ask if Jesus is indeed Joseph's son. LeFevre's notes that the question is posed in present-tense, indicating that Joseph is still alive.

From a procedural and traditional viewpoint, Jesus makes major mistakes beyond reading Scripture out of order. In Luke 4:23 Jesus quotes a proverb from Cicero, a well-known pagan Roman Senator who died in 43 BC. This proverb was spoken as part of Cicero's defense before the Roman Senate in 51 BC when he was accused of disloyalty by Mark Antony.

LUKE 4:23

²³ And he said unto them, Ye will surely say unto me this proverb, Physician, heal thyself: whatsoever we have heard done in Capernaum, do also here in thy country.

Antony asked Cicero why he felt obliged to preserve (soothe) the tormented souls of Rome's beleaguered citizens. Cicero replied,

"You, my most esteemed Antony, will say of me, 'Physician, pre-serve your own self, not us. For what you have heard done in Capri, do so as well in Rome.'"

Cicero had been sent to Capri by Julius Caesar, to secure the region's loyalty. Cicero succeeded. He prevented a riot in Capri and convinced the people to pledge allegiance to Caesar.

The Roman Senate was so moved by Cicero's defense that they unan-imously acquitted him of all charges.

Jesus uses this proverb, changing *Capri* to *Capernaum* and *Rome* to *his own country*, but the intent is the same.

It is vital to understand that it was *inexcusable* to quote a pagan like Cicero in God's holy sanctuary. To make matters worse, by uttering this quote Jesus is stating that he is being maligned without cause, just as Cicero was.

Jesus still isn't done. In verse 24, he makes another "mistake." He quotes a well-known aphorism (spoken in 335 BC by the renowned Greek philosopher Aristotle): "No prophet is accepted in his own country." To quote a pagan Greek philosopher at this point was like rubbing salt in an open wound.

But wait...things get worse. Jesus audaciously likens himself to two of the greatest prophets in Jewish history: Elijah and Elisha. He says that just as Elijah was not sent to a Jewish widow but to a pagan widow— and Elisha was not chosen to heal a Jew of leprosy but, rather, a General of pagan Syria, so the people of Jesus' community will be rejected by God, in favor of pagans. Indeed, pagans are far more qualified to receive God's blessings than those calling themselves *God's chosen people*.

Not surprisingly, the people rush Jesus and seize him, intending to throw him off a cliff and into a quarry pit. They don't succeed. The Bible states that Jesus passes through the midst of them and goes on his way.

How did Jesus escape? Did he use supernatural powers or did the people's fear of this bold man make them think better of their intentions?

It's unfortunate that more of LeFevre's translation didn't survive. Only two pages. What was written on all those *lost* pages?

After this event, the Gospels are silent on Jesus' life until the late summer of AD 26.

A Wedding in Galilee

At this time, Jesus and his two disciples attend a wedding in Cana, just north of Nazareth. John's Gospel reports that this wedding is the site of Jesus' first miracle, turning water into wine.

I found hundreds of stories, commentaries, and sermons about this wedding—but none more fascinating than a document I discovered in Antakya, in southern Turkey.

Today, Antakya is the capital of Turkey's Hatay province. In New Testament times, it was known as Antioch. Antioch was founded in 300 BC by Seleucus I. Pompey the Great conquered it for Rome in 64 BC, and by 40 BC it had become an important trade center for the Roman Empire. Because of its history, Antakya affords many Greek, Roman, Crusader, and Ottoman ruins.

During my research, I planned to visit some of these ruins before continuing toward the Syrian border. On my drive to the ruins, I got a flat tire, just as I passed an old mosque.

I limped my car into a vacant lot next to the mosque and started to change the flat. Moments later, I discovered my spare tire was flat too. It was Sunday. (Most of the city's residents were Muslim, but Antakya still honored Sunday as a holy day, as it had for the past 500 years.) Thus, every business in town was closed. I wasn't going anywhere until Monday.

I locked the car and started walking toward the mosque. When I reached the door, it opened from inside, hitting me. The man who opened the door was startled. We looked at each other for a moment. Then we shared a good laugh.

The man recognized that I was either European or American, so he spoke in a formal style of English, which made me feel like a hick.

He introduced himself as Amad, the mosque's mullah (priest). He told me that the mosque was originally an Orthodox church, built in the sixth century. Mehmet the Conqueror had turned it into a mosque back in the fifteenth century.

After I introduced myself, Amad asked how he could help me. I told him about my tire problem, and he confirmed my assumption that no repair shops would be open until Monday. I nodded and asked him for the location of the nearest hotel. He dismissed my question. He told me that my breaking down was a sign from Allah: Amad was to take care of me. I was to be a guest in his home until the tires were repaired.

We walked back to the car, where I retrieved my duffel bag and briefcase. Meanwhile, Amad had crossed the street and was talking to a young man. Within a couple of minutes both of them approached me. Amad introduced me to Izerim, who had agreed to watch my car overnight. (I would learn later that Amad paid Izerim the equivalent of $20 dollars for this task.)

We then walked the four blocks to Amad's house. Along the way, he asked me why I was in Antakya. I told him that I was an American historical researcher on my way to Syria—but that I wanted to see Antioch's ancient ruins first.

I added that I was hungry for any information that would help me confirm the Gospels' account of Jesus' life.

Upon hearing this, Amad said he wanted to show me an ancient manuscript he had found about 30 years previously, when a gas explosion damaged part of his mosque's foundation. While surveying the damage, he found a small cavity in one of the building's original support columns.

Inside the cavity, he found a pottery jar containing two parchment scrolls and one fleece manuscript. The scrolls and manuscript were written in Greek. Amad noted that he hadn't told anyone about his find for fear that it would be confiscated. He added that he had spent 10 years translating the documents into Turkish, a task he had yet to complete.

Before he could tell me more, we arrived at his home, where he introduced me to his wife, Betra, and explained my plight. She bowed her head submissively and quickly set about preparing a mid-afternoon lunch.

Amad excused himself. He returned 10 minutes later with the two scrolls and the fleece manuscript. The scrolls were so fragile that I did not want to handle them. I asked Amad to unroll one of them, but as he began, pieces of the parchment broke off.

I wasn't surprised at the scroll's fragility. Because it was found in one of the mosque's original support columns, it had to date back to at least the sixth century.

Amad explained that the scroll began with the author's introducing himself. Apparently, he said, the scroll was a long letter to a group of people in the city of Patara, in the Roman province of Lycia.

I knew that an earthquake had destroyed Patara in AD 93. The scroll had been written before that.

Amad said that author identified himself as "Lucius of Iconium, a slave and unworthy servant of my risen and living Master." Evidently Lucius was a first century Christian. The most legible part of the scroll offered a message of encouragement to the worshippers in Patara, urging them to remain devoted in their faith, even to the point of death. Also decipherable was a eulogy to "our brother in the faith, Titus, who had been martyred in the blood games of Domitian in the circus at Dyrrhachium."

I knew that ancient Dyrrhachium was present-day Durres, Albania. Located in Durres were the ruins of a first century Roman amphitheater where local tradition holds that St. Titus, the companion of Paul, was martyred. Dyrrhachium was the site of many first, second and third century martyrdoms and deadly amphitheater games.

However, AD 86 marks the first record of Christian participation in the games at the amphitheater-nine years after the traditionally accepted date of Titus's death. Thus, Titus might have been martyred in Dyrrhachium, but not at the amphitheater.

As fascinating as this scroll was, I found the sheepskin manuscript even more intriguing.

Amad unrolled the sheepskin and began to explain it to me, using his Turkish translation. This sheepskin manuscript was written in Greek and appears to be a letter of petition addressed to the Roman administrative magistrate in Sapphires. The style of writing is compatible with first century Roman texts. So, the manuscript could date back to the time of Jesus' life."

I was amazed at Amad's sophistication and intelligence. I quickly began taking notes.

The letter requested that the Roman magistrate intervene in a commercial dispute between a Jewish woman from Nazareth and a Roman merchant from Cana. The woman had ordered 30 ephah (about 180 gallons) of wine for her daughter's wedding, scheduled to be held in Cana during the late-summer month of Elul. The wine was to be delivered directly to the wedding celebration, and the woman had paid the merchant in advance.

However, the merchant delivered only 12 ephah (5 ephah of *kalos* wine and 7 ephah of *halos* wine). The woman wrote that this wine shortage could have caused a problem, had not her son, a rabboni, produced an additional 27 ephah (162 gallons) of *kalos* wine. (The letter didn't specify how her son had "produced" the wine.)

The letter went on to say that when the woman visited the merchant (accompanied by her rabboni son and stonemason husband), he refused to make restitution for shorting her order. She added that her rabboni son and two of his brothers planned to move to Capernaum to expand the family stonemasonry construction business. Thus, the purpose of the letter was twofold: 1) To receive permission for expanding the family business and 2) To settle the dispute with the wine merchant.

"Neither Mary's nor Jesus' name is mentioned in the manuscript," Amad noted, "but the events recorded in the document are suspiciously similar to those that took place at the marriage at Cana attended by Mary, Jesus, and his disciples and recorded in your Bible's Gospel of John, chapter two."

I was amazed by what I'd just heard. True, I had no way to verify the sheepskin's authenticity, but Amad told me that manuscript was either the original document, written by Mary, Jesus' mother, in AD 26, or a copy, probably made in AD 35.

Amad added that the marriage traditions represented in the story are still practiced in Muslim countries today.

Next, he elaborated on the wedding at Cana, quoting, from memory, Scripture from John chapter 2.

JOHN 2:1-11
¹ And the third day there was a marriage in Cana of Galilee; and the mother of Jesus was there:

² And both Jesus was called, and his disciples, to the marriage.

³ And when they wanted wine, the mother of Jesus saith unto him, They have no wine.

⁴ Jesus saith unto her, Woman, what have I to do with thee? mine hour is not yet come.

⁵ His mother saith unto the servants, Whatsoever he saith unto you, do it.

⁶ And there were set there six waterpots of stone... containing two or three firkins apiece.

⁷ Jesus saith unto them, Fill the waterpots with water.

¹¹ This beginning of miracles did Jesus in Cana.

"According to this portion of the Christian holy writings, the marriage took place about three days after a conflict in a Nazareth synagogue. Jesus and his two disciples attended the marriage. In this portion of the Christian writings, it is stated that the mother of Jesus was there. The word translated *there* in the King James Version is the word *soryi*. This word means '*sponsor* or *patron* or *initiator*.' In this case, the word was used to indicate that Jesus' mother was the sponsor, the one in control of the celebration.

"And if Mary was the sponsor of this celebration—and if we consider the traditions of the day—that means this celebration was held in honor of Mary's daughter, Jesus' sister.

"At this time, you see, the bride's mother was responsible for organizing the marriage feast.

"Tradition would also dictate that Jesus, the oldest brother, was responsible for giving the wedding-feast benediction and the '*Be fruitful and multiply*' blessing to the newlyweds.

"Typically, the celebration and feast began at sunup. Fresh and dried fruit, olives, bread, garlic-seasoned olive oil, and cheese were the first of five courses of food served, along with *kalos* wine. *Kalos* means sweet, beautiful or clear. *Kalos* was a sweet, strained wine whose sugar had not yet turned to alcohol. This portion of the feast normally lasted most of the morning.

"Near mid or late morning, various vegetable, seed, and bean dishes were served as the second courses. The other three courses were served during the afternoon and evening. Each of the final four courses was served with *halos* wine. *Halos* means less sweet, or worse. The sugar in halos wine had begun to ferment into alcohol.

"After all five courses had been served, the older brother stood and offered the feast benediction and the marriage blessing.

"After this, the bride and groom excused themselves and went into isolation for the next month. Western Christians get their honeymoon tradition from this custom. After the bride and groom were sent off, with much fanfare, the guests were invited to stay and celebrate well into the night."

Amad continued, "For the next seven days, food and wine were continuously served. Guests came and went, often bringing gifts for the new couple.

"Some time during the first day's celebration, Mary ran out of wine. She told Jesus about the shortage, hoping that, as the older brother and likely a co-sponsor of the celebration, he could address the problem.

"Jesus responded by saying that it was not appropriate for him to tell the guests about the wine because it was not yet his time to address the people. In essence, he was saying, 'Wait until it is my turn, and I have given my benediction. Then I will do something.'

"Mary probably assumed that after Jesus completed his benediction, he would either go to the wine merchant in Cana to get the rest of the wine, or he would buy wine from someone else.

"At this celebration stood at least six stone water troughs, which were used to cleanse implements used in religious ceremonies. Each trough held about 27 gallons of water. Jesus told the servants to fill the troughs with water. (It probably took them a long time to carry enough water to fill all six troughs with a total of about 162 gallons.) After they had filled the troughs, Jesus told them to serve some of the water to the 'governor of the feast.' This man was the public spokesman representing the groom and was usually the 'best man' or at least a close friend of the groom. He kept things on schedule.

"After the wine was served to the governor and he had tasted it, he was amazed that Mary had chosen to serve *kalos* wine *twice*. *Kalos* wine was usually served only in the morning, with *halos* wine being served for the remainder of the feast. The governor also commented that Mary had kept the best *kalos* wine for last.

"The Christian writer John states that the miracle at Cana was Jesus' first. Therefore, the multitude of stories proclaiming Jesus' boyhood miracles are, according to John, nothing more than fabrications."

With that, Amad re-rolled the sheepskin manuscript, setting it and his translation aside. Amad then picked up the last scroll and unrolled it. I noticed that it didn't seem as fragile as the others.

CAPERNAUM

Amad began,

"This scroll was apparently written by a scribe who was court transcriber for Alexus Rufus, judicial tax administer for the Galilee, under Tiberius Caesar. I won't go into detail about this scroll. I'll just say that it confirms, through new-resident tax records, that in the winter of AD 26, the rabboni Jesus from Nazareth, his mother, two of his brothers, and two non-family companions moved to Capernaum in the Galilee and opened a stonemasonry business."

"That is all that needs to be said about this scroll," Amad said as he re-rolled it and set it aside. "But I have a few more things to tell you. You can write them down if you want."

"Please," I said, "keep going." Amad continued:

"Capernaum was located in the fertile plain of Gennesaret, which extended from the northern part of the Sea of Galilee around to the eastern part of the sea. In that plain, there were many towns and villages, both large and small. There, Jesus carried on the bulk of his early ministry. One of the larger cities in the region was Capernaum. The city became Jesus' vocational and ministry headquarters.

"I have found no record to indicate that Joseph moved to Capernaum with Jesus, Mary and the family. If Joseph was a master stonemason or an architect specializing in stone construction, why *would* he choose to leave Nazareth, with all of its stone quarries?

"In AD 756, John of Damascus wrote that Joseph, Jesus' father, was a stonemason/architect who constructed many buildings in the new Roman imperial city of Tiberias, as well as in Capernaum, Scythopolis, and Magdala. He said that Jesus was Joseph's construction supervisor on many of these projects (which could explain Jesus' good relationship with the Roman authorities) and that he represented Joseph in the new stonemasonry business in Capernaum.

"The Gospel of Philip, from the Apocrypha, says that Jesus was a master stonemason and engineer who learned the trade from his father, Joseph. This gospel says that Jesus' moving to Capernaum was a business decision. Joseph was contracted by a Roman centurion in Capernaum to build a synagogue there. Jesus was given the responsibility of supervising the project. Philip also claims that this synagogue was funded by the Roman centurion whose servant Jesus later healed. (See Matthew 8:5-13). If this is true, perhaps Joseph sent Jesus to Capernaum to conduct the final inspection so that the synagogue could be opened. Whatever the case, we know that Jesus moved to Capernaum, but Joseph did not.

"Nothing more is recorded about Jesus' activities from the winter of AD 26 when he moved to Capernaum, until the spring of AD 27, when he attended the Passover celebration in Jerusalem. This may be because Jesus was so busy with the synagogue that there was nothing of note to report."

"That is all I have to say. Do you have any questions?"

I had hundreds of questions, but I did not know where to start. I hadn't met anyone like Amad. He didn't act superior, but I felt inferior in his presence. I told him I would defer questions for later.

For the rest of the evening, we talked about other things. The next morning, Amad helped me buy a new tire and fix the spare. At noon, I left Antakya for Syria.

As I drove, my head was swimming in a vast sea of information.

I had learned so much about the famous wedding and more:

The wedding at Cana was probably Jesus' sister's wedding.

Mary was the sponsor of the wedding.

Two very different wines were served.

A wine merchant shorted Mary on her order.

Jesus was responsible for giving a benediction at the wedding.

Jesus and Mary, along with some of Jesus' brothers and his disciples, moved to Capernaum.

It's likely that Jesus opened a branch of the family business in Capernaum.

Jesus was construction supervisor of a synagogue in Capernaum—which was funded by a Roman centurion.

All of these facts could be corroborated by the Gospels or at least inferred by reading between the lines.

For the rest of the day, I felt in a daze as I contemplated all that had just transpired. I was curious too.

Why wasn't information like Amad's part of the contemporary church's body of knowledge? Yes, this information might threaten the dogma of Mary's perpetual virginity, but certainly not Jesus' divinity.

I drove on, wondering what I might learn next.

Ruins of a synagogue in Capernaum. The visible ruins date back to the 3rd century AD, but the foundation dates to the time of Jesus—Israel.

❧ ❧

CHAPTER 15

Jesus' Second Year of Ministry

PART 1 — AD 27

THE YEAR AD 27 MARKS the second year in which Jesus ministered and it is his first *full* year of ministry.

That year's Passover sparked another key event in Jesus' life. To fully appreciate the significance of what happened, it's important to understand Rome's political climate at the time.

TIBERIUS CAESAR MOVES TO CAPRI

At Oxford University's St. Edmund Hall, I found something that certainly turbo-charged my political understanding. At the prestigious university, I found a bound set of about 30 ancient maps, each with a page or two of explanation. The volume's introduction credited Arthur of Durham (a monk of the Henry V era) as the author/compiler. This would date the set's creation to the early fifteenth century.

One map I found particularly intriguing depicted Rome, along with the troop-encampment locations of Sejanus' forces during the reign of

Tiberius Caesar. Sejanus claimed that these encampments were established to protect the city against rebellion. In reality, his soldiers held Rome's citizens hostage to the general's whims and demands. The map was titled: *AD 27 The Years of Embitterment—Tiberius Flees*. The accompanying pages noted that in AD 27, Tiberius fled Rome and settled in the island of Capri (a fact we learned earlier).

The explanation also included this text from the Gospel of Luke, chapter 3, verses 1 and 2:

LUKE 3:1-2

[1] Now in the fifteenth year of the reign of Tiberius Caesar, Pontius Pilate being governor of Judaea, and Herod being tetrarch of Galilee...

[2] ...and Caiaphas being the high priest, the word of God came unto John the son of Zacharias in the wilderness.

This Scripture helps us determine the genesis of Jesus' ministry. If his ministry began during the 15th year of Tiberius's reign (Tiberius lived from 42 BC to AD 37) and Tiberius had become Emperor upon the death of Augustus (August 19 of AD 14) then we can estimate that Jesus began his ministry sometime between August 19 of AD 26 and August 19 of AD 27.

The writer then details Rome's political condition at the time Jesus' ministry was launched.

In the summer of AD 26, Emperor Tiberius left Rome and retired for four months to Campania—at Sejanus' prompting. During Tiberius' absence, Sejanus quickly consolidated his allies and began to flex his political muscle, accusing all who opposed him of sedition and treason. Upon Tiberius' return to Rome, he was so disgusted with the political situation and with the total lack of responsibility shown by the Senate that (in February AD 27) he set up a Prince's Council to serve as guardian of Rome's political affairs. He then relocated his court of administrative rulership to Capri. This left Rome's fate in the merciless hands of Sejanus.

From Capri, Tiberius tried to rule the Empire. However, because he had little contact with Rome, many of his decisions were unwise, or motivated by revenge or spite. For example (as noted earlier), he declared that he would not overturn any Governor's judgment of sedition or conviction of treason.

Before this announcement, Tiberius was known for his fair judgment and mercy. Many times, he overturned provincial governors' convictions of treason whenever he felt a conviction was unjustified or based on vindictiveness rather than hard evidence.

During the first few months of his voluntary exile, Tiberius was inundated with requests to veto a judgment or overturn a treason conviction. He ignored them all. His clear message: Whatever the governor, procurator, or Senate decides is final.

With that, the explanation and description of this map ended. With this political backdrop established, let's return our focus to Jesus' early ministry.

In AD 27, Jesus began to be recognized as a true servant of God. Soon his popularity skyrocketed as did his infamy with certain religious groups.

The Jewish historian Joseph Klausner in his book *Jesus of Nazareth* writes:

> "That his name was Yeshua of Nazareth; that by some accounts he was a Roman by adoption of our Roman representative to our honorable Sanhedrin, Joseph; that he performed miracles and beguiled and led Israel astray; that he mocked at the words of our wise; that he expounded Scripture in the same manner as the Pharisees; that he had five close disciples, but many followers; that he had said that he had not come to take from the Law or to add to it; he cleared the Temple of merchandisers during the Passover causing a commotion that caused fear of revolt; he healed the sick; he overruled the power of the demonic; and he taught as a Rabban although he was not a Rabban but a Rabboni newly anointed by Caiaphas, the High Priest."

It had been about a year since John the Baptist had proclaimed, *"Behold, the Lamb of God..."* Now that Lamb was ready to expand his ministry from his base in Capernaum.

THE TEMPLE

The Passover in Jerusalem would be Jesus' first contact with non-Galileans since his ministry began.

We don't know when Jesus and his disciples left for Jerusalem or when they arrived, but John 2:14 suggests that Passover was already in full swing.

Upon their arrival, Jesus and the disciples visit the Temple.

At the Temple, Jesus becomes furious with the merchandising going on inside the compound. (It's important to note that he wasn't *surprised,* as this kind of activity had been going on for 100-plus years.)

Jesus' reaction suggests that he had maintained a long-smoldering resentment toward this activity but now his rabboni position gave him authority to do something about it.

This event was the first of three in which Jesus drove merchandisers from the Temple. (After the Passover of AD 27, Jesus didn't clear the Temple again until four years later, when he purged the compound twice in two days.)

Why the gap? It's possible that Jesus made such an impression the first time that it took the merchants and money lenders four years to overcome their fear of him.

My personal knowledge of Jesus' cleansing the Temple was greatly expanded by a man I met in Rotterdam in The Netherlands, at a Society for Investigative Truth. His name was Dr. Olav Gates, a brilliant professor of Ancient Middle Eastern History at the University of Oslo.

Dr. Gates told me that he had knowledge of Roman Syria from the Roman viewpoint. However, he knew very little from the Jewish perspective and nothing about the Jews' obsession with the physical Temple. Things changed when he read a Roman satirical work written in AD 65 by Junius Juvenalis.

The satire's topic was the weakness of the God of the Jews, who stood by and did nothing while one man drove *His* worshipers from *His* Temple.

Dr. Gates was not a Christian or follower of any religion, but this work convinced him that there was something to this Jesus fellow.

As we talked, he referred to the first scriptural record of Jesus cleansing the Temple. Here is that passage:

JOHN 2:13-17
[13] **And the Jews' passover was at hand, and Jesus ...**

[14] ... found in the temple those that sold oxen and sheep and doves, and the changers of money sitting:

[15] And when he had made a scourge of small cords, he drove them all out of the temple, and the sheep, and the oxen; and poured out the changers' money, and overthrew the tables;

[16] And said unto them that sold doves, Take these things hence; make not my Father's house an house of merchandise.

[17] And his disciples remembered that it was written, The zeal of thine house hath eaten me up.

Dr. Gates explained to me that the Temple was built by Herod the Great, and it was huge. He began construction in 18 BC, and at the time described in John, construction was still ongoing.

Today, the Temple site is occupied by *The Dome of the Rock* and the sacred courtyard that surrounds it, *The Harem*. The Dome was built over the site where Muslim teaching says that Mohammed ascended to heaven.

Herod's Temple comprised three levels, each one progressively higher and smaller. At the center of the highest level was the sanctuary.

Inside the sanctuary stood the Altar of Incense, the seven-branched Menorah, and the golden table where the priests placed shewbread. Behind a pentagonal door, always covered by a thick, heavy veil, was a small dark room called the Holiest of Holies, which only the High Priest was allowed to enter, once a year, on the Day of Atonement. A vestibule reserved for the priests, called the Priests' Court, surrounded the sanctuary. The court was separated from the larger area (about two acres) and surrounded by a wall. This was called the Men's Court. In this court, male Jewish worshippers could gather. A stairway with 15 steps led down to the lower platform, the Women's Court, which was considerably larger, at just over four acres. A second 12-step stairway led down to the great 35-acre trapezoidal courtyard, called the Gentile's Court. This area was open to all worshippers. The court's two longest sides measured 1,640 feet (almost a third of a mile) and 1,050 feet, respectively. On the east, it ended at a line of 162 huge pillars of white marble, which became known as Solomon's Portico. This was the only part of the original Temple of Solomon that had survived destruction by Nebuchadnezzar more than 500 years previously. (Nebuchadnezzar let the Portico remain as a lasting warning of the consequences of rebellion against Babylon.)

Solomon's Portico had three colonnades, collectively called the Merchants' Quarter. Here, hundreds of merchants would lease space to sell sacrificial animals, food, incense, oil, wine, grain, and various other religious and secular merchandise. Such merchants were common at feasts, celebrations, and religious observances.

During Passover, the entire Temple area teemed with thousands of people. On a typical day during Passover, the Court of the Gentiles *alone* would host 200,000 to 300,000. Add to this number the thousands of tourists, another 8,000 Roman soldiers, the 1,300-man Temple Guard, the hundreds of merchants, and up to 25,000 priests. Try to picture the scope of this scene.

And this is just the *people*. According to the historian Josephus, about 200,000 animals were typically sacrificed during Passover.

According to Dionysius Exiguus, a sixth century historian, the AD 31 Passover celebration (the one that marked Jesus' death), boasted an attendance of well over 4 million people.

"Along with all of these multitudes," Dr. Gates said, "the chief priests allowed the Court of the Gentiles to be used as a short-cut so that people could pass from one side of the city to the other without having to go around the Temple complex. The merchants or travelers would pay a fee to the chief priest stationed at the main gate, allowing them to pass through the Gentiles' Court 'short-cut.' This was a very lucrative and tax-free (Rome did not tax religious institutions) form of revenue for the High Priest and the Temple.

"When he arrived at the Temple, Jesus was infuriated by all the commercialism. He found some rope and braided a whip. Then he drove the merchandisers and moneychangers out of the complex, kicking over the money tables and setting the animals free.

"It's amazing that none of the thousands of people, especially the Roman soldiers, tried to stop Jesus. This purge could have taken him several hours, and it would have made a tremendous disturbance. Yet he remained unchallenged.

"In essence, Jesus was bucking a tradition that had been authorized by the High Priest himself (hence, endorsed by God Himself, according to the priests and Sadducees). This newly commissioned rabboni, from the Galilee of all places, had disrupted the Holy Passover and challenged the highest Jewish religious authority. Also, can you imagine the mad rush as hundreds of people scurried to collect the thousands of loose coins that scattered across the floor when Jesus kicked over the tables?

"Perhaps Jesus' good relationship with the Romans saved him, or maybe people were afraid to confront him physically. Maybe it was God's protection. Maybe all confusion made it impossible to pinpoint blame.

"I can certainly understand the Sadducees' concern about this event. What gave this Galilean rabboni the right to provoke Roman authorities and cause their anger to come down on the people?

"When questioned, Jesus does not answer the Sadducees the way they expect. He says that if they destroy this temple (he was probably pointing to himself), in three days he will raise it up.

"Although they may have understood what he was implying, they disregard it and focus on the physical Temple. Perhaps they choose to attack Jesus this way because he was a well-known builder and would know how long it would take to construct such a building.

"The Sadducees tell Jesus the Temple has been under construction for 46 years. How could he rebuild it in three days?

"Jesus does not respond to their sarcasm. He probably just walks away and departs the area."

After Dr. Gates finished his discourse, we discussed this incident in depth. I had always viewed the Temple purge as a minor occurrence in Jesus' life. I was astonished to discover the truth.

NICODEMUS

After Passover, Jesus and his disciples remain in Jerusalem for about two months. During this time, Jesus teaches and performs many healing miracles. As a result, many hundreds believe in him. This puts him on the radar of the Pharisees.

The Pharisees become so curious that one of their most-distinguished representatives, Nicodemus, pays Jesus a visit. He might have been sent by the Pharisees or by the Sanhedrin (of which he was a member), or he might have been motivated by personal curiosity.

Thanks to a security guard at the Church of Notre-Dame-des-Victories-du-Sablon (in Brussels, Belgium), I learned more about Nicodemus' conversation with Jesus than I was prepared to mentally digest. It took me at least three months to fully appreciate the implications of what I learned in Brussels.

The Church of Notre-Dame-des-Victories-du-Sablon is a beautiful example of fifteenth century Gothic architecture. While touring this church, I struck up a conversation with an elderly security guard named Roger VanRavenswa. Soon our talk turned to my search. VanRavenswa informed me that the church housed a large (and private) rare-book and ancient-manuscript library, which was used only occasionally by local university professors. He asked me if I wanted to see it.

You know my answer.

As we descended the steps to this library, I asked to do some research there. VanRavenswa said that it should not be a problem; however, he would have to consult with the church's rector/bishop.

My guide excused himself, then quickly returned with good news: I would be allowed to investigate any two books, documents, or manuscripts of my choice. I could not take anything from the library, and I could not take any photographs or use any recording device. I could research that day only, and I had to be finished by the 10 p.m. closing time. The guard would be with me all the time, as I took longhand notes. I quickly agreed to the terms.

VanRavenswa led me into the small, well-stocked library, with its solid maple shelves. The library had an old-fashioned card catalog filing system. The documents were cataloged by author, subject, key words, and theme.

Not knowing where to start, I looked up these words: *Gospels, Jesus, ministry*, and *Roman*. Then I cross-referenced the documents this search yielded. I focused on resources matching at least three of my four key words.

After eliminating three "contender" manuscripts, I considered a bound seven-page vellum document written in Latin in 1140 by an Irish teacher named Malachy O'More. The document retold Jesus' confrontation with Nicodemus and offered commentary from O'More.

As I read the document, VanRavenswa told me that he might be able to help me, if I trusted him. "I know Latin very well," he offered, "and it would save you time if you will allow me to read the document to you. Then you can make your notes. Of course, you will have to trust my translation abilities."

I accepted his offer. "It appears that this document," he said, "was used by O'More to teach students studying for the priesthood. In quickly skimming the lesson, it seems to me that O'More had a much better grasp of this confrontation than anyone I have ever read. But there is an interesting statement in the margin of the introduction's final paragraph. It is written in black ink and sealed with a red ecclesiastical seal. The statement says that because of O'More's opinions on Nicodemus and the way he presented the concept of being *born-again*, this document has been removed from the (Catholic) church's list of recommended theological education documents. The document may be used as history but not as a theological or doctrinal resource. The statement is dated and sealed, September 13, 1933. I guess that means that until 1933, the document was used as a doctrinal resource approved by the Church. Then the church changed its mind.

"Let's read on and find out why." With that, Van Ravenswa began translating Latin into English. I will paraphrase his translation for you.

During the first two months Jesus ministered in Jerusalem, Nicodemus came to him at night. This confrontation took place in the late spring of AD 27. The Gospel of John 3:1-12 records the confrontation.

JOHN 3:1-12

[1] There was a man of the Pharisees, named Nicodemus, a ruler of the Jews:

[2] The same came to Jesus by night, and said unto him, Rabbi, we know that thou art a teacher come from God: for no man can do these miracles that thou doest, except God be with him.

[3] Jesus answered ... I say unto thee, Except a man be born again, he cannot see the kingdom of God.

4 Nicodemus saith unto him, How can a man be born when he is old? can he enter the second time into his mother's womb, and be born?

5 Jesus answered ... Except a man be born of water and of the Spirit, he cannot enter into the kingdom of God.

6 That which is born of the flesh is flesh; and that which is born of the Spirit is spirit.

7 Marvel not that I said unto thee, Ye must be born again.

8 The wind bloweth where it listeth, and thou hearest the sound thereof, but canst not tell whence it cometh, and whither it goeth: so is every one that is born of the Spirit.

9 Nicodemus answered and said unto him, How can these things be?

10 Jesus answered ... Art thou a master of Israel, and knowest not these things?

11 Verily, verily, I say unto thee, We speak that we do know, and testify that we have seen; and ye receive not our witness.

12 If I have told you earthly things, and ye believe not, how shall ye believe, if I tell you of heavenly things?

Nicodemus was a highly respected Jewish rabboni, a member of the Pharisee sect, and a member of the Sanhedrin. According to 1st-century tradition, he was a close friend and Sanhedrin associate of Joseph of Arimathea.

We have no idea why Nicodemus came to Jesus by night. The church has heaped an undue amount of criticism on Nicodemus for coming to see Jesus this way. Perhaps he was motivated by shame, as the Church has speculated, but nothing in God's Word supports this. Maybe Nicodemus was busy during the day and Jesus was quite busy during the day too. Night might have been the only time *he* was free. It is unlikely Nicodemus came to Jesus at night because he was afraid of the Sanhedrin. Later, he stood up to the entire Sanhedrin body and defended Jesus.

John's Gospel strongly implies that the Sanhedrin sent Nicodemus to meet with Jesus, possibly because he was a friend or an acquaintance of Jesus, through Joseph of Arimathea.

If the Sanhedrin sent Nicodemus, it was probably to discover who Jesus was and how he justified his actions and revolutionary teachings. The powerful Sadducees were exasperated with Jesus because of what happened in the Temple during Passover, and it was a *major* mistake to be at odds with the Sadducees.

It was to the advantage of the Sanhedrin, whose membership comprised 70 percent Sadducees, that peace be maintained in Jerusalem. The Sanhedrin might have even guaranteed Pilate and the Roman authorities that this type of disturbance wouldn't happen again. A meeting with Jesus could secure that guarantee.

According to John 3:2, the Sanhedrin acknowledged that Jesus was a teacher sent from God. No one could perform such miracles otherwise. Yet, Jesus seemed to defy all the rules approved and/or instigated by the High Priest, who was *God's* acknowledged representative to the Jews.

So, how could a man be sent from God but blatantly defy the rules and worship rituals established by the High Priest? The High Priest claimed that he was God's one and only representative.

In John chapter 3, Jesus does not directly respond to Nicodemus' query. This, plus the statement he makes in verse 12, has prompted theologians and historians to speculate that not all of Jesus' conversation with Nicodemus was recorded. These scholars insist that a large portion of the conversation is missing from the biblical text. I (O'More) must agree. I think that at least half of the conversation between Jesus and Nicodemus *is* missing. Perhaps the writer of John's Gospel did not feel the entire conversation was important enough to record, or maybe some of the content disappeared over the years. After all, this conversation took place at least 70 years before it was recorded. We do know that Jesus told Nicodemus that he must be *born again* to see God's kingdom.

Nicodemus hadn't *asked* to see God's kingdom. Nor had he made *any* inquiry about this kingdom. So, the "born again" response surprised him.

The term *born again* and the *death and reborn* philosophy had their origins in ancient Babylonian religious mysteries, and they are foundational teachings of many belief systems, including Egyptian mysticism, Zoroastrianism, Hinduism, and Buddhism.

Such terms were not key to orthodox Judaism although most Pharisees believed in some form of reincarnation.

No wonder, then, that Nicodemus was disarmed by Jesus' statement. How could Jesus hold the office of rabboni, yet adhere to pagan beliefs?

The word Jesus used for *see* is the Greek *eidon*. The word means to perceive fully or to comprehend. It *does not* mean to see with one's eyes.

Nor does it refer to "seeing" heaven or going to heaven. What Jesus meant was *unless you are born again, you cannot comprehend the things of God, the purpose of God, the concepts and principles of God, His kingdom as it relates to the hearts of men, or to the future.* In short, *see* has nothing to do with salvation.

BORN AGAIN

Unfortunately, a current school of thought asserts that terms like *salvation, saved, born-again, redemption, confession of sin, cleansed, washed in the blood of the Lamb, new creature, children of God, conversion,* and *born-again Christian* refer to *salvation.* Nothing could be further from the truth.

For the first 1,000 years after Jesus' resurrection, these words held different meanings. It was not until this past century (O'More's eleventh century) that the same meaning was applied to *all* of these words.

I paused to contemplate the significance of what I had just learned. Then I asked my translator to proceed with more of O'More:

Over the past 100 years, scriptural words and phrases that previously had different meanings began to be used to denote salvation.

A simple word study would be more than adequate to show that many of these terms have different meanings, but factions in the Church have blindly accepted the premise that these words and phrases all mean salvation.

Let's look at one feature of this ridiculous assumption. The Church agrees that salvation was made possible through the shed blood of Jesus, and that eternal life with him was assured upon his resurrection. However, at the time of Jesus' conversation with Nicodemus, he had not shed his blood and died. Thus, he had not been resurrected. So, if born-again and saved mean the same thing, how was Nicodemus to be saved, given that the provision for his salvation had not occurred?

Nicodemus' question about being born again could be rephrased as, "Please explain what you mean by citing a doctrine rooted in mystical paganism." He was *not* asking, "How is being born again accomplished?" Because this born-again philosophy had been taught for more than 2,000 years by almost all pagan religions, Nicodemus wanted Jesus to clarify what he meant. Was Jesus saying that the pagan philosophies were correct?

Jesus then explained that Nicodemus needed to be born-again to *perceive* the true Kingdom of God. Jesus was saying that it was good that Nicodemus believed on him and acknowledged that he was God-sent, and it was good that Nicodemus was a godly man who knew God's Law, but this was not enough. If Nicodemus took more steps, he would reach a new level of spiritual awareness. He would understand God's plan for the universe. To get to that level, the first step was to be born again.

The phrase born-again implies death. Death must occur before there can be a rebirth. Jesus later confided to his disciples that this death is a violent death, a "take up your cross" type of death. It is agonizing, humiliating, and dreadful physically, emotionally, and spiritually. In this death, God (seemingly) forsakes the one dying. Jesus addressed the subject of born-again three different times in his ministry: the first was to Nicodemus, the second time was to three apostles at the Transfiguration in AD 29, and the third was in AD 31, when Jesus was telling his apostles about taking up their cross daily.

Jesus implied that if Nicodemus was content to live in spiritual mediocrity and be respected by the people, that was okay. If he wanted to experience the fullness of God's plan, he had to face the harsh born-again experience. The born-again experience *is not* salvation. It is separate. It is the result of a disciplined maturing process that usually takes years of faithful commitment and it would be worth the hardship.

With this, my elderly guide completed his translating "That is all that our Irish bishop has passed down to us in this document," he explained, "but I'm sure this is not all he wrote."

I finished writing my notes. Then I leaned back in my chair. My head was swimming again. All my life I had been taught that when you say you are saved, it means you've been born again. O'More now said this doctrine emerged in the eleventh century. Before that, Christian teaching proclaimed that salvation was attained by confessing sin, believing Jesus rose from the dead, and believing Jesus was God's Son and that through Jesus one could have forgiveness of sin and salvation from eternal death.

After salvation, there was *another* experience that a saved person could strive for, but it had nothing to do with salvation or eternal life. Only salvation through faith, belief in Jesus Christ and in his sacrifice could guarantee eternal life. The *born-again* experience was about spiritual maturity. It was an experience in which a person dies emotionally, spiritually, and psychologically through a painful death cycle that can take years to complete.

As I pondered O'More's words, I realized he had a point. Why would Jesus, four years *before* the crucifixion, tell Nicodemus that he had to be born again, if being born again was synonymous with salvation and salvation was based on Jesus' death and resurrection?

I think O'More gave a convincing argument, yet it had fallen on deaf ears. If eleventh century church leaders had taken a stand against doctrinal contamination, we wouldn't be dealing with the salvation versus born-again confusion we face today.

As a result, ever since the twelfth century, the assertion that born-again and salvation are the same thing (e.g. when a person is saved, he is born-again too) has become an ingrained doctrine of evangelicalism.

This raises an important question: If there is indeed a salvation experience, which is later followed by a separate born-again experience for those who seek it, why haven't any of the world's great theologians taught or written about it?

The past 250 years have seen the emergence of some great theological minds but the notion of salvation versus born-again has not been discussed or debated. I can't find any evidence that it has even been considered.

Did some twelfth century schemers conspire to cover up the true meaning of salvation or is the contention that salvation and born again are two different experiences an attempt to complicate the simplicity of salvation, as presented by the Gospels?

As I wrestled with these questions, I realized that I wasn't quite convinced that salvation and born again are two different experiences. I would hold the position that the new birth is an assurance of salvation from eternal death. After receiving the assurance of salvation, an individual can choose to advance through levels of spiritual maturity. This process of growing spiritually is *discipleship*.

I shared my position with VanRavenswa. He looked at me and said, somewhat apprehensively, "*Born again* is not the only thing about this Scripture that will surprise you."

I told him that he might as well lay it on me. I couldn't become any more unnerved than I already was.

Here's what he told me: "Ever since the mid-1700s, when a pastor named Sylvester Connolly claimed that the Apostle John appeared to him in a dream and told him that Jesus was the author of John 3:13-21, this portion of Scripture has been acknowledged as a continuation of Jesus' conversation with Nicodemus. Before that time, it had been assumed that this passage was John's personal testimony of Jesus. So, events relating to Nicodemus ended with verse 12 and the historical events didn't resume again until verse 22. The entire affirmation between verse 13 and verse 21 is not Jesus speaking about himself in foresight of what is to come. It is John's testimony about Jesus, about who he was and what he had done for humankind. This testimony was written 70 to 250 years after the events took place."

"So, John 3:16 was *not* spoken by Jesus?" I asked.

"No," came the response. "It was written *about* Jesus *by* John. That doesn't make it any less true, but it was not spoken by Jesus."

Again I had to ponder what I had just heard. While I was thinking, a young lady approached our table and whispered something to VanRavenswa. He shook his head, and the lady walked away. A few minutes later, he told me he had to leave to deal with an emergency. He apologized to me for the interruption.

I told him no apology was necessary. In about two hours, I had already learned enough to keep my head spinning for days.

Those days turned into months. Day after day, I researched and re-read the Nicodemus story and all of John 3. Eventually, I came to grips with the fact that O'More might have been right.

After many more weeks of studying John 3, I concluded that much of Jesus' conversation with Nicodemus *was* missing from the biblical text and if O' More was right, then:

1. Salvation and being born-again are two different experiences.

2. Salvation is necessary and mandatory for forgiveness of sin and to ensure eternal life.

3. One must choose to undergo the born-again experience.

4. The born-again experience *is not* salvation. It neither brings salvation, nor does it guarantee eternal life. It is a spiritual maturing process.

5. To clearly understand God's kingdom, God's will, purpose, and plan, one must be born-again.

6. The born-again experience is an agonizing death-and-rebirth cycle. It's not for everybody. It is only for those who are willing to forsake *all* this world has to offer. It takes extreme discipline and dedication.

7. If one chooses *not* to progress to the born-again experience, he or she is not any less saved or any less assured of eternal life. That person's intimate relationship with Jesus won't be jeopardized. He or she can still grow in the Lord and serve him whole heartedly. However, this person will probably never advance to a high level of spiritual maturity.

With these realizations, I completed my in-depth study of John 3 and chose to expand my research into other areas of Jesus' early ministry.

BAPTISM DISPUTES

Jesus and his disciples stayed in Jerusalem until late spring of AD 27. They probably would have stayed longer, but the Sadducees were becoming too curious. They wondered, "Is this Jesus to be taken seriously and feared or is he just another religious zealot whose flash of influence and popularity will probably evaporate quickly? Should we just leave him alone and avoid acknowledging him?"

Jesus chose not to tempt his nemeses. He left Jerusalem to avoid conflict. Someday, he would have to challenge the Sadducees. Some *later* day.

Although Jesus left Jerusalem, he did not leave the general area. For another month or so, he and his disciples stayed in the surrounding countryside. While ministering here, Jesus saw a controversy developed between John the Baptist's disciples and a Jewish religious leader, probably a Pharisee. This controversy centered on a comparison between John and Jesus.

At this time, John was baptizing in Aenon (See John 3:23.) Aenon was located west of the Jordan River, about 55 miles northeast of Jerusalem.

John's disciples came to him, complaining that Jesus was baptizing more people.

Note that both John 3:22 and 26 say that Jesus was baptizing. However, John 4:2 says that Jesus did not baptize—only his disciples were baptizing. How can this apparent contradiction be justified? Unless we read between the lines of John's record, it cannot.

If we take some assumptive liberties, we can conclude that Jesus was baptizing during the time indicated in John 3:22 and 26, but, in the interval represented in John 4:2, he ceased baptizing because of the "purification controversy" between the Pharisees and John's disciples.

Responding to his disciples' complaint about Jesus, John the Baptist offers his unconditional support for Jesus and his ministry, saying, "He must increase, but I must decrease" (John 3:30).

When Jesus heard about this controversy, he decided that he and his disciples would leave Judaea and return to the Galilee, to avoid the perceived competition. As Jesus was preparing to depart, John was arrested by Herod Antipas and imprisoned at Herod's mountain fortress.

SAMARIA

As we have learned, Jesus and his disciples decided to return to the Galilee after John's arrest. During this journey, Jesus stops to rest at Jacob's well. He sends his disciples into town to buy food for their midday meal. At the well, Jesus confronts a woman who has come to draw water.

I found some convincing early Christian documentation confirming the Gospel of John's record of this event. My discovery came while helping my friend Aziz Afifi identify some ancient manuscripts in Sur, Lebanon.

Afifi is a general contractor in Sur, and five years after meeting him, I found myself driving from Turkey to Israel. I decided to stop and visit my friend.

When I arrived at Afifi's house, his wife told me that he was working at the Church of St. Thomas. Three weeks before my arrival, a flash flood had damaged several of the area's ancient landmarks, including this eighth century church. Part of its foundation had been washed away, and the church's bishop contracted Afifi to handle the repairs.

When I arrived at St. Thomas', I couldn't see anyone. "Aziz! Aziz!" I called. Finally, I saw my friend crawl out of a hole in the floor, near the church's north wall.

After we greeted one another, I asked Afifi, "Where are your employees?"

He explained that the previous day's work had uncovered an underground vault, dating to the eighth century or earlier.

He further explained that the vault's stone entrance was cracked, and he had removed enough loose stones to squeeze his way inside. There, he found ancient Christian amulets, pieces of jewelry, and four bound volumes. Each volume was made of leather sheets bound between two cedar boards and held together with small leather cords. These articles were placed in the vault before the church was built, because the vault was built into the foundation.

Realizing the importance of his find, Afifi halted the work and reported the discovery to the church's bishop. The bishop became worried. He knew that Lebanese officials would confiscate anything they deemed valuable, citing "national treasure conservation."

"So," Afifi told me, "the bishop and I cleaned out the vault carefully and took its contents into the church and hid them in a safe in his office. He was planning to contact an archaeologist friend in Istanbul but, now that you are here, maybe *you* can tell us if these items are authentic and valuable. Bishop Ohan thinks the early Christian trinkets and the bound volumes are from the third century, perhaps even the first or second century."

I replied, "I am not an expert in ancient artifacts, but I will do my best to date them and evaluate their authenticity."

Afifi led the way to the bishop's office.

After introductions, Bishop Ohan welcomed me enthusiastically, saying, "A friend of Aziz is also a friend of mine. If he places his trust in you, so do I."

The bishop seated us at a wooden table and brought the artifacts to us. "Take your time," he said.

I spent more than an hour studying the amulets and various trinkets. Without a doubt, these were first or second century Christian.

I moved on to the bound volumes. Each one consisted of sheepskin leaves, bearing Latin text. The first leaf of each volume explained that its text was a Latin re-write of a lesson originally penned in Greek by Vitus of Sicily (whom I knew died in AD 303.) The re-write was by Bartholomew, servant of Damian, Bishop of Tyre. (I knew that Damian died in AD 710.)

One of the volumes was composed of six sheepskin leaves. Two volumes had eight leaves, and another had 11.

Bartholomew claimed in each of his introductions that he had copied Vitus's lessons verbatim but as I studied the texts, it appeared that Bartholomew had inserted some of his own thoughts along the way.

I carefully examined each volume. Finally, after a few hours, I told the bishop and Afifi that the volumes appeared to be authentic Latin re-writes of older texts. These re-writes seemed at least 1,000 years old.

I added that the six-leaf volume described the annunciation of Gabriel to Mary, Jesus' mother. One of the eight-leaf volumes told the story of Emperor Constantine's conversion to Christianity. These would probably not benefit my research efforts.

The other two, however, held more promise. The eight-leaf volume was a lesson covering Jesus' calling of Philip. However, as I read, I realized that the information added little to what I already knew. The 11-leaf volume was a lesson centering on Jesus' confrontation with the woman of Samaria at Jacob's well.

I asked Bishop Ohan for permission to take notes on these two volumes. He agreed and even volunteered to read the texts to me.

We started with the 11-leaf volume. I decided I would alternate between transcribing directly and paraphrasing what I heard. The bishop read:

Jesus had been ministering in the state of Judea with his disciples. Shortly after his confrontation with Nicodemus, Jesus discovered that the Pharisees were upset about his increase in popularity. So, he decided to go back to the Galilee the quick way, through Samaria, a route typically by-passed by Judean religious leaders.

Samaria was considered off-limits to many Jewish religious leaders in Judea, because it was occupied by a mixed population of Israelites and descendants of Assyrian colonists.

The Samaritan Jews professed Judaism, but they had broken all religious ties with Judea and Jerusalem, and they refused to be a part of the cult of the Temple in Jerusalem. Approximately 30 percent of the total population in Samaria's four major hill cities was Jewish. The remainder of Samaria had a Jewish population of less than 5 percent.

As Jesus and his disciples traveled through Samaria, they stopped at Jacob's well. Here, Jesus rested, while his disciples went into the city to buy food.

Jacob's well was about 30 meters deep. It maintained a constant 3 to 4 meter depth of water, regardless of season. Tradition holds that this well was dug by Jacob himself and that it was where Joseph was cast by his jealous brothers.

Jesus and his disciples had traveled about 30 miles by the time they reached the well. They were tired, thirsty, and hungry.

At this point, it is important to understand that because Jesus was from the Galilee, he had no animosity against the Samaritans. Nor did his disciples. Although Jesus was aware of the regulations imposed by the Jewish religious leaders, they did not govern *him*.

The woman he met at the well did not seem to know he was from the Galilee (although his dialect should have betrayed him). When she saw the distinctive blue thread in the tassel of his garment belt identifying him as a Jewish rabboni, she quickly assumed he was a rabboni from Judea. After all, why would a rabboni hail from anyplace besides Judea? As such, she believed he would be subject to the restrictions of the religious law, which governed the social interaction and interface of the Samaritans. So she must have been shocked when he struck up a conversation with her.

You see, it was socially unacceptable in Parthian domestic law for a lone man to initiate a conversation with a lone woman unless he was interested in her as a potential wife.

Jesus explains the eternal spiritual living waters that he could give the woman, ensuring that her spiritual self would never thirst for satisfaction.

She responds sarcastically, assuming Jesus is talking about *physical* water, Jesus then tells her to call her husband. She confesses that she has no husband. Jesus then reveals that she has been wife to five men and that the man she is with now isn't her husband.

There has been much speculation about this woman. It has been assumed that she was a woman of the world or a harlot. There is no evidence to confirm this. Yes, this woman came to the well by herself at noon. (Women usually came in groups to draw water in the morning.) But this doesn't mean that other women didn't want to associate with her. In fact, John's Gospel doesn't state that she came *alone*. There might have been many other women at the well.

Moreover, there is no indication that Jesus judged this woman as immoral. The fact that she had been a wife to five husbands is usually cited as the reason for the assumption.

At this point, Bishop Ohan paused to inject a personal note.

"Some years ago, I discovered that in the Parthian culture a woman had many more rights than women did in Roman or Greek culture," he said. "In Roman or Greek culture, a woman was not allowed to divorce. Only a husband could divorce. According to Augustus's divorce law, if a husband divorced his wife, she could not remarry as long as her former husband lived, under penalty of being classified an adulteress and outcast from society. In Parthian culture, a woman was not allowed to divorce during the first two years of marriage. After two years, she gained that right. She could divorce and remarry up to five times. This meant that she could have a different husband every third year, and have up to five husbands. This did not include husbands lost due to death, or to husbands who divorced her.

"Thus, a woman could marry and divorce five husbands, be widowed twice, and be divorced by three husbands. She could have had ten husbands and still not be considered immoral according to Parthian standards. Nevertheless, after marrying and divorcing the fifth husband, she was not permitted to marry again. However, she was allowed to share living quarters with a male relative or friend, without breaking civil and domestic laws. So, the woman at the well was within her legal rights to have had five former husbands and to be living with a man who was not her husband. So, perhaps, we merely have an unlucky woman who was unable to find happiness in marriage."

After these personal comments, the Bishop resumed translating:

"Jesus' knowledge about her convinces this woman that he is a prophet of God. So she seizes the opportunity to ask a question that has been plaguing the Jews of Samaria: Where is the most acceptable place to worship God: Mount Gerizim or the Temple in Jerusalem?

"Jesus does not answer directly. He says that true worship isn't based on where or when it is offered. It is worship that conforms to each individual's personality. It is the outward expression of something felt deep within. It is worship unrestricted by a specific time, place, situation, or circumstance.

"The woman is not satisfied with Jesus' answer. She disregards it, saying, 'It doesn't matter anyway, because when the Messias gets here, He will tell us the truth. He will tell us where the acceptable place of worship is.'

"Jesus then disarms her by declaring *he* is the one, the long-awaited Messias.

"Then the disciples return, and the woman runs back into the city. She tells some men about Jesus, encouraging them to go see for themselves.

"The word used for *men* here implies that they were city authorities.

"Later, as Jesus looks up and sees a crowd coming toward him, he offers his great evangelistic challenge to his disciples, to 'look on the fields; for they are white already to harvest.'

"Jesus and his disciples stay in Sychar two more days and minister to the people. (Sychar was located just south of the city of Samaria.)

Bishop Ohan looked up, indicating the lesson was complete. I thanked him and spent the rest of the afternoon talking with him and Afifi about the vault's treasures and about Jesus' interaction with the woman at the well.

HEALING A HERODIAN'S SON

After leaving Sychar in Samaria, Jesus and his disciples continue on to the Galilee. Upon their arrival, they are welcomed with open arms

JOHN 4:45
45 Then when he was come into Galilee, the Galilaeans received him, having seen all the things that he did at Jerusalem

Obviously, the details of his ministry in Samaria and Judaea had preceded him.

Next, Jesus and his disciples travel to Cana, where he had turned water into wine. John's Gospel doesn't tell us why Jesus returned to Cana. Perhaps he wanted to visit his sister and new brother-in-law.

We do know that word rapidly spread throughout the Galilee that Jesus was in Cana. Even the House of Herod in Capernaum received the news.

According to John 4, a member of Herod's household, a Herodian whose son was ill, heard the news. This Herodian father set off for Cana.

I discovered validation of John's Gospel account while researching at the academic library of Egypt's Ain Shams University, in the heart of downtown Cairo.

At this library, I found a two-page thirteenth century Arabic manuscript. The vellum document's notes claimed it was a rewrite of a sermon penned by Gothard, an eleventh century Abbot at a Bavarian monastery. The Arabic scribe who translated Gothard's sermon called himself Babos.

The sermon centers on the healing of the Herodian's son. Gothard begins by citing the scriptural text for his sermon (John 4:46-53). He then explains that a similar event was recorded in the Gospels of Matthew (8:5-12) and Luke (7:1-10). However, the episode recorded in John is separate, occurring months, if not years, apart.

JOHN 4:46-53

[46] So Jesus came again into Cana ... And there was a certain nobleman, whose son was sick at Capernaum.

[47] When he heard that Jesus was come out of Judaea into Galilee, he went unto him, and besought him that he would ... heal his son: for he was at the point of death.

[48] Then said Jesus unto him, Except ye see signs and wonders, ye will not believe.

[49] The nobleman saith unto him, Sir, come down ere my child die.

[50] Jesus saith unto him, Go thy way; thy son liveth. And the man believed the word that Jesus had spoken ... and he went his way.

[51] And ... his servants met him, and told him, saying, Thy son liveth.

[52] Then enquired he of them the hour when he began to amend. And they said unto him, Yesterday at the seventh hour the fever left him.

[53] So the father knew that it was at the same hour ... Jesus said unto him, Thy son liveth: and himself believed, and his whole house.

Gothard notes that upon returning to the Galilee, Jesus and his disciples intended to stay in Cana for a while.

Capernaum, which figures prominently in this story, was a predominately Roman/Greek city, and a tax and commerce center for the province of Syria. At the time of Jesus' ministry, Capernaum boasted some 300,000 residents.

Herod Antipas, the Roman Tetrarch of the Galilee, maintained an enormous palace complex in northern Capernaum.

John's Gospel says that a nobleman heard Jesus had returned from Judea and was residing in Cana. The Greek word for nobleman, *basilikos*, refers to a title used by Syrian Roman authorities for officials and members of Herod's royal line. Perhaps this nobleman was a Herodian prince. He was certainly a man of stature.

John's Gospel says this Herodian left his palace home in Capernaum and traveled the 20 miles to Cana, hoping Jesus would heal his sick son, who was at death's door.

Gothard speculates that this Herodian was part of the Theophus Commission and had been sent to investigate Jesus as a possible Theophus. However, John's Gospel says this man went to Cana to persuade Jesus to heal his son. Who is right, the gospel writer or Gothard?

According to the scribe Babos, the answer is both. In his margin notes, Babos asserts that the Herodian's son was indeed gravely ill. However, because of an Imperial decree, the importance of the Theophus search trumped everything. That is the main reason the Herodian left his ailing son.

Still, this father hoped his trip would provide an opportunity to accomplish *both* goals. After all, he reasoned, Jesus was a Jewish resident of the Galilee, so it would be illegal for him to refuse a Herodian's demand to return to Capernaum for cross-examination. Then, if Jesus was a true miracle worker, he could heal his son while in Capernaum to face questioning.

Whatever was on the Herodian's mind, he arrives in Cana with a heavy heart. His son is dying. The Herodian finds Jesus around 1:00 in the afternoon and asks if Jesus will come to Capernaum and heal his son. Jesus responds with a question/statement designed to uncover the father's true motive. Is he truly concerned about his son, or is this just a ploy connected to the Theophus search?

The Herodian says, in essence, "Sir, this is not a game! Yes, I am commissioned to investigate The Theophus, but this is no trick. My son is gravely ill. If you do not come and heal him, he will surely die."

Jesus doesn't make the trip. Instead, he sends the Herodian home, telling him his son is alive. Healed.

Of course, if Jesus was a Roman citizen, he was under no obligation to obey the Herodian. On the other hand, if he was *not* a Roman citizen, Jesus violated a long list of Roman restrictions.

For example, he deliberately disregarded the Statute of Authority of the Roman administrators. Thus, the Herodian could have had Jesus arrested and imprisoned for disobedience.

Additionally, we see that Jesus unceremoniously sends the Herodian away with a promise that his boy has been healed. It is *highly* unlikely that the Herodian would have tolerated such an audacious statement unless Jesus was a Roman citizen, and a citizen of some renown. Consider the context. The Herodian meets a strange man, yet he trusts his words so much that he returns to Capernaum without insisting that Jesus accompany him. It's important to understand that Herodians were, by nature, skeptical. They trusted no one, no god, no government, and no religion. They had a reputation for being heartless. They were dedicated to almost nothing, except Caesar.

Given this, can you imagine what is on the Herodian's mind and heart as he makes his way back to Capernaum? It is possible that he will arrive at his home, facing the sad fact that he has failed Caesar *and* his son.

En route, the Herodian's servants meet him, bearing amazing news: His son has been healed. The Herodian asks when the boy's health turned around. The answer: About 1:00 in the afternoon of the previous day. The Herodian lets the truth sink in. This was when Jesus declared the boy healed.

Gothard goes on to say the Herodian believed and his whole house believed. However, he points out that the Gospel doesn't specify the *object* of this belief. Did they believe in Jesus, or did they just believe a miracle had happened? Perhaps they believed that Jesus was The Theophus.

We don't know the answer to any of these questions. But we do know that from summer of AD 27 until the last few months of Jesus' earthly ministry (spring of AD 31), the Herodians maintained a relatively uneventful relationship with Jesus.

Less than a year after Jesus' death, ambassadors representing Tiberius' Theophus Commission arrived in Jerusalem and questioned Herod Antipas, Caiaphas, the Jewish Sanhedrin, and Pilate about Jesus, his works and miracles, and his death. This forces me (Gothard) to conclude that it was not coincidence that the Herodians' interest in Jesus' activities came four years after the miraculous healing of the Herodian boy.

Here, the Gothard document ends abruptly. Clearly, he had written more, but it has been lost or destroyed.

SEA OF GALILEE

After Jesus' encounter with the Herodian, we find another gap in the record of his life.

Not until August do we find Jesus on the shores of the Sea of Galilee (or, as Luke 5:1 states *the lake of Gennesaret*) preaching to a crowd of people. August also marks the time Jesus calls Peter, Andrew, James, and John as disciples. The summer of AD 27 brings another miracle, too.

At the National Museum in Luxembourg City, Luxembourg, I was shown documentation of the calling of Andrew, Peter, James, and John. This resource also described an unusual, unexplainable event, something that inspired these men to drop everything and follow Jesus.

The documentation was a book written in 1890 by Dr. Louis Henrii Ranhugel, a Lutheran minister. Titled *The Miracle of the Call*, the book is based on a sermon Dr. Ranhugel addressed to the European Lutheran Missions Board conference of 1888.

Dr. Ranhugel preached from Luke 5:1-11 and Matthew 4:18-22. Those familiar with the New Testament know that the setting for these Scriptures is the western shore of the Sea of Galilee, a large lake known for its abundance of fish. It is 700 feet below sea level, and about 7.5 miles long at its longest point and 3.5 miles wide at its widest point.

Dr. Ranhugel writes:

"Jesus is preaching to a large throng of people, who have crowded him to the point of being pushed into the water. He asks to use Peter's boat so that he can preach from the sea. Peter, who is cleaning his nets, agrees. So, Jesus gets in the boat, pushes out into the water, and finishes his sermon.

"Afterward, Jesus advises Peter to launch out into the deep and fish. The Sea of Galilee had three depth distinctions:

- The *shore* (the area from shoreline to about 200 feet) had a maximum depth of about four feet.

- The *deep* (the area 200 feet from shore and extending about a half mile) saw its depth increase gradually from four feet to about 20 feet.

- The *depths* (or the center of the lake) boasted waters 600 feet deep, if not more.

"This lake's fish supply was so abundant that, on a given day, dozens of fishing boats patrolled the waters in hopes of a big catch.

"This brings us back to Jesus' urging Peter to launch out into the deep, more than a half mile from shore, and let down his nets."

"Peter has just finished the tedious and time-consuming task of cleaning his nets and laying them out to dry. After an unsuccessful all-night fishing venture, he is tired and frustrated. He doesn't want fishing advice from Jesus. Nevertheless, for some reason, he submits to Jesus' command. He loads up his gear again and launches his boat.

"The result? An unforgettable day of fishing.

"Classical historians Suetonius Tranquillus, Tacitus, Paolo, and Marcus Valerius Martialis all marked August 11 of AD 27 as a red-letter day in Roman history. All of them noted that something very strange happened to the Sea of Galilee (or Lake of Gennesaret). Paolo called it a "bubbling up of the sea," adding "the event was foreseen and presaged by a Jesus from the Galilee, a religious teacher of the Jews, the adopted son of Joseph the Jewish royal who was Rome's citizen Senior Senator representing Britain."

"The strange event on the lake was witnessed by members of the Theophus Commission, including Marcus Omerigus, a Senator from Rome; Claudius Maximus, a special tax envoy sent from Tiberius; and Marcus Antonious Somintous, a Roman military commander. These men had accompanied Herod Antipas to a work site in the city of Tiberias. (Tiberias was located on the western shore of the lake, just a few hundred feet south of where Jesus was teaching.) Herod Antipas wanted to show off the construction of this new city, hoping his guests would return to Emperor Tiberius and give a good report.

"It's important to understand that this body of water was "born" thousands of years before, due to the rifting of the Jordan River valley. This rifting created deep lava pits. Millions of tons of water poured into one of the pits as the centuries went by. Eventually, this water-filled lava pit became known as the Sea of Galilee.

"A shallow crust of rock that formed at the bottom of the pit sealed off the molten lava and allowed the waters to cool. As the lake filled, its waters spilled over into the surrounding shallow areas and formed a ledge (of less than 20 feet) called the deep. Fish bred in these relatively shallow waters. Thus, "the deep" offered the best fishing.

"Occasionally, this body of water experienced a "bubbling up," caused by pressure that built up under the rock crust at the lake's bottom. As pressure built, cracks formed in the crust. If the pressure was great enough, the crust would split open, releasing a huge bubble of sulfuric gas and boiling water. When the bubble broke the water's surface, the cooler atmospheric air was forced outward rapidly and violently. As the bubble continued to rise, cooler air filled its void, creating gale-force winds.

"Any ships unfortunate enough to be caught in the middle of the lake during this bizarre act of nature faced severe peril. However, vessels closer to shore (e.g. the deep) were safe because the ledge protected them.

"As you might imagine, when such a storm hit, thousands of fish tried to escape the scalding water by frantically swimming from "the depths" to "the deep." Thus, a fisherman trolling "the deep" during a storm could find himself with an embarrassment of aquatic riches. He could catch a year's quota in a few minutes. According to some reports, commercial fishing nets burst from their loads. What's more, an agile fisherman could exit his boat and walk to shore over a thick carpet of fish.

"This is why Simon Peter harvested so many fish so quickly.

"The question then becomes not how did Simon catch so many fish, but rather how did Jesus know that the bubbling up of the sea was about to take place? It was unpredictable and happened unexpectedly.

"Jesus' prediction so impressed Simon, Andrew (Simon's brother), and their business partners James and John that, at Jesus' bidding, all four immediately left their business and followed him. And it so impressed the Roman officials present that they insisted the event be recorded in Rome's permanent annals."

Dr. Ranhugel concludes his book with a surprising statement:

"Peter, Andrew, James, and John were personally called by Jesus to be his disciples, but then they were nothing more than four out of many, perhaps hundreds, who became followers of Jesus. They may have had 'Jesus' ear,' but they did not occupy a special inner-circle position at this time. They did not attain a special position until three of the four (Peter, James, and John) were selected by Jesus to accompany him to the Transfiguration, which occurred quite some time after they had been appointed as apostles. Even in their selection as part of Jesus' twelve apostles, they were picked out of a multitude of other disciples."

The Sea of Galilee, looking east from Tiberias.
The Golan Heights is in the background—Israel.

CHAPTER 16

✦

Jesus' Second Year of Ministry

PART 2 — AD 27

NOT LONG AFTER THE "bubbling up of the sea," Jesus and his disciples return to Capernaum. One Sabbath day, they go to a synagogue, where Jesus begins to teach. Jesus' knowledge and authoritative teaching amaze the people. While Jesus teaches, a man with an unclean spirit interrupts. (See Mark 1:21-28 and Luke 4:33-37.) Jesus responds by casting the unclean spirit out of the man.

I increased my knowledge of this event, courtesy of Dr. Harriet Blanch, Education Director at North Side Assembly Church and Director of Research and Investigative Resources at the University of Chicago's library. Dr. Blanch became so fascinated with my search that she spent an afternoon and evening helping me find corroborating documentation of the Gospels.

One of the resources she showed me was a 600-page book titled *Not Against Flesh and Blood*, written in 1880 by Gustave Doren, a former

Methodist pastor turned writer and painter. (Doren was a friend of the great pastor and writer Charles Spurgeon.)

Doren states that much of his book is composed of paraphrases from the writings of Polycarp, Bishop of Smyrna from AD 150 to 155 (and martyred in AD 155). Early Church tradition holds that Polycarp was a personal disciple of the apostle John. According to Doren, the Polycarp source document was titled *Divisions*.

Dr. Blanch explained to me:

> "To date I have not found a copy of the Polycarp document or even a copy of a copy. All that is known about *Divisions* is what the early church fathers Tertullian and Origen have written. Both acknowledge that Polycarp wrote a document titled *Divisions*, about four years before he was martyred. It was distributed to Christians in Italy and Greece, warning them of the subtle and deceptive evils at work in the court of Antoninus Pius, the so-called 'Gentle Aristocrat.' Doren's book covered a variety of subjects. However, its primary focus was the levels of authority in the evil-spirit world."

UNSEEN POWER STRUCTURE

In a particularly interesting section, Doren seeks to prove that Jesus knew about these levels of demonic authority and that he actively fought against them. In this section, Doren cites two key Bible references: Mark 1:23-28 and Luke 4:33-37.

MARK 1:23-28

23 And there was in their synagogue a man with an unclean spirit; and he cried out,

24 Saying, Let us alone; what have we to do with thee, thou Jesus of Nazareth? art thou come to destroy us? I know thee who thou art, the Holy One of God.

25 And Jesus rebuked him, saying, Hold thy peace, and come out of him.

26 And when the unclean spirit had torn him, and cried with a loud voice, he came out of him.

27 And they were all amazed, insomuch that they questioned among themselves, saying, What thing is this? what new doctrine is this? for with authority commandeth he even the unclean spirits, and they do obey him.

28 And immediately his fame spread abroad throughout all the region round about Galilee.

LUKE 4:33-36

[33] And in the synagogue there was a man, which had a spirit of an unclean devil, and cried out with a loud voice,

[34] Saying, Let us alone; what have we to do with thee, thou Jesus of Nazareth? art thou come to destroy us? I know thee who thou art; the Holy One of God.

[35] And Jesus rebuked him, saying, Hold thy peace, and come out of him. And when the devil had thrown him in the midst, he came out of him, and hurt him not.

[36] And they were all amazed, and spake among themselves, saying, What a word is this! for with authority and power he commandeth the unclean spirits, and they come out.

Dr. Blanch told me that the setting of this event is when "Jesus and his disciples were in Capernaum. On a Sabbath day in late summer of AD 27, they go to a synagogue, where they encounter this 'spirit of an unclean devil.'

"According to Doren's book, exorcism was well-known at this time. It was practiced by a few Jewish priests and a select number of Pharisees. Polycarp claimed that Solomon originally established the principles and techniques of exorcism. According to some sources, Solomon created a school/clinic dedicated to exorcism's study and practice. This institution claimed a clientele of thousands, from throughout the world. Where Solomon and the exorcists of his day learned their art is unknown. Perhaps it was divinely given.

"By the time Jesus began his ministry, most exorcisms were performed by specially appointed exorcists on behalf of the High Priest. They were chosen from the ranks of experienced Pharisees and priests. Because Jesus did not have the official title of exorcist, his exorcisms did not carry the blessings of his religious overlords. Consequently, this exorcism could have been interpreted as insubordination. This could have resulted in Jesus' dismissal from his position as rabboni, his exclusion from synagogue worship, and his excommunication.

"In AD 27, exorcism was a long and agonizing process lasting at least five days—up to several months. The primary method of exorcism was to strip the demoniac naked and bind him in chains. Each time the person became violent and uncooperative, the exorcist would douse him with frigid water (blessed by the exorcist priests) until he calmed down. This was accompanied by a never-ceasing oral recitation of the Law of Moses, the words of the prophets, the Psalms, and Solomon's proverbs. Four exorcists would each take a shift reading. Two priests would take turns reciting the prayers and lamentations of David, Isaiah, and Jeremiah, for up to ten hours a day.

"Eventually, the demoniac was supposed to calm down and return to normal. History has little to say about the effectiveness of this process, but, most likely, this method was effective in only a fraction of exorcism cases."

At this point, Dr. Blanch interrupted her reading to emphasize the demoniac at Capernaum recognized Jesus immediately: "He tries to discredit Jesus by associating him with Nazareth. Then he seeks to slander Jesus by implying that he is in partnership with the demon.

"Doren further contends that (according to Luke's Gospel), the demon was an evil or unclean spirit of a devil. This implied that the spirit possessing the man was a servant of a higher level of evil authority (e.g. a devil.)

"It appears that Doren's book suggests something contrary to today's assumptions. Today, those who believe in demons believe that people can be demon-possessed. These demons have a leader named Satan, also known as The Devil and Lucifer. Doren strongly believes that the three entities are different from each other. There are levels of authority among them."

"Now, let's move on to Doren's explanation of the Luciferian hierarchy," she said. At the time of his writing (1880), evil influences were called by different names: demon, devil, evil spirit, The Devil, or Satan, but these terms were synonymous. However, the early church fathers disagreed. Their writings assert that there has always been a well-organized and extremely disciplined hierarchy of evil.

"In the first century, the Pharisees, priests, and rabbis referred to general evil influences by the Hebrew word *mazzikim*, meaning 'evil spirits' or 'evil influences,' but when they referred to a *specific* evil influence, they used a Greek, Latin, or Chaldean word or phrase. The phrase for demon was *pneuma akatharton* (Chaldean). The word for devil was *daemonium* (Greek). The phrase for an evil or unclean spirit was *spiritus immundus* (Latin). Each of these had a different definition, reflecting a specific type of evil.

"Doren lists the three evil influences in order of authority, separating each group into specialized classes or *castes*.

"Although devils, demons, and evil/unclean spirits monitor, observe, and torment humans and perform their respective responsibilities world-wide, Doren chooses to focus on their dealings and relationships with believers in Christ, just as Polycarp did."

"Now," Dr. Blanch said, moving her eyes from Doren's book to my face, "I am going to proceed much more slowly. I want you to write down everything I am going to read to you."

With this, she began to read Doren's description of the evil-spirit world. I will paraphrase this description for you, for the sake of brevity:

DEVIL (Daemonium) This is the highest level of the three working levels of authority. Devils receive their authority directly from the Luciferian hierarchy. Within this class, there are four castes or levels of authority.

1. **Diabolos:** The word means adversary, accuser, and slanderer. Diabolos is superior within the devil caste. These beings continually stand before God and accuse true believers, who, in the *Diaboloses'* opinion, have failed. This is the only devil caste that does not invade Earth's atmosphere. This caste has three levels of authority within its ranks.

   - *Dilos* is the highest-ranking level. These beings deal directly with God in presenting a case against believers.

   - *Daalos* is the next level of authority. They are responsible for developing a case against a believer.

   - *Daima* is the lowest level. These are devils that collect slanderous information about a believer (from observing devils). They present this information to the Daalos.

2. **Disaliuon:** The word means ruler or dominion. They seek to rule specific geographical locations on earth (called strongholds.) Their power can be defeated by mature believers.

- *Dissali:* highest level of authority and rule empires, countries or a race of people.

- *Dosimia:* second level of authority, who rule a region with an area controlled by Dissali.

- *Desmoni:* third level of authority who control a district within the Dosimia region.

3. **Diamonion:** The word means observer and tempter. If a believer does not resist a particular temptation, he will be continually tempted in that area in an attempt to get that believer to sin or to commit iniquity.

   - *Demus:* the highest authority and deliver information about a believer's failure to the Daimonion.

   - *Deema:* second level of authority. When a believer begins to incubate a temptation rather than rejecting it, then he is turned over to Das Maus.

   - *Das Maus* is the third level. It records the believer's reactions to concentrated temptation and passes the information up the hierachy.

4. **Diasalos:** This devil caste is fourth in superiority. They are evil warriors who fight against the warrior angels of God and against powerful believers. There are three levels, similar to military authority:

   - *Dia Nunus* is quivalent to a general.

   - *Dammia* is equivalent to a subordinate officer.

   - *Deiaslo* is equivalent to a fighting warrior or soldier.

DEMONS (pneuma akatharton): This evil influence is the second of the three working levels of authority. Their main priority is to torment a believer in an attempt to cause him to forsake the true Godhead. Incapacitating believers is their priority. Tormenting all humans is their secondary priority.

   1. *Diamon:* evil possessor of feeling. These specialise in emotional tormenting, including hopelessness, loneliness, worthlessness, faithlessness, guilt, depression and

self-condemnation. This is oppression, harassment and torment. The demon leech can be eliminated through prayer and with the name and authority of Jesus.

2. *Sair* means mind manic. Psychological problems and phobias and self destruction.

3. *Shed* means flesh manic. Although they can be blamed for some disease and sickness that affect the physical body, they are NOT the cause of all sickness.

4. *Shair* means enchantment worship. Filling the spiritual need of mankind and steering attention away from the purpose of Jesus Christ.

EVIL (UNCLEAN) SPIRIT (spiritus immundus): The third class of working influences. There are four castes:

1. *Rialos:* The word means emissary. The Rialos travel along earth's geophysical force fields or ley lines and direct demons on assignment.

2. *Diablos:* The security guards. If powerful believers threaten a physical land territory these evil spirits will defend the territory for the devils until deiaslo arrives.

3. *Milos:* Prevent travel. They are responsible for intercepting a believer's prayer, which would threaten the Luciferian system and its plans.

4. *Resalos* or presence: These evil spirit reside in a specific geographical location, city, territory, area or country. They do not leave the area unless forced to do so by powerful believers.

Dr. Blanch told me, "Doren turned his attention to the Luciferian system. Polycarp merely stated that the system existed, so for information on the system I have relied upon the writings of the eighteenth century Luciferian, Adam Weishaupt, and Satanist, Sir Francis Dashwood."

"According to Weishaupt and Dashwood, the three highest levels of authority seldom intervene on earth. That responsibility is left to the spirits commissioned to do that particular job."

THRONES: are the highest level of Luciferian authority: There are four thrones:

1. *Satan:* the founder of all deception, unholy, man-centered false religions.

2. *Balial:* an evil god who controls conflicts and disturbances in areas of emotional and psychological sensitivity

3. *Leviathan:* controls conflicts and disturbances in areas of knowledge and intellect.

4. *Lucifer:* holder of mankind's light, physical, emotional, psychological and spiritual. Whenever Lucifer is referenced, the name implies the whole Luciferian godhead and power structure.

DOMINIONS: two Dominions each rule over four Principalities.

PRINCIPALITIES are eight Authorities that rule the 24 Powers.

POWERS are the lowest level of authority. There are 25 ruling Powers; 12 rule and supervise the Dissali (controlling empires and people) and 12 rule and supervise the Dia numus (military generals). The 25th Power rules the Diablos, who are continually bringing accusations about the believer before God.

"Doren goes on," Dr. Blanch continued, "to describe the difference between devils, demons, and evil spirits. Again, he repeated that he received the bulk of the information from Polycarp. He says that **devils** are 'beings' created by God. They were originally angels, but they joined the Luciferian rebellion against God. Thus, they were evicted from heaven. They became 'fallen angels.' Since they were created as angels, they lack the ability to possess people. Like angels, devils have different levels of authority.

"**Demons** are the disembodied souls of past unrighteous/evil inhabitants of the earth. Because they are disembodied souls, demons must possess a body to function at maximum capacity. Demons are evil forces that directly influence humankind, by oppression or possession.

"**Evil (unclean) spirits** are also created beings. Perhaps they fit in the same category as cherubim. They joined the Luciferian rebellion, just like the devils. They do not possess people. They are messengers, guards, or caretakers. They typically operate within a specific geographical area unless they are cast out and forbidden to return to that area."

Dr. Blanch went on to further explain the Luciferian power structure, before pausing to note that "Doren spends about 200 pages, going into great speculative depth about how the Luciferian system works and how it influences humankind. He even presents a theoretical power structure of the Trinity and the godly system. He claims that his theory is based on Polycarp's writings. He lists levels of authority for godly spirits and suggests their functions on earth as well as on other solar systems and universes."

With this summary, my research at the University of Chicago ended.

My introspection on Doren's book would not end so soon. I had never encountered so much detail about the spirit world. Levels of authority? Devils, demons, evil and unclean spirits, each different from the other? A godly power structure at work in other universes? It was all too much.

Yes, it's reasonable that the kingdom of evil would be organized, just like God's kingdom. If Lucifer was an archangel cast out of heaven, wouldn't he establish a systematic order of evil?

I thought about Jesus' dealing with demons, about Daniel's confrontation, about the man Legion, and about the Isaiah, Jeremiah, Ezekiel, Genesis, and The Revelation Scriptures that deal with the issues of Satan, evil spirits, and the like.

I continue to think on these things. I confess I am not sure what I believe. The Bible states that devils, demons, Satan, Satan's kingdom, and evil exist. Therefore, I believe it. I believe that evil influences humankind. I believe that demons can possess someone. I believe evil forces war against the forces of good. I believe that human souls are a prize sought by both the kingdom of God and the kingdom of Satan. How evil influences humanity, how it wars against good, how Satan's kingdom operates—these things I do not know.

A comforting thought to me was that the Creator God who made all things has the ultimate power and authority in all things. Jesus, the Christ, conquered all the forces of hell and openly displayed his authority over them after the cruxifiction, before taking his rightful place in the Heavenlies. All authority in heaven and on earth belongs to Jesus, who has delegated His authority to the believers on earth. For every fallen angel working for the Luciferian system there are TWO working to accomplish the plans and purposes of God our Father. Be encouraged and pray!

EPHESIANS 6:12

12 For we wrestle not against flesh and blood, but against principalities, against powers, against the rulers of the darkness of this world, against spiritual wickedness in high places.

COLOSSIANS 2:15

15 And (Jesus) having spoiled principalities and powers, he made a shew of them openly, triumphing over them in it.

HEALING A CENTURION'S SERVANT

A while after his confrontation with the demoniac, Jesus is approached by a centurion who has a sick servant.

I discovered a book explaining this miracle at Franklin College in Lugano, Switzerland. *Sacrificia de Jesus* was written in 1637 by John Eudes, the founder of the Society of Jesus and Mary.

The book is an anti-Semitic treatise, detailing how Jesus ministered to, and on behalf of, Romans, tax collectors, outcasts, and Herodians instead of the Jews.

Eudes includes this text from Matthew 8:5-13:

MATTHEW 8:5-13

5 And when Jesus was entered into Capernaum, there came unto him a centurion, beseeching him,

6 And saying, Lord, my servant lieth at home sick of the palsy ....

7 And Jesus saith unto him, I will come and heal him.

8 The centurion answered and said, Lord, I am not worthy ... speak the word only, and my servant shall be healed.

9 For I am a man under authority, having soldiers under me: and I say to this man, Go, and he goeth ...

10 When Jesus heard it, he marvelled, and said to them that followed, Verily I say unto you, I have not found so great faith, no, not in Israel.

11 And I say unto you, That many shall come from the east and west, and shall sit down with Abraham, and Isaac, and Jacob, in the kingdom of heaven.

12 But the children of the kingdom shall be cast out into outer darkness: there shall be weeping and gnashing of teeth.

[13] And Jesus said unto the centurion, Go thy way; and as thou hast believed, so be it done unto thee. And his servant was healed in the selfsame hour.

Eudes claims "that this centurion was Rustus Flabian, the senior Roman centurion in the military district that included Capernaum. The servant's name was Nehem, a Galilean Jew who was Flabian's brilliant financial manager. Under Nehem's management, Flabian had become one of the wealthiest people in northern Galilee. To reward Nehem, Flabian granted him his freedom and told him that he would give him anything within his power to bestow. Nehem requested that a new synagogue be built in Capernaum, where Galilean Jews would be proud to assemble.

Flabian wanted the best contractor available, and he was eventually referred to a certain Nazareth-based man named Joseph. Then, given the synagogue's aggressive building schedule, Joseph delegated the job to his son Jesus. Work began in AD 21.

According to Eudes, Jesus worked on the synagogue for four years. Then in AD 25, he reduced his role to that of an overseer/construction manager.

In the winter of AD 26, Joseph suggested that Jesus, his mother and his brothers establish a permanent branch of the construction business in Capernaum. Jesus jumped at the opportunity. (It's worth noting here that Jesus was regarded with suspicion in Nazareth, but he was welcomed warmly in Capernaum.)

The synagogue's construction was completed about six months after Jesus moved to Capernaum. On the day the synagogue was dedicated to the Lord, Nehem was to be the guest of honor. It is not known whether Jesus attended this dedication celebration.

As Nehem was riding to the synagogue celebration, his horse became frightened and threw him off. When Nehem hit the ground, his spinal cord was broken, paralyzing him from the neck down. (Flabian was on military assignment, so he did not know what happened to Nehem.)

The dedication began without Nehem and lasted most of the day. Then, late in the afternoon, Nehem was found lying paralyzed at the site of the accident. He was taken to Flabian's home. He was not expected to survive. Months later he was still alive, though paralyzed and weak.

Meanwhile, Flabian had become impressed with Jesus' character, professionalism, and ability as a construction supervisor. Moreover,

Flabian had heard that Jesus was a wise teacher and that he had exorcised demons and performed other miracles.

By September of AD 27, Nehem's condition was so poor that it seemed death was imminent. Flabian sought Jesus' help.

At this point, Jesus and Flabian had known each other professionally for about five years. It's possible that Jesus knew something of Nehem's plight. Whatever the case, when Flabian pleaded for his servant's healing, Jesus said he would come to Flabian's house and heal Nehem.

To Jesus' surprise, Flabian said he was not worthy (the word translated worthy means holy or spiritually pure) of Jesus' entering his home. Clearly, Flabian recognized Jesus' authority and power. He realized that Jesus didn't need to be in Nehem's physical presence. A verbal command would suffice. Flabian lived in a world of authority. He believed Jesus had authority over sickness, even death.

Jesus was amazed by Flabian's faith in him. Perhaps Jesus had never seen this side of the man. Jesus let everyone know how much this show of faith impressed him, a faith he had not seen in any Jew in the area.

Now, Jesus' healing command was a smack in the face to any Jew who heard it. And Jesus didn't stop there. He said that people like Rustus Flabian would qualify to be part of the Kingdom of Heaven before the Jews. And that many Jews wouldn't ever make it into the kingdom.

Jesus then quoted a passage from the Roman poet C. Valerius Catullus (87-54 BC) titled, Annals of Truth. The poem portrays the folly of believing one's Roman citizenship places him above the law. Catullus contends that Romans who take advantage of the poor, disrespect the government, break the law, and despise the righteous should not inherit citizenship's privileges. Instead, they should be placed in the vilest of all prisons.

By quoting Catullus, Jesus was insinuating that many Jews were cut from the same cloth as these Roman citizens. Catullus, incidentally, was a well-known Roman poet. His works were mandatory study for any Roman seeking a position of authority, including centurion.

This incident marks the first time Jesus directly ministers to (or heals on behalf of) a Roman. And Flabian was no common Roman. He was a centurion—a military captain with authority over 100 soldiers.

Imagine what the Pharisees thought when Jesus said openly that a Roman centurion, whom the Judean religious leaders considered evil, had more faith than those who considered themselves to be God's representatives. Jesus went on to say that there would be those from the Empire's western-most parts (Romans, Greeks, Illyrians, etc.) and the eastern-most parts (Persians, Parthians, Arabs, etc.) who would see the kingdom of heaven long before the 'holy and righteous children of God' (as the Pharisees proclaimed themselves) if they were to see it at all. He concluded by saying that people from pagan countries would sit down with the ancient Jewish fathers in the kingdom.

According to Eudes, "Jesus prophetic statement has literally occurred. Multitudes in the West and the East came to believe in Jesus as their Christ and Messiah before the destruction of Jerusalem and the subsequent dissolving of the Jewish State, and many more multitudes have done so since. At the same time, the Pharisees suffered destruction because of their refusal to believe.

After this, Jesus sent the centurion away, saying that the servant was healed. The servant was restored completely."

With this statement, Eudes's account of this event ends.

After Nehem's healing, Jesus and his disciples again disappear from recorded history for a brief while. They don't re-emerge in Capernaum until about three weeks later, just in time to greet the Bubonic Plague.

BUBONIC PLAGUE

Roman history records that tens of thousands were stricken with this deadly disease. However, only one plague victim of note is recorded in the annals of Christian history: Simon Peter's mother-in-law, the lady Jesus heals in late September or early October of AD 27. (See Matthew 8:14-15, Mark 1:30-31, and Luke 4:38-39.)

I discovered an extra-biblical account of this healing at Turkey's Ankara University. The manuscript was written in Latin, but it had been translated into Arabic, Turkish, English, and Greek.

Disibod, an Irish monk/bishop and founder of Germany's Disibondenberg monastery, wrote the manuscript in AD 670. It is the only surviving manuscript out of dozens that Disibod allegedly wrote about Jesus' miracles.

As I read this manuscript, I quickly realized that this was no ordinary re-telling of an event in Jesus' life. Disibod goes into great detail describing the historical backdrop, and his writing is free of church dogma. Here was a free thinker, about 1,000 years ahead of his time.

Here is the Gospel of Luke's account of this healing:

LUKE 4:38-39

[38] And he arose out of the synagogue, and entered into Simon's house. And Simon's wife's mother was taken with a great fever....

[39] And he stood over her, and rebuked the fever; and it left her: and immediately she arose and ministered unto them.

Disibod writes:

"In September and October of AD 27 the (bubonic) plague made an appearance in Syria and in the Galilee. Many workers laboring on the new cities of Tiberias and Julias died from the plague. This resulted in construction being halted. Simon's mother-in-law may have become infected with this most fearful of plagues.

"The most dreaded diseases in the Galilee/Decapolis regions at that time were bowel conditions, malarial fever, skin eruptions, smallpox, pruitus, leprosy, eye diseases, blindness, diseases of Venus (venereal disease), deafness, decay of organ and skin (cancer), swollen and painful joints, nerve disorders, convulsion disease (epilepsy), lung and heart disorders, and the plague.

"In the Galilee/Decapolis districts, those afflicted with such diseases were treated (both medically and emotionally) as you would suppose one should be treated.

"But in Judea the Jewish religious leaders claimed these diseases (were) curses of God for punishment of personal or inherited sin. The word used for any of these diseases was *het or hattaah* (referring to) *guilt for sin* or for breaking some religious rule. Jewish religious leaders taught that because of breaking laws and rules, God inflicted diseases. Thus, the cure for any of these diseases was possible only if God granted His pardon, which could only be sought through special rites of purification and through offerings given at the Temple in Jerusalem.

"By January of AD 28, the plague had run its course and had taken the lives of more than 3,000 people as it spread across Syria.

"In Judea, the Pharisees claimed the epidemic was God's punishment upon the people, because Jews who were working on the cities of Tiberias and Julias had submitted to Roman authorities and consented to construct the cities rather than refusing to work. The Judean Pharisees felt that it was better to refuse to work and face death, rather than build 'imperial' cities for the Romans.

"It appears that Jesus was in a synagogue in Capernaum when he was summoned to Simon Peter's house. Jesus, knowing the true nature of the disease, did not demand repentance from Simon Peter's mother-in-law, nor did he demand specific purification rituals. He simply healed her showing no fear of the infectious disease, knowing that she had been stricken through no fault of her own.

"It is not known how many (similar) people Jesus healed. What is known is that the plague exited the area much more rapidly than in times past. We also know that work on the cities was resumed by November of that year, which was an impossibility without divine intervention.

"After Jesus had healed Simon's mother-in-law, and perhaps countless others, of the dreaded (bubonic) plague, his fame spread throughout Roman Syria. He healed all who came to him of all manner of diseases and sicknesses."

Given this swelling fame, Jesus felt it necessary to take his disciples away from the crowds and minister to them privately, teaching them what they would need to know to minister to the needs of the people. This teaching was different from and contrary to what the Pharisees and scribes taught. This is the first of two key lessons Jesus gave to his disciples, which is now known as *The Sermon on the Mount.*

SERMON ON THE MOUNT-THE STRAIGHT GATE

In my research, I found a mountain of information on the Sermon on the Mount. Two resources stand out.

I had spent two days researching at Jerusalem's Hebrew University library and, I was dissatisfied with what I had found. I decided to devote one more day, then I would drive down to Be'er Sheva' and visit Ben Gurion University.

On my third day at Hebrew University, Dr. Abram Luwenstein, the head librarian of the university's climate-controlled rare books and manuscripts vault, asked me to accompany him to the vault room. He wanted to show me something.

I followed him to the vault and sat at one of its long tables. Dr. Luwenstein excused himself and returned a few minutes later with a large volume, about two feet-square. The volume consisted of vellum leaves bound between two oak boards.

According to Dr. Luwenstein, Peter Abelard had written this volume in about 1123. Titled *Theologia Historia*, this French-language work had been unavailable for public viewing, as it was being translated into Hebrew, Arabic, and English. The librarian offered to give me a few hours with the book.

I spend about an hour with the original French document, before turning to the English translation for the bulk of my research.

The *Theologia Historia* attempts to trace the development of Christian theological thinking, from Jesus' teachings until the time of the volume's production (the year 1123).

I found Dr. Luwenstein, Jewish by birth, to be open-minded when it came to the historical Jesus. Realizing that I could easily spend weeks "digesting" the huge volume, he suggested I focus on a hot theological issue during Abelard's day: Jesus' teaching on the "straight gate," as presented in the Sermon on the Mount.

Abelard begins his treatise by quoting St. Augustine (who contended that the *Sermon on the Mount* was probably not a single sermon). Rather, it was a compilation of sermons from the first two or three years of Jesus' ministry. Later, Matthew summarized the sermons into maxims.

Here is the scriptural setting for the controversial teaching. Jesus said:

MATTHEW 7:13-14

¹³ **Enter ye in at the strait gate: for wide is the gate, and broad is the way, that leadeth to destruction, and many there be which go in thereat:**

[14] Because strait is the gate, and narrow is the way, which leadeth unto life, and few there be that find it.

Below, I will paraphrase Abelard's insights on this passage:

The word translated *enter* is the Greek *agonizomai*. It means to *agonize as in a wrestling match*.

At the time of this lesson, consecrated shepherds, priests, and Levites had the responsibility of raising sheep. Out of their herds would be selected the sheep and lambs to be sacrificed during Passover. Every seven years, a new herd of consecrated sheep was started. Because God demanded that sacrificial animals be strong and healthy, only the best were chosen. An appointee of the High Priest supervised the selection of sacrificial sheep and lambs, held every seventh year in the Hinnom Valley, south of Jerusalem.

Selection took six days. From sunup to sundown, herds of sheep were led into the Hinnom Valley. Midway through the valley, a High Priest appointee would stand on a platform at a junction in the path. Here, two gates were established. The left gate was very wide, and the path leading to it offered little resistance. The right gate was different. It was narrow, so narrow that a full-grown sheep could barely squeeze through. To get to that gate, the sheep had to endure a narrow, steep climb. Only one sheep at a time could navigate the path.

When the entire herd had congregated around the appointee's plat-form, he would order both gates to be opened. The sheep that went through the wide gate and up the wide path were sold to merchants for butchering and wool. Those that went through the narrow gate and continued up the steep and narrow path without falling off or turning back were selected as consecrated sheep when they reached the hilltop. They were worthy for God's purpose.

Abelard explains that Jesus informed his disciples (six at the time) that they had a choice. As his sheep, they could choose the path of least resistance and minimum spiritual hardships—the choice of most of Christ's followers. On this path, there is room for Christ, as well as all other religions and philosophies, but at the path's end, destruction awaits.

If they chose the narrow and challenging path, with room for only Jesus, they would be rewarded with eternal life.

I was intrigued by these insights. Dr. Luwenstein told me that he, too, admired how Abelard made his point.

In my notes, I wrote, "If Peter Abelard's insight is correct, Jesus was saying that on the wide path there is room for him, and for Buddha, Tao, Confucius, Krishna, Eastern Mysticism, Transcendental Meditation, and everything else related to man's spiritual nature. The walk up that path will continue unchallenged until it comes to a destructive end. However, on the narrow path there is room for Jesus *only*. Behind him multiplied millions can line up. It is a path that is agonizing and non-compromising, but if a person maintains his walk up that path, behind Jesus, eternal life is guaranteed at the end.

After I finished writing, Dr. Luwenstein informed me that my time with *Theologia Historia* was up. I thanked him for the privilege he had given me.

The second intriguing Sermon on the Mount document presented itself to me at Greece's University of Ioannina's Museum of Middle Eastern Anthropology. An eight-leaf vellum manuscript I found there featured pages laminated in plastic. The university had translated the original Latin text into Greek, English, and French and provided brief historical information about the manuscript.

According to this information, the eight pages were all that remained of a larger (100-plus pages) document written in 1241 by Alexander of Hales, author of the renowned *Summa Universea Theologiae*.

Alexander declares his authorship in the first paragraph of the first page. He dedicates the document to Duns Scotus, whom he calls "a worthy adversary," with an apology to the reader for discussing *every* aspect of "Jesus' sermon as delivered to his disciples on the mount."

As I read the front and back of the surviving eight pages, it became obvious that Alexander of Hales *was not* the typical Catholic scholar of his day. He didn't blindly accept the dogmas declared by church hierarchy. Also amazing was how Alexander used historical information to explain the Sermon on the Mount's spiritual points and practical applications. It's tragic that most of this work vanished. If the surviving eight pages are any indication, the original document must have been the most exhaustive examination of the Sermon on the Mount of its day, perhaps of all time.

Alexander doesn't approach the Sermon on the Mount in a systematic manner, verse-by-verse, chapter-by-chapter, or subject-by-subject. He writes as if addressing individual topics and answering questions that emerge on the way.

SALT

He writes (and I will paraphrase), In the late fall of AD 27, Jesus took six of his disciples into a mountain. This seems to indicate that he took them into a cave or a cleft of the mountain to teach them.

This was the first of many times Jesus and his disciples isolated themselves. Although all of this sermon may not have been spoken at this particular time, the portion known as the beatitudes and the principles for greater righteousness was most likely taught by Jesus at this time."

Apparently, Alexander's discussion of the beatitudes is missing, because the first thing that he discusses is Jesus' describing his disciples as the salt of the earth and the light of the world. (See Matthew 5:13-14.) Alexander explores each of Jesus' analogies separately.

MATTHEW 5:13-14
¹³ Ye are the salt of the earth: but if the salt have lost his savour, wherewith shall it be salted? it is thenceforth good for nothing, but to be cast out, and to be trodden under foot of men.
¹⁴ Ye are the light of the world. A city that is set on an hill cannot be hid.

Discussing the disciples' being called the salt of the earth, Alexander notes that Jesus was calling these men the most precious of all elements and the preservers who protect others from spiritual decay. He then provides historical background:

Alexander the Great used salt in large quantities to preserve meat during his long military campaigns. By the time of Julius Caesar, salt had become such a mandatory element in Roman life that it was considered by most citizens of wealth to be more precious than gold. It was in so much demand throughout the Roman Empire that military expeditions were sent to the far corners of the world. Countries were conquered for the sake of salt. Rome was shaft-mining salt in what is now Austria. Salt was also mined in Africa, Anatolia, Greece, and Gaul.

The Empire's largest concentration of exposed salt reserves was in the area of the Dead Sea (the Salt Sea) salt flats. This area had so much salt that Judaea was allowed by Rome to pay a large portion of its provincial tax burden in salt. The salt was collected, transported overland, and loaded on ships in Ascalon, Caesarea Maritima, Joppa, and Tyre. From there, salt was shipped to Rome. Ships would travel to Rome in large caravans of 20 to 30, from each of four ports. After a ship was loaded with salt, it was covered to prevent water contamination.

At the time in Judea and in the Galilee, bands of revolutionaries wanted to overthrow their Roman overlords. These revolutionaries sabotaged Rome's administrative and military efforts. Consequently, as the salt-laden ships were resting at anchor in harbor, waiting for a caravan to be formed, the rebels would sneak aboard the ships and, under cover of night, mix dirt with the salt. This is what Jesus meant by the *salt losing its savor*. It meant that dirt in the salt compromised its usefulness.

This "unsavory salt" was worthless except to be used as road fill where it was trodden under foot of men.

Alexander explains, "This taught the disciples that they must be pure. They must not allow the things of the world (symbolized by the dirt) to mix with their life of discipleship (symbolized by the salt). To God, these disciples were most precious in His eyes. Hence, they cannot allow themselves to be compromised by the things of the world."

LIGHT OF THE WORLD

Next, Alexander explains what Jesus meant when he identified his disciples as lights of the world, noting that a light on a hill cannot be hidden.

He writes, "Jesus probably pointed to the warning city of Acaba, which could have been seen from the cave, if the cave was located on the north side of the mountain.

"Such square-shaped warning cities were built on the highest points of surrounding areas. These cities existed throughout Herod's kingdom. They were situated so that one warning city could be seen from another. The cities warned of approaching danger. Because a warning city was built on a high point, it could be seen from any place in the area. During the day, the warning cities signaled danger by displaying large red banners. In the days of Herod the Great, the banner of peace was yellow and was always waving above the north wall. If a red banner waved, an enemy had been sighted. Red banners waving above the north and east walls signaled an enemy advancing. Red banners waving above the north, east, and west walls meant that the area was under attack. Red banners waving above all four walls meant that the regional warning city was under attack. If all banners on all walls had been lowered, it meant that the city had fallen.

Night-time warnings were different. If there was peace, a torch would burn above the north wall. If two torches burned on the north wall, an enemy had been sighted. If there were two torches lighted on the north wall and one on the east wall, an enemy was advancing. If two torches were lighted above the north wall, one on the east, and one on the west wall, it meant that the region was under attack. If all torches were extinguished, the city had fallen.

"Jesus was trying to point out that his disciples were like regional warning cities built on hills. The cities' sole purpose was to warn. People had a choice whether to live in the warning city, but once they made the choice, they were obligated to be the region's warning city. Jesus told his disciples that they, too, were warning cities. Their commission was to warn and to guide. They had a choice to accept his invitation to follow him, but once they made that decision they had an obligation. They could not hide their light, nor allow their light to go out. Too many people were looking to them for hope, help, and guidance."

GIVING

Later in the document, Alexander explores Jesus' strong warning to his disciples about the kind of giving intended to gain human acclaim. (See Matthew 6:1-4.) The accepted practice of the day was to announce one's giving of alms to the poor. The Temple offered three collection receptacles. The most prominent collection box, made of solid gold, was set up in the Men's Court. The second most prominent box, plated with silver, was located in the Women's Court. The third box was plain fir-wood and located in the Court of the Gentiles.

Alexander notes, "This wood box is where the widow gave her two mites, inspiring 'Jesus' lesson on humility.' Those who had a small amount to give would place their gift in the wooden box. A larger gift was placed in the silver-plated box. A 'telecaster' would call attention to the gift by clanging cymbals and announcing the amount of the gift and the name of the giver. The largest gift was placed in the gold box. Announcing this gift, the telecaster would shout the name of the giver and the amount given. This announcement was accompanied by a lengthy anthem of trumpets and the crashing of cymbals, followed by great applause of those gathered."

In his lesson, Jesus tells his disciples that those seeking the praise of others have already received their reward. They are hypocrites. Their identity comes from superficial recognition. God will not reward this kind of giving.

Mammon

Alexander emphasizes this point when he focuses on Jesus' statement about mammon.

"*Mammon,*" he writes, "is a Semitic word that was used in the first century BC through the first century AD by Syrian/Greek school masters and teachers when they explained the concept of a 'substitute god.' Jesus uses mammon when he warns disciples that they cannot worship God and a substitute god."

I thought about this for a moment. I had always thought that Jesus was talking about money or wealth when he spoke of mammon, but according to Alexander, Jesus referred to *anything* (or anyone) that takes God's rightful place.

Alexander continues, "Jesus said that his disciples would have to fight this temptation throughout their lives. He wanted them to be totally absorbed in God. They, however, were often absorbed with ministry, the needs of the multitudes, keeping schedules, politics, religious observance, and money.

"Whenever they substituted those things for God, they started to worry. If they kept focused on God, they did not worry because they knew God would take care of them."

After I finished reading Alexander's manuscript, I sat in the library for another hour or so, contemplating his words. I wished I could have read his complete discourse on the Sermon on the Mount.

The Worship of a Leper

After this time of teaching, Jesus and his disciples descend the mount. A great crowd meets them. Among these people is a leper who approaches Jesus, falls before him, and worships him (See Matthew 8:2-4, Mark 1:40-45, and Luke 5:12-15.) This is the first record of Jesus' being worshipped and of his dealing directly with a leper.

Apparently, Jesus receives this adoration without objection. The leper tells Jesus that if he wills, he can heal him. The word translated *wilt* in each Gospel account is the Syriac *sqarui*. It had three meanings: choose, plan, and want to. So, the leper said either, "If you choose," "If it is in your plan," or "If you want to."

Which meaning is correct?

When Jesus touches the leper, his response has been translated in our Bible, "I will; be thou clean." However, this response should have been translated, "I choose to heal you because it is within my plan and I want to do it for you. Be clean." This statement included elements of three different languages Greek, Persian, and Latin.

With these words, the leper is instantly cleansed.

Jesus then instructs the man to avoid telling anyone. Instead, he is to go to the priest and be pronounced clean, as instructed in the Law of Moses. If this event took place in the midst of the crowd, multitudes would have witnessed it. So, why did Jesus caution the leper?

Two possible reasons emerge: First, Jesus wanted the man to follow the rules established by Moses. This would allow the man to be officially welcomed back into society. Second, Jesus did not want the man to tell anyone *how* he had healed him—neither the words he used, nor the technique. Jesus didn't employ traditional Jewish/Pharisaical methods for cleansing a leper. Nor did he use a method approved by the Sadducees and priests. Thus, his warning was meant to avoid controversy.

But this man does not keep quiet. He tells everybody. Thus, Jesus cannot enter any city without creating fanfare and controversy.

It's possible that Jesus' arrival at a city created an uncontrollable mob. Such chaos would have sparked the wrath of the Roman military. Especially in the Galilee, where Pilate had forbidden large assemblies.

Moreover, Jesus' healing probably created resentment and controversy among the cosmopolitan population of the Galilee.

From the time of the leper's healing until mid-winter of AD 27, we find another gap in Jesus' life.

INHERITANCE

The Gospels pick up the story as Jesus and the disciples prepare to cross the Sea of Galilee and sail to Gaulanitis to seek respite from the huge crowds.

On the Sea of Galilee, Jesus and crew are almost capsized by a storm (See Matthew 8:23-26.) Jesus calms the storm, and the voyage continues.

Upon arriving at the other side of the sea, Jesus is confronted by two demoniacs. He heals them both.

I found great information about these events in Avignon, France in another book by Hans von Dohnaniy, the brother-in-law of Dietrich Bonhoeffer. Titled *Inheritances,* this essay collection compares the superiority of a heavenly inheritance to an earthly inheritance. (A secondary focus is Jesus' miraculous calming of the storm on the Sea of Galilee.)

Jesus' teaching on a heavenly inheritance is found in Matthew 8:19-22 and Luke 9:57-62. Von Dohnaniy writes,

> "According to both the Matthew 8 and the Luke 9 setting, it appears that as Jesus and his disciples were preparing to board a ship to cross the lake, he was approached by a scribe who said that he wanted to follow Jesus. Jesus answered, saying that he had no home and that if he wanted to be a disciple, then he, like Jesus, must be willing to give up his home and all that he had. It is not recorded whether the scribe followed him. However, upon hearing this answer, two disciples approached Jesus. Second and 3rd century church tradition says that these two disciples were Jesus' cousins James and John, the sons of Zebedee.
>
> "Zebedee, Jesus' uncle, was very wealthy and owned a fishing business. Apparently, he had become sick or he was elderly, and it was assumed that he would soon die. James and John were both concerned about their inheritance.
>
> "One of them approached Jesus and said he would follow Jesus without question, but he wanted to wait until after his father died so that he could oversee the distribution of Zebedee's estate and ensure

he received his portion. Jesus responded: 'Follow me. Let the dead bury their dead.'

"Jesus' statement is self-explanatory. It means, 'do not let the affairs of this life distract you from your mission.' However, the second portion is more confusing, unless we consider the possibility that the King James translators mistranslated a word. In the KJV, the word used in Jesus' response is *metha*. This is an Aramaic word that means *the dead*. Many of the earliest manuscripts, including the Vulgate, translate this word as matha, an Arabic word that means *the villagers*.

"If this latter translation is correct, Jesus was saying, 'Follow me. Let the people of your father's village bury him.' This seems much more logical."

This was immediately followed by the other brother asking Jesus for permission to go back home and tell the family good-bye. In reality these brothers wanted to go back home to make sure that all was in order. They wanted to follow Jesus, but they also wanted to make sure that they got their share of Zebedee's inheritance.

Jesus answered the brother by saying that no man, having put his hand to the plow and then going back, is worthy of God's kingdom. If you claim that you have given up all for me and then change your mind and choose to become involved in the things of the world, then you are not worthy to be part of my apostolic disciple corps. It is okay to be involved in the things of the world, along with being a follower of me, but if you have claimed you are willing to give up all then you must not turn back."

Jesus had decided to sail with his disciples over the Sea of Galilee to the district of Gaulanitis. While sailing, they fell victim to a storm.

STORMY SEAS

Jesus and his disciples arranged passage on a large Roman troop-carrier ship. These carriers were common on the Sea of Galilee.

We do not know why Jesus booked passage on a Roman troop carrier. It was not customary for a Roman military carrier to allow non-military passengers, but these ships were known to accommodate Roman citizens of some renown.

Thus, Jesus and his disciples met the criteria.

Almost immediately upon setting sail, Jesus went below deck and went to sleep. While he was sleeping, a massive storm blew up.

The word Matthew used to describe this storm was *seismos*, a Greek word that meant *earthquake or earth tempest.*

Some theologians have taught that this upheaval was an unnatural event caused by Satan in an attempt to kill Jesus, but I believe that it was a natural earthquake that took place periodically along the fault line beneath the sea.

Nevertheless, we do know that all on board were terrified. From the disciples' point of view, they could have been suspicious of the cause of this storm—the same type of storm that overcame Jonah when he was running from God. As in Jonah's case, the storm was a direct result of disobedience. The disciples' words betrayed their thoughts. They rushed downstairs and awoke Jesus with the terror-stricken cry, "Don't you care that we perish?"

These disciples' words indicate a deep-down question about whether Jesus had displeased God. Jesus had taught and performed contrary to the law of the Sadducees and Pharisees. He had ministered to Romans and had healed Romans, the oppressors of God's chosen people. He had used pagan history and mythology as allegories. He had collaborated with tax collectors and sinners. Maybe enough was enough. Maybe now he had to pay for his defiance. Perhaps the only hope for survival would be to throw Jesus overboard.

The disciples awakened Jesus, in desperation: "Jesus, help us. Is this your fault? How can you sleep? Do whatever you need to do to save us."

Jesus awakened and asked them, "Why were you afraid to face your fears, questions, and suspicions? Why were you so timid about confronting me so that I can prove to you my authority?"

Jesus was then faced with a dilemma. Of course he could calm the storm, but he had to do it in a way that assured the disciples that their faith was not a mistake. He also had to relate to the Romans, who represented the majority of the ship's occupants. He wanted them to know he was their friend and deliverer as well.

Tacitus records how Julius Caesar was asleep in his troop carrier as he and his troops were making a dangerous crossing from Apollonia to Brindisi. Midway through the crossing, a storm arose. The crew and the troops were convinced that they would sink, so they rushed downstairs and awakened Caesar. He rushed on deck and encouraged the pilot of the ship. He then turned to his troops and encouraged them: "Have no fear. Caesar is with you. Peace be with you. Peace I leave with you."

Soon the storm subsided, and his troops were convinced that their general was a special gift from the gods.

This story was taught as part of Roman history in every school in the Empire. To the Roman soldier, the story had special meaning because it proved that Caesar and his army had been chosen by the gods to bring liberation to the oppressed, freedom to the enslaved, and enlightenment to the uncivilized.

As Jesus stood on the deck in the midst of the raging storm, he stretched out his hands and with a loud voice thundered the same words that all Romans learned, the words used by Julius Caesar. Instantly the storm calmed.

Jesus could not have said anything more comforting for both his disciples and the Romans. For the storm to cease was something that convinced every Roman that Jesus truly was a chosen vessel of the gods. It convinced his disciples that he was indeed a special servant, and possibly the Son of the most high God.

The ship sailed the remainder of the journey in relative peace and calm. Yet nobody who was on board that evening would ever forget the astounding events of that trip.

DEMON-POSSESSED PIGS

After this journey, Jesus and his disciples walked right into another adventure. In von Dohnaniy's words:

"Two demon-possessed men ran out screaming at Jesus.

"In the area of a city called Gergesa, there were three large caves in the side of a mountain, used as a penal colony. The prisoners were former Roman soldiers who had committed murder or other crimes of violence. These men had been declared insane. As two of these demon-possessed men ran out to challenge Jesus, he stood his ground and commanded the demons to come out of the men. The demons asked permission to enter into a herd of pigs grazing in the area. Jesus gave his permission, so the demons departed out of the men and possessed the pigs. The pigs then went wild and ran the two miles or so to the Sea of Galilee, where they ran off the mesa and drowned.

"The event caused a commotion, resulting in city officials confronting Jesus. A portion of the city's livelihood had been destroyed, and the officials feared a response from the Roman military. So they asked Jesus to leave.

However, the local Roman authority, who could have been the commander of the troops who joined Jesus on the journey across the Sea of Galilee, did not reprimand him. The issue was dropped.

We do not know what became of the two criminals. Nor do we know how long Jesus stayed in the area before he and his disciples returned to Capernaum. It is not known if the Roman commander authorized a private return of Jesus and his disciples to Capernaum. Somehow Jesus and his disciples were granted permission to sail back to Capernaum on a Roman troop-transport vessel."

With this, von Dohnaniy ends his exploration, and we have reached the end of Jesus' first *full* year of ministry.

The village of Hallstatt. Salt mines located in the mountains overlooking Hallstatt provided Rome with more than half of her annual salt needs during the reigns of Julius Caesar, Augustus. Tiberius, and Caligula—Austria.

CHAPTER 17

꧁ ꧂

Jesus' Third Year of Ministry

PART 1 — AD 28

WE RESUME THE STORY of Jesus' ministry early in AD 28. AD 28 marks the third year in which Jesus ministered and his second *full* year of ministry.

Jesus has been invited to speak at a great religious conference held in Capernaum. This conference provides the setting for one of Jesus' most memorable healing miracles.

THROUGH THE ROOF

For many years, I thought Jesus healed a paralyzed man who was lowered through the roof of the disciple Peter's house or the home of another disciple. I couldn't have been more wrong.

I discovered the truth while visiting Fustat, a heavily barricaded Coptic Christian area of Cairo, Egypt. I began my research here by touring the Ahmed Ibn Tulun Mosque, claimed by many to be the city's first mosque. From there, I walked to The Church of St. George, then to St. Sergius Church, built over a spot where Joseph, Mary, and Jesus might have stayed after fleeing to Egypt during Herod's murder of the innocents. Then it was on to St. Barbara's Church and the Ben Ezra synagogue, where Jeremiah is alleged to be buried. Then I visited the Coptic Museum. The churches were beautiful, but I enjoyed the museum most.

The museum was simple, but its paintings, sculptures, tapestries, and other artifacts were exquisite. A painting that grabbed my attention depicted a man turning his back on a table full of coins. It was titled *Matthew Forsakes All*.

I was so impressed with the painting that I stopped and studied it for quite a while. After a half hour, I was approached by a museum employee. He asked if he could tell me about the painting. "Please," I said, "tell me everything you know."

"The painting," he said, "is the work of a St. Catherine's Monastery monk named Benjamin. It dates to AD 648. Apparently, Benjamin was so moved by a sermon delivered by John Climacus, (Abbot of the Mount Sinai monastery) that he wanted to capture it in a painting which Benjamin planned to present to Climacus. Before Benjamin finished painting, Climacus died (in AD 649). After the abbot's death, Benjamin left the monastery and lived as a hermit in a cave.

"No one knows exactly when Benjamin died, but in AD 670 his bones were discovered in a cave in the Sinai desert. Also found in the cave were a last will and testament, the finished painting, a handwritten transcript of Climacus's sermon, and a testimonial explaining how the sermon changed his life and inspired the painting.

The painting has been housed in various locations in Egypt since its discovery."

The museum overseer then asked if I was interested in reading Benjamin's testimonial and his transcript of the sermon. My answer should be obvious by now.

I followed him to his office, where he retrieved a volume from near the top of his bookshelf.

We both sat at a table, and the overseer began to read, translating Latin text into English as he went.

Although Benjamin's testimonial was fascinating, I decided not to include it in my notes. However, the record of the John Climacus sermon was so intriguing that I felt obliged to paraphrase it. That paraphrase follows below:

The Scripture Climacus uses is Luke 5:17-29. However, he doesn't quote this Scripture. He merely refers to it occasionally. Apparently, Climacus was a great admirer of Origenes Adamantius (Origen), the head of the Catechetical School in Alexandria, for he cites him and his work liberally.

Climacus sets the stage for the events of the religious conference by quoting directly from Origen's historical records. According to Origen, Emperor Tiberius ordered a great religious conference to be held in Capernaum, in the early part of AD 28. The conference was to be the crowning event of Tiberius's search for The Theophus in Roman Syria.

Similar conferences (27 of them) were held throughout the year in other parts of the eastern Empire. Apparently, Tiberius believed that the true Theophus would reveal himself at one of the conferences.

The conferences typically lasted three days. Representatives from every religion and religious philosophy in the region were invited. There were numerous discussion groups and exchanges of religious ideas. Caesar's Religious Delegation invited six guest speakers to each conference. One of these speakers addressed the attendees at midday. Another addressed them at sundown. Tiberius's Theophus Commission had identified each speaker as a potential Theophus candidate. Jesus, a Jewish rabboni, was invited to address the Capernaum conference.

Origen adds that Jewish religious leaders from all over the Galilee and Judaea attended the conference, along with leaders representing other religions.

More than 70,000 people attended the Capernaum conference, which was held at the huge *Foria Consortium*, a large open-air, marble-column-lined auditorium. At least 30,000 people could stand in the main facility. Another 20,000 could stand under roofed porches. Others could congregate beyond the porches.

Origen claims that Jesus was the only Jewish-born religious leader invited to address the conference. Jesus spoke at midday on the second day and drew the largest audience of all the speakers.

No doubt Jesus was greatly ridiculed and resented for his participation in this conference, although any Jewish leader would have readily accepted the invitation to speak, considering it an honor.

Jesus' participation suggests several things:

- He was well known by the attendees.

- He was well known by the Romans, who had invited him.

- He had been identified by Tiberius' Theophus Commission as a potential Theophus candidate.

- His invitation was approved by Tiberius Caesar. Hence, his ministry and acts were known to Tiberius.

- Of the thousands of accomplished religious leaders in Syria, only one Jew, the non-traditional, non-compromising rabboni Jesus, had been chosen by the venerable Religious Delegation of Caesar to address this conference.

Climacus's sermon includes Origen's description of how a conference speaker addressed attendees:

LUKE 5:18-19
18 And, behold, men brought in a bed a man which was taken with a palsy: and they sought means to bring him in, and to lay him before him.
19 And when they could not find by what way they might bring him in because of the multitude, they went upon the housetop, and let him down through the tiling with his couch into the midst before Jesus.

Jesus is answering questions and discussing issues related to healing when some men arrive, carrying a paralyzed man on a *somorti*. A *somorti* was a couch—a very special couch. It was an extremely expensive Roman commemorative item, the type usually given as a gift by the wealthy Roman aristocracy to recipients who had proven themselves loyal to Caesar or to the Roman cause. Wealthy Romans often arrived at special events on somortis carried by porters. Few non-Romans were wealthy enough to own one. So, the man being carried to Jesus was a Roman, a Roman ally, a Herodian, or a wealthy Roman sympathizer.

When this man's porters arrive at the conference, they try to squeeze through the crowd and get to Jesus. This proves impossible. So they hoist the man on top of the auditorium roof and began to rip a hole in the roof.

According to Climacus, this process probably takes several hours. The porters must create a couch-sized hole in the thick tile roof. Meanwhile, Jesus continues to teach and interact with the crowd. Obviously, the Roman authorities have plenty of time to stop the porters, but they are allowed to continue dismantling the roof. This indicates that the paralyzed man is probably a high-ranking Roman.

At this point in the narrative, Climacus interrupts the story line to interject a personal note regarding his theory of the paralyzed man's identity.

LUCENIUS APPOLONIUS

According to the third century bishop of Neo-Caesarea, Georgory Thaumaturgus, *The Day of Tribute* for the eastern Empire was scheduled to be held in the military city of Nain on August 29. Lucenius Appolonius was to represent the Roman Senate and the Emperor.

Lucenius Apollonius was known to have become paralyzed, but then he made a miraculous recovery while on a trip to Syria. Senator Apollonius and his lavish entourage left Rome in late February AD 28, bound for Capernaum via Caesarea Maritima. The senator was to be the guest of Herod Antipas until the Day of Tribute (August 29), when he and his entourage, along with Herod Antipas and his company, would travel to Nain.

En route Apollonius and his caravan were attacked. The attackers were successfully rebuffed, but the senator took an arrow to the back. The caravan was within a day's sail of Caesarea Maritima, so the senator demanded that they continue on. Upon their arrival in Caesarea Maritima, the senator was treated by the best doctors, but they were unable to help him. He was paralyzed from his neck down. Nevertheless, he insisted on being transported to Capernaum, where he would represent Tiberius at the Day of Tribute ceremonies.

Apollonius arrived days before the religious conference began. Perhaps this paralyzed senator was healed by Jesus. Apparently, Apollonius had heard about this Jesus, a possible Theophus, who was speaking at the conference. He reasoned, Jesus could prove he is a worthy Theophus candidate by healing a paralyzed man.

If Senator Apollonius was the paralyzed man brought to Jesus, that would explain why no one questioned his order for the roof to be torn apart. It might also be why the Pharisees were so angry with Jesus for forgiving the man for his sins.

With this, Climacus returns to the main focus of his sermon.

Let's return to the sermon paraphrase:

If the auditorium Jesus was speaking in was typical of the era's construction, the roof tiles would have been between a half-cubit and a cubit thick (12 to 26 inches).

Thus, after what might have been hours, the men create a hole large enough for the *somorti*. They lower the man through the roof, right in front of Jesus.

Jesus is amazed at the faith demonstrated by these men, but, rather than healing the paralyzed man immediately, Jesus looks at him and says, "Man, your sins are forgiven." The word Jesus uses for *man* is the formal Greek *anthropinos*.

This word was seldom used in normal conversation. It was forbidden by Roman law to be used by any non-Roman when that non-Roman was addressing a Roman. It was a ceremonial term used to describe or address a citizen of high political rank in Rome. In 42 BC, Julius Caesar used the word to describe Cicero. In 23 BC, Augustus Caesar also used the word to describe Cicero. In AD 26, two years earlier, Tiberius Caesar used the word to describe Lucenius Apollonius. In a 100-year period, these are the only three recorded instances of *anthropinos* being used publicly.

Jesus uses the word and tells the man, perhaps Apollonius, that his sins are forgiven.

The scribes and Pharisees who hear this are upset. They consider Jesus' behavior inexcusable because:

• Only God can forgive sin.

- The Pharisees taught that paralysis was a curse from God, as punishment for some appalling sin.

- The man is a high-ranking Roman oppressor. Jesus should curse him, not forgive and heal him.

The scribes and Pharisees dare not criticize Jesus openly, but he knows their thoughts. He knows that they believe paralysis is God's curse. So he asks them, "Which is easier, to heal or to forgive sin?" They do not answer.

Jesus then announces he will do something to prove the Son of Man has the power to forgive sin. He instructs the man to pick up his *somor* (a wool fleece cover placed on the *somorti* to prevent bed sores) and walk.

Now, the term *Son of Man* was reserved for Caesar. However, the term translated *son of man* in the Hebrew language was the phrase *ben-adam* (*ben-nasha* in Aramaic). Both phrases meant *a man born to another man*. The term referred directly to the high priest succession through the line of Levi.

Thus, Jesus implies that he is the ultimate High Priest, *the* Son of Man. To prove his point, he heals the man. The Pharisees taught that only the Messias has the right and the ability to forgive sin, reverse a curse, and heal the cursed in a single action.

Climacus states,

"When Jesus healed the man, he showed that he had been given the ability by God to heal, that he had the authority to reverse a so-called curse imposed by God, and that he had the authority to forgive sin. Even the sin of a hated Roman."

It is certainly understandable, then, why the people who witnessed the miracle were amazed and filled with fear. Did this healing signify that Jesus was the Theophus? Had the *Romans* become God's chosen people? If so, there was no stopping them. Had God's patience with the Jews finally run out?

Fear, excitement, and confusion swept through the crowd, spilling into the streets and moving through the city.

As Jesus left the conference, a huge crowd followed him. As he walked, he passed the office where taxes were collected. Jesus stopped and focused his attention on an exceptionally wealthy tax collector named Matthew, the son of Alphaeus.

MATTHEW THE TAX COLLECTOR

The museum overseer interrupted his reading to address me: "Here, Climacus breaks from his story of Matthew's calling to explain the tax system in which Matthew was involved. My guide informed me that according to Climacus

"The tax district of Capernaum was located on the main trade route connecting the Mediterranean coast with Damascus. It served the Roman province of Syria. Here, Roman taxes were levied and collected on all transit goods. These taxes were collected by Roman military personnel and used for the support of the military. None of these tax revenues benefited the local government or the local economy.

"Capernaum also served as a local customs center where taxes were levied on goods passing through the area.

"All told, the residents of Judaea and the Galilee were paying about half their income and net worth in mandatory taxes and another 10 to 20 percent in 'strongly suggested' taxes. Residents of Judea were paying 60 to 70 percent of their income/net worth in taxes."

Upon completing this explanation, Climacus returns to Matthew's story.

"When Jesus encounters Matthew, this district tax assessor is busy collecting taxes. Matthew was hated, especially by people of his own lineage. Rabbi Gellial called Matthew and his ilk 'despised bloodsucking vermin who fatten themselves on the innocent blood of their fellows.'

"Jesus stops in front of Matthew, in full view of his adoring crowd, and invites him to be one of his disciples.

"Immediately, Matthew follows Jesus. He makes an about-face. He leaves everything. His life, his profession, his wealth, his position, and his promising future.

"Jesus plummets in the eyes of the common people. He tumbles from the highest levels of prestige to the lowest levels of contempt. He is a friend of tax collectors.

"Although God's Word does not tell us *exactly* how the people reacted, one can speculate. The Pharisees and other enemies of Jesus see renewed hope for his demise.

"Those who fear that Jesus is aligning himself with the Romans see those fears increase. Those who see Jesus as a savior who will free them from political and economic oppression see the tide turning, and *not* in their favor.

"Meanwhile, to show his appreciation, for Jesus' invitation, Matthew gives a feast in Jesus' honor.

"Matthew invites all of his friends. (Because Matthew is a tax collector, the only friends he has are Herodians, Roman tax assessors, Roman military personnel, Roman officials, and other tax colleagues. Consequently, the feast is a Roman affair, complete with Roman traditions and grandeur.) Matthew also invites local Pharisees who, in turn, invite some Judean Pharisees. More than 100 guests attend.

"The Pharisees called the Jewish tax collectors *ame ha-erets*, which modern translations have rendered *sinners*. The original word meant, *men of dirt, scum, fool, or reprobate*. The first century AD rabboni Hamel of Hebron asserted that tax collectors who served God's enemies and robbed God's people were garbage."

My overseer friend again interrupted his reading of the sermon to share an important insight. "At this time in history," he said, "the Middle Eastern law of hospitality said that you became a friend for life with whomever you ate. So by accepting Matthew's invitation, Jesus, is saying, 'I choose you as lifelong friends' to everyone at the feast. This incensed the Judean Pharisees."

Then the overseer returned to his reading of the Climacus text (which I will continue to paraphrase):

While Jesus and his disciples dine at the feast, some scribes and Pharisees complain that they should *not* be eating with sinners and tax collectors. They dare not challenge Jesus. He is the guest of honor. Moreover, Jesus has already shown his power and his refusal to play by Pharisaical rules. So, these critics *indirectly* challenge him by grousing to the disciples.

"Why does he eat and commune with tax collectors and sinners?" they protest. The disciples don't answer, but Jesus does.

He explains that healthy people do not need a physician, and that he did not come to call the righteous. Rather, he came to call sinners to repentance. The word translated call means to pull together into a company, as with a Roman army, or to assemble a fighting force. In other words, Jesus says he did not come to raise an army of the righteous; but rather sinners to repentance.

Jesus goes on to rebuke the scribes and Pharisees, comparing their doctrines to his teachings. He tells them that trying to incorporate his teachings with the Pharisees' doctrines is like sewing a piece of unshrunken woolen cloth onto a garment whose cloth had already been shrunk. The doctrines of the Pharisees look fine until they are challenged, like a cloth that is washed, and then allowed to dry in the hot sun. It soon becomes obvious that the old cloth and the new cloth are not compatible.

"With that, John Climacus ends his sermon," the overseer informed me. He then excused himself, as he had a meeting to attend. He left the office, telling me I could stay as long as I wanted. "Just close the door behind you when you leave," he said.

I sat awhile, collecting my thoughts and reviewing my notes. The conference in Capernaum and Jesus' call of Matthew represented a major turning point in his ministry.

HERODIAN'S DAUGHTER

Soon after Matthew's calling, a Herodian arrives at Matthew's house and approaches Jesus. He asks Jesus to raise his daughter from the dead. (See Matthew 9:18-25.)

MATTHEW 9:23-25

23 And when Jesus came into the ruler's house, and saw the minstrels and the people making a noise,

24 He said unto them, Give place: for the maid is not dead, but sleepeth. And they laughed him to scorn.

25 But when the people were put forth, he went in, and took her by the hand, and the maid arose.

At the National Autonomous University of Mexico in Mexico City, I found a unique resource related to this event.

My research at the university unearthed a thin book detailing the history of some Christian artifacts displayed at the 900-year-old monastery Cartuja de Miraflores, located in Borgos, Spain. The book featured drawings of the artifacts along with detailed explanations (written in Spanish, French, and English). The book bore no author, but the university's research staff believed it was created by several Cartuja monks over a period of 200 years during the seventeenth and eighteenth centuries.

The book's index listed 15 artifacts, but the following pages contained drawings of only seven and descriptions of just two.

The subjects of the drawings included:

- A chip of bone allegedly from the thigh of St. Hippolytus.

- A piece of cloth from a shawl said to have been used by Elizabeth to wrap the body of John the Baptist.

- A mud brick, allegedly from the home of Clement.

- A lock of hair from (allegedly) the daughter of the Herodian, whom Jesus raised from the dead.

- A piece of cloth, supposedly from a garment worn by Jairus's daughter when Jesus raised her from the dead.

The surviving descriptions related to the last two artifacts.

According to the book, the incident involving the Herodian's daughter occurred in February of AD 28, while the raising of Jairus's daughter occurred in the winter of AD 30.

The two relics apparently made their first appearance in Spain in 1055. They were possessions of King Ferdinand. The relics disappeared in the 13th century and did not resurface until after the anti-Semitic rebellion in Barcelona (in August of 1391). Fearing for their lives, Barcelona's Jews fled to the royal castle. There they were besieged by an anti-Semitic mob. Many were killed. Following this purge, the relics were found in the ruins of a house used as a synagogue in the Jewish ghetto region of Barcelona. Later, the relics became the property of Ferrant Martinez, an administrator of the diocese of Seville. They remained in Seville until 1519, when they were given to the newly ascended Holy Roman

Emperor, Charles V of Spain. Charles placed the items in the monastery of Cartuja de Miraflores for safekeeping. In 1918 the monastery placed the relics on public display.

Let's take a close look at the events related to these two relics.

In February of AD 28, Jesus and his disciples are invited to a feast at Matthew the tax collector's home. Someone from the House of Herod shows up and interrupts Jesus as he is speaking. As an official of Herod, this man was entitled to show up uninvited at any home. Because the Herodians were considered protectors against anti-Roman sedition, they would often pop up at various gatherings, especially those with many guests. However, this Herodian, upon finding Jesus, worships him. This is remarkable!

According to the monks' book, this Herodian's daughter had already died. She was at the family home, probably receiving the customary lamentations from official mourners.

The Herodian asks Jesus to accompany him to his home, to raise the girl from the dead. This is a first in Jesus' ministry. At the time, it had been 800 years since the last recorded instance of anyone being raised from the dead. There was no reason to believe that Jesus could resurrect someone unless he was The Theophus.

Jesus says that he will go heal the daughter. His disciples follow him.

When Jesus, the Herodian, and the disciples arrive at the Herodian's home, the official mourners are in the midst of their lamentations with flutes squealing and voices wailing. Jesus dismisses the mourners, saying that the girl is not dead but only sleeping. (The mourners, of course, know the girl is dead. She died hours ago.)

The mourners mock Jesus' "ignorance." However, it is important to understand that the word Jesus uses for *sleep* means *soul rest*. The word implies physical death, but not spiritual death. To him, the girl's body was dead, but her soul lived on.

This "soul rest" contradicted Herodian beliefs. Herodians were agnostic, though they did believe that, at death, the soul went to a place of testing and trial at the center of the earth. Here, the soul would be judged by an inquisitor panel, which would determine if the soul was worthy to enter the restful realm of the dead. If not, the soul would be cursed to wander the inner earth in total darkness and isolation.

Jesus isn't bothered by the mourners' scorn. After they leave, he takes the girl's hand. She rises. News of this miracle spreads rapidly.

To the Herodian, this miracle confirms Jesus as The Theophus.

JAIRUS'S DAUGHTER

Now, let's jump ahead to a similar miracle related to the second artifact in this section. The raising of Jairus's daughter, (recorded in Mark chapter 5) occurs in the winter of AD 30. Jesus and his disciples have just returned to Capernaum from Gadara.

Upon this return, Jesus and his disciples are welcomed by a huge crowd of joyous people. Jairus, an overseer in a local synagogue, is among them.

Jairus approaches Jesus sharing the news that his 12-year-old daughter is dying. Jesus does not respond directly. Instead, he and the disciples follow the overseer to his home, followed by a huge crowd.

Along the way, Jesus pauses to heal a woman afflicted by severe bleeding. Meanwhile, a messenger from Jairus's house arrives with tragic news: The girl has died. Jesus speaks to Jairus, telling him not to worry, but to believe. He dismisses all the followers, except Jairus, Peter, James, and John.

According to the monks' book, Jairus needed this encouragement from Jesus, as he probably thought that Jesus' stopping to heal the woman had prevented the group from reaching his daughter in time.

When the group arrives at Jairus's house, the professional mourners have begun their lamenting. Jesus tells them to be quiet, as the girl is only sleeping. (Note the similarity to the earlier episode involving the Herodian's daughter.)

In this case, the word Jesus uses for *sleep* is a Syriac word meaning *soul occupation of space*. The implication is that the girl's soul has not departed.

Again, the mourners scoff. Again, Jesus dismisses them from the home.

Then he leads Jairus, the girl's mother, Peter, James, and John into the room where the girl lies. He takes her by the hand, saying, "*Talithacumi.*" Mark's Gospel translates this command: "*Damsel, I say unto thee, arise.*"

According to the monks, *Talithacumi* is a Chaldean word used by the Babylonian Chaldean magi as part of a post-death incantation spoken over a deceased Babylonian king or a priest. The incantation was intended to give the deceased's soul permission to proceed to the after-life, to the abode of the gods.

These magi believed that a common man automatically entered the after-life within four days of death because he was no threat to the gods. The king and the priests, however, were considered earthly embodiments of the gods. Thus, their souls presented a threat to the gods' divine power. Hence, the need for the incantation. If a dead king or priest did not receive the incantation, his soul would wander throughout the earth, searching for permission to proceed to the after-life.

"*Talithacumi,*" the monks wrote, "actually meant, '*I say to thee, 'Soul, arise and proceed.'* It is obvious that although the Babylonians knew the right words to say, they had no clue how to use them correctly as Jesus did."

The girl responds to Jesus by rising and walking. Jesus tells the onlookers to give her something to eat. (Jesus' insistence that the girl be fed has led some to conclude that the girl was in a diabetic coma. However, Mark's Gospel clearly states that she was dead. Remember that this Gospel was probably written by Jesus' brother James.)

Jesus charges those present to keep quiet about what they have witnessed. Note that Jesus does *not* warn them to keep quiet about the healing itself. He doesn't want them to talk about the *method* used to resurrect the girl. If they did, their safety would be jeopardized given that Jesus' method directly conflicted with the commonly accepted practices of the Jewish religious leaders. And Jairus, as we have learned, was a synagogue leader.

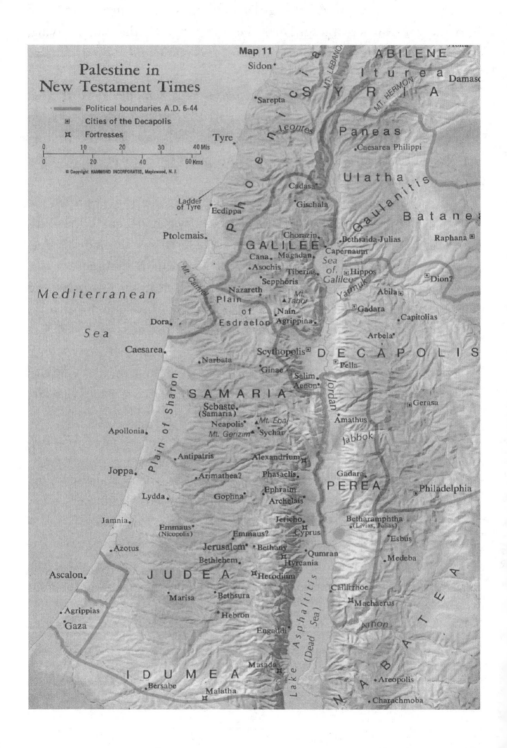

Map 11

Palestine in
New Testament Times

Political boundaries A.D. 6-44
◙ Cities of the Decapolis
⌘ Fortresses

0   10   20   30   40 Mls
0   20   40   60 Kms
© Copyright HAMMOND INCORPORATED, Maplewood, N.J.

CHAPTER 18

❦

Jesus' Third Year of Ministry

PART 2 — AD 28

THE NEXT FEW MONTHS of Jesus' ministry find him traveling throughout the Galilee teaching, preaching, and healing.

In mid-spring of AD 28, Jesus and his disciples leave the Galilee and travel to Jerusalem to celebrate Passover.

In the midst of Passover, a special ceremony, called the Ritual of God's Grace, was conducted annually at the Pool of Bethesda. Jesus and his disciples attend this ceremony.

In the small but extraordinary research library at Jerusalem's Albright Institute, I found documentation substantiating the Gospel of John's account of the events surrounding the Ritual of God's Grace during Passover of AD 28.

The corroborating resource was a book titled *Bethesda*, written in 1819 by Dr. Moshe Weizmann, a Jewish historian. During a trip to Jerusalem, he wrote of the miracles ascribed to the healing attributes of the pool called Bethesda. Many pen-and-ink sketches accompany his writing.

The book's first chapter tells the history of the pool, which dates back to King David's day. Chapter 2 describes Jesus' healing a man at the pool. (The rest of the book was interesting, but not directly related to my research.)

In the paragraphs that follow, I will paraphrase Dr. Weizmann's insights, quoting him directly at times.

THE POOL OF BETHESDA

Dr. Weizmann begins by asserting the most famous miracle related to the Pool of Bethesda had no connection to the pool itself. The event occurs on the High Sabbath before Passover, when Jesus and his disciples arrive at the Pool of Bethesda (or place of mercy) to take part in the *Ritual of God's Grace* ceremony.

Weizmann says this pool, also called the Sheep Pool, was located near the Sheep Gate, the place where blood from burnt sacrificed animals and the corpses of non-burnt animals were discarded during Passover. (Only one of 100 animals killed for sacrifice was actually burned.) The corpses of the other 99 were discarded, through the Sheep Gate, into the Kidron Valley, where the poor collected them for food. The day before Passover, the gate was used as an entrance through which the animals to be sacrificed would filter into the Temple complex after being washed in the Pool of Bethesda. After this washing, the High Priest declared the pool off limits until after the *Ritual of God's Grace.*

"The *Ritual of God's Grace* originated in the days of King David," writes Dr. Weizmann. After David's adultery with Bath-sheba, he discovered that he had been infected with a venereal disease. However, it is doubtful that Bath-sheba gave him the venereal disease. The Talmud records that David contracted the disease as a result of a relationship with a harlot. The Talmud says that Bath-sheba was infected by David, rather than the reverse, and that the Lord healed her of the disease two years later, so that she would be able to conceive and bear Solomon.

"Once a year, at Passover, the priest Zidok would accompany David to the brook of Camiel, where tradition holds that David first saw Bathsheba. This brook was the source of water for the Pool of Bethesda. When they arrived at the brook, Zidok would pour a drink offering of sour wine followed by a cup of blood from a sacrificed lamb mixed with water into the brook as he quoted the *Lament of the Diseased,* (or the 38th Psalm). This ritual became known as the *Ritual of God's Grace.* It was offered in supplication as an act of penance for David's sin of adultery and murder.

"According to the Talmud, Zidok performed this ritual every year. At the *Ritual of God's Grace* ceremony that occurred 38 years after the prophet Samuel's death, Zidok was quoting the 38th Psalm when David was miraculously healed of his venereal disease. (Samuel, you may recall, was the prophet who anointed David as king.)

"After David's healing, the place became known as *Beth-shalom*, the place of peace. It soon became a pilgrimage destination for those suffering from venereal disease.

"Solomon built a small but elegant chapel at the site. There, a priest would administer the *Ritual of God's Grace* to diseased pilgrims. Upon Jerusalem's destruction by Babylon, the chapel was destroyed and the ritual was abandoned.

"In 209 BC, the ritual was reinstated, but the chapel was not rebuilt. This reinstated ritual was performed on behalf of those suffering from venereal diseases, during the Passover celebration *only.*

At the exact site of Solomon's chapel, Herod the Great, rebuilt the pool, which was dubbed The Pool of Bethesda (or *"the pool of peace"*).

In *Bethesda's* second chapter, Weizmann continues:

By the time of Jesus' ministry, the *Ritual of God's Grace* had become one of the Passover celebration's most popular rituals. It had expanded to include not only those who were suffering from venereal disease but also all who were impotent, lame, or diseased. All of them were invited to participate in the *Ritual of God's Grace*, which was administered on the High Sabbath preceding Passover. The lame and the afflicted were brought to the pool complex with hopes of being healed.

The Pool of Bethesda was, in reality, two large rectangular pools, separated by a stone wall. The pool complex included five covered areas leading from the Temple compound level to the pools.

At the dawning of High Sabbath. the High Priest would leave the porch of the Temple's Holy Place, followed by a herd of priests,

Sadducees, and other religious leaders, and proceed to the water, carrying a silver cup filled with a mixture of sour wine, lamb's blood, and water from the Pool of Bethesda. A long blast of trumpets would signal the beginning of the *Ritual of God's Grace*. The High Priest would quote the 38th Psalm as he made his way through the crowd of the afflicted and diseased. Then he would take a small hyssop, dip it into the cup, and scatter drops of the mixture into the crowd. Other priests would identify those on whom a drop of the mixture had fallen—usually about 50 or 60 people. These fortunate souls were told to assemble around the two pools. Temple guards made sure no one touched the water before the appointed time.

Next, the High Priest recited a prayer as he walked the center wall between the two pools. At the wall's midpoint was a hole that emptied into both pools.

When he finished his prayer, the High Priest would shout, "The death has passed. Lord send your angel of healing and mercy and give life to the one chosen to obtain His mercy." The High Priest would then pour the mixture into the hole in the wall, noting which pool received the mixture first. At the first sign of the mixture's bubbling up, the High Priest stirred the pool's water with his hyssop. (King James renders this act "troubling the waters.")

At this point, the priest quoted Psalm 51, returned to the covered pool area, and shouted, "Give mercy Oh Lord." Then he would throw the hyssop into the pool he had stirred. Only the people surrounding that pool were eligible to be healed. Immediately after the hyssop hit the water, the afflicted would rush forward. Only the first one in the water would be healed.

With this stage set, let's return to Passover of AD 28. At the *Ritual of God's Grace,* Jesus meets a man lying ill by the pool.

The King James translators use the word 'infirmity' to describe the man's affliction, likely a venereal disease.

John's Gospel notes that this man has suffered for 38 years. The scribes and Sadducees taught that if a man had a venereal disease for 38 years, he was incurable. The sin that caused the disease was unforgivable.

In John 5:6 Jesus asks the man, who is lying on a *sick bed*, if he wants to be cured. Jesus uses the word *whole*, which is a root of the Persian word *qiami*. It was used to encompass all aspects of life: physical, psychological, emotional, spiritual, and intellectual. Jesus is offering the man healing of body and spirit.

The man responds by saying that he cannot be healed because he cannot get to the water fast enough.

Jesus looks at the man and instructs him to "take up his bed and walk." The man obeys. He is healed. He picks up his bed and walks away.

The Jewish religious leaders' response to the miracle? They reprimand the man for carrying his bed. In essence, they tell him, "You have had all night to carry your bed to this place. It is now too late. It is the High Sabbath and the ritual has begun. You cannot break the law of the Sabbath."

The man protests, "It's not my fault. The man who healed me *told me* to take up my bed."

Later, Jesus finds the man in the Temple, telling him, "You are whole *qiami* (body, soul, and spirit), go and sin no more, or a worse thing will come upon you."

Next, the man finds the religious leaders and tells them that Jesus healed him and told him to pick up his bed and making him break a Sabbath law.

The Jewish leaders become furious at Jesus. To them, Jesus' disregard for the law is punishable by death.

Dr. Weizmann observes,

> "It seems quite strange that the orthodox Jewish religious leaders would be so fanatical regarding the Sabbath considering that until the time of the giving of the law at Mount Sinai, the Sabbath was not a statute by which one must live. However, at the time of Jesus' ministry, the law of the Sabbath was strictly obeyed. During Pompey's siege of Jerusalem the Jews refused to bear arms and defend themselves on the Sabbath. This hastened the Roman victory.
>
> For his part, Jesus did not object to this law, which was instituted by Moses. He objected to the additional restrictions created

by the religious leaders. Faced with the choice of performing a good deed or violating a Sabbath rule, he did not hesitate to do good."

At this point, I should note that some theologians argue that the Pool of Bethesda never existed. Others acknowledge its existence but deny its healing powers. I had doubts myself until I read this small book by Dr. Weizmann. Here was a Jewish historical educator who made no claim of Jesus' divinity. He wouldn't profess belief in anything that couldn't be documented. I am convinced Jesus' miracle at the pool is valid. I am equally certain that John's record of the event is genuine and accurate.

SABBATH

After Passover, Jesus and his disciples stay in the area for several months. During this time, the disciples pick corn (or wheat) and eat it on the Sabbath.

Not surprisingly, the Pharisees confront them for working on the Sabbath. Jesus defends his disciples. He compares their actions to David's eating of the Temple shewbread, implying that his followers are equal to the most honored of all Jewish kings. He then adds that he is *Lord of the Sabbath*. (See Matthew 12:1-8, Mark 2:23-28, and Luke 6:1-5.)

During this time, Jesus heals another man on the Sabbath, a man with a withered hand. Matthew's Gospel implies that this healing occurs on the same Sabbath that the disciples are caught picking corn.

About 20 years into my research, I was introduced to an Arab historian named Dr. Amed Kori, a retired professor of ancient history at the University of Jordan. Dr. Kori invited me to accompany him to the university's Archaeological Museum, where he showed me an ancient scroll depicting Jesus' healing of the man with a withered hand.

As he unrolled the fragile leather scroll, Dr. Kori said it had probably been written by an unknown monk or hermit in the third or fourth century. The scroll's Latin text had been translated into Arabic, Turkish, and English. He gave me a three-ring binder containing the translations.

"You will be surprised at what you will discover in this manuscript," Dr. Kori said, smiling broadly.

I spent a few minutes examining the original scroll before allowing Dr. Kori to return it to storage. Then I focused on the scroll's English translation.

As I read and re-read the translated text, I was amazed at the author's depth of understanding and his knowledge of Roman/Jewish history and Jewish culture.

The translation included Luke's record of the miracle:

LUKE 6:6-11

⁶ And it came to pass also on another sabbath, that he entered into the synagogue and taught: and there was a man whose right hand was withered.

⁷ And the scribes and Pharisees watched him, whether he would heal on the sabbath day ...

⁸ But he knew their thoughts, and said to the man ... Rise up, and stand forth in the midst. And he arose and stood forth.

⁹ Then said Jesus unto them, I will ask you one thing; Is it lawful on the sabbath days to do good, or to do evil? to save life, or to destroy it?

¹⁰ And ... he said unto the man, Stretch forth thy hand. And he did so: and his hand was restored whole as the other.

¹¹ And they were filled with madness; and communed one with another what they might do to Jesus.

Setting the stage for this miracle, the author writes:

"During the reign of Herod the Great, the magnificent Jewish Temple was enhanced and enlarged by Herod, making it one of the great architectural and engineering wonders of the eastern part of the Roman Empire. Herod spared no expense in its construction, hiring the most talented master builders. These master builders numbered 217.

"Construction went smoothly until 5 BC, when Herod had a premonition that he would die before the Temple's construction was completed. Thus, Herod ordered work to continue around the clock, even on the Sabbath.

"Jeshu ben See, Herod's hand-picked construction overseer, gave his approval for the Jewish master stonemasons to work on the Sabbath. Jeshu ben See convinced the High Priest, Joazar, to support the decision. Hence, the stonemasons worked on the Sabbath with the approval of the High Priest, the Sadducees, and the most powerful Jewish religious leaders.

"Herod died in 4 BC, without seeing the Temple completed. Under Archelaus, Herod's successor, ben See maintained his position as supervisor. Within four years, the master stonemasons had completed their part of the work on this first phase of construction.

"Although the stonemasons had completed their first phase portion of work on the Temple itself, Herod's Tower of Antonia had not yet been completed. Roman Governor Coponius demanded that ben See continue the seven-day work week. The overseer then convinced the new High Priest, Elazar, to issue the Sabbath of Weeks proclamation, which allowed the stonemasons to work an additional 126 consecutive Sabbaths.

"When work on the Tower was complete, all of Judea celebrated. The *Sabbath of Weeks* proclamation expired in March AD 2. On the Sabbath following this date, ben See invited all the stonemasons and their families to the Temple complex, where they would be honored."

"However, after the stonemasons were honored, ben See declared, 'Working on the Sabbath is forbidden, according to our law, but working on the Sabbath was permitted so that work on the first phase of the Temple could be completed. For that you will not be punished, but for working on the Sabbath to complete the Tower of Antonia you will be punished.'

"With that, ben See had the right hands of all 217 master stonemasons smashed, instantly destroying their livelihood. This punishment violated the laws of the Sabbath, which forbade any type of cruelty that would ruin a man's livelihood. He then ordered that the eyes of the stonemasons' children be gouged out and that their wives have one eye gouged out and the fingers on their right hands cut off. The wives were also condemned to work in the garbage dump of Gehenna for the rest of their lives. The children were forced to beg on the streets. Their parents would never see them again.

"The stonemasons were ordered to spend every Sabbath in their local synagogue, where their crushed right hands would serve as warnings to anyone who might break the law of the Sabbath. Further, they were not allowed to raise their heads in public or look at anyone for as long as they lived. Like their children, they were to beg for food.

"According to Elazar, this proclamation came directly from God.

"The stonemasons' families would be forgiven of the sin, but the stonemasons would never be forgiven. The stonemasons were forced to live the rest of their lives convinced that God had forsaken them. The proclamation further said that the stonemasons were allowed no conversation with anyone.

"When the Roman authorities were alerted to Jeshu ben See's act of punishment, they tried to stop the cruelty, but, by the time Roman soldiers arrived at the Temple compound, the carnage was over."

According to the scroll, "One of these unfortunate stonemasons was confronted by Jesus, on a Sabbath, as recorded in Luke chapter 6. At the time, almost 30 years had passed since the man's hand had been smashed. It was withered and lifeless. Everyone at the synagogue knew the story behind the man's affliction.

As Jesus assesses the situation, he alludes to the original judgment proclaimed by the High Priest more than 20 years before: *Is it lawful on the Sabbath days to do good, or to do evil? To save life, or to destroy it?* In other words, is it acceptable to do good by building the Temple on the Sabbath, but evil when the same type of work was done on buildings other than the Temple? Is it evil, as Leviticus says, to take away a man's livelihood on any other day except the Sabbath?

Then Jesus heals the man. This healing demonstrates that the man had not sinned, nor was he cursed. He was merely a victim of ruthlessness. According to the scroll, "The healing vividly supported Jesus' message of doing good on the Sabbath, by forgiving sin and healing the physically handicapped.

Jesus has not changed, nor have his desires and priorities changed. Jesus is still more concerned with the individual than he is with the institution. He is still a Savior who can heal the unhealable and forgive the ones who are seemingly unforgivable. Even if people feel that God has forsaken them, Jesus can make a difference in their lives. He still heals the physically damaged. He still re-creates the life that has been destroyed."

After reading these concluding remarks, I sat and talked to Dr. Kori for a while. This was one of the greatest sermons I had ever read, and it was more than 1,700 years old.

Truly, the gospel is timeless. It is alive and relevant, regardless of time, culture, or social system.

THE TWELVE DISCIPLES

In the summer of AD 28, the number of Jesus' close disciples (or apostles) reaches 12.

Dr. Stefus Kenwanjuni, President of Kenya's East Africa School of the Bible, helped me understand the unique character of each of these apostles. I met Dr. Kenwanjuni at a mission's conference in Houston, Texas. We became fast friends, and he shared some invaluable information with me one night over dinner. I will paraphrase this information:

In mid summer of AD 28, while Jesus and his followers were in eastern Judaea, he chose, out of the ranks of hundreds of disciples and followers, the twelve he would call apostles. The event is recorded in Matthew 10:1-15 and Luke 6:13-49. At this time the chosen were commissioned and sent out to minister to the Jewish people in Judaea *only*. This commissioning was the first of two times that twelve were commissioned and sent out.

The second time, the apostles were told to expand their efforts into the Galilee and the Decapolis. Jesus charged them to preach that the kingdom of heaven was at hand, to heal the sick, to cleanse lepers, to cast out demons, and to raise the dead. Even Judas received this power. They were to travel in pairs and stay in the homes of friends.

According to Matthew 10, Mark 3, Luke 6, and Acts 1, the 12 selected on this second occasion were Simon (later called Cephas), Andrew (Simon's brother), brothers James and John (the sons of Zebedee), cousins of Jesus, Philip, Bartholomew (perhaps the nathanael mentioned in John 1:45), Thomas, Matthew (or Levi), James (the son of Alpheus), Thaddeus, Simon the Canaanite, and Judas Iscariot, the only non-Galilean chosen. The Luke 6 and Acts 1 listings of the 12 apostles do not mention Thaddeus. Instead, they name Judas, the son (or brother) of James. (Over the years, Catholic tradition has sought to clarify the difference by saying that Thaddeus was the surname of Judas.)

Kenwanjuni said let's look at each of these twelve men.

Simon was a fisherman from Bethsaida. He was married and lived in Capernaum. Along with his brother Andrew, he was a junior partner in a fishing business owned by Zebedee. Catholic tradition holds that Simon went to Rome and established the first Christian community. Later, he died a martyr under Nero. The Bible, however, implies that Simon went to Babylon, not Rome.

Clement of Alexandria says that Simon's wife was Perpetua, and that they had three children. Perpetua and the children were martyred some time after Simon's death. One questionable Catholic tradition claims that one of Simon's disciples wrote *The Gospel of Mark*, as well as *I and II Peter*. More believable is that Simon personally authored *I and II Peter*, but had no part in *The Gospel of Mark*.

Simon was probably a follower of John the Baptist, before being called by Jesus. Although Catholic tradition claims that Simon was crucified upside down by Nero in Rome, historical documents do not confirm this, but they do confirm that Simon Peter was martyred, probably by crucifixion.

Andrew was Simon's brother, a fisherman and a disciple of John the Baptist. Eusebius reports that Andrew preached in Scythia. Jerome and Theodoret say that he preached in Achaia (Greece). Peter the Hermit says Andrew founded churches in Dalmatia, while Nicephorus says that he preached in Asia Minor and Thrace. Tradition says that Andrew was crucified at Patrae, on an X-shaped cross.

James was one of two sons of Zebedee, Jesus' uncle. (Thus, James was a cousin of Jesus.) James and his brother John were junior partners in Zebedee's fishing business. According to Acts 12:2, Herod Agrippa I (in AD 44) ordered James to be killed. Until the Council of Bishops (AD 1215) it was taught that Herod also killed John at this time. At the council, however, John was proclaimed to have lived until AD 104. He was boiled in oil during the reign of Domitian in AD 95, but he survived the ordeal. He was exiled to the Roman penal colony on the Isle of

Patmos. After his release, he settled in the city of Ephesus, where he died of natural causes.

Like James, John was a cousin of Jesus. As stated earlier, John did not "become" the author of the biblical books attributed to him until the Council of Bishops in AD 1215. The Catholic Church holds that Polycarp, Ignatius, and Papias were disciples of John. (Kenwanjuni believes that John was killed, along with James, by Herod in AD 44.)

Philip was a Greek, and the first apostle to be called by Jesus. In a letter written in AD 190 by Bishop Polycrates, it is noted that Philip, while living in Upper Egypt, wrote his own *Gospel of Jesus*. According to St. Epiphanius, after preaching in Scythia, Galatia, and France, Philip returned to Hierapolis, where he was martyred by crucifixion.

Bartholomew does not appear in the *Gospel of John* unless he is the nathanael confronted by Jesus in John 1. If so, he was introduced to Jesus by his friend Philip. Coptic tradition says that Bartholomew ministered in Arabia. Armenian tradition claims that he preached in India. It is said that Bartholomew was flayed alive and then crucified upside-down in Armenia.

Matthew (often called Levi) was a tax collector. He was probably a mix of Hebrew and Greek. Matthew's authorship of the Gospel bearing his name is based on statements by Bishop Papias, circa the mid-second century. Beyond these statements, no evidence supports this authorship. The Gospel of Matthew was probably written by a second century or late first century Jewish convert, perhaps an early church leader.

This Gospel is far from being chronologically correct, which leads me (Kenwanjuni) to believe that its major purpose was to preserve the teachings, character, and purposes of Jesus and his ministry. Eusebius says that Matthew preached for 15 years in Judea and then traveled east. Ambrose says that Matthew left Jerusalem after the Lord's ascension and went to Persia, where he preached for 40 years. Clement claims that Matthew suffered terribly when he was martyred. Over a period of five days Matthew was methodically dismembered and chopped to pieces with an axe.

Thomas was a Zoroastrian philosopher of Syrian ancestry. He eventually evangelized throughout Persia, Arabia, and India. He was best-known for his skepticism of Jesus' resurrection. An apocryphal Gospel, *The Gospel of Thomas,* has been credited to him. Some biblical scholars contend that this work deserves to be called The Fifth Gospel. I disagree. First-century Christian tradition says that Thomas preached in Parthia, India and Persia. Thomas was martyred in India either by stoning or by being run through with a spear, then with a sword.

James (Yakob) was called "the less" or "the little" because of his physical stature, or because he was a younger brother. It can be argued that this James was Jesus' brother. This relationship is implied by the historian Josephus, as well as by Eusebius of Caesarea, in his 4th-century *History of the Church.* Eusebius refers to him as *"James, the son of Joseph, the husband of Mary, the mother of Jesus the Christ."*

By the eighth century, though, the notion that Jesus was an only child was gaining strength. As a result, the rosters of the apostles in Mark and in Luke were amended and James was called "the son of Alpheus."

If this man was indeed Jesus' brother, he became the leader of the early church in Jerusalem and one of the most authoritative Christians of the first century. Virtually all theologians and Christian historians agree that he authored the book bearing his name. Evidence also suggests he authored *The Gospel of Mark* and the *Letter to the Hebrews.* Hegesippus records that angry scribes and Pharisees threw James off the roof of the Temple in Jerusalem. He was then stoned and bludgeoned with a fuller's club.

Thaddeus (or Jude Thaddeus) is a mystery disciple. Little is known about him. Some say he was the brother of Jesus and James and the author of The Epistle of Jude. Tradition says that he evangelized Persia, Mesopotamia, and Arabia. He is said to have been martyred in Syria.

Judas, the son or brother of James, is also called Thaddeus. (Luke and Acts both refer to this disciple as Judas.) Tradition says that he was a strong Roman sympathizer and that he founded the Church in Edessa. He was martyred in Mesopotamia.

Simon was called the Canaanite (from the Aramaic *qana* which means *daggerman* or *assassin*). These *daggermen* were the radical faction of the Zealots, a Galilean revolutionary group that staged an unsuccessful coup against Roman authority in AD 6. The Zealots were continually harassing the Romans, Herodians, and Sadducees by guerilla warfare. They were known to assassinate Roman sympathizers and Sadducees. Given this Simon's political pedigree, it is shocking that Jesus chose him to be an apostle. Tradition says that Simon the Zealot ministered in Egypt, Cyrene, and Mauritania and that he was crucified in Judaea, during the reign of Domitian.

Judas Iscariot is perhaps the best known of Jesus' disciples. By the 12th century, it was assumed that Judas was a Zealot, but no historical evidence supports this.

According to Luke, after Jesus commissioned these twelve, they all went up a mountain to pray. After prayer, they descended into a valley plain. There, Jesus taught them what has become known as the *Sermon on the Plain*, recorded in Luke 6:13-49. The instructions given to the 12 are very similar to instructions that Jesus gave his six original 'called' disciples in what has become known as *The Sermon on the Mount*.

A CONTROVERSIAL EXORCISM

This brings us to Jesus' memorable healing of a demon-possessed man. (Matthew 12:22-30,43-45; Mark 3:22-27; Luke 11:16-20,24-26)

While researching in the library of an old Norman church called Annunziata dei Catalani, in Messina, Sicily, I found information validating the Gospels' account of this healing.

Most of this church library's manuscripts were from the Middle Ages, and they dealt with church doctrine and politics, but I did find an intriguing letter, written by the prophet Dorotheus the Younger, the founder of the monastery of Khiliokomos.

According to background information provided by the library, Dorotheus the Younger penned this letter to answer a question about the "unforgivable sin." In 1037, a woman named Cunegund wrote to Dorotheus, because she feared her husband, Henry, might have committed this sin.

Dorotheus responded by writing to Cunegund and sending his letter with a servant named Eloi. En route, Eloi was robbed and killed. Among the items taken by the attacker was the letter, which went missing for more than four centuries.

Finally, in 1499 the letter reappeared. An orphan boy found it in a small bookcase (or book closet), which he had stolen while its owner was taking a bath. The boy gave the letter to a teacher named Jerome, who kept the document until his death in 1537. Upon Jerome's death, one of his student teachers, Malchus Marillo, took possession of the letter. Marillo went on to found an orphanage, and somehow the letter found its way into an empty wine bottle, which was sealed with wax. Then the bottle was hidden in a small carved-out hole in the wall of a wine cellar. For some reason, the hole was plastered over. Thus, the letter was forgotten again for hundreds of years.

In 1908, an earthquake cracked the wine cellar's walls, and the wine bottle tumbled from its hiding place and broke, revealing its contents. The letter was then placed in the Sicilian church's manuscript library. In 1958 it was transferred to the manuscript museum.

A large leather-bound book offered the English translation of this letter (originally penned in Latin). I sat at a table and began to take notes: Dorotheus writes:

"After Jesus had sent the 12 out to minister in Judaea, he returned to Capernaum. There, a man who was demon-possessed, manifested by blindness and muteness, was brought to Jesus. Jesus immediately recognized the source of the man's ailment and cast the demon out of the man. The man was immediately healed.

"Shammaite Pharisees from Jerusalem, along with some Temple scribes, witnessed the exorcism, but because Jesus had not followed the accepted practice for exorcism, they dismissed the healing contemptuously. They claimed that the reason Jesus was able to exorcise the demon was that he was allied to Beelzebub, or Baal-zebub. This Baal-zebul was known to the early generations of Canaan dwelling Israelites as the god of excrement and filth.

"By the time of Saul, the Philistines called this god Baal zebub, the god of flies, corruption, and infection. The god's name evolved to Beelzebub, a Greek name. At the time of Jesus' ministry, the god had evolved into a prince (not *the* prince) of devils. Beelzebub commanded demons that specialized in the spread of filth, corruption, disease, and putrefaction. Many people in the Galilee believed that Beelzebub had to be propitiated in order for infection and corruption to be neutralized and for disease to be healed.

"Whether the Pharisees really thought Jesus believed in Beelzebub is arguable, but they knew that many of the Galileans believed in this god. If they could convince people that Jesus exorcised the demon with permission from Beelzebub, they could discredit him, his authority, his methods, his teachings, and his mission.

"Because these Shammaite Pharisees were unfamiliar with the rituals of the cult of Beelzebub, they made fools of themselves when they identified Beelzebub as the prince of devils. Almost any Galilean would know that Beelzebub was not the prince of devils, but rather a prince of the devils.

"The Gospels' account does not claim that these Pharisees openly accused Jesus of casting out the demon through Beelzebub's permission. Rather, Jesus knew their thoughts and intentions. However, I (Dorotheus) imagine that they did accuse Jesus openly.

"After the Pharisees had made fools of themselves, Jesus forced them to wallow in their disgrace by confronting their ineptness right in front of the people who had just witnessed the exorcism.

"Jesus did not confront them from an emotional position, but he confronted them logically. He stated that if a nation, kingdom, or organization was to survive, it could not be divided against itself. He went on to say that the forces of evil could be overcome only by an antithetical power. It was through the power of God that Satan could be overcome. So, to say that evil can overcome evil is blasphemy, because it negates the need for God's intervention."

Dorotheus goes on for sentence after sentence, explaining God's power over evil. Then he returns to the letter's central subject: the unforgivable sin: blasphemy against the Holy Ghost.

THE UNFORGIVABLE SIN

Dorotheus reiterates that the Pharisees accused Jesus of casting out a demon by the authority of the prince of devils. Thus, he notes they *consciously* attributed the work of God to Satan. These Pharisees knew that it was God's power that cast out the demon, but they refused to believe that Jesus could be used by God in such a way.

He then describes the sin of blasphemy against the Holy Ghost.

"This sin is not the rejection of the Spirit's prompting. Nor is it habitual sin. Rather, it is to '*premeditatively, willingly, and knowingly ascribe the work of God the Holy Ghost to the work of Satan.'*

"Dorotheus assures Cunegund that unless her husband had committed a premeditated, willful act like that of the Pharisees, he had not committed the unforgivable sin.

With that, Dorotheus concludes the letter.

DAY OF TRIBUTE

Let's move on now to August 29 of AD 28, an unforgettable Day of Tribute for Senator Lucenius Appolonius and all who witnessed the events.

On this day, Jesus accepts an invitation from a high-ranking Roman military official (possibly Senator Lucenius Appolonius, whom he had healed six months earlier) and travels to the military town of Nain, followed by a large number of supporters and disciples (these did not include the 12 that he had commissioned and sent out, as they were still ministering in Judaea). Here, he raises a widow's son from the dead.

For years I had assumed Nain was a typical Galilean city and that the widow was a typical Jewish resident whose husband had died some time earlier. Now her young son had died too. Tragic circumstances, but not unusual for the times.

When I began to carefully study the Luke 7 account I discovered that things did not mesh with my assumption. Some of the unexplainable things that I discovered were:

- *The gate of the city*: Nain did not have a wall around the city, so how could it have a gate?

- *Much people were with her*: The word translated people by the King James translators was *giiaoi*, which was a Phoenician word that meant *armed horde or military personnel*.

- *Touched the bier*: The word bier was a Latin word that described a ceremonial burial platform on which a sarcophagus would rest. It was used for ceremonial burials only; and ...

- *Young man:* It was a term of respect and honor used by non-military residents when addressing a Roman officer.

None of this made sense if Nain was a simple Galilean city, occupied by some Jewish residents, and this boy was nothing more than a young son of a Jewish widow. There had to be something more.

Then I visited the Archaeological Museum in Thessaloniki, Greece.

In The Thessaloniki Room, one of the museum's 10 rooms, I found an ornamental piece of jewelry, probably intended to be worn as a necklace. Painted on an oval-shaped silver ornament was a representation of a soldier rising from what looked to be a bier, with a man standing nearby, with his arm outstretched. The ornament intrigued me, so I asked one of the museum attendants about it.

The attendant left to retrieve an informational binder. Then he welcomed me to have a seat at a study table and peruse the binder for as long as I wanted.

According to the binder, Jacob of Amphipolis painted the ornament in AD 282 and gave it to Theognostus, head of the Catechetical School in Alexandria, who was gravely ill at the time. The artwork commemorated Theognostus's most-renowned sermon. The sermon's topic: the resurrection of a widow's son in Nain.

The binder included a transcription of this sermon, which I will paraphrase for you:

Nain was a Roman military garrison that spawned a town. It was located in the Galilee, near the northern border of Samaria on the Roman Imperial Military Highway called the via Augusta (the Augustan Way). Non-military traffic (trade and local traffic) was allowed on the highway by paying a large transit toll to the Romans. Non-military travel was not allowed at night or during times of celebration (there was a restriction on pilgrim traffic traveling to Jerusalem for Passover).

The city of Nain and the garrison were located just over one mile east of the Augustan Way. The city was connected to the Augustan Way by a broad straight road. At the point of intersection between the Augustan Way and the road that led to Nain was a military checkpoint and toll station. In the Bible, this checkpoint was called the gate of the city. It was not a gate but rather an inspection station, military checkpoint, and toll station where the non-military traffic would pay a transit toll to use the Augustan Way.

By Jesus' time, Nain served as a headquarters for a portion of the 7th and the 10th Roman Legions and the families of the officers. Non-military people were not allowed into the city unless they were members of an officer's family stationed at Nain, or by special permission of the Roman authorities.

Emperor Tiberius, being a military man, declared that special recognition would be given to Roman soldiers who had been killed in action. Generally, Roman soldiers killed in action were cremated in the region where they were killed. Under Tiberius, every 100th officer who had been killed was honored with an elaborate ceremony and burial. Once a year, the emperor declared a Day of Tribute, wherein an officer was ceremoniously buried and special recognition was given to the Roman soldiers who died while serving in each of four regions: Europe, Africa, Asia and the East.

Each of these four ceremonies was directed by a Roman Senator and featured an imperial burial processional called *Caesar's Processional of Honor*.

These processionals included members of the emperor's personal guard, two priests from Rome, local priests, the officer's family members, hundreds of soldiers, and various dignitaries.

In AD 28, the *Day of Tribute* ceremony in the east was held in Nain under the direction of Senator Lucenius Apollonius, whom Jesus had likely healed of paralysis just months before.

Preparations for the *Day of Tribute* began 30 days before the ceremony. The body of the dead officer was prepared for burial. This included removal of the brain, spinal cord, heart, lungs, tongue, eyes, and liver. These organs were dried in the sun for 20 days. They then were placed in a bronze container in a vinegar/myrrh/honey/salt solution. The Roman Senator who led the processional carried this container. After the organs were removed, the officer's body was drained of blood, and a vinegar and honey solution was pumped through the body. The body was then immersed and soaked in a salt/olive oil/honey/myrrh solution until the night before the ceremony. On this night, the body was washed in vinegar, then in a salt solution, and, finally, in a scented oil-and-wine solution. He was dressed in ceremonial military apparel and placed on a gold silver and brass-inlaid cedar bier, which would be carried by the emperor's guard for burial outside of the city, in a marble sarcophagus.

The processional departed Nain at daybreak.

No one was allowed to speak during the processional. Once it began, it was forbidden for the processional to stop for *any* reason. *No one* was allowed to touch the bier or any member of the processional. To do so brought immediate death.

On the *Day of Tribute,* the section of the *Augustan Way* that passed near Nain would have been closed to all non-military traffic. Thus, it seems that Jesus had received special permission and was leading a large group of dignitaries and friends to Nain to participate in the processional.

According to Luke (7:12), it appears that Jesus and his companions arrived too late to be a part of the processional, for as they neared the gate of the city, the Roman checkpoint where the road to the city met the Augustan Way, the processional was just clearing the checkpoint and was on its way to Scythopolis.

Jesus saw the weeping mother of the dead soldier. Luke 7 says that this woman was a widow. It meant that with the death of her son, the Roman officer, she had no means of support. Overcome by compassion, he literally placed his life on the line. He not only spoke to the woman telling her not to cry, but he also touched the royal bier and stopped the most solemn of all ceremonial processionals. The processional stopped and Jesus spoke to the dead corpse of the Roman officer (a corpse that had not had life for 30 days) and told the officer to arise

Jesus knew about Caesar's Processional of Honor. He knew that the organs of the Roman officer had been removed, dried and placed in the brass container that was being carried by Lucenius Appolonius. Yet, in front of this great crowd of people, 99.9 percent of which were non-Jew-ish and did not believe in the God of the Jews, Jesus told the officer to arise. Instantly, the young man was restored to life. Not only restored to life, but Jesus had re-created blood in place of the vinegar/honey solu-tion, and had created a new heart, lungs, brain and spinal cord, liver, eyes, and tongue so that the soldier was able to sit up and to speak. All of this instantaneously! It is little wonder that the soldiers dared not try to kill Jesus for interfering with the processional.

I finished reading the sermon, filled with a much-deeper appreciation for the magnitude of this miracle. No wonder this sermon was Theognostus's most famous.

Associated with this miracle, Justin Martyr, in his *Dialogue with Trypho*, explained that following Jesus' great miracle of the raising of the widow's son, fear spread over the crowd. The officers and the soldiers in the processional feared greatly what Tiberius would do if he ever found out what had happened. The Roman authorities feared that a man who possessed such great power could be the personality around which a rebellion could be fomented. The handful of Jews who witnessed the event feared because Jesus had the power to raise their Roman enemy from the dead. They could also have feared that Tiberius would punish the Jewish nation, because one of their religious leaders defiled the solemn processional of Caesar. The people feared because they could not understand how the power of creation, and power over death could be given to a man. The non-Roman, non-Jews feared Jesus' apparent good relationship with the Romans. Senator Lucenius Appolonius feared that he would not be able to get back to Rome quickly enough to convince Tiberius that he had truly found that Theophus. He knew that resentment against Jesus by his own religious leaders was growing stronger daily, and he feared that Jesus may be delivered into their hands for chastisement before he had the opportunity to plead Jesus' case before Tiberius. So, among all who had witnessed this great event, fear spread and was all consuming. Thus Jesus was allowed to leave unmolested and unquestioned. His fame most definitely spread throughout Syria.

No wonder the Romans feared him and the Jewish religious leaders hated him. He was a Jewish/Roman enigma that defied all logic and reason.

FEAST OF DEDICATION

After this event, the record of Jesus' life is blank again, until the winter of AD 28.

At a small church called the Chapel of St. Kilian (in Ulm, Germany), I found some intriguing artwork related to this season in Jesus' ministry.

Specifically, I found four large sandstone carvings, each depicting Jesus' participation in a dinner. A monk named Brother Paulus carved these works over a 53-year period from 1411-1464.

As I was the only visitor the morning I visited the chapel, a guide gave me a private lecture on the carvings.

One of the carvings depicts the feast given by Matthew in Jesus' honor. Another portrays the feast at Simon the leper's house. The other two carvings depict two separate Feast of Dedication celebrations. The first carving is a depiction of Zerebell Hazzel, the Chief Pharisee's Feast of Dedication Sabbath meal, to which he invited Jesus. It is recorded in Luke 14:1-24. Jesus healed a man with dropsy and taught a parable based on a wedding feast. It took place in December of AD 30. The second carving is the one that commemorates a Feast of Dedication Sabbath meal that was held in Capernaum two years earlier in December of AD 28. Jesus was invited to this feast by Simon the Pharisee. It is recorded in Luke 7:39-50 and 11:37-53.

As the guide told the story of the Feast of Dedication carvings, he repeatedly used the phrase, "Contrary to Pope Gregory the Great."

After he finished speaking, I had to ask him about this deliberate repetition.

"Sir, you are very observant," he responded. "I did make that statement on purpose, but few ever catch the emphasis, or care enough to ask me. You are one of a small handful who have questioned me in the nine years I have worked here. I am Dr. Karl Richenburger, a retired professor of Roman History from the University of Cologne, and I will be pleased to explain what I mean by the statement."

My guide sat down on a bench and welcomed me to join him. I asked if I could take notes. He did not object. He offered a wealth of information on all four carvings, but I will focus on the second one he showed me. Its subject: a Feast of Dedication Sabbath meal held in Capernaum in December of AD 28. Dr. Richenburger began and I will paraphrase:

Originally, the celebration was confined to Jerusalem and lasted two days, However, by the time of Jesus' birth, the celebration had expanded to eight days and was celebrated by Jews throughout Judaea, the Decapolis, and the Galilee but not in Capernaum. For years, Herod Antipas feared that the celebration could lead to a riot in Capernaum, so it was not until AD 27 that he allowed this city to participate.

The Feast of Dedication or Hanukkah, was celebrated annually on the 25th day of the month of Kislev (some time between the middle and end of December). The Sabbath meal was served on the final day of the seven-day celebration. The celebration commemorated the 164 BC re-consecration of the Temple in Jerusalem by the Maccabees. This was six and a half years after the Temple's Holy Place was destroyed by the Syrian king, Antiochus Epiphanes. Antiochus offered 400 boiled pigs on the altar of sacrifice (Jewish tradition claims that this is the abomination of desolation prophesied by Daniel). When Herod later rebuilt the Temple, he enlarged the altar to offer one hundred sheep at a time. When the Romans destroyed Herod's Temple in AD 70, they used the altar stones to construct the Temple of Ventanius, dedicated to the god Mars and the goddess Venus.

For the first seven days and seven nights of the celebration, the celebrants were abandoned to continuous uninhibited drinking, feasting and wild joyous celebration. The seven straight nights of dusk to dawn celebration were sometimes called the Feast of Lights, because the celebrants would carry torches as they celebrated in the streets and moved from place to place. Only on the Sabbath, at the conclusion of the celebration, were there peaceful and solemn festivities.

In Judaea, everyone could participate, Jew and non-Jew alike. In Capernaum, Herod insisted that:

- All who planned to be involved in the celebration must register their intent well in advance of the celebration.

- The participants be Jewish born.

- The celebration participants pay a celebration fee to Herod's tax representative equal to seven days' wages of a common laborer.

- Anyone sponsoring a Sabbath meal had to pay an additional tax equal to one day's wage for every guest invited to the meal.

- In the year AD 20, the High Priest gave special permission for the Feast of Dedication celebrants to eat the concluding

Sabbath meal with entertainment during the feast, providing the cooking, serving, and entertaining was done by non-Jews, and as long as the sponsors complied with the following:

- Invite at least one stranger, Jew or non-Jew, to the meal.

- Invite at least one guest whom the sponsor considered to be an enemy.

- Open their doors to the poor, the afflicted, and outcast so they could partake of the leftover food.

- Respect the viewpoint and the values of all those present by encouraging their verbal interaction and not ridiculing or belittling the guests' viewpoint, if it happened to be different from the sponsor's. The common method used by a sponsor to show displeasure or disagreement was to remain silent. If the sponsor remained silent, even though he was addressed directly by a guest, it indicated that the sponsor vehemently disagreed, to the point of repugnance, with the guest's point of view.

In Jerusalem, these stipulations were strictly honored, but during the three celebrations that were allowed to be held in Capernaum, the sponsors may or may not have chosen to honor them.

At the time of this celebration, very few Pharisees, and only three inner circle Shammaite Pharisees, called the Galilee their home, One of these Shammaite Pharisees was Simon, who invited Jesus. We know that Simon held Jesus in utter contempt, so he could have invited him as the token enemy.

At this meal, couches were arranged in a U shape around a central serving area. The guests reclined on couches, while servants offered food and drink.

While Jesus and the other guests were dining, a woman, whom Simon identified as a *sinner*, knelt at the foot of Jesus' couch. She began to cry, letting the tears fall on Jesus' feet. She then used her long hair to dry the tears. Next, she anointed his feet with an expensive ointment called spikenard. Jesus allowed this show of adoration without objection. However, Simon and the other Pharisees, scribes, and lawyers present were appalled.

While Luke's Gospel (Luke 7:36-50, Luke 11:37-53) doesn't identify this woman, Pope Gregory identifies her as Mary of Magdala.

Now, the word translated sinner by the King James Bible is *eros caritus*. The word was used by the local non-Jewish Greco-Roman residents to identify:

- A consecrated follower of the goddess Venus. Some of these women were religious prostitutes.

- An entertainer, usually a dancer, who performed at celebrations. Afterwards, many of these performers made themselves available for intimate encounters with men.

- A courtesan, usually an unmarried female between the ages of 12 and 35 who was paid by a household to provide sexual favors to the master of the house, as well as to other adult male household members. She lived in the home and was considered to be an essential member of the household. Any children she bore were considered children of the household and heirs of the estate, just as the children of the official wives. She was expected to serve food and drink at feasts and to entertain the guests by dancing or playing musical instruments. The Pharisees justified the practice by referring to Abraham's relationship with Hagar.

- A widowed or single woman with no way to support herself. She would wander the streets in search of something that she could sell to buy food or shelter. Such a woman was allowed to enter a house during the Sabbath meal of the Feast of Dedication and gather all the leftover bread and meat she could carry.

As for the woman who approached Jesus, she will probably remain a mystery, but this much is certain: She was not Mary of Magdala or Mary of Bethany, contrary to what Gregory the Great thought.

The ointment the woman used to anoint Jesus' feet was probably spikenard, a precious spice gum ointment. Pure spikenard gum comes from the Indus River Valley in Pakistan and India. Approximately every eight to ten years, the Indus River floods. As the waters recede, a bacterium that lives in the water attaches itself to, and attacks the roots of, the rare river valley grass that grows predominately on the western and northern shoreline of the river. To fight off the attack of the bacteria, the roots of the grass secrete a sticky gum, spikenard gum. This gum dries and hardens into brownish transparent crystals. The crystals are gathered and melted in oil to form a sticky spikenard suave (about 150 pounds of crystals are needed to make less than a quart of suave). To make pourable spikenard ointment, a small amount of spikenard oil is mixed with myrrh oil, frankincense oil, olive oil, spiced water, and clove oil. The mixture is then permanently sealed in either an alabaster box or an alabaster cask.

Spikenard was the world's rarest and most expensive ointment; perhaps this might still be true. It would take about 30 ounces of pure spikenard gum per 18,000 gallons of solution to make a vat of Faberge's Brute cologne.

The alabaster box or cask containing an ounce or less of spikenard anointing ointment carried a price tag equal to twice the annual salary of the average laborer.

In Jesus' time, only the exceptionally rich could afford to purchase a container of spikenard. Sometimes, a very wealthy man would give a container to a woman as a sign of his undying love.

This alabaster box of spikenard was a gift so precious that it would be passed down from generation to generation, generally from mother to daughter. If a woman's loved one died, she might show her love by breaking open the box and pouring its contents on the deceased.

We don't know how the woman in this story came to possess her spikenard but we can deduce that it was the most precious possession she would ever own. She chose to use it on Jesus.

Simon and the others present didn't speak their contempt, but Jesus knew what they were thinking. This prompted him to tell them a parable about a creditor who forgave the debts of two debtors. One owed an amount equal to 500 days wages. The other owed an amount equal to 50 days of wages. Jesus then asked Simon which debtor loved the creditor more. Simon's answer: the one with the largest debt. Jesus then used Simon's answer to condemn him, noting that he didn't afford Jesus even the minimum amount of respect indicated by the law of hospitality. Yet, the "sinner woman" offered her most precious possession.

Next, Jesus forgave the woman all her sins. This caused quite a stir. Those present believed that only God could forgive sin.

This led to a verbal duel between Jesus, the Pharisees and scribes. One of the scribes (scribes interpret the law), stood up and asked Jesus to explain to him what he had to do to inherit eternal life. Because Jesus had just forgiven this woman and, in essence, assured her of eternal life, this lawyer was curious. He believed that he had done many good deeds in his quest to become worthy of eternal life, so he was curious which *one* was the key.

Jesus told him to answer his own question. The lawyer quoted Deuteronomy 6:5 and Leviticus 19:18. *Love the Lord your God with your whole heart, soul, strength, and mind; and to love your neighbor as yourself.* Jesus told him that he was correct and that if he kept those commandments, he would inherit eternal life. But the lawyer, wanting to put Jesus on the spot, asked, *If I am to love my neighbor, then who is my neighbor?* This question led to Jesus' parable of the Good Samaritan.

THE GOOD SAMARITAN

Irenaeus (who was appointed Bishop of Lyons in AD 177) asserts that this parable was based on an actual event. In AD 15, Valerius Gratus was appointed Roman Procurator of Judaea. Gratus then appointed a nephew, Marcus Antonius Sparitacus, to the post of Minister of Taxation for Judaea.

Because of Gratus's ruthlessness and his extreme tax-collection methods, opposition against his rule began to build. Finally, in AD 21, rebels from Samaria and the Judaean wilderness area formed an alliance. The rebels aimed to block the flow of tax revenues into Gratus's (and, ultimately, Rome's) coffers. Thus, Rome would be upset with Gratus and replace him with a more compassionate procurator.

Marcus Antonius Sparitacus employed more than 100 customs officers, charged with ensuring all tax revenues were collected and safely delivered to Caesarea Maritima. But by AD 21, the rebels had killed at least 60 customs officers, intercepting the tax revenues and bringing Gratus's administration to his knees.

In September of AD 21, a large tax receipt shipment was due to arrive in Caesarea. The shipment was to be accompanied by 100 Roman soldiers. However, Gratus hatched an alternative plan: He would use the guarded shipment as a decoy. The real tax receipts would be carried by the lone Marcus Antonius Sparitacus, who would take the Jerusalem to Jericho to Antipatris to Caesarea Maritima highway, at night. He would reach his destination one day after the decoy contingent arrived. At first, all went as planned. Sparitacus left Jerusalem and headed for Jericho on the night after the decoy procession's departure.

As expected, the decoy procession was attacked by rebels. The ensuing fight was devastating to the attackers. More than half of them were killed or taken prisoner. The survivors escaped to the hills of Samaria. Meanwhile, Sparitacus was well on his way to Jericho.

However, the lone traveler became uneasy about being alone on the dark highway. When he was only an hour's ride from Jericho, he decided to hide the tax revenues before proceeding to Jericho, where he would spend the night. He planned to retrieve the funds the next day and complete his journey.

But shortly after Sparitacus finished hiding the money, a pack of robbers attacked him. The attackers took his personal funds and stripped him of his expensive Roman clothing. Then they beat him unconscious and left him lying by the roadside.

As morning dawned, a priest from Jerusalem, en route to Jericho, saw the wounded man. However, because the victim looked to be Roman, the priest declined to help.

Later, a Levite (who were commanded by God to show mercy to their enemies and comfort the injured) encountered Sparitacus. However, the Levite did the same thing as the priest before him. He passed by on the other side of the road.

The third man to encounter Sparitacus was a Samaritan silk merchant named Narciss, who was on his way to Jerusalem to appeal to the regional customs officer about reducing his tax burden. Narciss had no love for the Romans. They had nearly taxed his business into bankruptcy. He stopped and cared for the Roman's wounds and took him to an inn in Jericho.

The Samaritan paid for the Roman's lodging and medical care. He told the innkeeper that upon his return from Jerusalem, he would settle up any additional expenses.

It is vital to understand that it took Sparitacus a year to recover from his wounds. Throughout the process, Narciss continued to cover all expenses. He didn't know the victim's social standing or occupation—only that he was a Roman.

Meanwhile, the recovering Sparitacus sent a message to his uncle: He was alive and the tax revenues were, presumably, still safely hidden.

Gratus sent officers to retrieve the funds. However, he left his nephew in Jericho, to continue healing. He made sure the officers didn't reveal his nephew's identity or government position.

Finally, Sparitacus was well enough to travel. He invited Narciss to Caesarea, saying that he wanted to repay the generosity. Narciss reluctantly accepted.

Upon their arrival in Caesarea, Marcus revealed his true identity, and he told his uncle about Narciss's hospitality and generosity. Gratus responded by declaring that Narciss's tax load would be relieved for life. Also he pledged that his entire court would buy all its silk from the good Samaritan. Narciss was shocked to learn the victim's full identity, and he was flabbergasted to reap such rewards simply for showing kindness and compassion.

Thus, Jesus used a *true* story to answer the lawyer's question. "Who was the true neighbor?" he then asked. The lawyer answered correctly.

Jesus acknowledges the correct response, but he asserts that the lawyer must do likewise if he intends to fulfill the commandment to love one's neighbor as oneself.

With that, my guide ended his explanation.

We chatted for a few minutes before being interrupted by some tour visitors. I thanked the guide for his time, and then left him to serve his next customers.

The Plain of Esdraelop, located in the Galilee. The Roman military town of Nain was located on the slopes of the hill, in the far background. The ruins of the Augustan Way military highway are located at the foot of the hill, running left to right—Israel.

CHAPTER 19

❧❧

Jesus' Fourth Year of Ministry

PART 1 — AD 29

THE YEAR AD 29 DAWNS with John the Baptist's disciples burying his body after his execution. This event profoundly affected Jesus and his disciples.

By far the most thorough corroboration of the Gospel record of John's arrest, imprisonment, and death came from a Muslim acquaintance of mine: Dr. Mehmet Abassi, who was teaching at Hadassah College in Jerusalem when I had a chance to interview him in his home. Dr. Abassi is probably the Middle East's foremost expert on the history of ancient Moab and Ammon, but his passion is John the Baptist lore. I paraphrse Dr. Abassi:

In AD 27, Herod Antipas left his magnificent palace in Capernaum and installed himself in his garrison at Amathus, where John the Baptist had been ministering, to lead a war against his father-in-law, Aretas, king of the Nabateans (ancient people of Jordan).

ZOLLERAS

The reason behind the war? Antipas had married Aretas's 12 year old daughter, Zolleras, in AD 13. She was called 'the bent beauty' because of a disease that left her bent over, yet she was considered one of the most beautiful women in the world.

While in Rome to visit his brother Philip, Antipas fell in love with Philip's wife, Herodias. This development resulted in the two brothers working out a deal. Philip became even wealthier, and Herodias accompanied Antipas back to the Galilee.

CAESAR'S DAY OF AMNESTY

Herod Antipas and Herodias were married. Antipas *then* divorced Zolleras, paying Aretas the equivalent of $2 million in gold as compensation for divorcing his daughter. The gold didn't placate Aretas, who pledged to take the matter up with Caesar. Antipas, in turn, became furious with Aretas, saying that he would not be threatened for doing as he pleased with the two women. Herod raised an army and planned to attack Aretas. Rome remained neutral in the matter, claiming that the whole thing was below the Empire's dignity.

Shortly after Antipas set up military headquarters in Amathus, John the Baptist began to criticize publicly the intra-family military conflict and the reason behind it: Antipas's adulterous private life. Antipas responded by arresting John and throwing him in an underground dungeon, a fortress called Machaerus.

Zolleras, who admired John, lived at Machaerus for half of each year while awaiting a Nabatean divorce (neither she nor her father honored Antipas' divorce that he obtained in Rome). However, she probably had no knowledge that John the Baptist had been arrested, as she was visiting her father in Nabatea at the time.

When Zolleras returned to Machaerus and discovered that John was in prison, she ordered that he could have unlimited visits from his disciples and that he was to be fed from her own table. Zolleras, of course, supported John's condemnation of Herod Antipas for divorcing her and marrying Herodias. She did not have authority to free him, but she did begin a process of appeals to secure his release.

In December of AD 28, Zolleras received word that her appeal succeeded. John's prison sentence had been reversed. He would be released on *Caesar's Day of Amnesty*, January 9 (AD 29.) Believing John was safe, the relieved Zolleras traveled back to Nabatea to be with her father.

"In her absence, Herod took up residence at Machaerus, where he planned to celebrate his birthday (January 3).

"Please understand," Dr. Abassi explained, "Antipas did *not* hate John, despite the vocal criticism. He admired the itinerant preacher and his faithfulness to his principles. He often visited John in prison. He would also grant John temporary release so the two could visit in the ruler's chambers. But Herodias hated John. She wanted him dead.

"Roman law dictated that four times during the year (January 9, April 9, July 9, and October 9), individuals whose convictions had been overturned by the Roman High Court could be released. The dates were called *Caesar's Day of Amnesty*. On January 9 of AD 29, just six days after Antipas's birthday, John the Baptist would be a free man.

"Herodias, fearing that John would return to his public excoriation of her and Antipas, hatched a plot. She tried to convince her husband that there was just cause for an appeal of the High Court's decision. After all, John was a threat to Roman stability. Herod resisted her.

"But Herodias would not be denied. She hastily developed another plan. She believed that if John was executed while still under Herod's guardianship, her husband could successfully defend his actions before a Roman tribunal. She unleashed her plot during Herod Antipas's birthday celebration.

"During the last few days of AD 28 and the first few days of AD 29, Herodias threw a 10-day birthday celebration. According to some historians, more than 3,000 attended this drunken orgy.

On January 3, Herodias scheduled Salome, her daughter, to dance for Herod. Salome, age 17 or 18, was a radiant young woman with beauty so dazzling that Lucian of Antioch, a 3rd-century teacher, gushed, 'The grandeur of the sun, the moon, and the stars all pale in their luster when compared to the splendor of her beauty.'

"Antipas was also captivated by her beauty. He was involved in a licentious relationship with the girl, with Herodias's knowledge and consent.

"The dance that Herodias told Salome to perform was what the Greeks called The Dance of Eros, and what the Romans called The Dance of the Seven Veils.

"The dancer began, dressed in a variety of seven translucent silken veils or scarves. The music began with a soft and gentle melody. Then the music gradually built to a frenzied epicurean climax. During the build-up from a soft love melody to a pulsating sensuous apogee, the dancer's movements would gradually transform from a fluid promenade into an arousing voluptuous gyration. She peeled off veil after veil until all that remained between her and total nudity was one transparent gold silk veil.

"So moved was the drunken and sensuously disconcerted Antipas that he offered Salome up to half his kingdom as a reward. (Anticipating this response, Herodias had prompted Salome to ask for the head of John the Baptist.)

"Antipas was taken off-guard by the request, but, for the sake of his reputation, he ordered John the Baptist to be beheaded that night.

"Tradition says that Herod dismissed his birthday celebration after John was beheaded and that he sank into a long period of depression. This depression, which was probably evident when he questioned Jesus before his crucifixion (more than two years later), would eventually cause Antipas to divorce Herodias.

"Ten years later (AD 39), Herod Antipas was denounced to Emperor Gaius (Caligula) by his nephew Agrippa, as a treasonous plotter against Rome. This resulted in Herod being deposed from his Tetrarchy and exiled. He died in exile.

"Zolleras was influential in the reversal of the charges brought against John the Baptist and she was instrumental in convincing Gaius, the Roman presiding judge who ruled on behalf of John the Baptist, to bring charges against Herod before the Roman Senate. Some historians consider that Zolleras was in love with Gaius and wanted to marry him, but for political reasons and to form a non-aggressive political alliance, her father chose to give her in marriage to Antipas, Gaius, in turn, settled for Zolleras's half-sister.

"Incidentally, tradition holds that Herodias' hatred for John the Baptist was so intense that she took his head and had it pickled in vinegar and honey and placed in a brass container. She slept with the container by her bed for the rest of her life.

"Shortly after John's death, Salome, not able to live with the coldness and ruthlessness of her mother, returned to her stepfather, Philip, in Rome. In AD 30, she married Philip, who was at least 35 years her senior."

At this point, Dr. Abassi paused and walked to a room at the back of his house. He returned a few minutes later, carrying a small file. As he sat down he said, "In 1690, a scroll was discovered at the University of Istanbul. It was titled *Herod Antipas, Defense Before the Roman Senate in Regard to the Execution of John the Baptist.* The scroll was Antipas's answer to charges of insubordination, disregard for the High Court of Rome's authority, and unauthorized declaration of war upon an ally of Rome (Aretas). The charges were brought by Gaius, the Presiding Judge of the High Court Tribunal that declared John's innocence and mandated his release."

Dr. Abassi continued, "Apparently, the charges were brought before the Senate after Herod's defeat at the hands of Aretas. The charges were supported by Agrippa, a junior magistrate, and by Pontius Pilate, who seemed to be more concerned about Jesus of Nazareth and about how Herod's actions could potentially cause a revolt than whether John had been an innocent victim of a vengeful woman. If you want, I will read to you Herod's defense, according to the scroll."

HEROD'S DEFENSE FOR BEHEADING JOHN

I asked him to continue, so he began to read Herod's defense.

"The letter starts with an introduction:

To Tiberius Augustus and the Senate of Rome.

My Noble Lords, Greetings:

It is true, as my enemy asserts, that I was defeated in battle with Aretas, King of Arabia, but I was forced to fight when unprepared for the conflict. I either had to fight or have the country overrun by this wicked people. It is true I was defeated, but it was owing to the want of time and better preparation. Aretas came upon me without warning. Notwithstanding my defeat, his army was so crippled that he had to withdraw his forces from the field, and has not been able to rally them since. So our country was saved from the devastation of a foreign foe.

I understand that the superstitious Jews say my defeat was for my wickedness in the death of John, called Baptist. My understanding of the God of the Jews is that He does not chastise the innocent for the crimes of the guilty. What did my actions have to do with the poor, suffering soldier?

The facts in the case are about as follows: John, called Baptist, had set a new mode of religion altogether different from the Jewish religion, teaching baptism instead of circumcision; which had been the belief and custom of the Jews in all ages past.

Now, John had no authority from his God to do what he was doing. All his authority came from his words, saying, 'He that sent me to baptize is true' but he could not tell who *He* was. Then his going into the desert land: the Jewish God had by their myth spoken to Solomon to build the finest temple of its time in all of this part of the world, and made promises that whoever came to that temple with an offering and a sacrifice, his prayers should be heard and answered. This temple had been the place of the Jews meeting for hundreds of years.

Now see the difference:

- John had no authority to preach a different religious practice.

- He changed the place of worship to their God from the Temple to the desert.

- He changed the doctrines of Abraham and Moses.

- He changed the mode of application from circumcision to baptism.

These troubles on the Jewish mind were very heavy, and gave such respected religious leaders as Hilderium, Shammai, Hillel, and others great concern. And no matter, for in their judgment it was vacating the temple of religious worship; it was blocking the road to heaven, and driving the poor and unsuspecting to ruin, as well as destroying the whole nation. So it was, by their request that it was better to execute one to save many from a worse fate. And this is the true reason for the deed, and not to please the whim of a dancing girl, as you have heard.

As to what Pontius Pilate says in regard to my cowardice and disobedience in the case of Jesus from Nazareth, I will say in my own defense: I was informed by all the Jews that this was the same Jesus that my father aimed to destroy in his infancy; for I have in my father's private writings and accounts of his life, showing that when the report was circulated of ambassadors inquiring where was he that was born King of the Jews, he called together the Hillel and Shammai schools, and demanded the reading of their sacred scrolls; that it was he that was to be born in Bethlehem of Judea, as read and interpreted by Hillel. So when my father learned that there had been a birth of a male child in Bethlehem two years previous, under strange circumstances, he had the male children slain that were near his age. Afterward he learned that his (Jesus') father and mother had taken him and fled to safety. For this attempt to uphold the Roman authority in the land of Judea, the Jews in Bethlehem and Judea have not ceased to curse him to this day, and yet the Caesars have done a thousand times worse things, and done them thousands of times, and it was all well. As to Pilate's saying that Jesus was a Galilean, he is mistaken. Jesus was born in Bethlehem of Judea, as the records show. As the adopted son of his Roman Senator uncle, he traveled from place to place. He learned soothe-saying while with his Rabban in Egypt and in Persia and the Indias, to perfection, in so much that the Theophus Commission of Ambassadors of Tiberius convinced themselves that he was he (The Theophus). So this is my defense.

I submit it for your consideration of the facts. I pray for clemency.
Antipater of the House of Herod
Tetrarch Servant of Augustus and Rome"

"Whether the scroll is authentic or not we probably will never know," Dr. Abassi confessed. "We do know that Antipas did escape the wrath of the Roman Senate. According to almost all historical references, Antipas talked his way out of this crisis by casting doubt upon the validity of the accusations and by shifting blame from himself to other circumstances, just as the scroll's text seems to indicate.

"It seems fairly obvious that Zolleras was influential in the reversal of the charges brought against John the Baptist and that she played a part in convincing the judge Caius, to bring charges against Herod before the Roman Senate. Caius, by the way, was Zolleras's brother-in-law, having married her half-sister.

"I will conclude by noting that after suffering his military defeat, Herod returned to Capernaum. It was during this time that Zolleras was healed of her disease. Many claimed that Jesus healed her."

As Dr. Abassi stopped speaking, and I reviewed my notes, I could not help but wonder at Dr. Abassi's admiration for John and his high regard for Jesus. Although Muslim, he seemed to honor Jesus as much as most Christians and more than some.

Like Zolleras and so many others, Jesus was profoundly affected by the news of John the Baptist's death.

Perhaps sensing that this tragedy was the beginning of severe persecution against those who proclaimed the good news. Jesus led his 12 disciples into a desert place.

WALK ON WATER

After this retreat, the Gospel record on Jesus is silent until the spring of AD 29, when he takes his disciples to a fish-drying-field near the city of Tiberias. Jesus performs the miraculous feeding of the 5,000 (See Matthew 14:13-21; Mark 6:33-44; Luke 9:10-17; and John 6:1-14.) Immediately after feeding the crowd, Jesus insisted his disciples get into a boat and go ahead of him to Bethsaida.

Halfway into the disciples' trip to Bethsaida, a storm erupts and threatens to capsize them. Jesus sees that the rowers are struggling with the oars. He approaches the boat, walking on the water (Matthew 14:24-33; Mark 6:47-51).

Some theologians believe this to be Jesus' greatest miracle, and I learned more about it at the University of Glasgow in Scotland, where I met Dr. Christian Craddi, a physicist at the university. For years, Dr. Craddi had been studying the unnatural and unexplainable phenomenon of Jesus walking on water.

Central to Dr. Craddi's efforts was a manuscript featuring a sermon written in 448 by Peter Chrysologus, Archbishop of Ravenna. (For 10 years, Dr. Craddi had poured over an Old English draft of the sermon, which was originally rendered in Latin.) The sermon's topic: *Jesus' walking on water.*

As I talked with Dr. Craddi, he informed me that Jesus performed this miracle at least twice, and perhaps three times.

Then he began to list all the 'unnatural' aspects connected to the miracle. All told, he spent about three hours with me, during which I took page after page of notes. Below, I will provide a paraphrase of this discourse. Occasionally, I will quote Dr. Craddi as well.

After the feeding of the 5,000, the disciples buy passage on a large passenger ship. They are probably afraid to return to Herod's jurisdiction, given what has recently happened to John the Baptist. Also, they recently endured a near-capsizing the last time they sailed.

After the ship departs, Jesus walks up into the mountains about 10 miles west of the seashore to pray.

At about three in the morning, halfway into the disciples' journey, a furious storm hits. Jesus is more than 10 miles away, but, somehow, he sees the ship in peril.

For Dr. Craddi, this is the first of many mysteries about this story. How could Jesus, deep in prayer and meditation, and many miles away from the ship that was in the middle of the sea, know what was happening in the midst of the Sea of Galilee? It was three o'clock in the morning and pitch-black, with the wind blowing hard and the waves breaking so violently that the huge passenger ship was being tossed back and forth. Surely, a man who could predict the bubbling up of the sea could have foreseen how violent this storm would have been? Rather than warning them, Jesus had insisted that they got in the boat.

If Jesus could have run the distance that separated him from the boat at a rate of 10 minutes a mile, it would take about two and a half hours. Yet the Bible says that he came to them *walking* on the sea. Of all Jesus' miracles, this is the one that most strongly defies logic.

How did Jesus *see* the boat about a dozen miles away in the middle of the black sea? There were dozens of vessels on the lake. How did he know which one was occupied by his disciples?

As we ponder these questions, let's return to my paraphrase of the Archbishop Chrysologus sermon:

When Jesus' disciples see him walking on the water, they are terrified. According to a popular legend of the day, the ghost of a drowned seafarer would appear to a sailor who was destined to die by shipwreck. This ghost would appear, walking on the water, just moments before the shipwreck.

Thus, the disciples assume two things:

- Jesus has recently drowned, and his ghost has arrived to warn them of a similar fate.

- That fate was imminent.

No wonder they are terrified.

Dr. Craddi notes that the miracle of walking on water was unprecedented. Food-multiplying had been done by both Elijah and Elisha. Both of these Old Testament figures had raised people from the dead. Healings of various kinds had been recorded on many occasions. Moses and Elijah dramatically illustrated power over the forces of nature.

Some scientists believe that our universe has six *in* holes and six *out* holes. Gravity is zero here. However, these holes have never been known to move. They are stationary. Jesus walked on the water. Thus, the neutralizing (or reversal) of gravity had to be *mobile*.

We have no historical precedence for such a miracle, nor do we have a logical explanation. Not once, but twice in this one setting, did the miracle occur. Not only did Jesus come to them walking on the water, but Simon Peter walked to Jesus on the water and they both walked on the water back to the ship. Since there is no logical explanation on how the miracle was accomplished, the miracle can only reside in the realm of the miraculous phenomena that can neither be explained nor comprehended.

After this statement, Dr. Craddi paused for a few minutes, appearing to organize his thoughts. Then he continued to educate me: "Even if Jesus had used ley lines to accomplish the miracle, ley lines do not move. Nor is there record of them ever neutralizing the laws of gravity. Yes, Jesus somehow used these geophysical forces to accomplish his miracle. *How* he did this is a mystery that will probably never be revealed."

I allowed myself to imagine the scene for a few moments. I was pulled back to the present when I heard Dr. Craddi saying, "and what was amazing about Jesus' character is that he did not chastise Peter for sinking in the water when he looked around him and saw the storm raging. All he said to Peter was 'Did you doubt? Why did you not believe that I could come to you regardless of circumstances?' This was truly amazing! Jesus was an amazing man! He and Peter then walked back to the ship together. The moment they boarded ship, the stormed ceased. I have always wondered why, if Jesus had the power to still the storm, he didn't do it *before* he walked on the water to meet the disciples? Why not calm the water, so that he and Peter could walk back to the ship together, without taking the chance that Peter would panic again? Why did he subject his disciples to such danger if he had the power to calm the storm?"

Then Dr. Craddi added, "I am not a religious man, but, if I chose to be a religious man, I would choose to believe in a deity that had the power to reverse and bewilder the universal laws of nature."

I was gratified to hear these words. I regretted that my being lost in thought had caused me to miss some of Dr. Craddi's discourse, but I sensed that I had caught the most important part.

Dr. Craddi then began to formulate his opinions concerning the second record of Jesus walking on the water, recorded in John 6. After they had been blown off-course as a result of the first storm when Jesus and Peter walked on the water, they landed in Gennesaret, on the northeast shore of the Sea of Galilee, or the Lake of Gennesaret, so called by the Roman military. Gennesaret was a fertile plain that extended from the sea to about three miles inland. It served as an unofficial buffer zone between the northern settlements and the Roman military lands.

There, Jesus preached, healed, and performed many miracles. Because of these miracles, the people wanted to take him by force and proclaim him as their king. Upon discovering their intentions, Jesus left the people and went up into a mountain alone to pray. As evening approached, Jesus' disciples went down to the lakeshore to wait for his return. He did not send them; they went on their own.

As it became dark, the disciples went on board a small ship, not as large as the one they had arrived on. The ship was probably a 20-passenger boat. There were several of these boats on the Sea of Galilee and they were used for short excursions. The boats were about 25 to 30 feet long, approximately 10 feet wide with a small sleeping and storage quarters underneath the main deck. On the boat, they waited for Jesus to join them, so they could sail back to Capernaum. When nightfall overtook them, Jesus still had not joined them. Of course he never said that he was going to join them and he never told them that he wanted to sail back to Capernaum. They just assumed that to be the logical course of action.

With the fall of the blackness of night, the wind of another storm began to howl. Before long, the wind reached critical proportions. To prevent damage to the small ship or harm to the occupants, the disciples released the ship from dock and rowed out into the open water of the lake about two or three miles from shore, supposing that Jesus would understand that they had to leave and that he should meet them in Capernaum later on.

As they struggled with the ship in the midst of the lake, in the middle of the steadily increasing treacherous storm, Jesus came to them, again walking on the water. When they saw Jesus this time, they were more surprised than they were frightened. Surely this could not happen twice in a lifetime, much less twice within a time span of two days? But twice it was!

As soon as Jesus entered the little ship, the storm ceased and the boat and all of its occupants were instantly and immediately transported about three miles to the northern shore. In an instant of time, quicker than a micro-millionth of a second, the boat and its entire load and occupants were transported more than three miles. One moment they were in the middle of the sea and the next they were at shore.

"How?" asked Dr. Craddi. "Only God knows. Again, it happened within less than a week of one another. Truly what manner of man was this Jesus?"

I agreed, and felt it unnecessary to add anything to Dr. Craddi's obvious admiration of Jesus.

TWO BY TWO

The mid-summer of AD 29 finds Jesus selecting his 12 apostles (from the ranks of the disciples) and sending them out to minister.

After commissioning the 12 apostles, Jesus appoints another 70 disciples and sends them out to minister, in like manner with the apostles.

He sends them out two by two, with the power to teach, preach, heal, and cast out demons.

When the 12 return to Nazareth, in late October or early November, Jesus leads them to Caesarea Philippi, about 30 miles north of the Sea of Galilee. Here, Peter confesses that Jesus is the Christ, the Son of the Living God. This is also the site of Jesus' transfiguration. (See Matthew 16:13-25, Mark 8:27-29, and Luke 9:18-27.)

Dr. Pil Klensberg, the Historical Research Director of the Kunstmuseum in Bern, Switzerland, introduced me to documentation validating this portion of the Gospel records.

During my visit, Dr. Klensberg told me that the museum had few resources related to my quest. "However," he said, "I have a private document in my office. It might interest you. It relates to Peter's confession at Caesarea Philippi."

I followed Dr. Klensberg to his office, where he pulled a slim volume from his bookshelf.

The document featured 10 leather leaves, bound between two oak boards. The author was Peter of Tarentaise (circa 1147), the Archbishop of Tarentaise. Accompanying the author's words was an ink sketch depicting the apostle Peter kneeling before Jesus. The sketch was titled *Peter's Confession*. Dr. Klensberg didn't share how he came to possess this twelfth century work, but he had translated it (from the French) and researched it for 32 years.

I sensed that he was very protective of the document, so I didn't ask to study it. Instead, I requested that he read it to me and share what his research had revealed while I took notes. The following is a paraphrase of those notes:

CAESAREA PHILIPPI

In late October or early November of AD 29, after the return to the Nazareth area of the 70 (or 72) that Jesus had sent out, he and his disciples left the area and traveled about 30 miles north of the Sea of Galilee to the Roman city of Caesarea Philippi, located in the Roman district of Panias. It should be noted that Jesus had returned to Nazareth after he had helped his mother settle his father Joseph's estate.

Caesarea Philippi was originally called Paneus, the city of Pan (the Greek/Roman god of wild animals, material goods, and sexual pleasure). The city had been built around the Paneion grotto, the source of the Jordan River.

It was an open city in which everything (except murder and stealing), was tolerated. Romans from all over the Empire would vacation in Caesarea Philippi to indulge in every licentious and sexual pleasure. The entire city was completely given over to gross decadence and sexual debauchery.

It was also a religiously tolerant city and residents worshipped virtually every god, goddess, or religious philosophy known both in the Empire and beyond. Caesarea Philippi's nick-name was The Gates of Hades (Hell) (Matthew 16:13).

When Jesus arrived in Caesarea Philippi, the Festival of Pan was in full swing. It lasted from the time of the first changing of the leaves (October or November) until the winter solstice in December. The festival was a mourning festival in which the observers would celebrate the death and hibernation of the Earth. Winter, or the time of non-productivity and non-reproduction, was set aside for blatant homosexual activity and bestiality; Pan had supposedly decreed that reproduction was not advisable during the time of non-production. The first sign of spring signaled the beginning of a carnival atmosphere of fun, music, love games, and wild heterosexual activity.

I'm sure that the disciples were bewildered why Jesus had brought them to such a wicked and perverted city. They did not stay in the city itself but they were close enough to the city so that the point could be driven home.

Sometime after they had arrived in the area of Caesarea Philippi, Jesus went away by himself to pray (Luke 9:18). After a while, his disciples came to him as he was praying. As they gathered around him, Jesus asked them, "Whom do men say that I am?

They tell him that some believe he is John the Baptist reincarnated. Others say Elijah. (At this time, most Jews believed in reincarnation.)

Then Jesus asks the disciples, "Who do you think I am?" Peter answers quickly: "Thou art the Christ; the Son of the Living God."

So, for the first time, Jesus is recognized for who he truly is—the Messias, the Christ; and Messiah, the Son of the Living God. In one person.

Jesus acknowledges that Peter could not have known this truth unless God revealed it to him. Jesus then addresses him as Peter ("Simon meaning a reed was transformed into Peter, meaning a chip of granite rock"). Jesus is saying that Peter is a chip off the rock. Jesus is The Rock, upon which the church will be built.

Then, Jesus (probably) points at Caesarea Philippi, saying, "And the gates of hell will not prevail against it (the church)." The statement was one that indicated an offensive position. The church will become so powerful that its members will literally storm the gates of hell (symbolized by Caesarea Philippi) and lay siege. They will be successful against every defense thrown up by the forces of evil. As a powerful conquering offensive force, the church was destined to break the defenses of hell and bring the forces of evil to its knees.

Jesus said that he has given Peter (and the other disciples) "the keys of the kingdom," making them heirs to and owners of the kingdom.

The one who had the keys, owned the kingdom. Because they were heirs and owners, anything they loosed on Earth would be loosed in heaven and anything they bound on Earth would be bound in heaven.

In other words, because they had the authority of the kingdom that Jesus had given them, and authority that they would continue to possess as long as they remained in him and he (Jesus) in them, they had the right to dictate when, where, how, how much, and under what circumstances, now and in the future, warfare with the forces of evil would take place.

Dr. Klensberg interjected, "Unfortunately for the most part that authority was abdicated to the organized church, with its dogmas, doctrines, and ritualistic traditions. The church in turn crushed it and allowed it to drain away until all that was left was an empty shell that looked impressive on the outside, but inside it was, and still is, empty and filled with void and/or corruption."

After proclaiming the disciples' new authority, Jesus shares that he will someday have to face death. At this point, Peter, perhaps prideful because of what he has just heard, "corrects" Jesus.

Jesus responds by rebuking Peter and the spirit that is influencing him. Apparently, Peter's pride has made him vulnerable to Satanic corruption. Jesus told Peter to get under authority and maintain the proper line of priority authority; and he demanded of Satan that he quit trying to detour the plan of God, because it is going to happen, regardless of how he (Satan) might fight against it or try to disrupt its fulfillment.

Jesus then explains what the disciples must do if they truly want to be *born again*. He implies that they must die emotionally, psychologically, and spiritually. Only after this excruciatingly painful process can they be *born again*.

After Dr. Klensberg finished reading his private document to me, I spent another hour asking him questions about Jesus and about Peter, who was soon to see Jesus in a unique light.

The city of Jerusalem, looking west from the Mount of Olives—Israel.

CHAPTER 20

❦

Jesus' Fourth Year of Ministry

PART 2 — AD 29

SIX DAYS AFTER Peter's confession, Jesus takes Peter, James, and John to Mount Hermon, where he will be transfigured. (See Matthew 16:28-17:16, Mark 9:1-13, and Luke 9:28-36.) My investigation of this event in Jesus' life brought me to Turkey.

At the Church of St. George in Istanbul, I found a four-leaf manuscript written by Peter Damian in 1066 while he was in seclusion at Fonte Avellana. In 1046, Damian had supported Emperor Henry III's decision to depose two Popes and replace them with one of his own choosing. Twenty years later, Damian found himself forced to defend his support of Henry.

In a letter to Pope Gregory VII, Damian not only defended his position, but also used the transfiguration of Jesus to support his position. Although most of the portion that explained the historical event of

Jesus' transfiguration was intact, the portion dealing with his use of the transfiguration story as part of his defense had long since disintegrated

The manuscript, written in Latin, was displayed in a small room next to St. George's main church building. Near the display was a leather-bound notebook with English and Greek translations, along with some background on the letter's history.

TRANSFIGURATION

The letter begins, "Eight days after Jesus and his 12 appointed disciples had arrived in Caesarea Philippi (Luke 9:28), and six days after Peter's confession, Peter, James, and John accompanied Jesus to Mount Hermon. This was the first time that Jesus had separated these three from the others.

"Mount Hermon rose 8,500 feet above the city of Caesarea Philippi. The top portion was covered with snow most of the year." Damian continued, "Although Matthew says that they went into the mountain, it is not known whether they went into a cave on the mountain, were under some other place of protection, or were on top of the mountain. Wherever it was, Jesus was transfigured and was launched into the last phase of his ministry.

"Matthew used the Greek word *metamorphoo*; it meant *to change form*. Did Jesus transform from flesh into spirit? Did he change from mortal to immortal and then back to mortal? Jesus was transfigured in front of them.

"Suddenly, appeared the forms of Moses and Elijah. The two men began to talk to the transfigured, or glorified, Jesus. According to Luke they talked to Jesus about his death and his ministry from that time until his death. Moses probably represented the Law and the Old Covenant and the promise of salvation; Elijah probably represented the prophets. Both gave honor and subservience to the glorified Jesus.

"Peter spoke to Jesus, telling him that it was good that they were there to witness this event. Was he implying that no one would believe this unless they saw it with their own eyes, or that they deserved to be there because they were most qualified to be witness to these events.

"Peter then suggested that he build three sanctuary shelters. There were hundreds of sanctuary shelters scattered around the mountain, the grotto at the foot of the mountain and other places throughout the city of Caesarea Philippi that were dedicated to various gods, goddesses, holy men, or philosophers, and were used in the worship of those to whom they were dedicated.

"Peter was suggesting that all three were worthy to be worshipped. Although Peter had said that Jesus was the Christ, the Son of the Living God, he perhaps did not completely believe it. If he had then he would have been convinced that Jesus alone was the only Christ, and the one and only Son of God, who stands alone (not with Moses and Elijah) as worthy of honor and worship. In Peter's eyes, Jesus' position was most assuredly exalted, but it was exalted to a level equal to Moses and Elijah, not necessarily above them, but certainly equal to them.

"While Peter was speaking, a bright cloud engulfed them. Then out of the cloud a voice spoke (whether the voice was the personality of God the Father or God the Holy Spirit or both, we do not know; but the voice belonged to God). It said that Jesus was His beloved son, in whom He was pleased and that they should listen to him (Jesus only). The disciples fell face down on the ground, terrified. This indicated that Moses and Elijah or the Law and the prophets were not equal to Jesus; but rather Jesus, his ministry, and his teachings were superior to both. He and he alone is the one who must be served, listened to, followed, exalted, and honored. All else and all others are subject to him, even the Law and the prophets.

"His instructions concerning discipleship (Matthew 16:24-25) are true and must be followed if one is truly to be a disciple of Jesus. That discipleship is more than a conversion experience or more than just being saved. It is a born again experience. Born again is not the same as conversion. Born again implies that there must be a death, and then a rebirth. It is a step beyond conversion. It is a step that leads to discipleship."

I paused as I read this portion of Damian's letter and thought about what Peter was saying. This was the second time that Jesus had talked about the born again experience. The first time he was addressing Nicodemus. This second time he was addressing three of his disciples. Apart from these two occasions, expressed by the writings of two different men at two different times in history, I had never heard this concept before. (The Irish teacher Malachy O'More in 1140, concerning

Nicodemus, and the second by Peter Damian in 1066, concerning the disciples at the transfiguration.) So, knowing that I could not resolve the issue right then, I returned to Damian's letter.

"The disciples remained face down on the ground terrified, until Jesus came and touched them and told them not to be afraid. When they looked up, Jesus was back to normal, Moses and Elijah were gone, and the cloud and the voice had left.

"Whether immediately or the next day, they descend the mountain. Jesus told them not to tell anyone what they had seen until after he was raised from the dead. This was probably because Jesus did not want this experience to be identified with the mythological stories of the prevalent pagan religions. In Egyptian mythology, Osiris was transfigured and in his transfigured state Isis spoke to him, telling him that he was chosen to live again. In Babylonian mythology, Marduk was transfigured; and in Phoenician mythology, Baal was transfigured. All three were worshipped and honored in Caesarea Philippi. What better way for Jesus to be discredited than for his disciples to begin spreading the news that he had been transfigured in Caesarea Philippi?

"As they descended the mountain the disciples asked Jesus that if he was the Son of God, Messias, The Christ, Messiah why did the teachers of the Law say that Elijah must first come before Messiah is revealed?

"The traditional eschatology teachings of the teachers of the Law, based on Malachi (4:5-6), said that Elijah must appear before the coming of Messiah. If Jesus was that one who was to come, why had not Elijah come first?

"Jesus answered that Elijah had come before him, but the religious leaders did not recognize him; instead they consented to and even applauded his death. The disciples realized that Jesus was referring to John the Baptist, and that he would die just as John the Baptist had died. Just as John was not recognized by the teachers of the Law, so Jesus would not be recognized by them. Instead they would consent to and applaud his death.

"Jesus and the three disciples returned to where they had left the others. There is no record that the three told the others what had happened on the mountain, until after Jesus had resurrected."

At this point, Damian transitions to his personal defense. Unfortunately, much of this part of the letter had disintegrated. Thus, there is a gap between the defense and the conclusion of the letter, which portrays Jesus' healing of a boy in Caesarea Philippi. Damian writes:

"Some time after the transfiguration, Jesus and his disciples walked to Caesarea Philippi. As they approached the city, a man ran out to meet him. The man had a son whom the town's people classified as lunatic.

"The man pleaded for Jesus to heal the boy, saying that he had asked some of his disciples to heal him, but they could not. The traditional belief at that time was that a person with the type of disease from which the boy was suffering was lunatic, or 'moon-struck.' The moon caused the disease; thus the disease usually manifested itself during a full moon.

"Caesarea Philippi was known to be the center for those who suffered lunacy. It was the madness capital of the Empire. With open promiscuity and a welcome to all pagan worship it was not surprising.

"Jesus healed the boy. Knowing that the moon had not caused the problems, Jesus did not rebuke the moon. Instead, he cast out the demon that caused the disease.

"Jesus then used the disciples' inability to heal the boy as an opportunity to teach a lesson on faith.

"Pointing to a mountain covered with mustard plants, Jesus used the mustard plant and the mustard seed as an example of faith: Against overwhelming odds, the mustard plant becomes 'victorious' over the mountain, through patience, confidence, determination, discipline, and consistency."

At this point, the manuscript deteriorated again. It would have been interesting to see how Damian used events from Jesus' life to defend himself, but his historical corroboration of the Gospel records was far more useful to me.

LIKE A CHILD

In late November or early December, after healing the moon-struck boy, Jesus and his disciples head toward the Galilee.

As they travel, Jesus warns his disciples that he will be delivered into the hands of those who consider him their enemy. Then he will die.

Sometime after the return to the Galilee, Jesus' disciples come to him with a question: Which of them is most important to the kingdom of heaven? (See Matthew 18:1-34 and Mark 9:33-37.)

Jesus responds by summoning a child. He places the child in the middle of the group and teaches the disciples a lesson on who is *truly* greatest.

I discovered a unique painting that depicts this event at The Cinquantenaire Museum of Art and History in Brussels, Belgium.

When I arrived at this museum, I spent at least two hours studying the various rooms featuring Roman, Greek, and Byzantine art, before coming to the Renaissance section. One of the rooms in the Renaissance section was the Taormina Room, which featured the 40-year efforts of Sulius of Taormina, who, in the fourteenth century, produced a series of 11 paintings that he titled *Daily Life of the Saviour*. Each of the 11 paintings depicts Jesus in a different daily activity. Below each painting was a brief description.

I spent quite some time studying the paintings. One, however, held special interest for me. It shows Jesus sitting on a stone wall and holding a young child on his lap. Four other children gather around him. In the background, four men look on contemptuously. The painting was titled *Becoming Ta*.

I did not understand the title, but I assumed that it had something to do with Jesus blessing the little children. I asked a security guard if I could review the painting's reference notes in the museum's research library.

"I'll give you one hour," he told me.

Fortunately, the museum's research information was cataloged in chronological order. I found an 1851 essay on the *Ta* painting, written by a Dr. Jensin Ginozzi.

Dr. Ginozzi cites the entire 18th chapter of Matthew in his essay, but he notes that the first three verses will be his focal point. I quote:

MATTHEW 18:1-3

¹ At the same time came the disciples unto Jesus, saying, Who is the greatest in the kingdom of heaven?

² And Jesus called a little child unto him, and set him in the midst of them,

³ And said, Verily I say unto you, Except ye be converted, and become as little children, ye shall not enter into the kingdom of heaven.

"The 12 disciples were disputing among themselves about who was the greatest asset to the kingdom. Jesus did not address their argument directly. Instead he took a little child and sat the child in the middle of the group. The child was a *ta* child. The KJV translated this word to mean 'little,' but the Greek word *ta* means handicapped or mentally afflicted. It was usually used to describe a 'Down syndrome' child or one who was mentally handicapped.

"In the Greek-culture-dominated Galilee, *ta* children were usually responsible for washing the feet of visitors or guests before they entered a home. Because this job was considered one of the most demeaning of all tasks, it was given to a ta child.

"Ta children were also used as 'sex slaves' by many brothels that catered to upper-class residents. Because the ta children were outcasts, no one really cared.

"The name tasim, meaning one cursed with ta, was used to describe a person who was despised. In the Galilee, it was the most insulting name one could be called."

According to Ginozzi, Jesus, through his actions and statement, was teaching his disciples to give up all pride, all worldly loyalties, and all selfish desires. Instead, they should be willing to be despised by the world. Only then could they be truly great, on earth or in heaven.

Jesus wanted his disciples to go to the furthest extreme to avoid offending another person, especially one who was spiritually, mentally, or physically handicapped. This was a lesson contrary to Pharisees' teachings. (Pharisees taught that ta children had been rejected and cursed by God. They had no worth. Whatever was said or done to them was acceptable.)

Dr. Ginozzi concluded his essay by explaining how confusing such a teaching must have been to the disciples. For generations, the Pharisees' viewpoint on ta children had been dominant. After all, these religious leaders proclaimed that their doctrine came directly from God.

Thus, the disciples faced a dilemma: Jesus and the Pharisees couldn't both be right.

I was fascinated by Dr. Ginozzi's essay. I had never heard this explanation about ta children. His words held up logically. His description of the event matched Jesus' character and Dr. Ginozzi had significant documentation to support his points. At the very least, his perspective merited serious thought and thorough investigation.

The Eastern Gate in Jerusalem. It is through this gate that tradition says the Messiah will enter Jerusalem at the end of the age—Israel.

CHAPTER 21

𝔧𝔬𝔮

Jesus' Fifth Year of Ministry

PART 1 — AD 30

THE NEXT MAJOR EVENT in Jesus' life occurs in the winter months of AD 30: the raising of Jairus's daughter. (We covered this miracle back in Chapter 17.)

Not long after this miracle, scribes and Pharisees (who have come to Capernaum from Jerusalem) approach Jesus and complain to him about his disciples' failure to wash their hands before eating.

This washing involved scooping water into one's cupped hands, then letting it run down the arms and drip off the elbows. This was a 100-year-old tradition established by the scribes in Jerusalem.

The scribes contended that this tradition was equal to or even more important than the words of the prophets and the Law. A first century BC Jewish Rabban said, "The words of the elders as recorded by the scribes is more weightier than the words of the prophets." His assertion was only one of several such contentions recorded in the Talmuds.

Thus, dishonoring the traditional washing of hands was inexcusable.

Jesus does not make excuses for his disciples. Instead, he turns the tables on the complainers. He tells them they are just as guilty as his disciples because they choose to keep the traditions of the elders, but they dishonor God's commandments.

He warns those assembled to be careful about what the Pharisees are teaching because they are like the blind leading the blind. Eating with unwashed hands does not defile the spirit, he says, but listening to the Pharisees' teachings does defile.

Soon after this confrontation, Jesus feels the need to leave Capernaum and go someplace where he and his disciples can rest without being a public spectacle or without having to minister to multitudes. He decides to bring them to an unexpected place: Phoenicia (specifically, the cities of Tyre and Sidon (Matthew 15:21-29; Mark 7:24-31).

A SYROPHENICIAN WOMAN

While researching at Illinois' Wheaton College, I was studying one of the many biographies written about Charles Albert Blanchard, which the college library housed in a school-history section (Blanchard was president of Wheaton College for 43 years.) While reading, I found a statement that intrigued me. It said that when Blanchard was pastor of the Chicago Avenue Church (from 1891 to 1893), he wrote three long treatises about the life of Jesus, but all had been lost except a small portion of the second treatise. The small portion dealt with Jesus' trip to Phoenicia. The statement went on to say that the surviving portion of the treatise was reproduced in the appendix of the volume I was reading. So, I turned to the appendix and read Blanchard's account. It was so fascinating that I read it twice before I began taking notes.

Blanchard began the surviving portion of his treatise with Jesus' journey to Tyre and Sidon.

> "It seemed that for some unspecified reason, Jesus felt it necessary to hide out for a while and that neither the Galilee, Judaea, Peraea, nor the Decapolis was where he and his disciples needed to be. He had to find a place that was so inconceivable that there would be no thought that he could possibly be there. He could have gone north into the mountains or south into the desert, but instead he chose the most

illogical of all locations and destinations: the most morally depraved region in the eastern Mediterranean, Phoenicia. The most corrupt and profligate region in all of Phoenicia was the region of Tyre and Sidon. So, crossing the rugged spurs of the Anti-Lebanon Mountains, he and his disciples crossed the border into Phoenicia in April of AD 30." This is recorded in Matthew 15 and Mark 7. Blanchard quotes from the Mark account:

MARK 7:24-30

24 And from thence he arose, and went into the borders of Tyre and Sidon, and entered into an house, and would have no man know it: but he could not be hid.

25 For a certain woman, whose young daughter had an unclean spirit, heard of him, and came and fell at his feet:

26 The woman was a Greek, a Syrophenician by nation; and she besought him that he would cast forth the devil out of her daughter.

27 But Jesus said unto her, Let the children first be filled: for it is not meet to take the children's bread, and to cast it unto the dogs.

28 And she answered and said unto him, Yes, Lord: yet the dogs under the table eat of the children's crumbs.

29 And he said unto her, For this saying go thy way; the devil is gone out of thy daughter.

30 And when she was come to her house, she found the devil gone out, and her daughter laid upon the bed.

"Tyre and Sidon were the principle cities of Phoenicia. They were located on the Mediterranean coast about 20 miles apart. Tyre, the closer of the two to the Galilee, was about 40 miles northwest of Nazareth. Both served as important seaports for Rome. In addition, both cities were centers of worship for the Roman deities Venus, Isis (adopted from Egypt), Mercurius (Mercury), and Neptune, among others.

"The Romans called the residents of this area of Phoenicia Syrophoenicians, to distinguish them from the Phoenicians of the North African coast, who were called Libyophoenicians. The vast majority of the population was Greek, Greek/Roman, or Greek/Phoenician and was very pagan.

"In Tyre, the priestesses and female devotees who worshipped Mercury (with sexually perverse rituals) were called Syrophenician. Such was the woman who approaches Jesus about her possessed daughter.

"As we consider this event in Jesus' life, it is important to note that Syrophenicians and Jews hated each other. Because of this intense hatred, Roman authorities had decreed that no Jew (unless he was a Roman citizen) was allowed to enter any city or village in all of Phoenicia except for Tyre and Sidon, and then only if the Jew was a male merchant. The ruling was made to preserve the peace. Even as a merchant, the Jew was not permitted to stay for more than two days or the Roman authorities would imprison him. So, it is odd that Jesus brings his disciples to this most corrupt and hostile region in Phoenicia.

"Jesus and his disciples stay in the region for two months, perhaps three. Here again is evidence that Jesus was either a Roman citizen, or he had been granted special permission to stay in this region by Roman authorities.

"We don't know how the Syrophenician woman locates Jesus, or how long he and his disciples have been in the region before she finds them. What we do know is that the Gospels' calling her a Syrophenician indicates that she was a priestess or at least a ceremonial devotee from Tyre's massive temple of Mercury.

"Religious devotees like this woman were scorned by most Jews. (Most Jews had never even seen a Syrophenician. Their contempt was based mostly on reputation. Women like the one Jesus encounters were called 'dogs' and 'vultures.')

"When the woman approaches Jesus, requesting help for her daughter, it seems that Jesus and the disciples treated her contemptuously at first. Jesus simply ignores her until his disciples ask him to send her away. Then, when he speaks to her, he addresses her with the typical contempt that a Jew had for such women. He informs her '*it is not right for him to share God's blessings with dogs.*'

"It seems that the woman has expected this answer. Her response so impresses Jesus that he speaks to her with admiration. More important, he heals her demon-possessed daughter. Jesus says the woman has great faith. (He makes this comment about only three people—none of them Jews. The two others were centurions in Capernaum. All three of these people came to Jesus with the absolute faith that he would meet their needs and help them.)"

Nothing else is recorded about the two or three months that Jesus and his disciples spend in Phoenicia.

When Jesus and company depart Phoenicia, they travel to the Sea of Galilee and sail to the Decapolis. Here, Jesus ministers to and heals all who come to him, including a man who can neither hear nor speak. (See Matthew 15:29-31 and Mark 7:31-37.)

Then, sometime between April and September, Jesus travels to Bethsaida, where he heals a blind man (Mark 8:22-26) and a boy possessed by an evil spirit (Mark 9:15-29).

RIVERS OF LIVING WATER

September of AD 30 finds Jesus in Capernaum, where some of his brothers approach him to taunt him. They ask him, contemptuously, if he is going to the Feast of Tabernacles in Jerusalem, scheduled for September 15th to 22nd. He tells them no.

Two days later, Jesus leads his disciples to the feast, secretly.

Once present at the Feast of Tabernacles, Jesus causes another ruckus. This brings us to another manuscript discovery.

At England's University of Nottingham, I found a five-page vellum manuscript written in the late-fifteenth century by William VII of Troyes. Its title: *Feast of Tabernacles*. As I read William's account of Jesus' last Feast of Tabernacle celebration, I was intrigued by the historical background he brought to the narrative.

In the following paragraphs, I will paraphrase the manuscript, quoting William directly when appropriate:

After the AD 30 edition of the feast had begun, the religious leaders looked for Jesus, but he would not arrive in Jerusalem for two more days. When he did arrive, he went to the Temple and began to teach.

This became a pattern. He would arrive at the Temple, teach all day, and then leave at sundown.

"On the event's eighth and final day (called the Great Day), sacrifices were made for the Jewish people and the Jewish nation. The day's activities began at sunrise, with the solemn ceremony called the libation of water. This ceremony offered thanks to God for the harvest and for the rain that made it possible. The climax of the ceremony was marked by the High Priest's entreating God for his continued provision of rain. The High Priest also pleaded for God to have mercy on the people of Israel."

Just before dawn on this day, long trumpet blasts announced that a Chief Priest had been selected (a once in a life time honor) to draw water from the Pool of Siloam.

Then, at the first glimpse of the sun, another trumpet blast signaled that the priest was kneeling at the pool and drawing water into a golden vial. After drawing the water, the priest would rise.

A third round from the trumpets announced that the priest had begun his solemn walk back to the Temple. The priest walked slowly, carrying the vial with both hands to prevent spilling.

At the foot of the great staircase that led to the Temple compound's massive courtyard, the priest would stop. As he stood perfectly still, the multitudes that had lined his route, as well as the many thousands gathered in the compound, cheered and shouted, with thundering volume. The trumpets sounded again, and the priest began ascending the grand staircase leading to the Temple courtyard.

As this chief priest entered the courtyard, there was total silence, except for the rustle of his footfalls. Holding the vial, he made his way to the altar of sacrifice, where the High Priest, dressed in full ceremonial vestments, awaited him. The High Priest took the vial of water and poured it into two silver cups. Into one of the silver cups, the High Priest added wine. Into the other cup, he poured olive oil.

The High Priest then walked up the ramp that led to the top of the altar of sacrifice. When he arrived, the High Priest set one cup on the altar's east side and the other on the west side. The sacrifice had already been placed on the altar and positioned so that it would lie between the silver cups.

Next, a company of seven priests ascended the ramp, softly reciting Psalms as they walked. Everyone else was silent. At the top of the altar, the seven priests and the High Priest circled the altar seven times, continuing with their Psalms.

The High Priest then took both cups and held them up to heaven and quoted a portion of Isaiah (the 12th chapter). He took the water and wine mixture and poured it into the cup containing the oil and water. He then poured the mixture of water, wine, and oil upon the altar and the sacrifice as he quoted another portion of Isaiah (the 55th chapter). All this time, the people stood still and remained silent.

Next, the High Priest set the sacrifice on fire. As the sacrifice began to burn, the High Priest removed a portion of the Law from a small golden chest and read it aloud. He then threw the animal skin on which a portion of the Law had been written into the sacrificial fire and shouted to the Lord. This was a signal for the entire multitude to begin cheering and singing praises to the Lord.

After corporate praising and singing, the High Priest concluded the ceremony by placing another small animal skin (on which another portion of the Law was written) in a gold, jewel-encrusted chest and then hid it under stones near the top of the altar.

There the skin would remain until the next Feast of Tabernacles celebration.

This year, as the High Priest began to pour the water, wine, and oil mixture onto the sacrifice, the silence was shattered by Jesus' thundering voice. *"If any man thirst, let him come unto me and out of his belly shall flow rivers of living water."*

With these words, Jesus proclaimed that he was the provider of the indwelling Holy Ghost whom the Sadducees and Pharisees taught could be provided only by God. Thus, amid an audience of thousands, Jesus claimed equality with God.

These words sparked a great commotion. Many in the crowd believed in him, but the Pharisees and religious leaders began to plot how they could use the Roman political system to put Jesus to death.

Jesus' words pushed the moderate *and* the conservative Shammaite Pharisees to band together and demand that he repent and make amends for all the damage he had done.

Jesus, meanwhile, remained in the Temple, teaching for the rest of the day. The religious leaders wasted no time in trying to remove Jesus from his public platform.

ADULTERY

Later that morning, some scribes and Pharisees brought a woman to Jesus. They said that she had been caught in the act of adultery, and they hoped that Jesus' reaction would trap him into flouting Rome's authority. (It's important to note here that the Greek word translated *woman* in the Gospel of John's account is *anakom,* used to describe a Roman lady of high social rank.)

These men told Jesus that the Law of Moses required that the woman be stoned.

Now, if Jesus confirmed that she should be stoned, he could be held in contempt of the local Roman court, which was the only authority that could carry out capital punishment. If he disagreed with this punishment, the scribes and Pharisees could use that against him and accuse him of undermining the Law of Moses. (Regardless that Moses' law applied only to Jews, and this woman was Roman.)

Jesus refused to be trapped.

According to William VII:

"This woman was a young lady by the name of Livia. She was the 22-year-old daughter of Plinius Coponicus, the Roman Governor General of Syria, whose administrative base was located in Peraea. The Governor General was the military's executive administrator of a region and Coponicus was the administrator of all Roman military activities in Roman Syria. It was common knowledge that Livia was having an illicit sexual relationship with Justus, the married adopted son of Annas, the former High Priest. These religious leaders were so determined to eliminate Jesus that they sought out Livia, forcibly brought her to Jesus, and tried to provoke him into passing judgment upon her.

"They were so blinded by their rage that it seemed they considered any vengeance that the Roman governor could heap upon them for humiliating and dishonoring his daughter to be worth the cost, if it meant that their actions would guarantee the eradication of Jesus.

"This caused the entrapment scenario to thicken even more. Would Jesus condemn a Roman citizen of high rank? Would he say that Livia was not guilty and allow blatant sin with the son of God's anointed High Priest to go unpunished?

Before William details Jesus' response, he points out that this portion of John's Gospel (John 7:53-8:11) was not included in the earliest biblical manuscripts of the first three centuries. For this reason, many Bible historians of the fourth century through the tenth century believed that the story of Livia was added to the Gospel either by a disciple in the third or fourth century, or by St. Jerome in the fourth century. We know from the Roman court historian Practicus (court scribe and historian for

Governor General Coponicus), that the events of the story themselves are true. He was in Jerusalem accompanying the Governor General for the Feast of Tabernacles celebration that year, AD 30. A Galilean Jewish rabboni of some distinction, the only rabboni in Syria who was a Roman citizen, did challenge the Pharisees who had brought Livia to him in the Temple compound, having caught her and Justus in the midst of sexual fornication.

This Roman/Jewish rabboni did not defend Livia. Instead he challenged those who had brought her to him, that they should take her life only if they had no sin within them for which they could be charged. None who had brought Livia to him sought her death any further. Then, left with no accusers, the rabboni dismissed Livia, with a charge to commit no more acts of fornication.

It's noteworthy that, even after the fourth century, when the story was included in the Gospel of John, the portion where Jesus said, "Neither do I condemn thee. Go and sin no more" was not read in public, because it seemed to suggest a lax attitude to adultery.

William then focuses on Jesus' response.

"Jesus did not respond in judgment to the Pharisees' and scribes' accusations," he writes. "He merely stooped down and began drawing in the sand and said that he that is without sin, let him cast the first stone.

"The concept and the spirit of the statement that Jesus made to the Pharisees and scribes were being taught in the Rabbi School of Hillel. However, the Stoic philosopher Lucius Annaeus Seneca, in a letter that he wrote to Cornelius Tacitus the elder, was arguably the first to make the statement, 'If one is to fully understand this law of forgiveness then one cannot be first to cast a stone, if he too has that deficiency or fault that itself would be worthy of stoning.'

"Afterwards, Livia's accusers walked away without casting stones or making further accusations."

After this event, nothing more is written in either the Gospels or in William VII of Troyes manuscript about Jesus' activities until later in the evening.

SIN

William did go into a lengthy discussion about the difference between sin, iniquity, transgression, and trespass. He used the 51st Psalm to confirm Jesus' position on the subject and to show that there are four different offenses for which we must ask God's forgiveness daily.

As I began to read William's explanation, I found myself feeling that again we, the current Christian society, had somehow been left in the dark concerning some key foundational truths that centuries ago were taught as basic doctrines of the faith. All my life I had been taught that sin is not acceptable to God, which is true, and that sin is sometimes called transgression, sometimes iniquity, and sometimes trespasses. Essentially they are all the same thing—sin. According to William, this assumption is far from correct.

He said that Psalm 51 shows that there are differences of offense and diverse wrongdoing that require us to deal with each differently. Jesus recognized the difference between the four primary offenses and we must deal with each, daily in prayer.

William then explained the difference between the four offenses. I will quote him directly.

"**Sin** is an offense that if left unconfessed and unforgiven will condemn to hell. These are offenses that damn the soul. These could include conscious rejection of Jesus as Savior, blasphemy against the Holy Ghost, trying to purchase salvation with deeds, rather than accepting it by faith as a gift from God, and maliciously taking the life of the innocent.

"**Iniquity** is a lack of righteousness or justice. It is an unjust action or word that is hurtful. An example would be that I hurt another brother in Christ and I knew that I hurt him, but I justified it by saying that he needed to be hurt or that he needed to hear what I had to say, even though he was offended by it and it hurt him. So, it is willful hurting. This willful hurt, if left unconfessed and if no attempt is made to rectify the hurt, will eventually evolve into sin.

"**Transgression** is overstepping or breaking the established rules, law, or principle. It means to go beyond the limits, most times unknowingly or without realizing that the rule or law has been broken. Sometimes this means that I may offend another with my speech or actions, but I did not realize that I have offended. For this reason we must ask our Lord to forgive our transgression daily just in case we have offended and are not aware that we have offended.

"**Trespass** means to knowingly (compared to transgression which means, unknowingly) go beyond the limits of what we know to be right, lawful, moral, ethical, and right. It is also an encroachment or intrusion upon or against another person. This means that the person offends, but they usually try to justify the offense as needed, wanted, or necessary. This is similar to iniquity but not entirely the same. Iniquity results in hurt, sometimes deep and lasting hurt. Trespass results in offense, or a small hurt that only lasts for a short period of time. However, each must be confessed daily to prevent them from evolving into sin."

With that, William ended his description and explanation of the four offenses, and continued where he had left off with his record of Jesus activities for the remainder of the day.

William then turns his attention to trouble that occurs later the same day:

LIGHT OF THE WORLD

"By the year AD 25, the Jewish religious leaders had added a ninth day to the Feast of Tabernacles celebration, called The Day of the Light of the World.

"At sundown on the eighth day, the observers gathered in the Temple courtyard around the altar of sacrifice. As the observers watched in silence, the High Priest carried a small wooden chest and a small lighted oil lamp to the top of the altar. In the chest was a small scroll with a portion of the Law, a portion of the Psalms, and a portion of the Prophets written on it. The High Priest opened the chest and removed the small scroll and replaced it with the small lighted oil lamp, commemorating the sayings of Psalm 119:105 and Proverbs 6:23. This was followed by the High Priest leading the singing of Psalm 119. The lamp stayed in the chest all night. At sunup the following day, the ninth day, the High Priest placed the small scroll into the box and removed the lamp.

"While the High Priest was placing the oil lamp into the chest at sunset of the eighth day, Jesus again broke the silence with his thundering voice: 'I am the light of the world.'

"This phrase was the same Hebrew phrase used by God when He gave a description of the definition of His name to Moses, I AM. It was a phrase that was never heard and never mentioned in public, because it was so holy. The term was spoken by the High Priest only once a year, on the Day of Atonement in the Holiest of Holies. This name was never spoken in public.

"Of those who witnessed this interruption by Jesus, none had ever heard the term he used, except the High Priest, and no one had any idea what Jesus was talking about. If they had known, Jesus would have been torn apart immediately, but because they were ignorant they criticized Jesus only for interrupting the ceremony.

"Why the High Priest did not object is unknown, unless perhaps he had no explanation for how Jesus knew the word.

"What followed was a full-fledged verbal war of accusations and counter-accusations between Jesus and the religious leaders.

"Finally, after perhaps an hour or so of this arguing, the religious leaders had had enough. They picked up stones, intending to stone Jesus to death, with little concern about their actions being prohibited by Roman law. However, Jesus escaped the stoning. We do not know how. Did he hide? Did he supernaturally escape? Did the Roman military, which sought to prevent a riot, instigate his escape? Did his disciples, or friends, or followers rescue him? Did he use some form of self-defense? Any of these could be true. However, we are not told by historical records or by the Gospel of John.

"Afterwards, Jesus walked to the Mount of Olives. The following morning he returned to the Temple area."

With this statement, William VII of Troyes ends his account of one of the most incendiary days of Jesus' life.

CHAPTER 22

꒰ ꒱

Jesus' Fifth Year of Ministry

PART 2 — AD 30

FOR THE NEXT FEW WEEKS, nothing is recorded about Jesus' activities.

Then, in late September or early October, Jesus and his disciples encounter a man who has been blind from birth.

The disciples ask Jesus, "Whose sin resulted in this man's blindness, his, or his parents?"

Jesus corrects their erroneous assumption. The blindness is not a punishment for some sin. Then, to glorify God, Jesus decides to heal this man.

He spits on the ground, makes a bit of mud, and then smears it on the man's eyes. Next, he instructs the man, now healed, to go wash in the Pool of Siloam. The man's healing causes quite a stir as it marks another time Jesus heals someone on the Sabbath. (See John 9:1-37.)

I found a key extra-biblical source confirming the Gospel account of this miracle while doing some research in Toledo. Specifically, at the Synagogue of El Transito in Toledo, *Spain.*

Although this synagogue is no longer active, it houses a museum featuring many Sephardic Jewish artifacts, as well as artifacts and manuscripts reflecting Catholic doctrines and rituals.

Among these treasures, I discovered a four-leaf manuscript written in Latin, and bound between two pieces of thick leather.

According to the museum's director (who helped me by translating the Latin text), the four leaves were all that remained of a 100-page document.

The document was penned by Gregory Makar, an austere eleventh century hermit who resided at Pithiviers in Orleans. He titled his work *Pagan Practices Made Truth.*

Makar feared that the decrees of Pope Alexander II would result in historical records being altered in an unfortunate way. Specifically, Makar was concerned that these records would be purged of all references to Jesus' knowledge of healing practices of non-Jewish nations. (Pope Alexander had launched a search and destroy mission targeting any documents that portrayed Jesus healing by any methods that did not reflect the Catholic church's doctrine.)

In Makar's introduction, he writes that Alexander had destroyed hundreds of irreplaceable Roman, Greek, Syriac, Babylonian, and Egyptian documents in a nine-year purge.

In response, Makar set out to document, from memory, what he had discovered about some of Jesus' miraculous healings including how so many of Jesus' techniques mirrored those of non-Jewish healers.

Over a 20-year period, Makar wrote three copies of his 100-page work. Sadly, after the hermit's death, all three copies disappeared. Then, hundreds of years later, four pages were found in Toledo (in 1602). They were taken to the Synagogue of El Transito, where they remain to this day.

"These four pages," the museum director told me, "are the introduction and the first three pages of the document. These surviving pages describe the opening of a blind man's eyes."

Here is the Gospel record of this miracle:

JOHN 9:1-38

¹ And as Jesus passed by, he saw a man which was blind from his birth.

² And his disciples asked him, saying, Master, who did sin, this man, or his parents, that he was born blind?

³ Jesus answered, Neither hath this man sinned, nor his parents....

⁶ When he had thus spoken, he spat on the ground, and made clay of the spittle, and he anointed the eyes of the blind man with the clay,

⁷ And said unto him, Go, wash in the pool of Siloam... He went his way therefore, and washed, and came seeing....

¹⁰ Therefore said they unto him, How were thine eyes opened?

¹¹ He answered and said, A man that is called Jesus made clay, and anointed mine eyes, and said unto me, Go to the pool of Siloam, and wash: and I went and washed, and I received sight.....

¹³ They brought to the Pharisees him that aforetime was blind.

¹⁴ And it was the sabbath day when Jesus made the clay, and opened his eyes....

¹⁶ ... said some of the Pharisees, This man is not of God, because he keepeth not the sabbath day. Others said, How can a man that is a sinner do such miracles? ....

²⁴ Then again called they the man that was blind, and said unto him, Give God the praise: we know that this man is a sinner.

²⁵ He answered and said, Whether he be a sinner or no, I know not: one thing I know, that, whereas I was blind, now I see....

³⁴ They answered and said unto him, Thou wast altogether born in sins, and dost thou teach us? And they cast him out.

³⁵ Jesus heard that they had cast him out; and when he had found him, he said unto him, Dost thou believe on the Son of God?

³⁶ He answered and said, Who is he, Lord, that I might believe on him?

³⁷ And Jesus said unto him, Thou hast both seen him, and it is he that talketh with thee.

³⁸ And he said, Lord, I believe. And he worshipped him.

Writing about this Scripture, Makar observes that Jesus had created a spectacle by twice disrupting the solemn celebration rituals of the feast, by comparing himself to Moses, and by claiming equality to God. So incensed were the Jerusalem Pharisees that they plotted with the Temple scribes to have Jesus arrested and to have him condemned to death. Jesus was already on the Pharisees' enemy list by the time this miracle took place. They were looking for any excuse to accuse him of blasphemy or sedition.

Some time later, probably in October, Jesus and his disciples were walking in the Temple area on the Sabbath when they noticed a blind man begging. They may have seen this man before, because he was probably one of the many beggars who would sit every day and beg at the Temple gate called *Beautiful*. On this day, Jesus looked upon the man and healed him.

It is estimated that at this time in Judaea one out of every 30 people suffered from some kind of eye disease, many of which caused blindness. Blindness was one of the most common afflictions in Roman Syria.

The Jerusalem Shammaite Pharisees believed and taught that at death, pious and righteous souls were reincarnated as a reward, not as a punishment. However, the wicked were either put into eternal prisons to be tormented forever or they would be forced back into an imperfect, diseased, or afflicted body as a penalty for sins committed by them in a former life, or committed by their parents or grandparents before the person was born. The presence of physical infirmities (especially blindness, deafness, and lameness) were held by these Pharisees to be outward signs that sin was present and that the person must pay the full penalty.

The Shammaite Pharisees considered these physically afflicted to be cursed by God. Jesus' disciples even believed this. It was what they had always been taught from childhood and what the Jewish religious leaders had taught the people for generations.

When Jesus' disciples questioned him about who had sinned, Jesus told them that the Pharisees were wrong. This implied that all teachings on reincarnation, pre-existent sin, and physical infirmities, supposedly proving the existence of sin were false teachings. This man was blind, Jesus said, because he was *born* blind. It was a physical reason. He was not born blind because of sin or a curse.

Jesus then spat on the ground, made clay and rubbed it on the man's eyes, and told him to go to the other side of town and wash in the pool of Siloam. This pool was deep enough to dive into, and it was so far from the Temple that unless the man had help, it probably would have taken him, in his blind condition, two or three hours to walk to the pool.

For centuries it has been a mystery why Jesus rubbed mud on the man's eyes or why he had him walk so far. There were other pools much closer. However, the man obeyed and was healed.

My museum guide/Latin translator noted that for centuries there has been much speculation that this blind man was a non-Jew of Roman heritage. The ritual Jesus uses is consistent with this speculation.

The Romans taught that Janus, the twice-born son of Jupiter, created man by spitting on the ground and making clay. From the clay, he formed man and breathed life into him. The priests of Janus had used (since 107 BC) a healing school and clinic where they performed various rituals of healing and treatment for those afflicted and/or diseased. This institution was still active in Jesus' day.

In the ritual for the blind, the Roman priest would spit on the ground and make clay. The clay would then be rubbed on the blind person's eyes. This was known as *the ritual of the clay*. After the clay was rubbed on the eyes, the blind person would be escorted to the Tiber River, where he or she would wash off the clay. If Janus found favor with the person, he or she would be released from the curse of blindness. If the victim did not find favor, the blindness would remain. There are Roman records that claim healings from blindness through this ritual. Why and how people were healed, we don't know. Neither can we determine the accuracy of the Roman records."

According to Makar, "Jesus performed the same *ritual of the clay* that the priests of Janus followed. It was a ritual with which all Roman-educated people were acquainted. As such, the man would have obeyed Jesus' instructions without question, especially if he believed that Jesus was a holy man or an agent of Janus.

"The Tiber River was considered by the Romans to be a holy water source. In the same way, the pool of Siloam, whose source location was claimed by the Jews to have been given to Hezekiah by God in a vision, was also considered a miracle pool and considered sacred.

"If the man was a Roman or a non-Jew, Jesus would have received immediate cooperation from him by using a generations-old ritual of healing to gain his confidence. At the same time, Jesus showed that *he* was the one who had the power to heal and to neutralize a perceived curse, not the gods of the Romans.

"Jesus sent the man on his way, with mud over his eyes, to struggle to the pool of Siloam and be healed. Meanwhile, Jesus and his disciples went about their business.

"The Shammaite Pharisees were furious with Jesus for healing the man on the Sabbath. Moreover, he healed a man they classified as cursed by God. Before this man could be healed of his blindness, they believed, his sin's had to be forgiven and his curse revoked.

"Now, the fact that the blindness was healed was a sign that God's curse had been reversed. Only God or God's anointed could reverse the curse, and these men could *not* accept that Jesus was God's anointed. He broke the Sabbath regularly and disrupted sacred celebrations. They considered Jesus a sinner because he did not honor the rules and traditions they believed were established by God.

"Because they would not accept that Jesus had the authority and power to reverse the man's curse, they mercilessly interrogated the man.

"The man told them what Jesus had done and that he had used the technique used by the Janus priests. Immediately they labeled Jesus a sinner. They then searched out the man's parents to confirm his blindness, but the parents were of little help. Finally, out of sheer frustration, they threw the man out of the Temple compound.

"The episode must have caused quite a stir. The Feast of Tabernacles had just concluded, so there were probably still some 200,000 visitors in Jerusalem.

"When Jesus heard what had happened to the healed man, he sought him out and revealed himself as the Son of God. The man responded by falling down and worshipping him. Apparently, Jesus accepted this show of adoration.

"Jesus then exposed the sinfulness of the Shammaite Pharisees and unleashed his wrath upon them.

"In response, the religious leaders tried to detain Jesus, but, as in times past, he escaped (John 10:39).

"After this, Jesus and his disciples went to the east side of the Jordan River. From there, they must have ventured on to the Galilee, because the next recorded activity of Jesus is when he is departing the Galilee about a month after the events in Jerusalem.

"And that," the museum director said, "brings us to the end of Makar's document.

ZOLLERAS

Back in Chapter 5, I introduced you to Valleus Paterculus, the prominent Roman historian who was appointed by Tiberius to head The Theophus Commission.

In October of AD 30, Paterculus arrives in Jerusalem, according to a manuscript written by the Egyptian monk Pachomius. I found this manuscript while studying at the library of The Monastery of St Catherine in Sinai. Pachomius (AD 292-346) founded the Nile community of monks at Tabennisi. I will paraphrase Pachomius manuscript:

Paterculus questioned Roman officials about Jesus' whereabouts. The officials told Paterculus that they knew little of Jesus other than that he was a Jewish rabboni of Roman citizenship, due to his being adopted by Joseph of Arimathea.

According to Pachomius, Valleus Paterculus then questioned the Jewish religious leaders and civil leaders about Jesus' whereabouts. They told him that they had heard that Jesus could either be in the Galilee or in the territory of Herod Antipas on the east side of the Jordan.

This marks the beginning of the Jewish religious leaders' resolve to eliminate Jesus. They were convinced that if Jesus were somehow identified as The Theophus, the Romans would dissolve their nation and they would become wards of the Emperor. Hence, it was better for the Jewish people that Jesus die rather than for their whole nation to vanish. So, although many of the Shammaite Pharisees wanted Jesus dead because they held him in contempt, the Sadducees, the chief priests, the legal scribes, and the High Priest felt that Jesus must be removed as a matter of national identity and security.

Valleus Paterculus left Jerusalem, traveled to the Galilee, and met with Herod Antipas and the Herodians concerning the report given to the ambassadors by the House of Herod. There, Paterculus was told that Jesus was somewhere on the east side of the Jordan River, whereupon

Paterculus immediately left to search for Jesus. To show his support, Herod Antipas sent four of his court officials and 20 armed soldiers to accompany him.

Finally, about a month after he had arrived in Jerusalem, Paterculus found Jesus in the village of Machaerus.

While researching at Texas A&I University in Kingsville, Texas I discovered a small book titled *Venice Mustard Gold and Variations on the Mustard Plant,* which was the interpretation of an Italian manuscript that had been written by Laurence Justinian, the former Bishop of Castello. This book was the work of Rev. Theodore McKinney from Richmond, Virginia and threw more light on the healing on the Sabbath event.

Rev. McKinney began by quoting Luke 13:10-21. He then wrote:

"Justinian wrote that Herod Antipas had married the 12-year-old Zolleras, daughter of Aretas, king of Nabataean Arabia, in AD 13, to form a political alliance. Although an extraordinary beauty, she had a disease that caused slouching of her shoulders and back. This disease made its first physical appearance in the year she married Herod .

"In AD 26, leaving Zolleras in Sepphoris, Herod Antipas traveled to Rome to stay with his half-brother Herod Philip. In Rome, Antipas fell in love with Philip's wife Herodias.

"Antipas wanted to marry Herodias and offered his brother a large amount of money (equivalent to $2 million in today's money). Philip consented, and Herodias demanded that Antipas divorce Zolleras. Before returning home, Herod was granted a Roman divorce from Zolleras. Roman law, decreed by Augustus, said a divorced woman could not remarry as long as her former husband lived. If she did, she would be considered an adulteress. Herodias broke the law of Augustus by marrying Antipas. Zolleras was not officially notified of the divorce. Antipas had no contempt for Zolleras and invited her to stay as his guest in his Tetrarchy. The divorce was considered official in Rome, but in Nabataean Arabia it was not. A wife had to consent to a divorce, or, after ten years of the husband filing for divorce, the divorce became official. Herodias demanded that Antipas imprison Zolleras or put her to death. Antipas knew this would have meant war with Aretas, and he would have had to answer to the Roman authorities. So, he resisted Herodias's insistence."

HEALING ON THE SABBATH

The setting for this event was in a synagogue on the Sabbath Day, on the east side of the Jordan. In the state of Judea (on the west side of the Jordan), the synagogue was off limits to non-Jews. However, on the east side of the Jordan, much like in the Galilee, there was no such restriction. The population was so cosmopolitan that it was not unusual to find a person worshipping many different gods and observing different religious customs, including Judaism. The Jewish leaders in Jerusalem looked upon the leaders east of the Jordan with contempt, ignoring them unless they were guilty of defiling the Sabbath laws.

Zolleras occasionally attended synagogue in Machaerus. The synagogue leadership were honored that the wife of the Tetrarch would come to their Sabbath day observances.

Jesus was present at the observance on this Sabbath on which Zolleras decided to show up. Valleus Paterculus and the Theophus Commission of Ambassadors were also present, intending to interrogate Jesus. Instead, they became first-hand observers and eyewitnesses to one of Jesus' truly great miracles.

By now Zolleras has had the disease for 18 years and was so bent that she could not straighten up. Jesus called attention to Zolleras, a daughter of Abraham, and healed her.

Valleus Paterculus was so astounded that it is recorded that he became weakened at his knees and staggered when he left the synagogue.

This miracle created a dilemma for the leaders of the synagogue of Machaerus. Zolleras's healing would generate kingdom-wide attention. The report of The Theophus Commission representatives from Rome who witnessed the miracle could attract international attention. If the leaders of the synagogue said nothing about the miracle, it would imply their acceptance of the spectacle and the Jewish leaders in Jerusalem would call them into question for allowing the Sabbath day regulations to be violated. If they rebuked Jesus for his actions and for the miracle, they risked igniting the temper of Zolleras and the suspicion of The Theophus Commission.

The leaders realized that something had to be done. They decided not to attack Jesus directly but to condemn the act of healing on the Sabbath as a violation of the laws of Sabbath observance.

Jesus scoffed at their attempts at self-preservation and called them hypocritical. He knew that they were liberal in their observances, but he also knew that they were terrified of a censure by the Jewish religious leaders in Jerusalem.

He reprimanded them and told them why they were hypocrites. He said that there was no better day than the Sabbath for the healing of Zolleras, a daughter of Abraham (she, being an Arab, was from the line of Abraham through Ishmael, and the historical Nabataeans were from the line of Abraham through Isaac and Esau). The Sabbath was originally designated to be a commemoration of Israel's deliverance from Egypt.

McKinney continued with Justinians's explanation of the Sabbath Day's origin. He quoted Deuteronomy 5:15 and Exodus 12:17, adding:

"Whenever the leaders of the slave nation of Hebrews felt that the slaves needed a rest, they would petition the Egyptian authorities who would either grant or deny the request. The Sabbath was set aside for rest and any day could have been chosen. It was on one of these days of rest, April 15, that the Hebrews began their exodus. God told Moses to tell the people to dedicate the Sabbath to the memory of their deliverance, doing no work or business. They were to spend the day in contemplation and reflection upon God's miraculous deliverance.

"Jesus healed Zolleras on the Sabbath and delivered her from the bondage and oppression she had suffered for 18 years."

THEOPHUS COMMISSIONER REPORT

In January or February, AD 31, Valleus Paterculus returned to Rome and reported his findings concerning Jesus to The Theophus Commission. In late April, AD 31, he reported his finding and his Theophus conjecture regarding Jesus to Tiberius in Capri. But by then, Jesus had been crucified.

Justinian claimed that "Zolleras became one of the most compassionate and benevolent women in the history of Nabataean Arabia, and she became the primary witness for Christianity in Arabia, until her death in 58 AD. She also convinced her father that Jesus was The Theophus. Aretas opened up trade routes to India, which were used by men and women carrying the good news about the resurrection of Jesus.

"The events leading up to Valleus's encounter with Jesus are suggested in the Gospels of John and Luke 13:10. However, the encounter is recorded in the writings of Valleus Paterculus, Priscian, Tacitus, Dio Cassius, and Petronius."

Pachomius goes on to explain that Paterculus wrote a four-page report to the Theophus Commission and Tiberius Caesar about his encounter with Jesus. Only two paragraphs of that report have survived. Below is Pachomius's translated paraphrase of the first of the two paragraphs:

"Valleus Paterculus said that in the Syrian region of the Galilee/ Judaea he interrogated and witnessed the character of a Roman Jewish religious figure named Jesus, from the city of Nazareth. He followed him and witnessed and testified to his character, his works, his actions, and his teachings for 20 days and then reported his findings to a special calling of the entire commission in Rome and then to Tiberius Caesar. Valleus Paterculus wrote that Jesus was one of the most remarkable characters he had ever met and that he was more afraid of Jesus and his influence with the unseen powers that control the destinies of both men and nature, than an entire army of our (Rome's) most elite guard. He cured disease of all manners. He raised the dead of Jew, Roman, and Greek. His command was reported to subjugate the winds, the sea, and the elements of nature. He is feared, respected, and hated by his Jewish religious countrymen, but honored by his Roman fellows. Yet, even though it is reported or rumored that his uncle and conservator is none other than he who represents our Senate in Britain, Jesus seeks no authority, recognition, reverence, or office."

According to Pachomius, the only other surviving element of Paterculus's report is its conclusion. Below is what Pachomius states is the verbatim text of that conclusion:

"It is my (Paterculus's) opinion that it is within Jesus' power that if he chooses, an entire army could be raised by him in a single hour, which could sweep the world in conquest in a single day. Yet, he denounces all Earthly claims to rule or reign. I feel that of all who have been interrogated by this commission, Jesus only has the idiosyncrasy and the qualifications to fulfill the required Theophus character. However, we cannot suppose that he is that Theophus. I proffer to your most excellent Augustus Tiberius, son of our most

divine Augustus, that there must be another thorough interrogation of Jesus before representation from this commission, from our
treasury, and from our honored Senate, under the protection and
authority of our military magistrate, before such a proclamation is
affirmed upon any man. I propose to this commission and to your
most excellent Tiberius Caesar that after the winter celebration, two
years thence, I will lead this delegation to the region to interrogate
further this man, Jesus. If he will not submit to this investigation,
we must not distinguish him as that Theophus of whom your most
honored esteemed Augustus Tiberius and this commission seek."

Pachomius notes,

"Although we have no record of Tiberius's response or the
response of the commission, we know that Valleus Paterculus led a
delegation to Judaea in January, AD 33. This delegation questioned
Procurator Pilate at his palace in Caesarea Maritima, Tetrarch Herod
Antipas at his palace complex in Capernaum, and Caiaphas the High
Priest in Jerusalem. After hearing of Jesus' death, Valleus demanded
that Caiaphas, Pilate, and Herod report their actions in the matter
and justify their actions and that he, Valleus, would hand-deliver
the reports to the Commission in Rome and to Tiberius in Capri.
In addition, we know that Valleus did deliver the three letters to
Tiberius in Capri sometime in early AD 35.

"We also know that Tiberius recalled Pilate from Judaea in
AD 36 or 37 for the offense of brutality. Pilate had hundreds of
Samaritans slaughtered as they gathered on Mount Gerizim. They
had been lured there by a false prophet who had declared that he
would reveal the hiding place of the sacred vessels used by the
priests, which Moses was supposed to have hidden. Pilate, fearing
insurrection, killed them all.

"The court historian Protoian Anticlius said that Tiberius
recalled Pilate from Judaea because he had ordered the death of The
Theophus of Tiberius' obsession, whom he claimed was a rabboni
from the Galilee. Tiberius then had him exiled to Veinne in Gaul,
where he committed suicide during the rule of Nero Augustus."

GUEST OF A SHAMMAITE PHARISEE

In mid-December, about a month after his meeting with Valleus
Paterculus, Jesus and his disciples arrive in Jerusalem, where he is invited

to participate in the Feast of Dedication at the home of a Shammaite Pharisee.

While at the feast, Jesus heals a man of dropsy and for the first of two times, he gives his teaching on the wedding feast (Luke 14:1-24). The second time is during his last few days in Jerusalem before his crucifixion (Matthew 22:1-14).

The first time that Jesus was invited by a Pharisee to attend the Feast of Dedication was in Capernaum two years before. As you may recall, at the Chapel of St. Kilian, in Ulm, Germany, I discovered large sandstone carvings depicting two Feast of Dedication celebrations. You also might recall that my chapel tour guide was Dr. Karl Richenburger, a retired professor of Roman History. Dr. Richenburger did a wonderful job of illuminating the first Feast of Dedication celebration, and he was equally helpful on the second event. Here is his account:

> "It was the Feast of Dedication celebration in the year AD 30, to which Jesus was invited by the chief Shammaite Pharisee in Jerusalem, Zerebell Hazzel.
>
> "Hazzel was a very powerful man. He was a friend of the Romans, and under his leadership he somehow mended the rift between the Pharisees and the Sadducees. A fragile peace and semi-harmony between the two religious sects was maintained.
>
> "As they were eating, a handicapped man appeared, as was the custom, to partake of the food scraps left by the celebrants. The man had a disease that the King James translators identified as dropsy. Dropsy, or dropsical, was a kidney disease that caused the body to swell to grotesque proportions because of excessive water retention.
>
> "Luke said that Jesus asked the guests whether it was good to heal on the Sabbath. This seems to indicate that the man may have asked Jesus to heal him. If so, he recognized Jesus.
>
> "They did not answer Jesus. They remained silent, which indicated displeasure or disagreement.
>
> "Jesus then healed the man. Afterwards, (perhaps the swelling went down immediately, confirming the healing) he asked them another question regarding what is acceptable to do on the Sabbath Day. Again they all remained silent, showing their disagreement and their displeasure with him.

"Knowing that they held him in contempt for healing a physical outcast on the Sabbath, Jesus told them a parable that was intended to show the host as well as the guests just how dangerous it was to hold anyone in contempt and to show favoritism. The parable of the Great Banquet is recorded in Luke 14 of the Holy Bible."

After the completion of the Feast of Dedication, nothing more is recorded about the life of Jesus until mid-January of AD 31, when he and his disciples leave Jerusalem and travel back to Judea Beyond Jordan (Matthew 19:2-30; John 10:40-42).

CHAPTER 23

✦

Jesus' Ministry: The Final Year

PART 1 — AD 31

JESUS AND HIS DISCIPLES leave Jerusalem about mid-January of AD 31 and travel back across the Jordan River to Judea Beyond Jordan. While there, multitudes approach Jesus. He teaches and heals.

Of course, not everyone approaches Jesus with good intentions. After one of Jesus' lessons on the "born-again" experience, a group of Shammaite Pharisees and scribes begin to complain about Jesus' welcoming and associating with "sinners and commoners." Jesus answers them with a series of parables. (See Luke 15:1-17:10).

At Nancy, France's beautiful Eglise des Cordeliers cathedral, I gained new insight into these parables.

I had been touring the church for about an hour, when I heard a lady calling me by name. Who in Nancy, France knew my name? I turned to see a young lady employed by the hotel where I was staying. She had shown me to my room.

Marquette Lebeaux reintroduced herself to me (which was fortunate, as I had forgotten her name). Then she told me that she worked part-time as a tour guide at the cathedral.

I told her a little about my project and asked if the church had a research library or documents archive.

She told me about the church's private research library, which was available to church scholars and educators but off-limits to tourists. I was grateful that my background qualified me for access.

The library offered about a dozen glass-covered wood cases, each containing two or three bound volumes.

Most of the volumes were religious in nature, and I found one that dealt exclusively with Jesus' ministry. It was titled *Parables Given to the Pharisees in the Presence of Sinners*.

According to the book's explanatory notes, its pages contained a sermon written by Heribert, the Archbishop of Cologne, in 1021. The sermon was an attempt to combat the belief that because Jesus' parables were based on myths and fables, and couldn't be trusted as lessons of truth and holiness.

PARABLE

Heribert begins his sermon by defining and explaining parables. He writes,

> "During Jesus' ministry, the typical didactic teaching methods of the rabbis and rabbonis consisted of presenting a *halakah* (a precept or a rule), and then explaining the halakah by analogies and by referring to a particular current or past event. These analogy commentaries were called *haggadah*. But, on most occasions, Jesus went further than this and resorted to using imaginative illustrations called *mashals*, a complex descriptive form of figurative speech that incorporates comparisons, metaphors, historical facts, manners and customs, and allegories, called *parabole*. The combination of all four elements halakah, hagadah, mashal, and parabole was called a *parable*."

This explanation helped me understand why Heribert became so irritated when some religious leaders tried to discount Jesus' parables as nothing more than fables.

Heribert continues, "The setting for Jesus' parables is recorded in Luke's Gospel (15:3-17:10), when Jesus was invited to a gathering of Pharisees. Before long, sinners joined the gathering. Jesus welcomed them and began to eat with them. The Pharisees became furious because Jesus 'mixed' with these sinners, even though their own most respected leaders taught that they must have compassion on the sinner to bring him back into righteous standing before God. Of these that Jesus told, I (Heribert) have included six in this sermon: the lost sheep, the woman who lost a coin, the prodigal son, the rich man and his unjust steward, one cannot serve two masters, and the rich man and Lazarus. All six were based on well-known historical events, customs, or beliefs."

Heribert points out that Jesus was skilled in using actual historical events as the basis for his parables. Then, he would relate an event and its implications to his audience. In this chapter, we will explore three of Jesus' parables, as illuminated by Heribert.

THE LOST SHEEP

The first parable the archbishop examines centers on the lost sheep. In Luke 15:4, Jesus asks,

LUKE 15:4
⁴ What man of you, having an hundred sheep, if he lose one of them, doth not leave the ninety and nine in the wilderness, and go after that which is lost, until he find it?

Heribert writes,

"The parable of the lost sheep was a well-known allegory at that time. It was based on a historical event.

"Before the righteous king Josiah left Jerusalem with his army to meet the invading army of Egypt, he related a story of the lost sheep to his advisors. It was a personal event in his life when he was a young boy tending sheep for the family. In allegorizing the story, King Josiah said that the Lord's chosen people, the people who had drifted from the Lord, needed to be brought back into the sheepfold.

"With that, King Josiah set off to protect the villages, and restore them to the place God had intended for them. Unfortunately, King Josiah was killed and the villages came under Egyptian subservience.

"In 160 BC, just before Judas Maccabees left Jerusalem to meet the Syrians in battle, he related the same allegory to his military council and his family. He applied the allegory to himself. He said that he had been chosen to rescue the wandering few, those who had not joined his cause to throw off the yoke of Syrian oppression.

"Judas left Jerusalem, confident of victory, but he was killed in battle. The ones he went out to protect were annihilated by the Syrians.

"Jesus repeated this parable to the Pharisees. Why? What was he trying to imply? Jesus insinuated that the Pharisees who were critical of him for receiving sinners, the sheep of God's fold who had wandered away, were comparable to the militaries of Egypt and Syria whose purposes were to devour the defenseless sheep that had wandered from the fold. Jesus implied that the Pharisees and scribes should try to rescue sinners, yet they had not. However, he would rescue them. With each lost sheep that he brought back into God's sheepfold, there would be great rejoicing by God and by all the righteous in heaven, because they, the sinners, were lost but had been found.

"With this parable, Jesus was implying that he was the shepherd sent by God to bring his wandering sheep back into the fold before they could be devoured by their enemies, the ravaging Pharisees and religious leaders."

THE PRODIGAL SON

Heribert's sermon also includes what is perhaps Jesus' most famous parable: the prodigal son. (See Luke 15:11-32.)

Heribert contends,

"This parable was based on historical fact. Its history dates back to 800 BC, and it was taught throughout the eastern Roman Empire. The story's setting was the Kingdom of Urartu (present-day eastern Turkey, northern Iran, and western Armenia).

"The king of Urartu was Cherimachinus. His oldest son, Urrias, was the governor of Tushpa, and he also served as chief administrator of Urartu's western provinces. The younger son, Arrias, was the chief of defense for Cherimachinus's royal palace.

"King Cherimachinus and his two sons ruled with distinction and honor for many years. Then, when Arrias was 33 years old, his wife and infant son drowned in the Araxes River. Arrias went into deep depression. He decided to leave Urartu and the painful memory of his wife and son behind. Because he was determined never to return, he demanded of his father an 'inheritance settlement.'

"The right of an 'inheritance settlement' had been the 'law of the land' for more than 1,000 years. The law stated that a younger son of a king could demand an 'inheritance settlement' any time after his 25th birthday.

"Once the settlement was granted, it was final. Thus, a younger son would forfeit his royal rights and his family name. He also forfeited these rights on behalf of his descendants. In return, he would receive an amount equal to five years' family income.

"Upon receiving his inheritance," Heribert continues, "Arrias moved to Ashur in Assyria. There he 'lived it up' for three years, spending his entire fortune and running up a tremendous debt that he could not pay. It landed him in a debtor's prison.

"While in prison, a local official who had been befriended by Arrias a year previously paid off Arrias's debt and had him released from prison into his charge.

"Upon release from prison, Arrias had to pay off his debt to the local official. So, Arrias was obliged to work on the official's farm. Because the official was a supplier of meat to the Assyrian army, Arrias's job was to tend the pigs, cattle, and sheep.

"Arrias worked for four years, until the debt was paid in full. At this point he was invited to become overseer of the farm's meat production. He agreed.

"But then the official died, and his estate was sold. Arrias kept his job, but he soon found the new owner to be ruthless and overbearing. Arrias objected. The new owner responded by stripping Arrias of his position and reassigning him to feeding the pigs and cleaning the pigpens. Arrias continued to protest, so the owner imprisoned him in a pigpen, with no food or water.

"Knowing he would likely starve to death, Arrias escaped and fled north back to Urartu.

"During the eight years after he left his family, Arrias had no communication with his father. The king would sit in the upper chamber of his cliff palace and look out a window, day after day and year after year, watching and waiting for his son to return.

"The law and social custom of the time would not allow the king to go after his son since he had renounced his princely position;

however, the king could allow the son to return, if he returned voluntarily.

"During Arrias's absence, the king, who had ruled so brilliantly, began to neglect his kingdom.

"Finally the older son, Urrias, fearing for the welfare of the kingdom, decided to govern the kingdom in his father's stead. King Cherimachinus did not protest.

"Under Urrias's brilliant leadership the kingdom thrived. Within six years Urrias had brought Urartu from a state of ruin to being influential enough to be feared by the Assyrians, the Phrygians, and the Lydians.

"All the while, Cherimachinus spent his days in a depressed, trance-like stupor, gazing for hours out over the highland, hoping to see his younger son. One day, while Urrias was away on business, Arrias returned.

"King Cherimachinus saw him approaching from afar. Miraculously his depression lifted. He ran from his upper chamber and ordered the palace to prepare a great feast in honor of his returning son.

"Cherimachinus, who was greatly overweight, ran all the way down the steep road that connected the palace to the capital city, almost dying of exhaustion.

"When he got to the city, he ordered his personal guard to accompany him as he rode out to meet Arrias. The homecoming celebration that followed lasted for 21 days, but Cherimachinus was unable to enjoy it to its fullness because he was still trying to recover from his ordeal of running to meet his son.

"Nevertheless, in the midst of the celebration, the king called Arrias to him and, contrary to the law, restored his position as son and gave him a family signet ring. Yet, his heir position was not restored.

"News reached Urrias about his brother's return, his father's miraculous recovery, the celebration, and the restoration of Arrias. He was pleased to hear that Arrias had returned and that his father had recovered from his depression, but he became furious when he heard that Arrias had been restored to his position as son of the king.

"Urrias immediately returned to reason with his father about his unlawful decision. Urrias's pleadings were ignored.

"Cherimachinus offered to abdicate the throne and proclaim Urrias king and governor of the Kingdom of Urartu if only he would agree to the restoring of Arrias.

"Urrias refused and hurriedly returned to his city of Tushpa. There, he quickly gained the support of the people and seceded from the Kingdom of Urartu.

"Cherimachinus recovered physically and again began to govern with pride and dignity, with Arrias by his side. Because Arrias had given up his right of rulership, he was not permitted to hold a position of royal leadership; however, Cherimachinus restored him to his former position as chief of the defenses.

"Meanwhile, Urrias raised an army and marched against his father. He conquered all of the land between Lake Van and the capital city of Sehvanes—then laid siege to the city. Every occupant was killed or enslaved.

"Next, Urrias laid siege to the royal palace. Not fearing Urrias, Arrias attempted to reason with his brother by walking out to meet him, unarmed.

"Urrias refused to talk to him and instead cut his body in two with his sword and then cut off his head. Upon seeing Arrias killed, the king threw open the gates to the palace and ran out and fell upon his son's mutilated body. Then, while holding the decapitated head of Arrias in his hands, he begged Urrias to forgive and start anew. Urrias responded by decapitating his father.

"It is unclear," Heribert explains, "why Jesus told the Pharisees the parable of the prodigal son. It appears that he was comparing Urrias to the unforgiving Shammaite Pharisees, who rejected sinners as being unworthy of being accepted into the kingdom of God. They felt that God had no intention of welcoming sinners. They felt that if 'family' members turned away from the family, they could not return to be part of God's family.

"It also appears that Jesus compared God's forgiving nature to the compassionate forgiveness of King Cherimachinus. So, although the parable has been used for centuries as an allegory of a father's unconditional love in the face of rebellion and bitterness, Jesus' primary purpose for telling it to the Shammaite Pharisees seems to be one of indictment against their self-righteousness, unforgiveness, and judgment."

The Rich Man and Lazarus

The sixth and final parable of the sermon (and the *third* one we will cover) is that of the rich man and Lazarus, as recorded in Luke 16:19-31. Heribert writes:

"This parable was based on a true story. It is suspiciously similar to an allegory told in 210 BC by the great Jewish religious leader Meleshia, to his students in the school of Alexandria.

"Zeruthem was a Jewish religious leader who lived in Alexandria, Egypt. He died in 260 BC. Although Zeruthem was a religious leader, he was far from holy or compassionate.

"Zeruthem demanded that tithes, worship tax, and offerings be paid to him directly. Instead of using the funds to help widows and the needy, he used them to finance his own lavish lifestyle. He held the needy in the utmost contempt.

"The Law demanded compassion for sinners, which would encourage them to forsake their life of sin and return to the family of God, but to Zeruthem, they were a nuisance that needed to be removed from sight.

"When Zeruthem died, he received a fabulous Egyptian funeral. However, according to Meleshia, Zeruthem lifted up his eyes in the world of darkness and intense heat, being in torment in Hades.

"From that place of torment, Zeruthem could see a man who used to beg for alms at his gate. This could have been the beggar Lazarus, featured in Jesus' parable.

"The beggar Lazarus was in a place of peace, whereas the rich man was in a place of torment.

"Meleshia said that Zeruthem requested from the governor of the place of peace to have the beggar place one drop of water on his tongue to quench the horrible torment, but the governor refused his request.

"Next, he asked the governor to send someone back from the dead to warn his family so that they could avoid such a horrible place, but the governor told Zeruthem that they had the prophets, the Law, and the Scriptures. If they believed them, that was all they needed.

"Meleshia used the story to show the scholars that although they were working daily with the Holy Scriptures, if they did not believe and practice what the Scriptures said, they would end up in the same place as Zeruthem.

"Jesus had just told the Pharisees about the truth of the Scriptures, implying that they must live according to the entire Word of God, which by their contempt for sinners and their contempt for Jesus for showing these sinners love, compassion, and acceptance, they were forsaking.

"Almost to the last detail, the parable Jesus spoke to the Pharisees was the same as what Meleshia related to Alexandrian scholars more than two centuries before. However, Jesus did add a portion to Meleshia's allegory. He added that the rich man asked father Abraham that if someone who had risen from the dead would come back and speak to his family, they would listen and avoid that place of horror. Abraham said that even if someone rose from the dead and came back and preached to them, they still would not believe.

"With Jesus' last statement, he too implied that the Pharisees' rejection of the Scriptures, in favor of their own rules, would result in death, as it resulted in Meleshia's lesson.

"Without a doubt, the Shammaite Pharisees and the scribes became furious with Jesus for using the parable to condemn them."

With that statement, Heribert concludes his sermon.

Among my notes on Jesus' parables, I wrote this: "I have wondered for years concerning these parables, and now I have discovered that they were more than just stories or tales invented by him. They were based on actual events and used as tools for teaching, much like allegories or analogies. By using actual historical events, Jesus made the parables come alive with meaning, significance, and importance."

CHAPTER 24

Jesus' Ministry: The Final Year

PART 2 — AD 31

THE NEXT TIME WE READ about Jesus in the Gospels, it is late January of AD 31, and Lazarus, his friend from Bethany (the brother of Mary and Martha), has become sick.

Jesus is still ministering in Judea Beyond Jordan when he receives word from a messenger sent by Mary and Martha. "Come to us quickly," they plead, "or Lazarus will die."

However, Jesus delays his return to Bethany. By the time he returns, Lazarus has died (John 11:1-46). Thus, the stage is set for one of the greatest miracles in Jesus' ministry.

At the El Azhar Muslim University in Cairo, Egypt, I found some rock-solid confirmation of this miracle. (El Azhar, incidentally, is the world's top university for Islamic cleric studies.)

This university's manuscript vault is as impressive as it is beautiful. It houses Islamic manuscripts dating to the eighth century. But what was most amazing to me were the third and fourth century Coptic Christian manuscripts hidden away in dark underground granite and steel vaults.

As I descended the narrow stairs that led to the vaults, a university guide explained that the Christian manuscripts had been originally placed in the university's storage vaults in 980 AD, after the Vizier Yacub Ibu Killis had prophesied that Christianity would be extinct within one millennium.

To ensure that the *memory* of Christianity would not be eliminated, he demanded that 100 Christian manuscripts and documents be preserved, for the benefit of future generations. Of the 100 manuscripts and documents originally preserved, almost 40 remained intact, with an additional 20 or so preserved in fragments.

The area was very dimly lit, so it was difficult to see. Each vault had a plaque on its door, briefly describing the manuscript or document inside.

I could read only two manuscripts, one of which was written in Greek and another written in Latin.

The Latin document was a letter written by Cyprian of Carthage, addressed to the "beloved sufferers for Christ at the hand of Emperor Decius." Thus, if this letter was an original, it dated to 246-258 AD. (I knew Cyprian converted to Christianity in 246 and was martyred in 258.)

The letter encouraged the families and friends of those who were victims of Decius's purge. Cyprian also detailed his conversion to Christianity, through the influence of the presbyter Caecilianus. Interesting content, but not relevant to my search.

The second manuscript was a four-leaf Greek document—a sermon written by Tertullian (circa 160 AD to 225 AD.)

At first, Tertullian's identifying himself as the author confused me. All of his known works of 30 books and hundreds of sermons had been penned in Latin. I had heard rumors of Tertullian's "lost" Greek sermons, but many western-Christian theologians disputed their existence.

I sat down on the woven-rug-covered floor of a university study room and began to pore over the document. Tertullian directs his sermon to the local church at Carthage. His topic was Jesus' raising Lazarus from the dead.

During the seven centuries after Jesus' death, Tertullian was regarded as one of Christendom's greatest thinkers. (Some would argue that the word "Christendom" could be removed from the preceding sentence.) Tertullian was brilliant, having distinguished himself in history, literary education, legal matters, philosophy, medicine, and theology.

Knowing Tertullian's background, I should not have been surprised when I read the sermon. What Tertullian wrote about the resurrection of Lazarus was so amazing and so inspiring that nothing that I had seen, heard, or read, matched it.

I read this sermon three times.

LAZARUS OF BETHANY

Tertullian begins by quoting from the story's scriptural setting (John 11:1-44):

JOHN 11:1-44

[1] Now a certain man was sick, named Lazarus, of Bethany, the town of Mary and her sister Martha....

[3] Therefore his sisters sent unto him, saying, Lord, behold, he whom thou lovest is sick.

[4] When Jesus heard that, he said, This sickness is not unto death.

[6] When he had heard therefore that he was sick, he abode two days still in the same place where he was....

[14] Then said Jesus unto them plainly, Lazarus is dead....

[17] Then when Jesus came, he found that he had lain in the grave four days already....

[34] (Jesus) said, Where have ye laid him? They said unto him, Lord, come and see....

[39] Jesus said, Take ye away the stone....

[43] And when he thus had spoken, he cried with a loud voice, Lazarus, come forth.

[44] And he that was dead came forth, bound hand and foot with graveclothes: and his face was bound about with a napkin. Jesus saith unto them, Loose him, and let him go.

In the paragraphs that follow, I will translate and paraphrase Tertullian's brilliant sermon for you, quoting him occasionally.

Apparently, Lazarus lived with (or near) his sisters, Mary and Martha, in Bethany, near Jerusalem. Lazarus was well-known and respected by the political leaders, Roman and non-Roman, and the region's religious leaders. This Roman Egyptian/Jew was a close friend of Jesus.

When Lazarus became sick, Jesus was east of the Jordan River, probably trying to evade Herod Antipas, who sought to detain him on behalf of The Theophus Commission.

When Lazarus became gravely ill, it was natural for his sisters to send a messenger to find Jesus, so that he could come and heal their brother. They didn't imagine him hesitating to come to Lazarus's aid.

The messenger was unaware that Lazarus died the day he left to find Jesus. According to John 11:14 Jesus knew Lazarus had died even before the messenger had arrived.

Two days after departing Bethany, the messenger found Jesus and told him that Lazarus was near death. Jesus, of course, knew Lazarus was dead. However, he sent this message to the sisters: Lazarus's sickness was "not unto death" and God was going to be glorified.

Imagine the excitement that the messenger would have had when he arrived at the home of Mary and Martha and told them that Lazarus was not going to die, but he would recover so that God would be glorified. This then was immediately followed by the depths of despair, when he realized that Lazarus was dead already and had been dead since the day that he had left to find Jesus. Perhaps this was three days before Jesus had said that Lazarus was not going to die.

To make matters worse, Jesus did not even return with the messenger, but rather, he sent the messenger away, telling him to return to the sisters with news that ended up being nothing more than a false hope that ultimately turned into an untruth.

If Jesus had returned with the messenger immediately, he still would have been three days too late. However, Jesus did not leave immediately. Instead, knowing that Lazarus had died already, he chose to stay two additional days before he began his journey back to Bethany. By the time

Jesus arrived in Bethany, Lazarus had been dead for five days and had been entombed for four days.

During his sermon, Tertullian recounts his discovery of a papyrus he found among the ruins of the ancient Jewish settlement of Elephantine. (Elephantine was an island in the Nile River at the first cataract of the river in southern Egypt.)

When Nebuchadnezzar of Babylon was closing in on Jerusalem, some Jews fled to southern Egypt and established a settlement on the island of Elephantine. There they lived a life of relative peace under the dominion of first the Babylonians, then the Persians, and then the Greeks. They even built a temple of worship on the island.

By the time the Romans began to make an impact in the area, the community had evolved into an Egyptian/Jewish syncretistic community with worship offered to Yahweh, as well as to Anat-Bethel.

However, for some unknown reason, the community chose not to cooperate politically with the Roman/Greek Egyptian coalition. This led to the dissolution of the settlement and the dispersion of its inhabitants. Many of the former Elephantine Egyptian/Jews settled in the Jerusalem area and established the community of Bethany. For almost 300 years, from 100 years before Jesus' birth to almost 200 years afterward, the families and descendants of these Elephantine Egyptian/Jews occupied the town of Bethany.

Lazarus, Mary, and Martha were third-generation descendants of the displaced settlers from Elephantine. Bethany was unique in that the residents exercised a form of Judaism in their worship practices and religious observances, yet they were very much Greco-Roman/Egyptian in their customs, traditions, rituals, observances, and manners of dress. This Greco-Roman/Egyptian influence extended into the realm of burial practices, as well. Thus, when Lazarus died, he was not buried in the traditional Jewish manner, but rather he was embalmed and entombed in the traditional Greco-Roman/Egyptian/Jewish manner, with all of its rituals and uniqueness.

Thus, following the traditional rituals and arrangements that their ancestors had practiced in Egypt for hundreds of years, Mary and Martha prepared Lazarus' body for burial. First, the heart, the brain, the tongue, the eyeballs, and the lungs were removed and placed in a honey, wine, and olive-oil-filled pottery jar. The jar was sealed with beeswax. The body was drained of blood, coins were placed in the empty eye sockets, and the cavity where the organs had been located was filled with a mixture of honey, olive oil, and spiced wine. Afterward, the body was sewn up and coated with thick layers of resins, salts, and aromatic spices and wrapped mummy-style with dozens of wide strips of linen. The wrapped body was then placed in a tomb.

This tomb usually had two compartments or rooms. The first room was an area about eight feet square. On the day of death, the deceased's body parts were put in a pottery jar, which was then placed in the first room along with a loaf of bread and a vial of water. (These were to feed the dead person's spirit as he or she prepared for the afterlife.)

From the first room, a 40-step stairway led down to a larger second room. Here, the body would be placed in a stone vault or sarcophagus, with a stone or brick lid. The lid was sealed with tallow or wax.

As part of the burial ritual, the deceased's family would receive visitors from day two through day four. Many visitors brought gifts of condolences.

Tertullian notes on day five, the day that the body began to rapidly decompose, the official public funeral took place. The final burial benediction was pronounced and the tomb was closed by a huge stone that was rolled in front of the tomb opening. The huge tombstone was then sealed airtight with tallow and beeswax. This was followed by a Roman official's sealing of the tomb. It was unlawful for any unauthorized person to break the Roman seal.

Afterwards, the family accepted hospitality visits from the public for the remainder of that day, day five.

On this day that the tomb was sealed, Jesus appeared. He was not met with much enthusiasm. Everyone received him somewhat contemptuously, except for Mary and Martha. The two sisters received him with a combination of astonishment, sorrow, and faithlessness.

Jesus then requested that Martha remove the stone from the tomb opening.

Tertullian goes on to state the obvious. Jesus' request was physically impossible for Martha, and it was also emotionally and psychologically painful. At this time, there were probably hundreds of mourners gathered. One can only marvel at their reaction to Jesus' request of Martha.

However, Martha complied with the strange instructions and had the stone rolled away from her brother's tomb.

Then Jesus stood before the tomb and, after giving thanks to the Father for the miracle about to be performed, called in a thunderous voice: "*Lazarus, come forth*!"

Tertullian writes that we see Lazarus, standing at the entrance of the tomb, still wrapped in his burial bandages, with a separate wrap over his face.

It is unlikely that Lazarus just appeared instantaneously. One moment he was lying in the sealed sarcophagus and the next moment he was standing in front of Jesus.

Tertullian then offers a long explanation of how Lazarus somehow "kicked" the heavy lid off of the burial sarcophagus and struggled out of the vault, still bound tightly from head to toe. Lazarus then had to find a way to stumble up the 40 steps that led to the upper chamber.

Tertullian explains that we do not know how long it took Lazarus to struggle out of the vault and stumble up the stairs to appear still bound at the tomb opening. It could have taken hours, during which time Jesus waited silently and the crowd of spectators watched. It is doubtless that many of those watching and waiting were curious. Others stayed because they held Jesus in utter contempt and were certain that he would make a fool out of himself. Still others stayed because they did have a deep, but somewhat skeptical, hope that Jesus really could do something miraculous.

No doubt, many waited and waited, and seeing nothing happening, they turned away, thinking that Jesus was a fool and a failure. Others perhaps turned away, with their confidence in Jesus shattered, while still others perhaps turned away, thinking that this attempt was just too big, even for Jesus. But, those who remained became eyewitnesses to one of the greatest miracles ever recorded.

Tertullian concludes, "Lazarus had been given a new body, a new mind (the brain), new breath (the lungs), a new speech (the tongue), a new vision (the eyes), and a new heart, yet he was still bound and had to rely upon the help of his friends and his family members to release him from his bonds and blindness. We today can do no lesser a service for our brothers in Christ. He gives them new life, but we must loose them from their bonds and accept them into the brotherhood of the living."

After I had finished reading this manuscript for the third time, I sat there on the floor, amazed. This was probably the most powerful sermon I had ever experienced. I could certainly understand why Tertullian was so renowned in his day.

ZACCHAEUS

This brings us to another important encounter in Jesus' ministry. An encounter with a man named Zacchaeus.

I discovered documentation for this event at the world-famous Rococo Library in St. Gallen, Switzerland.

The library was located in an old abbey, originally built by the Irish disciple Gallus in the seventh century. Although much of the original abbey had been destroyed during the Protestant Reformation, the magnificent library, with its 150,000 religious volumes, manuscripts, and documents, had been preserved.

When I walked into the library, I was awe-stuck. I stood and admired the entire ancient complex. When I finally collected my composure and started investigating the library's vast collection of "literary gold," I felt I could stay for days. I ended up spending an afternoon studying an array of medieval religious volumes and I did not go beyond the first floor. Who knows what treasures I would have found on the second and third floors.

Late that afternoon, I became thirsty and went to the front reference desk to ask for the location of a drinking fountain. That's when I noticed a sign, written in German, English, and French, announcing that the library would be closing at 9:00 p.m. that day for inventory and re-cataloging. It wouldn't re-open for two weeks. I was so disappointed. I had planned to spend two or three days here. Now, I had only a few hours.

I quickly left the desk and walked to the card catalog files, kicking myself for not noticing the sign earlier, thereby wasting the entire afternoon. Now, I really had to focus my search.

By early evening, I settled on a small leather-bound volume written by Bernardino Realino, an Italian lawyer turned Jesuit. He served as rector of Jesuit College at Leece in Apulia. In 1600, he penned three works, rendered as legal opinions.

It appeared that these opinions were used as teaching tools for law students at Jesuit College. One of these works explored the conversion of Zacchaeus and the healing of Bar-Timaeus, the son of Timaeus

Realino writes that The Gospel of Luke (19:1-10) tells us that as Jesus and his disciples were walking through Jericho, a tax collector climbed a tree to see him.

JERICHO

Realino began his opinionated brief by describing the city of Jericho: "The city of Jericho is one of the oldest cities in the world due to its location in the midst of a large oasis of leafy palms. Jericho at the time of Jesus was located on the slopes and valley of a rugged horseshoe shaped mountain range north of the city. It had a tropical climate, which made it ideal for the growing all types of tropical fruit. It was the wealthiest city in the Roman Empire. Herod the Great built a magnificent summer palace in Jericho and at the time of Jesus' ministry, Herod Archelaus, son of Herod the Great, occupied the great palace.

> Jericho enjoyed a pleasant semi-tropical climate and had the Roman Empire's most elaborate irrigation network. As a result the streets of the city were lined with palm trees, almond trees, orange trees, African fig or African mulberry trees (the KJV of the Bible translated these trees as sycamore), lime trees, and lemon trees. North of the city, the mountain slopes were covered with groves of almonds, oranges, lemons, limes, pomegranates, date palms, balsam (from which was extracted myrrh), and bananas. On the ground growing between the groves of trees were thousands of vanilla orchids. The sweet aroma of all of these combined fragrances caused Ovid to comment that Jericho must be inhabited by the gods, for its sweet smell betrays them. Antony was so enchanted by the city that

he gave it as a gift to Cleopatra. She in turn built a dazzling summer palace there, which she never occupied.

"The city stretched southward from the mountain slopes. At the time of the death of Herod the Great, the city's length was more than 100 stadia (100 stadia was approximately equal to a five-hour walk at a brisk-pace) from the northern limits of the city to the southern limits. It had straight wide pedestrian-only avenues. The width of the streets varied from 50 feet to 140 feet and ran north to south and northwest to southeast (Jericho had only 13 streets that allowed animal, wagon or chariot traffic; and these were all located in the outer extremities of the city).

"Augustus was so enchanted by the city that by his decree it became a city of religion and all religious leaders living there were exempt from paying taxes. The common citizens of Jericho had to make up the taxes of the religious leaders so only the extremely wealthy had a home in Jericho. Out of a total population of 200,000 residents, there were nearly 50,000 priests of differing religions."

Jesus' reputation followed him everywhere he went, including Jericho. In Jericho, Jesus would be highly respected because of his Roman standing, and he would be accepted as an equal by the other religious personalities who lived there, because of his religious leader's position. A crowd would have quickly developed. Among this crowd was Zacchaeus

ZACCHAEUS

Realino explains:

"Zacchaeus was a chief tax assessor for the province of Judaea. He was employed by the Roman tax authorities in Caesarea Maritima. Although he lived in Jericho, he was the director of all tax assessment and tax collection for the entire province.

A third century tradition said that Zacchaeus was the wealthiest native Judean in Jericho. It seems quite obvious that he was very wealthy in that he lived in Jericho. The common Judean would never be able to afford a home in Jericho. Many non-Judean native Romans considered Jericho the most expensive city in the entire Empire.

Because of Zacchaeus' height, he was unable to see over the crowd of fellow religious admirers of Jesus. He ran on ahead of the crowd to climb up into either an African fig or African mulberry tree, from which he could see Jesus.

"When Jesus came to the tree he stopped and told Zacchaeus to come down because he wanted to go to Zacchaeus's house. This was a privilege that any Roman royalty or Roman citizen with administrative or legislative authority traveling through a city could demand. Zacchaeus quickly came down out of the tree to honor Jesus' demand. When Jesus' disciples and some of his more orthodox followers realized that Jesus was going to the house of Zacchaeus, they became angry with him. But Jesus went anyway.

"At the feast given in Jesus' honor, Zacchaeus stood and, without provocation by Jesus announced that half of all that he owned would be given to the poor."

Whether Zacchaeus actually gave one-half of his wealth is not known. However, Tantautius, an Arabic historian living in Jericho at Jesus' time, reported that Zacchaeus gave the equivalent of $27 million to the poor, and another $17 million to those he had taxed unfairly.

Whatever the case, at this point in the story, Luke's Gospel tells us that Jesus proclaimed to everyone present, "This day is salvation come to this house. For the Son of man is come to seek and to save that which was lost" (Luke 19:9-10).

Realino concludes that we do not know how long Jesus stayed with Zacchaeus, but upon leaving the house of Zacchaeus, Jesus with his disciples and followers, left the city and headed for Jerusalem.

BAR-TIMAEUS

As Jesus and his party were leaving Jericho, He was confronted by a blind man begging outside the city walls (begging was not allowed within the city limits of Jericho). This blind man was screaming "Jesus, thou son of David, have mercy on me" (Mark 10:47).

The Gospel account states that the man was blind and that he regained his sight, indicating that he had not been born blind.

From the writings of Tantautius the Arab, Realino notes, we discover that the healing of Bar-Timaeus by Jesus caused quite a stir in Jericho among the Roman officials. It was from this point on that the Romans began to view Jesus with suspicion. By the time he reached Jerusalem, the Roman authorities were monitoring the actions of this now common radical. What brought about such a change in attitude I had wondered? Realino states:

"The event leading to the blindness of Bar-Timaeus took place in AD 22, under the procuratorship of Valerius Gratus. Valerius Gratus, like most Roman aristocrats, maintained a residence in Jericho. Attached to his residence was a private armory of arms and military supplies that could be used by Roman troops in case of a local disturbance. His personal residence steward was Timaeus, a Greek/Roman.

"In AD 22, Timaeus's 24-year-old son, Infatius, led a night-time raid on the armory to steal the arms to sell to rebel Galilean factions. This was 'strictly business'—to steal and sell to the highest bidder. Infatius and his accomplices were caught in the act. Infatius's seventeen non-Roman accomplices were crucified on the northern hilltop overlooking the city. Infatius was a Roman citizen and could only have been crucified if convicted of treason. He was instead found guilty of profiting by sedition (This crime was not punishable by death, if the accused was a Roman citizen.) Instead, his eyeballs were burned out with a red-hot sword blade and he was forced to wear a red-stained tunic to indicate that he was suffering punishment for making a profit by actions against Caesar and Roman authority. Although he was not allowed to leave the Jericho area, he was not permitted inside the city of Jericho again. Instead, Infatius, identified as Bar-Timaeus in the Gospel of Mark, had to stay outside of the city and beg for his survival for the rest of his life.

"When Infatius heard that Jesus was passing through the city gate, he cried out loudly 'Jesus, thou son of David have mercy on me.' This was a Messianic title and implied that Jesus, whom many had said was that Messiah, would neutralize the great Roman authority and establish his own governmental structure.

"Jesus asked for the man to be brought to him. The man, in defiance of Roman authority, responded by immediately casting off the tunic he had been sentenced to wear for the remainder of his life and which represented Roman judgment and punishment.

"Jesus did nothing to prevent this contemptuous insult to Roman authority and its Imperial judicial decision. Instead, he asked the man what he wanted. The Gospel of Mark says that the man said that he wanted to receive his sight, but Tantautius said that Infatius replied 'that I may avenge my sight.' It was a political statement suggesting that he wanted reprisal upon his adjudicators. He had a hatred for the Roman authorities who had condemned him. Nevertheless, Jesus healed him and interfered with the official punishment sentence of the Roman authorities.

"Jesus then turned to continue his journey to Jerusalem, with the man who had just been healed following him. As he exited the city, he healed two blind men and then continued on his way.

"The Roman authorities were furious when they heard that Jesus, their friend, had countermanded the judgment of the Imperial Tribunal of Rome by healing the physical sign of punishment inflicted by the high court of Rome; encouraging the convict to throw off his tunic, the symbol of Roman judgment, leave the Jericho area and follow Jesus' group of followers.

"Word of this affront by Jesus quickly spread to Roman authorities in the area. By the time Jesus reached Jerusalem, word of his insult and disregard for Roman authority had already reached the Roman officials in Jerusalem. They carefully monitored and scrutinized every move that he made. Jesus' enemies would soon capitalize upon the Roman mistrust and suspicion of Jesus and use it to have him convicted of sedition."

"Before entering Jericho," Realino concludes, "Jesus had been honored and respected by Roman authorities from Syria to the Galilee, the Decapolis, and Peraea to Judaea and even as far as to Rome itself. After exiting Jericho, he was looked upon with suspicion by the same high-ranking Roman officials."

TWO TRIUMPHAL ENTRIES

Tuesday, March 13 of AD 31 finds Jesus making the first of two triumphant entries into Jerusalem. (See Matthew 21:1-11, Mark 11:1-10, and Luke 19:29-44.)

While researching at Southern Methodist University in Dallas, Texas, I discovered a thin bound volume, edited in 1829 by Dr. Wilkins Boothe. Titled *Letters from the Cedron*, the book presented 15 letters written by a Cappadocia-born monk known only as Sabas. Sabas wrote his letters circa 485, while in seclusion in a cliff cave overlooking a gorge in what was at that time Palestine and what is now Israel.

Sabas wrote to instruct a group of 150 fellow monks who were also dwelling in caves in the area.

According to editor/compiler Boothe, (whom I will paraphrase):

These 15 letters are but a fraction of the hundreds of letters of instruction that Sabas wrote as teaching lessons. Apparently from about 470 AD until about 492 AD, neither he nor the community of monks said a word, except in vespers at prayer. All instructions and teachings were in writing. Eventually, against his will, Sabas became recognized as the priest and religious authority of the cave seclusion community. These 15 surviving letters are teachings that dealt with the last couple of weeks before Jesus was crucified. They specifically covered Jesus' first and second triumphal entries into Jerusalem.

This sentence stopped me short: First and *second* triumphal entries? I had believed there was only one such entry, and it happened on the day we celebrate as Palm Sunday.

However, if there were two entries, it would certainly explain the conflicting accounts given by the Gospels of Matthew, Mark, and Luke with that of the one in the Gospel of John.

According to Dr. Boothe, The first of Jesus' two triumphal entries took place on what would be our Tuesday, March 13, AD 31. The incident is recorded in the Gospels of Matthew 21:2-8; Mark 11:2-10; and Luke 19:30-40. The second triumphal entry took place ten days later, on what would be our Friday, March 23, AD 31. This one is recorded in the Gospel of John 12:12-19.

Sabas began his letters by saying that in this particular year (AD 31), because of a well-justified fear of rebellion in the Galilee and in the state of Judea, Pilate had declared in January that the Jewish celebrations of the Feast of Tabernacles, Yom Kippur (the Day of Atonement), and the Feast of Dedication were that year forbidden to be held in Jerusalem.

To counter this unjust infringement upon Jewish religious traditions, the Sadducees in Jerusalem decided to incorporate the celebrations of the Feast of Tabernacles, Yom Kippur, and the Feast of Dedication into an expanded Passover celebration. The celebration would last for 17 days rather than the typical seven days. When the proposal was submitted to Pilate, he willingly approved it to discourage any kind of rebellion.

So, for the first and only time in the history of the Jewish people, four Jewish celebrations were combined into one national celebration that was approved by the Roman authorities. Thus, on Tuesday, March 13 of AD 31, Jesus found himself approaching Jerusalem, for the Feast of Tabernacles portion of the 17-day celebration was about to begin.

As Jesus and his disciples approached Jerusalem's municipal customs post, Jesus sent two of his disciples ahead into the little village that had grown up around the customs post. The name of the village was Bethphage, meaning *district customs house*. The disciples were to secure a donkey on which Jesus could ride into Jerusalem.

One of the primary traditional celebrations associated with the Feast of Tabernacles began at sunup, and was carried out on both the first day and the last day of the celebration. The people would gather at the Pool of Siloam, where a chief priest gave them green tree branches. They then would slowly walk to the Temple while waving the branches. As they walked and waved the branches, they lamented, mourned, and cried, begging for the Messiah to come and to save them. This was called the *Great Hosanna*. The *Great Hosanna* literally meant, *Save us; we beseech you.*

It was not a shout of joy but a loud lament, accompanied by crying and wailing, as if a loved one had just died.

This was another surprise to me. I had always been taught that *Hosanna* was a word of praise—a shout of joy. In truth, *Hosanna* was a lamentation, a cry for mercy.

Boothe (drawing from the Sabas letters) goes on to explain, that while the lamenting people were making their way from the Pool of Siloam to the Temple, Jesus and his followers were moving toward the Eastern Gate of the city. As Jesus and his disciples began their descent from the Mount of Olives toward the Eastern Gate, his followers began to spontaneously spread their clothes in front of the donkey that he rode, and they began to shout praises to him.

Upon entering the Eastern Gate, Jesus and his celebrating followers met the lamenting Feast of Tabernacles participants. As the two groups joined, they became a huge lamenting and praising throng. The disciples then joined the participants in shouting the *Great Hosanna*. However, they directed their words to Jesus, indicating that they recognized *him* as that great delivering Messiah. Eventually, the outer court of the Temple was filled with a massive crowd, crying and shouting to Jesus.

Jesus allowed this adoration to continue for quite some time. He did not try to stop it.

To the Sadducees, of course, this was blasphemy. Some years previously, this Galilean rabboni had caused a stir in the Temple when he drove some merchants and moneychangers out of the Temple compound with a whip.

Since that time, there had been no other Jesus-related event that the Sadducees felt was worthy of their concern, but now, Jesus had drawn attention to himself again. This act of receiving praise and adoration within the Temple compound was *the act* that caused the powerful Sadducees to regard Jesus as more than just another itinerant Galilean rabboni who claimed to be God-sent.

From that time onward, Boothe notes, Jesus' every action and every word would be evaluated with extreme scrutiny. The Sadducees were the ones that Jesus had to fear. They, not the Shammaite Pharisees, had the power to influence his arrest, his imprisonment, his trial, and perhaps even his death. The Sadducees were very tolerant of the hundreds of self-proclaimed Messiahs and saviors who were traveling throughout the Galilee and Judaea. These self-proclaimed saviors did not overly concern them because they knew that they were nothing more than religious fog, here this moment and gone the next.

This was not the case with Jesus, Boothe points out. When festival celebrants began to direct the *Great Hosanna* toward Jesus, and to proclaim his Messiah-ship through sacred ceremonies instituted by Moses himself, something had to be done. Then, when Jesus refused to silence those who were giving him adoration and instead, allowed it to continue, this was more than the Sadducees could take.

"It was one thing to dispute with the Shammaite Pharisees, the scribes, and the Galilean Sadducees," Boothe explains. "It was quite another thing to become an enemy of the extremely powerful state-of-Judea Sadducees and the Sadducee leadership in Jerusalem. Arguing with the Pharisees would be like dealing with an obnoxious fly. Contending with the Jerusalem Sadducees was like wrestling a wild bull or an angry Nile crocodile."

Eventually, the praises died down and Jesus made his way back through the Temple compound, heading toward Solomon's Porch.

CLEANSING THE TEMPLE

However, the more he walked, the angrier he became, until finally the anger resulted in the second of the three times that he cleansed the Temple of the moneychangers and traders. (The first cleaning of the Temple was during Jesus' Second Year of Ministry.)

"Hours later, after things had calmed down, Dr. Boothe continues, "following Jesus expulsion of the moneychangers, the children, or more rightly, teens, who were in the Temple compound, began shouting praises to Jesus. Whether they did this on their own or were simply mimicking the adult lamenting/praising celebrants, we cannot say, but, we do know that the chief priests and the scribes were quite upset because Jesus did not stop them from praising him. Shortly after this, he traveled to Bethany and spent the night there.

"A couple of days later (on Thursday, March 22 of AD 31) Jesus and his disciples left Greco-Roman/Egyptian/Jewish Bethany and traveled back to Jerusalem. While they were traveling, Jesus noticed a single fig tree a far off. Because he was hungry, he was expecting figs to be on tree, but as he approached the fig tree, all it had was leaves. Since figs normally appeared as the leaves grow, it was understandable why Jesus would expect the tree to have figs as well as leaves. When he saw that it did not have any figs on it, he cursed the tree (Matthew 21: 18-22; Mark 11: 12-26), which immediately began to wither and die from its roots up."

They then continued on their way to Jerusalem.

Arriving in Jerusalem, Jesus and his disciples went first to the Temple. When they arrived at the Temple, again the merchants and moneychangers were trading. So, for the third and final time, Jesus drove the merchants and moneychangers out of the Temple compound, again causing a stir with the scribes, chief priests, and the Sadducees.

He obviously made his point clear because the merchants and moneychangers did not return to the Temple until after the death of Jesus.

Later in the day, Jesus and his disciples returned to Bethany for the night. On their way back, they passed the fig tree that Jesus had cursed and noticed it had died and withered away. Some of the disciples commented about how quickly it died.

Jesus responded by teaching them a lesson on faith, by using the example of a mustard seed for the third time (Matthew 21:18-22; Mark 11:12-26). On all three occasions, Jesus emphasized the importance of a person's faith by comparing faith to a mustard seed and/or mustard plant. All three occasions took place at three different times over a two-year period.

Later that evening (Thursday, March 22, AD 31,) Jesus and his disciples were invited to eat at the home of Mary and Martha, the sisters of Lazarus, whom Jesus had raised from the dead (John 12:3-8).

JESUS ANOINTED WITH OIL

It is now nine days after the first triumphal entry into Jerusalem. Jesus and his disciples dine at the home of Mary and Martha.

After dinner, Mary kneels behind Jesus, who is reclining on a couch, and anoints his feet with spikenard.

According to Dr. Boothe, Martha was doing the serving while Jesus and his disciples and Lazarus were reclining on the couches that were so typical of Egyptian/Roman/Jewish culture. We do not know what Mary was doing until we see her come up behind Jesus and begin to anoint his feet. The ointment that she used was the same kind of ointment with which he had previously been anointed by a sinner woman at Simon the Pharisee's house in Capernaum (in the winter of AD 28).

This was the most expensive salve in the world; 12 ounces of it would have been worth about two years' income on the wholesale merchants' market and five to seven years' income on the retail market.

After anointing Jesus' feet and filling the whole place with the aroma of the ointment, Mary dried them with her hair.

The apostle Judas was incensed at what he considered a waste of expensive ointment, saying that it could have been sold and the proceeds given to the poor. Perhaps he mentioned the poor because, shortly before this, Jesus had given his great challenge about feeding the poor, helping the orphans, and visiting those who were in prison: *"In that you have done it to the least of these, you have done it unto me."* Judas felt safe in challenging this "waste" by using Jesus' own teaching, probably expecting Jesus to credit him for being so in tune with his ideas and philosophy.

However, Jesus knew that Judas' underlying motive was one of selfishness. Jesus defended Mary, implying that honoring him (Jesus) was a higher form of service than even that to the poor and needy. This stern rebuke of Judas, in front of all those present, was humiliating and infuriating.

It was probably after this open rebuke that Judas decided to get even with Jesus.

According to Dr. Boothe, "One of the Sabas letters covers Jesus and his disciples' traveling back to Jerusalem from Bethany on Friday, March 23. This was the last day of the Feast of Tabernacles' portion of the 17-day combined celebration. On this day, the second *Great Hosanna* lamentation takes place."

Boothe continues, "Jesus found a colt himself, sat on it, and led his disciples toward the Eastern Gate (John 12:12-19). Jesus again intercepted the *Great Hosanna* participants just as they were approaching the Eastern Gate. This time though, his disciples did not have to lead the way in worship and adoration to Jesus. The lamenting participants themselves recognized Jesus from 10 days previous, and they began to praise him and to direct the *Great Hosanna* toward him. Again, Jesus accepted the praise.

"Without a doubt, this was *the* final slap in the face to the powerful Sadducees. From that time forward, these Jerusalem Sadducees were determined to take Jesus' life.

"Less than two weeks later, their determination was realized."

With that statement, Dr. Boothe concludes his examination of the Sabas letters.

After his second triumphant entry, Jesus and his disciples spend the day in the Temple compound. Jesus teaches the Pharisees, scribes, priests, and anyone willing to listen.

The next morning, Friday, March 23, Jesus again traveled to Jerusalem and went to the Temple. This time there were no merchants, animals, goods, or money changers in the Temple. For the remainder of the day, Jesus stayed in the Temple and taught the Pharisees, scribes, and priests and the combined feasts celebrants. His lessons included the *parables of the two sons, evil servant, marriage feast* (the second time Jesus told the parable of the wedding feast), and the *wedding garments*; the lesson on *rendering unto Caesar that which is Caesar's, the greatest commandment* (the second time Jesus taught this lesson), the question of *marriage in the afterlife,* and the question about *who is David's son?*

OLIVET DISCOURSE

After a long day of teaching, Jesus and the disciples leave the Temple. Jesus informs the disciples that the magnificent structure will soon be destroyed. The disciples are shocked to hear this. They are speechless.

Later, the group crosses the Kidron Valley, climbs the Mount Olives, and sits down to rest.

As they rest, the disciples ask Jesus to explain his earlier comments about the Temple. When would the destruction happen? Would this be a sign of the world's end? Jesus' response to this line of questioning is called his *Olivet Discourse.* (See Matthew 24:1-51, Mark 12:41-13:2, and Luke 21:5-36.)

While studying at Southeastern Seminary in Louisville, Kentucky, I found a book edited by Dr. Alfredo Mozzini in 1938. This book featured sermons by Elijah Coleman Bridgman (1801-1861), America's first missionary to China. Jesus' Olivet Discourse was one sermon topic.

Bridgman begins this sermon with historical background information. This information was more important to my research than the sermon itself.

Bridgman explains:

"Jesus began this discussion with his disciples while they were still in the Temple compound. As they admired the grandeur of the Temple, Jesus told them that not one stone would be left on top of the other. It is not clear if Jesus was alluding to a physical future event or a symbolic event. Physically, this did take place with the destruction of the Temple in AD 70, when the Roman soldiers dismantled the Temple stone by stone to get to the gold that had melted, because of the intense heat. After the Temple was set ablaze, the melted gold ran down and had lodged between the joints of the stones.

"Symbolically, Jesus could have been alluding to a time when the existing Jewish religion would perish and be replaced by a new, purer, and less formal observance. After the destruction of the Temple, Jewish worship as they knew it disappeared. It was replaced with a different form of Jewish worship that was simple and far less ritualistic.

"Besides the 12 disciples, we do not know who heard Jesus make these statements. Most likely, it was only the 12, because if others had heard Jesus' remarks, it could have caused a panicked uproar."

We'll now skip ahead in the Bridgman sermon (I will paraphrase). Jesus and the disciples are on the Mount of Olives, and Peter, James, and John ask three questions: When will the destruction of the Temple take place? What will be the signs of your coming (or when will you set up your kingdom and reign as Messiah)? And when will be the end of time?

According to Bridgman, many Bible scholars think that major portions of Jesus' discourse have been lost. The primary reason for thinking this is that the Matthew 24 portion does not flow smoothly or clearly, which is different from most other discourses spoken by Jesus.

Another theory is that rather than some of the discourse being lost, the author of Matthew's Gospel did the same thing with this discourse as he had done with the Sermon on the Mount. He picked out parts from many different sermons and teachings from Jesus' teaching ministry and put them all together into one discourse.

Within the discourse can be found end-time catastrophes, judgment, the siege of Jerusalem, natural disasters, and the persecution of Christians. They are all thrown together in disorderly fashion. Hence, we must extract from this literary hodgepodge some type of coherent flow of events.

Here, the editor Mozzini interjects:

"Very little of the discourse had to do with future events that would be fulfilled in our (Mozzini's) time or some time beyond our time, regardless of what the reformers and revivalists have said over the past one hundred years.

"They have tried to mold this Matthew 24 portion into a predetermined theory, which has evolved into eschatology doctrine. This doctrine then must somehow fit into the prophecies of Ezekiel, Isaiah, Jeremiah, Daniel, I & II Thessalonians, and the Revelation, revealing events that are supposed to take place at the end of time, ushering in a world-renowned Anti-Christ. In our modern society this particular idea was introduced by the Anglican priest turned preacher, Rev. John Nelson Darby, in 1862. However, it was Darby's disciple and associate, Rev. Cyrus I. Scofield, with the publication of his Scofield Reference Bible in 1909, that raised the hitherto radical and unconventional philosophy to the level of fundamentalist doctrine.

"This reasoning and manufactured doctrine are absolutely ridiculous! All one has to do is to read this Matthew 24 portion and it becomes obvious that this revivalist-inspired, end-time prophecy teaching is nothing short of heresy.

"To me, it is obvious that the statements Jesus made have been enmeshed with many successive layers of revisions.

"The additions were not affixed to the beginning or to the end of the original discourse. Instead, they were added to the discourse in places where they would best conform to and emphasize the current doctrines of the church at a particular time in church history. As a result, we can readily recognize numerous 'out of place' statements by just reading the discourse."

According to Mozzini,

Mozzini adds, "One such example is Jesus' statement 'Now learn a parable from the fig tree.' The entire portion from 'Now learn a parable' in verse 32 through the statement 'Truly I say unto you' in verse 34 was added in the tenth or eleventh century. This portion had to do with the lives of the disciples not passing away before they would experience much of the horror that Jesus told them about. It is not the rebirth of Israel or the recalling of the Jewish people to their homeland.

"Jesus' original discourse dealt primarily with the immediate future. Jesus warned that the persecutions would begin soon after his resurrection and would continue for centuries. He also said that Jerusalem would be destroyed before the death of all of them who were there with him. After Jesus' resurrection and ascension, these disciples expected Jesus to return immediately and to set up his kingdom, meaning that all the things that he had spoken would be fulfilled.

"During the first century, there were numerous times when the early church believers could have concluded that Jesus' words were becoming a reality."

Mozzini gives several historical examples to support this point. Here are just a few:

- In AD 44, there was a widespread famine throughout Roman Syria. This ushered in many epidemics that, before the famine subsided in AD 48, claimed the lives of one out of every three adults and three out of every four children under age 12.

- In AD 53, a series of disastrous earthquakes rocked Phrygia, Galatia, and Cappadocia, destroying more than 300 villages and killing tens of thousands.

- In AD 64, a tremendous fire broke out in Rome. Nero blamed the Christians for the fire. As punishment for this "crime," he had hundreds of them put to death by the most horrible means.

- Of 29 sieges of Jerusalem, 16 took place after the Olivet Discourse. In each instance, thousands of Christians and Jews were tortured and killed.

- AD 81, Domitian began the most far-reaching general persecution of the Christians to date. For the first time, Christians were persecuted in all Roman provinces and in every region where Rome ruled. It is estimated that during this persecution, the Christian community throughout the Empire dwindled from 6 million to less than 2 million (by the time of Domitian's death in AD 96).

Mozzini then addresses false prophets and their role in signaling the end times. Mozzini agrees with Bridgman that there have been many false prophets/messiahs, dating back to Jesus' time.

Bridgman notes,

- A disciple of John the Baptist, a man by the name of Dositheus of Samaria, claimed in AD 34 to be the Messiah.

- In AD 63, Theudas of Hebron claimed to be the returned Messiah and had a following of over 4,000 dedicated disciples, who went two by two, spreading his message throughout the Roman world.

- Joachim of Floris said in 1130 that during the first century after Jesus' death and resurrection that no fewer than 380 men and three women claimed to be either the Messiah, the returned Messiah, or the reincarnated and returned Jesus.

So, although Jesus may well have referred to events that were to lead to the end-times, the majority of his Olivet Discourse was pointing to the immediate future concerning his disciples and how they were going to survive the immediate future.

According to Bridgman, "The end of the world, with a final judgment, was not unique to Jesus. The Babylonians, Persians, Assyrians, Hittites, Syrians, Greeks, Mayans, ancient Jews, and other peoples taught a future end, judgment, rewards for the righteous, and punishment for the wicked. What made Jesus' message unique was that he did not concentrate on the punishment side of judgment. Rather, he sought to open the hearts of his followers so that they would be spared punishment and be received into his new kingdom through faith in him and through forgiveness from God the Father and by being vigilant in their dedication to being 'doers' of what he had taught them."

Mozzini then breaks from his commentary on Bridgman's sermon and begins to talk about the times in which he lived. When Bridgman wrote this sermon, the Darby inspired fundamental dispensational movement, with its six or seven dispensation periods, rapture, and end-time prophecy, was in its infancy. It did not make much of a stir until after his death when it caught hold in America and spread like a wildfire and became the dominate thinking among American Protestants.

Although I knew some of the teachings that had originated with Darby and Scofield, there were many others that I did not realize derived from them. Some were fringe beliefs that were not worthy of serious consideration. However, once they were introduced as fact in his 1909 dispensational, premillennial Scofield Reference Bible, they became so solid that a doctrine could be built on them, irrespective of the foundational doctrines upon which the church fathers fomented their beliefs, more than 1900 years earlier.

As I reflected on the insights of Bridgman and Mozzini, I realized that, for years and years, I had been deceived. All of my life, I had been taught passages like Matthew 24 and the book of Revelation applied to the ultimate end of the world. Most people I knew believed this doctrine, which was taught by theologians like Scofield and Darby, and by almost every pastor and Sunday school teacher I encountered. My father was the rare exception. He did not swallow such teaching, because God's Word did not confirm it.

I determined that from now on, I wouldn't believe something was true just because someone said so. Absolute truth is attainable ONLY by studying God's Word. In His Word, God explains what he means. He doesn't need anyone to add to or twist His words.

THE TEN VIRGINS

After Jesus' *Olivet Discourse* teaching, he tells his disciples three parables about the 10 virgins, the five talents, and the importance of showing mercy.

At Notre Dame University in South Bend, Indiana, I found an essay written in 1899 by Dr. Leslie Pfeiffer. The essay was a commentary on a sermon by Thomas Becket, Archbishop of Canterbury from AD 1162 to 1170. Jesus' parables of the virgins and the talents are central to this sermon.

According to Dr. Pfeiffer, "The historical setting for both of these parables is the Mount of Olives. As Jesus concluded his *Olivet Discourse*, he told both of these parables to his disciples. The time was Saturday, March 24, AD 31."

Pfeiffer adds that although Becket was an Archbishop, he was a historian before he was a clergyman. As such, he had extraordinary insight and knowledge when it came to these parables. He believed that if the people could understand a parable historically, they would more fully appreciate its lesson.

Accordingly, Becket believed that the "10 virgins" parable was based on the marriage of Demeter, who was the daughter of Annius Rufus, a former governor of Judaea. The details of this wedding were well-known at the time of Jesus' ministry.

Pfeiffer writes,

"Demeter's wedding was scheduled for a specific day, March 15. However, her bridegroom, the military commander Sethius Octavia Seneacus, had to sail from Rhodes to Caesarea Maritima. Because of a perilous storm, Sethius was blown off course and his arrival was delayed by almost two days. He was unable to send word that he had been delayed. The guests could only speculate on what had happened.

"After a day of waiting, most of the guests became frustrated and left the wedding celebration. Among the ones that stayed were ten of the bride's best friends, who also served as the bride's personal care-maids.

"As the second evening wore on, discouragement began to set in. Then a messenger arrived, declaring that Sethius had been blown off course, but he was now on his way. He would arrive that night to take his bride.

"Demeter told her ten friends to travel up the main highway with a military escort, to meet Sethius and escort him to the wedding. Because it was night, the friends had to take lamps with them. Five of the friends had enough oil in their lamps to leave immediately, but the other five had to go into town and buy additional oil. However, while the friends were about their duties, Sethius suddenly arrived. Upon his arrival, he ordered the doors of the celebration hall to be closed, allowing no one else into the celebration. Those who had gone to buy oil were locked out.

"Jesus used this historical event to show that regardless of how secure a people feel that they are with the bride (the church), if they are not ready to enter into the joy of the Lord at the time of his return, they will not be allowed to participate. Closeness to the bride (the church) is secondary to closeness to the groom (Jesus)."

Five Talents

Dr. Pfeiffer's essay then moves to the second parable from Becket's sermon. This parable, too, was built on a historical foundation (Matthew 25:14-30).

According to Pfeiffer,

"This story was a favorite that was told in the Roman Imperial Schools of Economics and Finance to show economics students the absolute necessity of investing tax revenues in income-producing investments or interest-bearing bank accounts, so that the revenues would grow in value.

"Graduates of the Imperial Schools became 'tax lords.' This parable features one of these professionals: Craverius, the tax lord of the Roman province of Achaia during the reign of Augustus. Because of his unique ability to invest the province's tax revenues and to always make a huge profit, usually double the amount of taxes collected, and sometimes 10 times more.

"To reward this stellar performance, Augustus (in 10 BC) appointed Craverius to the honored position of tax lord over four additional provinces: Macedonia, Epirus, Thrace, and Dalmatia.

"To ensure that his performance would not suffer in the face of the added responsibility, Craverius divided the assessor respon-sibilities of the province of Achaia among his five district tax assessors, with instructions that the five assessors were to continue in Craverius's footsteps of investing and providing Augustus with many times more resources than were collected in taxes. After giving the five assessors their final instructions, Craverius left Achaia to visit his other four tax realms."

According to Becket's sermon, Pfeiffer writes:

"Craverius told his assessors that if they were successful, they would be able to attend a school of economics, and, eventually, become tax lords themselves." In the sermon, Becket reports, "Craverius was gone from Achaia for five years, expecting things to run under his five assessors as well as they had under his direct leadership. Upon his return, one of his first acts was to demand an accounting of the tax revenues and investment returns.

"Four of the assessors had been successful in making income on their investments. They went on to the schools of economics and eventually became tax lords. One did not want to risk the tax revenues on investments, nor did he trust the banks, so he did nothing with the revenues. Although he did not lose any money, the tax revenues that he collected did not grow. This assessor was condemned as a traitor by Augustus and was exiled to Moesia, where he worked in the unbearably hot and miserable sulfur mines (called outer darkness or utter blackness by the locals) for the remainder of his life, never seeing the light of day again.

"Jesus used this historical event as a basis for his allegorical teaching, which emphasized that his disciples should not be satisfied with the status quo. They must minister to the hungry, the naked, those in prison, and the hurting. In so doing, they would be investing revenues into interest-bearing accounts. The small investment that they would make would be multiplied far beyond their expectations, because they would be laying up treasures in heaven."

Becket commented that Jesus taught these lessons as they paused to rest on the Mount of Olives on their way back to the little town of Bethany.

Plotting a Death

Becket's sermon (and Pfeiffer's commentary) also cover what was happening in Jesus' life at the time he was teaching these parables.

Specifically, Pfeiffer reports, the religious leaders and the elders were conspiring with the High Priest on how to silence Jesus, even if it meant his death, but, they had a problem. If they arrested Jesus in the open during the day, his many followers would start a riot in his support and bring the wrath of Rome down upon them. It was forbidden to arrest a religious leader within the Temple compound grounds.

At night Jesus could not be arrested because he had been staying with influential friends in Bethany. Bethany had special protection from the Roman government, and it was outside of the jurisdiction of the Jewish Sanhedrin. The residents of Bethany hated the arrogant Jewish religious charlatans, especially those from Jerusalem. A Bethany town governor by the name of Cleopaulas Ceophus (in AD 23) forbade any Jewish religious leader from entering Bethany, under penalty of death, unless a resident of Bethany invited them to the town. A Jewish religious leader was permitted to pass through Bethany without an invitation, but he could not stop without a written invitation. At the time of Jesus' ministry, this restriction was still being practiced.

Faced with this dilemma, Becket says that these leaders "put the word out" that they would be willing to pay handsomely, up to 30 pieces of silver, to anyone willing to cooperate, This sum, interjects Pfeiffer, equaled about eight years' wages for a common laborer.

Becket notes that only Matthew's Gospel refers to the 30 pieces of silver. The Gospel of Andrew (from the Apocrypha), says that Judas was given a large sum of money, enough to make him among the ten wealthiest men in Jerusalem.

SIMON THE LEPER

Three days after teaching his final parables, (on Tuesday evening of March 27) Jesus and his disciples dine at the home of Simon the leper. There, Jesus is anointed for a third time (Matthew 26:6). Interestingly, twice Jesus was anointed on his feet. On this occasion, the oil was poured on his head. (Although the Bible refers to Simon the leper, it was not permitted for a leper to associate with those who were clean. Either he had been healed, or perhaps the early translators mistranslated the phrase and confused two similar Hebrew phrases, *the humble one*, for the word *leper)*.

The following day, Wednesday March 28, was the preparation day for the Passover portion of the expanded celebration. This was an exciting day for Jesus and his disciples, as it was for all Jews.

One of the most intriguing accounts of the Passover preparation was written by eighteenth century British nonconformist Philip Doddridge. Doddridge claimed to have gleaned his information from *De Trinitate*, a book by Hilary, Bishop of Poitiers (315-368).

I discovered Doddridge's book at Harvard University Library in Cambridge, Massachusetts. This book, published in 1749, was titled *Studies on the Opinions of the Fathers*. I found the text hard to follow, but it did provide a helpful, if sometimes *confounding*, timeline of Jesus' final days.

Early in his book, Doddridge explains that methods of counting time had changed between his time and that of Jesus. He writes,

"Typically, the seven days of unleavened bread and the Passover celebration began the evening of the 14th of Nisan (using the Jewish lunar calendar) and ended on the evening of the 21st of Nisan. Even though it was an expanded 17-day celebration in the year AD 31, the Passover portion of the expanded celebration remained the same. The daytime period of the 14th of Nisan was called the Day of Preparation. During this daytime period of the 14th of Nisan, the Passover lamb was killed. The evening of the 14th of Nisan was when the Feast of the Passover was observed.

"The next day, the Feast of Unleavened Bread was observed. This first 24-hour period was called a special Sabbath. Six days later, on the evening of the 20th of Nisan, the Feast of the Lord was observed. This feast frequently lasted all night. The following day, the 21st of Nisan, was the last day of the seven days of unleavened bread. This last 24-hour period was a High Sabbath because it was a special Sabbath that overlapped a weekly Sabbath. Jesus ate the 14th of Nisan Feast of Passover with his disciples but he did not eat the 20th of Nisan Feast of the Lord.

"The typical Jewish day was a 24-hour period that began at 6:00 a.m. (the 1st hour) and ended at 6:00 a.m. (the next 1st hour.) Each 24-hour period was divided into two 12-hour parts: the day period was from 6:00 a.m. (the 1st hour) to 6:00 p.m. (the 12th hour). The night period was from 6:00 p.m. (the 12th hour) to 6:00 a.m. (the 1st hour). Therefore, when we refer to Tuesday, we think of a period that began at midnight on Monday and ended at Tuesday's midnight. In the Jewish time frame, the same period of time would be composed of the last 12-hour night period of Monday and the first 12-hour period of Tuesday."

(Do you see what I mean by "confounding?") Doddridge then states,

"For the past two centuries (since the 1500s) all of the events of Jesus' last few days, from the Last Supper to the resurrection, have been compressed into four days (from Thursday evening to Sunday morning).

"However, the traditionally accepted viewpoint of the first 10 centuries placed the events from the Last Supper to (Jesus') burial in a five-day period with resurrection occurring THREE FULL 24-HOUR DAYS after burial.

"During the next five centuries, the traditional viewpoint of the period that covered these events fluctuated between three days and seven days, with resurrection of the body occurring two days later.

This tradition carried with it the belief that Jesus had two resurrections: one was the body resurrection and the other was the spirit resurrection. The two resurrections were separated by eight 24-hour days."

So, this leads us to acknowledge that we really don't know how many days it took for all the events from the Last Supper to the final (or only), resurrection to take place. I guess it really doesn't matter. All that matters is that it happened and Jesus arose from the dead.

THE LAST SUPPER

Next, Doddridge turns his attention from theories and timetables to actual events. Specifically, he focuses on The *Feast of Passover,* which was eaten after sundown, as the night period of the 14th of Nisan (6:00 p.m. on our Wednesday, March 28), the 12th hour, began. This meal, which Jesus shared with his disciples, is known by many as *The Last Supper.*

Doddridge writes:

"At the feast there arose a strife between the 12 over personal greatness,"(Luke 22:24-30).

"Jesus did not reprimand them for arguing and comparing; he merely showed them true humbleness by washing their feet (John 13:4-17).

"By washing their feet, he was implying that to obtain greatness, you must be willing to humble yourself and become a servant. He, being the Messias/Messiah, humbled himself. He was not only a regular servant, but the lowest of servants, the one who washed the feet of guests.

"Some time after this, Jesus foretold Judas' betrayal (Matthew 26:20-25).

"After the meal, it was customary for the host of the meal to take bread, sop out the meat dish, give the bread sop to different ones in the group, and give them a blessing as he fed them a piece of bread. One of the disciples Jesus picked to serve was Judas. As he gave him the bread, Jesus told him to go and do what he felt he should do. Because the blessing was always given to an individual, only he could hear it, none of the other disciples knew what Jesus had said to Judas. They assumed when Judas left, he was going to give money to the poor, which was a customary closing ritual to the Feast of Passover meal.

"Judas left the supper and went to the chief priests to betray Jesus. He took their money and told them where Jesus would be later that night. He later led them to the spot where Jesus was praying." (At this point, John's Gospel tells us that Satan entered Judas.)

"The chief priests had decided that if they could arrest Jesus he had to be interrogated before the Feast of the Lord, which was to be held on the 20th of Nisan (our April 2, AD 31). The 21st of Nisan (our April 3, AD 31) was the High Sabbath.

"After Judas had departed, Jesus gave the remaining disciples a new commission and a new commandment that they should love one another (John 13:31-34). He also instigated the Lord's Supper, which commemorated and became a permanent reminder of his sufferings and death. He also indicated that he would not eat the Feast of the Lord with them, which they were to eat on the 20th of Nisan, six days from then.

"Finally, they were finished and it was time to leave. Jesus asked about their weapons (Luke 22:35-38).

"They then sang a hymn and departed to the Mount of Olives. (See Matthew 26:31-35, Mark 14:26-31, Luke 22:31-39, and John 13:36-17-26.)

"On the western slope of the mount was located the Garden of Gethsemane, where Jesus was going to pray. It was a garden owned by a friend of Jesus. As they walked to the Mount of Olives, Jesus foretold that all of them would forsake him that night. Peter brazenly stated that he would never forsake him, even if all the rest did. That is when Jesus said that very night, before the peacock crowed three times, that Peter, would deny that he knew Jesus at least three times. Peter refused to believe that.

"As Jesus and the 11 continued to walk, Jesus encouraged them. The entire chapters of 14 through 17 of John record his conversation with his disciples, as they walked from the place where they had the Feast of Passover, to the Garden of Gethsemane.

"Upon their arrival at the garden, Jesus and his disciples entered. Leaving the rest of his disciples near the entrance, he took Peter, James, and John with him further into the garden. Jesus then left them, asking them to watch and pray, while he walked on by himself to pray."

According to Doddridge, Jesus prayed until about 9:00 that night, the 14th of Nisan (which is our Wednesday, March 28). Then Judas arrived, with a mob perhaps as large as 1,000 people, to arrest him.

Continuing archaeological investigations in Jericho—Israel.

CHAPTER 25

✺

Jesus' Arrest and Crucifixion

PART 1 — AD 31

"On the eve of Passover they hanged Yeshu of Nazareth. And a herald went before him forty days, saying, 'Yeshu of Nazareth is going forth to be chastened, since he has practiced sorcery and cheated, and led people astray. Let everyone knowing anything in his defense come and plead for him.' But they found no one in his defense, and they hanged him on the eve of Passover."
(from the Babylonian Talmuds)

ON THE FATEFUL NIGHT of his arrest, Jesus taught his disciples many lessons as they walked to the Garden of Gethsemane. Once they arrived at the garden, Jesus' long ordeal of pre-crucifixion torture began.

In the year 457, Pope Leo the 1st wrote a letter to "Cornelius of Carthage, sufferer for Christ." I discovered this letter while researching at the University of Manchester. It was one of several letters written by Leo the Great to be reproduced and translated from the original Latin into English, French, and Spanish and bound into a volume in 1817.

The volume was titled *Great Letters of Leo the Great*, and I found that the letter addressed to Cornelius did, indeed, greatly increase my understanding of Jesus' Gethsemane experience.

Leo begins this letter with a greeting and a prayer for God's grace and healing.

He then praises Cornelius for keeping the faith against overwhelming obstacles.

GETHSEMANE

Next, Leo reflects on Jesus' experience in Gethsemane. He writes,

"As Jesus went through so much for our sakes, then we too must be willing to go through the same for him." In the following paragraphs, I will paraphrase this letter, while including some direct quotes along the way.

"Jesus entered the Garden of Gethsemane, a large garden that fronted an immense olive grove (which contained an olive press.) The olive grove covered the entire north and most of the west of the Mount of Olives. Jesus left eight of his disciples in the garden near the entrance, and walked with Peter, James and John further into the grove, perhaps as far as the olive press,. Here, Jesus left the three disciples and walked on further into the olive grove to pray.

"When Jesus arrived at the place he was going to pray, he collapsed in spiritual torture and emotional agony. On two different occasions, about an hour apart, he returned to Peter, James, and John and found them sleeping, probably because the meal they had just consumed made them sleepy. He warned them to 'pray, that you enter not into temptation.' Although they were probably willing, the physical body would not cooperate."

Luke's Gospel records that as Jesus prayed, his sweat became as great drops of blood. "I feel, even though I am not a doctor," Leo writes, "that this was caused by Jesus' great emotional stress. This type of condition was a physical phenomenon known to the Greeks as hematidrosis, or bloody sweat. The condition occurs when a person is under extreme emotional stress to the point that tiny blood passages in the sweat glands break and mix with the sweat.

"This condition is rare, but it has been documented to occur amongst the Greeks, Romans, and Egyptians. Accompanying this condition comes extreme fatigue, weakness and the possibility of traumatic shock.

"Jesus prayed and asked the Father if it be His will, for the cup to be taken from him (Luke 22:42). This cup could have been the cup of intense suffering. However, Jesus knew that he was going to go through the most intense suffering that had ever been inflicted upon any man, so although he may not have been prepared for it to the fullest, he was aware that it would happen, and that it was supposed to happen. Therefore, I am not sure that this cup was the cup of Jesus' suffering. It could have been:

- The cup of death by the most inhumane means.

- The fact that Jesus knew his Father would literally turn His back on him, leaving him totally alone.

- The cup of shame, as he would be crucified naked, shamed.

- The fact that he knew his death would eventually culminate in the persecution of those whom he loved so dearly.

- That the cup was the cup of death inflicted upon him by Satan, before he got to the cross, right there in the olive grove. If Satan could kill him before he got to the cross, then God's redemptive plan could be short-circuited.

"The third time that Jesus came back to the olive press, he again found Peter, James, and John sleeping. But this time he did not ask them to pray as he had the other two times. This time he told them to sleep on because the hour was at hand for him to be arrested."

Some time later, Judas arrived, leading a huge procession of armed guards and civil and religious officials. The Gospel of John 18:3 and 12 indicate that an armed guard of 600 to 1,000 temple guards was sent by the High Priest to arrest Jesus. These, along with the local civil authorities and religious leaders, could have numbered well over a thousand.

It was predetermined that Jesus would be identified by Judas, who would greet him with the traditional kiss on each cheek.

Leo then writes about the admirable courage of Peter:

"When he realized what was happening, he drew his sword and attacked Malchus, the servant of the High Priest, to defend Jesus.

"For almost four centuries, there has been confusion about this attack. The Gospel of John says that Peter cut off Malchus' right ear. This could represent three different scenarios:

- Peter was left-handed, and he attacked Malchus while facing him.

- Peter was right-handed, but he attacked Malchus from the back.

- Peter attacked and killed Malchus and then cut off his right ear as a trophy of conquest (which was a typical action for victors of duels or arena blood games).

"I (Leo) believe that Peter was left-handed. However, the other scenarios could also be true, especially since many in the Church are now beginning to suppress any reference to Peter killing an unarmed man, even though he was protecting Jesus.

"Rather than thanking Peter for risking his life to save him, Jesus rebuked him. Jesus then healed (and perhaps raised from the dead) the man Peter had attacked.

"I (Leo) surmises that Jesus' response caused Peter to become angry. Peter's anger turned to resentment, which culminated in revenge, prompting him to repeatedly deny Jesus a few hours later.

"From the garden, the multitude led Jesus to the palace residence of Annas, a former High Priest (from AD 6-15) and the father-in-law of Caiaphas, the current High Priest.

"None of Jesus' followers supported him at the time. Perhaps they were afraid of the Temple guards, thinking that if they could arrest Jesus, surely they would arrest his followers too. Maybe they were afraid of Jesus and how he would react if they tried to support him. After all, look at what had happened to Peter!

"Since Jesus was a Jewish religious figure, the Jewish religious authorities were allowed to take the lead in dealing with him. Hence, it is most likely that they were given permission to arrest and detain Jesus. However, if the one arrested was highly regarded by Roman authorities, the Jewish religious leaders were forbidden to inflict excessive punishment.

"Jesus had already suffered intense emotional anguish, which left his body and spirit weak and vulnerable. This was only the beginning of an unprecedented journey of pain, torment, and agony that Jesus would endure over the next few days."

With that, Leo concludes his account of Jesus' passion.

The rest of the letter encourages Cornelius to use Jesus' passion as inspiration to press on.

I found another authenticating source for the events of Jesus' arrest, at England's London Bible College research library.

In 1237, Raymund of Penafort penned a 60-page Latin manuscript titled *The Historia Chronicon Pascale.* Raymund was a successful lawyer before becoming a Dominican monk in AD 1222.

A volume titled *The Order of the Mercedarian,* edited in 1937 by Sir Thurmon Kane, contains four surviving pages of Raymund's original manuscript, translated into Greek, French, and English. Along with the translations, Sir Kane added commentary and background information.

Today, the surviving vellum leaves of Raymund's thirteenth century manuscript are stored in The Vatican II library. (Vellum is a form of parchment, once made of animal skin.)

According to Sir Kane's background information, the main focus of Raymund's manuscript was to provide an exhaustive recounting of the passion, arrest, trial and crucifixion of Jesus. The surviving four pages cover Jesus' trial written as a legal summarization.

"It appears that Raymund of Penafort," Sir Kane explains, "had quite some insight into the judicial practices of both Jew and Roman at the time of Jesus' crucifixion."

"In his manuscript, Raymund summarized, in chronological order, the last days of Jesus' life before crucifixion. He then went back and forth describing in detail the events of those last days. The four surviving pages, written on the front and back, represent but a small portion of the first part, the summary."

Sir Kane then begins commenting on Raymund's document, which began in mid-sentence:

JESUS IS ARRESTED

"...the mob led Jesus, bound, from the Mount garden to Annas's palace.

"From the palace of Annas, Jesus was led to the palace of Caiaphas, the High Priest (John 18:13-14). There he appeared before the preliminary Court of Elders and Priests and was interrogated.

"As Jesus was being led into Caiaphas' palace, a disciple known by the High Priest, probably Judas, Nicodemus, or Joseph of Arimathea, followed Jesus into the palace. Peter stood outside of the palace. Not long afterwards, the disciple that the High Priest knew and who had followed Jesus into the palace, went out to get Peter and brought him inside (John 18:16).

"At the same time Peter was entering the palace, the lady door keeper asked him if he was one of Jesus' disciples. Peter said, 'No!' (John 18:17)

"Inside the palace, Peter joined a group of servants who were warming themselves by a fire. A girl said to the people gathered there that he (Peter) was with Jesus. Peter denied it. (Luke 23:56-57)

"As Jesus was being interrogated by the preliminary court, Peter was again asked if he was a follower of Jesus. For the third time he denied this. (John 18:25)

"Not long thereafter, a man said to Peter that he (Peter) was one of the followers of Jesus. Peter denied for the fourth time that he was one of Jesus' followers (Luke 22:58). Then a relative of Malchus, who Peter had confronted in the garden, challenged Peter. 'Weren't you in the garden with Jesus?' he asked. Peter denied it. Immediately following the fifth denial, the peacock crowed (John 18:27) the first of the two times."

After this quote, Sir Kane interjects this commentary.

"This cock was not a poultry rooster which we see so often depicted today. Chickens and roosters that we westerners so readily picture were not native to the Middle East. The chicken as we know it did not commonly appear in the Middle East until the second or third century AD. The bird in this story was probably a peacock or the 'fowl of conscience,' as Cicero called it.

"The trained peacock was used throughout the Roman Empire by the aristocracy and the wealthy for two reasons:

- The peacock was trained to crow approximately every two hours. So, approximately two hours after sunset, the peacock crowed for the first time and continued throughout the night every two hours until sunrise.

- Peacocks were trained as burglar alarms. Peacocks were allowed to roam freely throughout the house and throughout the grounds. If anyone who was unfamiliar to the bird tried to enter the home or the grounds, the peacock would start screeching and screaming its blood-curdling shriek, waking the members of the household."

Sir Kane then returns to Raymund's manuscript:

"From the time the peacock crowed the first time until it crowed a second time, two hours had elapsed. Sometime after Peter denied that he knew Jesus for the fifth time and the peacock crowed the first time, another man said that Peter was one of Jesus' disciples. Again he denied it and this time he cursed to emphasize that he was not a follower of this Jesus (Matthew 26:74; Mark 15: 70-71; Luke 22:60). Immediately the cock crowed a second time (Mark 15:71; Luke 22:60). As the cock crowed the second time, Jesus turned and looked at his disciple. Peter, remembering the words of Jesus, as well as his own words of guaranteed faithfulness to Jesus, ran from the palace of Caiaphas, and went out and wept bitterly (Matthew 26:75; Luke 22:61-62)."

An interesting point that Raymund brings out about cursing, Sir Kane explains, is that,

"Cursing is not part of a Christ-like character. So, the best way to convince people that one is not a follower of Christ is to curse. Regardless of what comes out of a person's mouth as praise, worship or admonition, the act of cursing will show to all that the person is not Christ's."

PILATE APPROVES A CIVIL TRIAL

Sir Kane continues with Raymund manuscript:

"Late that night the preliminary court reached a consensus of accusation and sent Jesus to Pilate, the ranking Roman authority, (who was obligated to be in Jerusalem for the 17-day expanded Passover) for his approval to proceed with a trial.

"After a brief interrogation, Pilate gave his approval for a civil trial, not a criminal or capital trial.

The Jewish religious authorities had no intention of proceeding with a civil trial. They insisted on a criminal trial. So Jesus' accusers

led him back to the High Priest for a private interrogation, as they
began to build their case for a criminal trial."

THE COURT OF ELDERS AND PRIESTS

Again, Sir Kane interjects personal comments concerning the Jewish
judicial procedures under the Romans:

> "The Sanhedrin, the legislative body of the Jewish nation, was
> divided into two bodies, the greater, which had 70 members, and the
> lesser, which had 24 members.
>
> "The Court of Elders and Priests had 12 members. Its chair was
> the High Priest. This court decided all appeals, and its judgment
> could not typically be appealed. It had exclusive jurisdiction for
> capital crimes, although under the Roman occupation, it could not
> carry out sentencing.
>
> "When an accused person was brought before the members of
> the Jewish judiciary, he first appeared before a five-member prelimi-
> nary interrogation panel made up of members of the Court of Elders
> and Priests. They held a preliminary interrogation to force a plea. If
> they could not obtain a plea, the accused was sentenced by the five
> members of the Court of Elders and Priests and was then sent to the
> ranking Roman authority for his authorization to proceed with a
> trial.
>
> "The Roman authority, in turn, ruled on whether the accused
> would receive a civil or a criminal trial. Although he could overrule
> the Jewish religious leaders' petition indicating that a trial was neces-
> sary, seldom was this done. Instead, he usually ruled whether the trial
> would be civil or criminal. Civil trials usually resulted in a moderate
> to heavy fine, a period of incarceration, or a period of closely scruti-
> nized probation and, in some cases, scourging. Criminal trials usually
> resulted in the convicted being scourged, imprisoned for a lengthy
> time, being charged a hefty fine or, in extreme cases, being executed;
> sometimes by crucifixion.
>
> "After the Roman authorities determined what kind of trial
> would be allowed, the accused was taken to the High Priest, who
> questioned him. If the trial was a criminal trial, the accused was sent
> by the High Priest to the Sanhedrin, where he was again interrogated.
> There the charges were written in the official records and corroborat-
> ing witnesses were interrogated."

The Raymund manuscript goes on to explain:

"If there were not two witnesses who corroborated each other's testimony, the accused was usually set free. If two consistent witnesses were found, then the Sanhedrin approved the recommendation of the preliminary interrogation panel, and the accused was sent back to the High Priest.

"At sundown on the day of approval by the Sanhedrin, the High Priest and the remaining seven members of the Court of Elders and Priests (who had not taken part in the original interrogation) would again interrogate the accused. They could find him innocent of all charges or blameworthy by suspicion. If found innocent, he would be released immediately. If found blameworthy, he would stand criminal trial before the entire Court of Elders and Priests. This Court was required to fast and pray for an entire day before the trial commenced.

"At sunrise, the High Priest brought the Urim and Thummim out of the Holy Place of the Temple and placed them before the High Priest's seat of judgment.

"The High Priest then excused himself and veiled himself in a dark room, with his back turned away from the accused. This act represented God's uncompromising, impartial justice. He would then be led out and seated in the Seat of Judgment. The Seat of Judgment, where the High Priest sat, was totally draped in a solid black veil so that it was impossible for the High Priest to see the accused.

"The High Priest then released the lactees. The lactees consisted of two men. One stood at the door of the court with a red flag in his hand, and the other sat on a white horse some distance down from the court, on the road leading to Gehenna, the place of execution. Each of these men would continually cry the name of the accused, his alleged crime, and the names of the witnesses who had sworn against him. This was followed by an appeal for any person (a non-family member) who knew anything to be said in the accused's favor, to come forward and testify.

"If two such witnesses testified in favor of the accused, the witness of the accusers would be neutralized, and the accused would be granted an appeal. In Jesus' case, no one came forward.

"These two favorable witnesses could come forward at any time during the trial, which could last from one day to months. After all testimony was heard and the accused was interrogated the eleven-member court would cast lots or vote. Then, the decision was presented to the High Priest. The accused could be convicted only by a unanimous vote.

"When the verdict was presented to the High Priest, he then would call for another vote of the members for their recommended penalty. Again a unanimous vote was required in favor of death. The result of the vote was then handed to the High Priest.

"The High Priest would remove the veils and pronounce sentencing to the convicted based on the two votes. If the verdict was for death, the High Priest followed his pronouncement by washing his hands as a token of the court's innocence, thus testifying to the fact that the convicted's own actions had condemned him.

"Once the High Priest had washed his hands, the Temple guards led the convicted to the Roman authority (in Jesus' case, this was Pilate), with the Court's recommendation for death.

"Even though the Roman authority (Pilate in this case) had authorized a civil trial only, if 100 percent of the voting Jewish judiciary chose to reject the civil trial mandate in favor of a criminal trial, the Roman authorities generally agreed.

"The Roman authority would then determine whether the convicted's crime was worthy of death. The Roman authority could not change or overrule the verdict, but he could decline the death penalty in favor of scourging or imprisonment.

"If the Roman authority determined that a crime was not worthy of death, he would transfer the convicted to a lesser Roman authority and civil court (in Jesus' case, Pilate referred him to Herod).

"That civil court would interrogate the accused and pass judgment, then carry out a lesser sentence or send the accused back to the higher Roman authority (Pilate) with either a 'no recommended judgment' or a 'judgment of agreement' with the Jewish court.

"If the higher Roman authority could find no justification for the recommended sentencing, he could dismiss the case or demand that the Jewish Court justify its judgment.

"If he felt that the accused was guilty of a crime but that the crime was not worthy of a sentence of death, he could have the convicted flogged to force an admitted guilt. If there was no admitted guilt, and if the accused lived through the flogging, Pilate could choose to set the accused free, send him back to the Jewish Court for re-trial, imprison him, or ratify the Jewish Court's recommendation and send him away to face death. If the accused died during flogging, it indicated that he must have been guilty.

"If the convicted was guilty of sedition, treason, or crimes against Caesar or the Roman State, he would face crucifixion.

"After death, all victims of crucifixion were forced to stay pinned to the stake or cross for up to 21 days or until their bodies were either greatly decomposed or had been eaten by scavenging animals. The body and bones that remained were then burned in the refuse fires of Gehenna."

According to the Raymund document, it was very unusual that Jesus' body was entombed. Official Roman court records from all over the eastern Empire, dating from 100 years before to 200 years after Jesus' death, note only three confirmed cases (out of a total of 9,784) in which a crucified person was allowed to be buried or entombed immediately after death.

THURSDAY 29TH MARCH AD31

Continuing his narrative, Raymund writes,

"At sunup the following morning (our Thursday, March 29) Jesus was again interrogated by the High Priest. Afterwards, he was sent to the judgment hall of the Sanhedrin for further interrogation. It was at this time that witnesses were allowed to make their accusations and Jesus was subjected to mockery and physical abuse. After all the witnesses were heard, the Sanhedrin confirmed the findings of the preliminary court. At sundown, the second preliminary Court of the Elders and Priests sent him back to the High Priest for additional interrogation."

FRIDAY 30TH MARCH AD31

"The following day (our Friday, March 30) was a fast day for the Court of Elders and Priests. No interrogation of Jesus was allowed. Jesus, however, remained bound.

SATURDAY 31ST MARCH AD31

"The following day (our Saturday, March 31) was the Sabbath, when typically there was no litigation. As this Sabbath would occur during the Passover week portion of the 17-day expanded celebration in which a High Sabbath would be observed, the High Priest gave permission for the Court of Elders to convene and for Jesus to stand trial.

"At the trial, Jesus was found guilty and sentenced to death. However, the Jewish court had no authority to carry out sentencing, so they had to send Jesus back to Pilate to ratify the decision of the Court of Elders and Priests.

"Pilate was appalled that Jesus had been found guilty of a crime punishable by death. He decided to interrogate Jesus personally. This was unheard of for a non-Roman. Roman procurators and governors personally interrogated only Roman citizens. Jesus remained silent during this interrogation.

"Appalled by the Jewish religious leaders unwarranted condemnation of Jesus and disagreeing with the ruling of the Jewish court, Pilate found nothing worthy of death for which to sentence Jesus. So, Pilate sent him to Herod Antipas, who was in Jerusalem for the first and only expanded 17-day Passover celebration. Pilate and Herod decided that Jesus should be tried on civil offenses, in which Herod would officiate.

SUNDAY 1ST APRIL AD31

"The following morning (our Sunday, April 1), Jesus stood trial before Herod for civil offenses, and for claiming to be The Theophus of Tiberius. Jesus was vindicated of all charges. After Herod's soldiers had mocked him and had physically abused him for hours he was sent back to Pilate.

"Before Pontius Pilate again at the Praetorium of the Fortress (Tower) of Antonia, the residence and governmental seat of Pilate while he was in Jerusalem, Pilate personally interrogated Jesus. Again, Pilate could find nothing wrong with Jesus and nothing worthy of death."

At this point, Sir Kane again interrupts the narrative to highlight differences among the Gospel accounts of these events.

"The Matthew setting suggests that Jesus was accused of blasphemy, a crime punishable (to the Jews) by death. Yet the Romans did not consider blasphemy a crime punishable by death. So the Jewish religious leaders had to come up with something else. The Jewish religious leaders considered that if they could convince Pilate that Jesus was a threat to the political power of Rome, they would accomplish their purpose. Consequently, they accused Jesus of trying to depose the ruling authority of Rome by claiming to be the King of the Jews.

"However, when the Jewish religious officials accused Jesus of claiming to be King of the Jews, Pilate considered their accusations a minor offense. Over the past four years, Pilate had encountered at least 28 men who had proclaimed themselves to be the King of the Jews. Of these 28 self-proclaimed kings, all had enjoyed a following, and all said that God had appointed them. Pilate dealt with each one with contempt and quickly squelched each movement. Seven of the self-proclaimed kings had large, rebellious followings.

"Jesus had no radical following, and those he considered his followers had forsaken him. One of his most trusted insiders betrayed him. He had no army in waiting, no political allies, and no one on whom he could call for any type of support. Surely, the Jews wanted him dead for spite. Although Pilate was not known for his compassion, he was not one to put to death an innocent rabboni. A flogging of 20 to 50 strikes would be typical and then he would be released.

"The Mark setting seems to be non-committal. In one sense it implies that the Jewish religious leaders did accuse Jesus before Pilate of claiming to be the King of the Jews, and then in another sense it seems that they accused Jesus of sedition and treason, a crime punishable by death. All accusations of treason were taken seriously and investigated by Pilate. If Pilate found the accused guilty of treason and insurrection, the accused would be flogged with 100 strikes and then crucified. Or he would be flogged with 200 strikes, which usually caused death long before the flogging was completed.

"The Luke setting indicates that Jesus had been brought before Pilate as a rebel who tried to incite the people to rebel against paying taxes to Caesar. This might be the most accurate account of why Pilate had Jesus flogged, then crucified as a treasonous enemy of the state. This sentencing by Pilate was confirmed by Seneca, Sirilius (the court recorder for Pontius Pilate), Livy, Plutarch, Cornelius Tacitus (the elder), Pliny the Younger, Suetonius, Thallus, Phlegon, and the satirist Lucian of Samosata, who all wrote authoritative records regarding the crucifixion of Jesus and the cause for which he was crucified.

"Some of these historians also said that the incident that sparked the fire that resulted in Jesus being condemned to crucifixion was the third time that he cleansed the Temple compound of merchandisers. The first time it took place (John 2:14-15), Pilate was not in

Jerusalem and no action was taken against Jesus. Almost four years later it happened again (Matthew 21:12-13) at the very beginning of the 17-day expanded Passover celebration. (Pilate had not yet arrived in Jerusalem for the celebration, nor had most of the celebrants.)

"At the height of the seven-day Passover portion's days of sacrifice, when the Temple compound could have been bursting with over one million worshipers, celebrants, sightseers, money changers, animals, merchants, priests, religious leaders, temple guards, and Roman military, Jesus, for the third time, came storming into the Temple compound and repeated the same cleansing ritual. Neither of the two previous Temple cleansings had been carried out in this type of setting with so many people and so much potential for a major uncontrollable insurrection.

"This time Pilate was in Jerusalem. From his residence at the Fortress of Antonia, he could have seen what was transpiring in the Temple compound. As such, it may not have taken too much persuasion to convince him that Jesus was a troublemaker who had the power, the personality, and the charisma to incite the people to rebellion.

"It is possible that Pilate and the temple officials, the Sadducees, had an understanding that if there was any trouble during these religious celebrations, especially this 17-day expanded Passover celebration which he had personally approved, it would be dealt with immediately and mercilessly and that the perpetrator of the trouble (whether Jew, Roman, Greek, or another nationality) would be dealt with swiftly and in severity. If this was the case, all the Jewish officials had to do was secretly arrest Jesus, so that such an arrest would not incite his followers, quickly convict him and send him to Pilate for sentencing. This would be done quickly, secretly, and conclusively.

"Considering the information recorded in Luke, one could conclude that the Sanhedrin, using the incident of Jesus' third cleansing of the Temple, found Jesus guilty of sedition. (Joseph of Arimathea abstained from voting. This was either because as a Roman appointee to the Sanhedrin, he had no vote in matters that involved Jewish religious leaders accused of capital offenses, or as the adopted father of the accused, he was automatically disqualified from casting a vote). Jesus was then sent to Pilate for ratification of the Sanhedrin conviction and for sentencing.

"The John record is, like Mark's, confusing and non-committal. It first implies that Jesus was accused by the Jewish leaders before

Pilate of blasphemy. Pilate tried to satisfy the Jews' thirst for Jesus' blood by ordering him to be flogged, implying that this was an optional punishment. This is contrary to Matthew, Mark, and Luke, and to Roman history, which records that all who were accused of treason, were crucified, and all who were condemned to crucifixion were flogged.

"Later, the Gospel of John begins to emphasize that Jesus had been accused and sentenced to death by crucifixion because the Jews had threatened Pilate, saying that if he did not convict Jesus and condemn him to death, then he was not Caesar's friend. Pilate, fearing he would be accused of treason, reluctantly submitted and sent Jesus away to be flogged and crucified. Knowing the type of person Pilate was and based on his record in dealing with the Jewish people, I (Sir Kane) cannot imagine Pilate succumbing to blackmail instigated by the Jewish religious leaders. I can see him ordering his troops to kill them all on the spot for trying to blackmail him but I cannot see him cowering down to their demands."

With this, Sir Kane ends his commentary on the Gospel records and returns to explaining methods of punishment:

FLOGGING

"The instrument generally used in flogging was a short whip called a flagellum or flagrum. The whip had several (from 10 to 30) single or braided leather thongs of variable lengths, in which small iron balls, iron chips, pottery shards, and sharp pieces of bone were tied. Although the Bible does not record the number of strikes to which Jesus was subjected, we know that 100 to 200 strikes were typically inflicted on one convicted of treason and condemned to crucifixion. If the flagrum had the larger count of 30 thongs and Jesus suffered the generally prescribed strikes of 100, Jesus would have been subjected to 3,000 individual stripes.

"In preparation for flogging, the prisoner was stripped of all clothing and was restrained in one of two ways. He could be tied with his hands above his head to an upright post, hanging with his wrists tied above his head. He was then pulled until his toes slightly cleared the floor. He could also be forced to bend over a stone or wooden bench, exposing the back and buttocks. The hands were then tightly chained to the feet.

"Before using the flagrum, a Roman legionnaire would beat the victim with a thick wooden stave. The number of blows was not consistent, so it could range from 10 blows to as many as 50. The purpose for the beating was to force the blood from the muscles to the surface of the skin, so that the whip could inflict the maximum damage.

"When the Roman legionnaire determined that the blood had risen close enough to the surface of the skin, he stepped aside and directed the flogging. Four strong slaves administered the flogging. Each slave was allowed 10 strikes at a time, until the strike allotment had been administered, or the prisoner died. After each strike, the flagrum was dipped into salt water, intensifying the victim's agony. (If a slave could kill the condemned with his allotted strikes, the slave would receive either a talent of gold or the condemned's weight in silver.) Thus, each slave tried his best to kill the prisoner.

"There was no reprieve if the prisoner collapsed into unconsciousness. If this happened, the prisoner would be revived and then the flogging would be continued. Half of the allocated strikes were administered to the back. Then the victim was turned over and the other half was administered to the front. The heavy whip was brought down with full force repeatedly across Jesus' naked shoulders, back, buttocks, and legs, reaching around the body on the sides, as well as the face, causing deep contusions and lacerating the skin and subcutaneous tissue. Before long the skin was hanging in ribbons, exposing the underlying skeleton, backbone, and skull, and some internal organs. In essence, the entire area that was being flogged became an unrecognizable mass of torn, bleeding tissue. After the flogging was complete, the victim was unshackled. Victims not killed during the flogging were destined to face death by crucifixion. So, in order for as much blood to be spared as possible, at least enough to keep him alive until he could be crucified, they rubbed the entire body of the victim with rock salt or they bathed him with salt water.

"In Jesus' case, after the beating, the Roman soldiers, amused that this weakened mass of torn tissue and blood had claimed to be a king, began to mock him by placing a scarlet or deep-purple robe on his shoulders, a crown of thorns on his head, and a wooden staff in his right hand. They knelt before him and mockingly paid homage by saying, 'Hail, King of the Jews.' They spat on him, they beat his head with a wooden staff, driving the 2-inch thorns deep into the scalp and forehead, causing severe bleeding and agonizing headaches.

They ripped out his beard by the handfuls. Finally they tore the robe from Jesus' back.

"The severity of the beating is not detailed in the Gospels," Sir Kane continues. "However, the Old Testament book of Isaiah mentions that Jesus was beaten so severely that his form did not look like that of a human being. He was so badly beaten that people were sickened to look at him.

"After the beating and the mockery, Pilate brought him out to the people and said 'Behold your king.' In other words, 'Isn't this enough?' The people demanded that the sentencing be carried out.

"So, as the day ended, Jesus' condemnation was confirmed by Pilate. The Roman Governor then washed his hands. The beaten and flogged Jesus was then returned to his prison cell to await crucifixion early the following morning."

The Garden of Gethsemane on the
Mount of Olives—Israel.

CHAPTER 26

✦

Crucifixion

PART 2 — AD 31

0600 - MONDAY APRIL 2

AT 6:00 ON THE MORNING of April 2, AD 31, Jesus was taken from his cell and led to Gehenna, to be crucified, along with 25 to 50 others. According to Sir Kane,

"The narrow street that led to the place of crucifixion was cleared of all traffic and observers early Monday morning. The only people allowed to observe were those who lived along the route or had places of business there. Generally, very few people were allowed to witness the transfer of prisoners from prison to the place of execution. So, contrary to tradition, only a few people witnessed Jesus' journey to Gehenna.

"Before the victims left the prison compound, each was obliged to carry across his shoulders the crossbar, the patibulum, to the place of crucifixion. His hands were chained to the wooden crossbar which weighed from 75 to 100 pounds and was treated with an oily creosote mixture. A Roman guard of seven soldiers escorted each condemned prisoner. An eighth soldier walked in front, carrying a titulus, which was a sign that announced the crime for which the prisoner had been condemned. In Judaea the titulus was written in Hebrew, Greek, and Latin (Matthew 27:37, John 19:19-22). This titulus was attached to the top of the cross at the crucifixion site. (Jesus' titulus read, Jesus of Nazareth, King of the Jews). Along with the eight-member personal escort for each prisoner, the entire processional was escorted by an additional Roman guard of 25 to 100 soldiers. A centurion led the procession. So, if there were 50 who were being crucified, then the entire processional that walked to Gehenna could have numbered over 500 individuals.

"From the prison compound, the condemned walked naked to the place of crucifixion. The fact that Jesus' garment was parted and then gambled away at the crucifixion site indicates that Jesus, being a religious leader, was allowed to wear his garment to the crucifixion site.

"Somewhere along the way, Jesus was unable to continue carrying his patibulum. Falling under the weight of the patibulum could have led to a heart contusion, predisposing his heart to rupture on the cross. Simon of Cyrene was compelled to help Jesus carry the crossbar.

"The Roman crucifixion practices adapted and conformed to the accepted practice of a particular area, so the Romans used the Latin cross (with the vertical piece extending above the horizontal piece), the tau cross, and the single impalement upright pole as instruments of crucifixion. The cross preferred by the Romans was called the low tau cross. This cross's vertical piece did not extend beyond the horizontal piece.

"In Judaea, the place of crucifixion was located outside the city walls, in an area called Gehenna, which served not only as the place of crucifixion but also as the garbage dump for Jerusalem. Only the immediate family members (no more than three at a time) and, in some cases, a few of the condemned's accusers were permitted to be present at the actual crucifixion site. These accusers would be allowed at the crucifixion site only after the condemned prisoners had been crucified and only for the first three hours after crucifixion. As many people as wanted to could watch the proceedings from the cliff tops that surrounded the area."

At this point, Sir Kane again interrupts his exploration of Raymund's manuscript and inserts observations from another source. He writes, "Before we go further with Raymund's document, I feel that it is crucial that I include comments made less than a century ago by the Danish thinker Søren Kierkegaard, who lived from 1813-1855. In 1848, Kierkegaard wrote two books and one discourse that revolutionized established Danish religious thinking. The titles of the books were *The Sickness Unto Death* and *Training in Christianity*. The discourse was titled *The Disease of Tradition*. The discourse is what I will refer to."

"According to Kierkegaard, at about 6:00 on the morning of Monday, April 2, AD 31, Jesus began his walk to the valley described as the Calvary (Greek) or the Golgotha (Hebrew and Aramaic). Calvary meant a place of death or a place of burnt bones or a place of the skull. Golgotha meant the place of skulls or the valley of bones or the place of death.

"The Romans carried out capital punishment four times per year: in the winter (January 2), spring (April 2), in the summer (June 2), and in the fall (September 2). Crucifixion and impaling were the typical methods of punishment.

"Although capital punishment was scheduled four times per year, Roman law dictated that there had to be at least 25 who had been sentenced before punishment could be carried out.

"This being the case, Jesus was most likely crucified with a minimum of 25 people who had been convicted of crimes against Rome or its citizenry.

"At the place of crucifixion, holes had been chiseled out of the exposed rock, about 18 to 20 inches deep. The holes were carved in a half-moon arrangement, about 8 to 10 feet apart. The vertical portion of the cross had already been fitted and secured in the holes by the time the execution processional arrived."

CRUCIFIXION SITE

"Although Kierkegaard did not describe the methods of crucifixion," Sir Kane continues, "he did make a revealing statement when he wrote:

'Although death by crucifixion was by far the most painful death inflicted by the Romans, many times death was not directly caused by crucifixion itself. More times than not, the condemned died from exposure and from being eaten alive by scavengers. Gehenna was filled with vultures and other flesh-eating birds, as well as wild dogs and jackals that would eat the flesh off of the dying prisoner. Generally within an hour or two after the condemned had been crucified, the birds would have already plucked out and eaten his eyes, while he was still alive. Considering that a condemned man usually stayed fixed to the cross from two to 14 days before finally dying, and 21 days before removal from the cross, this slow ravaging of the flesh would have been more torturous than any mind can imagine.'"

Kierkegaard then turned his attention to proving that the exact location of the site of crucifixion, as well as the burial place of Jesus, has been lost:

"In AD 70, when the Romans sacked Jerusalem, Titus had every tree in and around Jerusalem cut down and every building torn down. This included the trees in the present Garden of Gethsemane and in the Jerusalem locations of the various events connected to Jesus.

In AD 135, the Jews again rebelled. Hadrian (Roman Emperor from 117 to 138) had no mercy. Not only did he completely wipe out the city and scrape it clean to its foundations, but he also built a Roman city upon Jerusalem's foundations. The name of the city was Aelia Capitolina. By AD 139, the rebellion had been crushed and the city's construction was complete. Neither Jew nor Christian was allowed in the city. Pagan temples dedicated to Jupiter, Venus, Mars, and other Roman, Greek, Persian, and Egyptian deities were built upon the sites of the crucifixion, Jesus' burial, the Temple of Herod, and other locations considered holy by Jews and Christians.

In AD 313, Constantine issued the Edict of Milan, which moved Rome's recognition of Christianity from hostile neutrality to friendly neutrality. That year, Aelia Capitolina was opened to Christians and Jews.

For nearly three centuries, the actual crucifixion and burial sites of Jesus were lost. Then Constantine had his dream. In the dream, a man in white showed him the location of the two sites and told him to build churches or shrines on the sites, to preserve their locations.

In AD 326, Helena (Constantine's mother), traveled to Aelia Capitolina, which by then was unofficially called Jerusalem, to confirm Constantine's dream and to find the locations associated with Jesus' nativity, crucifixion, and burial.

Upon her arrival, Helena found it difficult to find anyone who could help her locate the sites. Finally, after offering a huge amount of money as a reward, a young Jewish boy named Judas told her that he had old family records that described the true location of Jesus' crucifixion and burial. He took her to the location of the crucifixion and burial site. A pagan shrine dedicated to Venus stood on the site, and all around the shrine the ground had been recently plowed. Judas told Helena that she should dig there and perhaps she would find something that would confirm his family's records. So, she had her servants dig in the freshly plowed soil next to the shrine. Miraculously, they 'discovered' three crosses in a state of perfect preservation. Constantine claimed that the site was the same as the one in his dream, so he proclaimed it to be Golgotha, the site of the crucifixion. He ordered the Venus shrine to be destroyed and removed and a church to be built. The Church of the Holy Sepulcher covers both locations proclaimed by Constantine to be the crucifixion and burial site of Jesus.

"Eusebius, the Bishop of Palestine at the time, strongly objected to Constantine's proclamation. He said the location was the burial site of the Maccabean priest/king John Hyrcanus.

"Constantine did not listen. He had the church built. Judas (the Jewish boy) converted to Christianity, and Constantine offered him the position of Bishop of Jerusalem, in Eusebius's stead. He was also given the name Judas Quiriacus. This Judas, over the next ten years, accompanied Helena as she traveled throughout the entire 'Holy Land' area of Nazareth, Bethlehem, Cana, Capernaum, Bethany, and so on. They 'discovered' many other locations associated with Jesus. In most cases, they built churches on the sites.

"In AD 614, the Persians attacked the area of Palestine and destroyed all of the churches and shrines that Helena had constructed, except the Church of the Nativity in Bethlehem.

"In the twelfth century, Crusaders ruled Jerusalem for 88 years. During this time, most of the churches that had been destroyed were rebuilt. The Church of the Nativity was modified to its present state during this time.

"The existing walls of present-day (Kierkegaard's day) Old Jerusalem were built from 1537-1541 by the Turkish sultan Suleiman the Magnificent. It was after this that the Via Dolorosa (Way of Sorrows) and the Ecco Homo gate (where Pilate was said to have condemned Jesus) were built and were established as shrines."

After this review of Kierkegaard, Sir Kane writes:

"I need to add a few explanatory notes of my own, concerning this topic. In 1867, Dr. Conrad Schick excavated an ancient tomb that had been hidden for centuries near the present Damascus Gate. The tomb had been cut in a rocky wall and was unusually large, signifying that the owner had been wealthy. Near the tomb was found an ancient wine press and a large underground water-collection system. The property was later converted into a beautiful garden. The tomb became known as The Garden Tomb and is identified today by many Protestants as the tomb of Jesus. In 1883, a British General (General Gordon) visited the tomb and noticed, as he surveyed the rocky cliff outside the tomb, a skull-shaped depression in the cliff. Due to the proximity of the tomb, he declared the place to be the actual Calvary."

"This ends my personal notes on this subject," Sir Kane explains. "I now feel I must return to Raymund's document."

EXECUTION PROTOCOL

According to Raymund:

"At the site of execution, the victim was offered a bitter drink of wine mixed with myrrh, as a mild analgesic. Jesus refused this drink. The offender was then violently thrown to the ground on his back, with his arms outstretched along the patibulum. Heavy, square wrought-iron nails were then driven through the wrists deep into the wood, firmly attaching the wrists to the crossbar. After the arms were fastened, the patibulum and the victim were lifted onto the stipes.

"After the crossbar was attached to the stipes, the titulus was attached. Next, a sedile or sedulum, a round wooden stake that served as a seat upon which the hip bones rested, was added. There were two ways that a sedile was used. The Romans would drive a sedile through the [victim's] bladder area, just below the hipbone and into the stipe. Upon this sedile, the hipbones and pelvic bones would balance. Or the Romans would take the body of the condemned and twist it 90° opposite his outstretched arms. Then the sedile would be driven through the fleshy part of the side of the buttocks into the stipe.

"If the offender was twisted 90 degrees opposite the outstretched arms, the feet were nailed to the vertical stipe in one of two ways. One way was to straddle the vertical stipe with the criminal's feet and nail one ankle to each side. The other way was to press one foot backward against the other foot, and with both feet extended a nail was driven through the arches of the feet into the stipe. If the victim was crucified with the sedile in the front, the left foot was pressed backward against the right foot, and with both feet extended, an iron nail was driven through both arches of the feet into the stipe.

"One of the most agonizing aspects of nailing the feet was that it affected every internal organ. The nerve endings that connect to every internal organ in the body collect at the bottom of the feet. If the foot is punctured from the top down, like with nailing the feet at crucifixion, the nerve endings are violently split apart and frayed. This sends an instant message of malfunction to the organs affected.

"Instantaneously and simultaneously, Jesus had the symptoms and the pain of hundreds of malfunctions and diseases such as a heart attack, brain cancer, gall bladder problems, a migraine headache, diabetes, lung cancer, and every injury to every internal organ in his body. Yet Jesus said not a word. He remained silent, as a lamb being slaughtered.

"Jesus was crucified in the midst of at least 25 others. In his immediate area were four offenders. Two of these condemned criminals were thieves and the other two were malefactors. Malefactor (Latin for 'squalid exploiter of a man') was a word used by the Romans to describe a non-Roman male prostitute with whom a Roman official had died while involved in sadomastic homosexual activities. (A malefactor was punished because a Roman high official died, not for prostitution.)

"Both thieves railed on Jesus, but only one of the malefactors did. The other malefactor believed that Jesus was who he said he was. Jesus told the believing malefactor that he would die that day and that he would meet him in paradise. Jesus forgave him of all sin.

0 9 0 0 – MONDAY APRIL 2

"It was 9:00 in the morning, and Jesus was now crucified. Jesus was naked, an unrecognizable bloody mass. He knew that none of his followers stood by his side, and he realized that soon even his own Heavenly Father would be turning His back. He hoped against hope that this would not happen. Yet, the first words that Jesus uttered after being suspended between heaven and earth were, 'Father, forgive them for they know not what they do.'

"As Jesus slowly sagged down, forcing more weight on the nails in the wrists, excruciating pain shot through the median nerves, along the fingers, and up the arms, to explode in the brain. As he pushed himself upward to avoid this torment, he placed his full weight on the nail(s) through his feet, causing searing agony as the nail(s) in the feet tore through the nerves between the metatarsal bones and the bottom of the feet.

"As the arms began to fatigue, waves of cramps followed in quick succession. With the cramps came his inability to push himself upward. Hanging by his arms, the pectoral muscles became paralyzed. Although air could be inhaled, it could not be exhaled, causing Jesus to fight desperately to raise himself to release even one short painful exhale. This caused the lungs to begin to collapse. Finally, carbon dioxide built up in the lungs and in the blood stream, and the cramps partially subsided. Spasmodically, he became able to push himself upward to exhale and to breathe in oxygen. It was during these short periods that Jesus uttered the last six messages before his death.

"After hours of waves of cramps, intermittent asphyxiation, and searing pain as tissue was torn from his back as he moved up and down the rough stipe, another pain began deep inside his chest. His pericardium slowly filled with fluid and began to compress his heart. Eventually, the loss of tissue fluids reached a critical level; the heart began to struggle to pump the thick blood. Meanwhile, the lungs struggled desperately to gasp small gulps of air.

"Finally, Jesus realized that death was upon him and in a tortured whisper he said, 'It is finished.' Then as he felt his last breath oozing from his body he took a deep breath and cried, 'Father! Into thy hands I commit my spirit.' Then he died. It was 3:00 in the afternoon. He had been on the cross for six hours."

1 5 0 0 - M o n d a y A p r i l 2

"His death was accompanied by an unusual darkness and a great earthquake that historians who lived at the time recorded. It was felt in Rome, Greece, China, Africa, in the Ural mountains of Russia, and in the Pyrenees of Spain."

Sir Kane reminds us:

"Jesus was a rabboni, and even though the Sadducees and High Priest may not have liked it, his position had been granted him by the High Priest. That fact could not be denied. Because he was an official religious leader, Jewish religious law would not allow Jesus to profane the High Sabbath by remaining on the cross.

"As far as the other criminals were concerned, it was standard practice for the Roman soldiers to inflict crurifracture (the breaking of their legs) upon those crucified after 12 hours. This expedited suffocation. With the breaking of the legs, the victim usually died within two to 14 days. The legs of all victims crucified with Jesus that day were broken. Jesus was already dead by the time they got to him. Apparently, to confirm that Jesus was dead, the legionnaire responsible for breaking the legs drove a lance through the fifth space between his ribs, upward through the pericardium, and into the heart, resulting in a flow of water-fluid mixed with blood. This indicated that Jesus had not died of suffocation, the typical cause of death. He died of heart failure, or a ruptured heart.

"Seeing their law forbade a religious leader from hanging on the cross past 6:00 in the evening, and because Jewish religious law forbade the desecration of the body of a religious leader, the representatives of the High Priest approached Pilate about taking Jesus from the cross. Pilate was surprised that Jesus was already dead, so granted their request.

"Soon thereafter, one of the most powerful men in Syria, the Roman Senator representing Britain, the Imperial Minister of Mines for both Augustus and Tiberius Caesar, the Roman representation and appointee to the Jewish Sanhedrin, and the adoptive father/grandfather of Jesus, Joseph of Arimathea, approached Pilate and demanded that he release the body of Jesus to him. Nicodemus, one of the wealthiest men in Judea, joined him. Without hesitation, Pilate released the body of Jesus. He had no choice.

"Nicodemus supplied expensive spices to temporarily preserve the body until after the High Sabbath, when they could return and prepare the body for burial more professionally. Jesus' body was then entombed in Joseph's family tomb. Jesus was the first family member to be laid to rest in the tomb of the family in which both Jesus and Mary were adopted members."

This statement concludes Sir Kane's commentary, explanation, and transliteration of Raymund of Penafort's manuscript.

After reading this heart-breaking account, I sat at the study table in the university library for an hour or more, tears in my eyes. I replayed the scene over and over in my mind. I couldn't believe the gruesomeness of the tragedy. Jesus endured all this suffering for me. For me and every person who has ever lived. Perfection submitted to death so that I, imperfection, could have a hope of being able to live for eternity with Him, the King of Kings and Lord of Lords.

The Revenge of Valleus Paterculus

Although Jesus' death had a sobering personal impact on his disciples and followers, it caused major *political* repercussions in the highest levels of Roman authority.

Upon his return to Rome, after witnessing the healing of Zolleras (see Chapter 19), Valleus Paterculus presented his findings about Jesus to The Theophus Commission. (At the time he reported to Tiberius in Capri, he was unaware that Jesus had already been crucified.) It is not known when Tiberius and Paterculus found out about Jesus' crucifixion, but based on a manuscript written by the fourth century Egyptian monk Pachomius (which I discovered at The Monastery of St. Catherine in Mount Sinai, Egypt), it appears that neither knew about the tragedy until Paterculus returned to Judaea in January AD 33, almost two years after the fact.

According to Pachomius (who founded the Nile community of monks), Paterculus led a delegation to Judaea in January of AD 33. The delegation questioned Pilate at his palace, Caiaphas the High Priest at his residence in Jerusalem, and Herod Antipas in Capernaum. While questioning Pilate, Paterculus learned that Jesus had been crucified. Pachomius, quoting the second century Roman court historian Dio Cassius and the first century writer Petronius, reports that upon hearing of Jesus' death, Paterculus became furious, warning Pilate that he would pay with his life. These men also wrote that after his confrontation with Paterculus, Pilate sunk into deep depression. He also became ruthless and irrational. He lost the ability to govern properly.

Paterculus demanded that Pilate, Caiaphas, and Herod write letters of explanation to The Theophus Commission and Tiberius Caesar, explaining their roles in Jesus' death.

Paterculus returned to Rome in March AD 35 and personally delivered the letters to the Theophus Commission. In April AD 35, he brought the letters to Tiberius in Capri.

We don't know how the Commission or Tiberius responded upon hearing the news that the *one* person who fulfilled all qualifications of The Theophus had been put to death. We *do* know that in June of AD 35, Roman authorities removed Caiaphas as High Priest. In AD 36 or 37, Pilate was recalled from Judaea. Herod was exiled by the Romans in AD 38 or 39 on the charge of treasonous incitement.

In less than a decade after Jesus' crucifixion, Valleus Paterculus had done what he could to avenge the death of the man he was convinced was The Theophus.

Pachomius's manuscript includes the complete text of the letters that Pilate, Caiaphas, and Herod were ordered to write.

CAIAPHAS'S DEFENSE TO THE THEOPHUS COMMISSION

Caiaphas addressed his defense to The Theophus Commission, Tiberius, *and* the Sanhedrin in Jerusalem. Here, with minor edits for the sake of brevity, is Caiaphas's official report, dictated to a Sanhedrin scribe named Eliezer Hiran:

"Joseph Caiaphas, High Priest of the Most High God, to the Theophus Commission of Ambassadors, our most honored of statesmen, Valleus Paterculus, our most respected Augustus, Tiberius Julius Caesar Augustus, and Masters of Israel, greeting.

"In obedience with demands by Valleus Paterculus for a reason for my action in the case of Jesus, a rabboni from Nazareth, and in defense of my conduct, I beg leave to submit the following for your consideration: I would assure you that it was not on account of personal malice, envy, or hatred nor for the want of a willingness upon my part to conform to the Jewish law in its strictest sense. I have but very little personal knowledge of the man from Nazareth. I hope you will investigate strictly on legal principles the reasons that I may give.

"So you may be able to see and weigh the question fully, and remember the responsibility that rests upon me according to the laws of our nation, I will ask you to go back to the chronicles of the history of our people. First, our dedication is pledged to one living and true God, this God being indescribable, unchangeable, incomprehensible, and unnamable.... He has been pleased to give us His name, or His several names, according to His relations to us... In His Holy Ark He records Himself Elaah existence without beginning or end. Again He says of Himself, Hhelejon unchangeable. Again He says His name Jah, knowledge that comprehends without being comprehended. Again

He says of Himself, Adonai full and free. A man cannot pronounce His name in its comprehensive sense.... Jesus could pronounce His name in His comprehensive sense, but he stole it out of the Holiest place of the Temple, so I am creditably informed.... Moses, that to make atonement for offenses must be by fasting for seven days, by an offering of oil and flour, and the sacrifice of a young bullock. Now, unless Moses was deceived, he has deceived us, or this Jesus from Nazareth in the Galilee is a false teacher; for he teaches metanoeite, as though a man's being sorry for an offense could make restitution to the offended.

"Jesus was called by his followers, although I have not heard him so say, that he is called the Son of God; and claims that he has been born of almah; that he and his Father, God, of whose name can not be uttered, are one and equal.

"Now this Jesus is a false teacher.

"Jesus ignored God's holy Temple, where He promised to dwell with His children, to hear their prayers, and to be pleased with their sacrifices. He sneers at the priests and scoffs at our holy ordinances and boasts that the gift will be destroyed.

"According to our laws I was made responsible, and stand before God between the people and God, to protect them from His consuming fire by doctrine and the Law. Jesus was well qualified to deceive the people. He had already led many to forsake the Temple, to hold the High Priest, the delegated authority of God, in contempt, to hold the ordinances of the Temple in derision, and to neglect the tithe to the Temple, but still encourage the payment of tax to the Romans. He appealed so to the unsanctified flesh of the pagan Galileans and the deceived Judeans that although he preached for less than five years he had more followers at his death than did Abraham during his life.

"So it seemed to me of necessity for him to be removed. That this may be evident to your minds, I ask you to contrast our present condition with the past. Jesus from Nazareth left his father's business of constructing and spent two years or more in Egypt under the instruction of Rabban Joshua bar Yeddesi, and learned the art of thaumaturgy (wonder-working) to perfection. If the reported miracles of Jesus are true, he must have learned how from Horus and Serapis, those pagan priests....

"Jesus embraced the doctrine of the Hillelites, presenting conspicuously the cosmopolitan spirit of the Jews. He taught that the dead would rise again and would live again in a future state of happiness or misery according as they have lived on Earth. Which doctrine is of the pagan Egyptians and Indus (Hindus). He taught future rewards and punishments; but he being present, how could he reward in the future? He taught the revelation of the prophets, but contradicted their teachings. He taught the eternity of God's laws and promises, but attempted to supersede them by living a life free from the rituals established by God. Even as rabboni, the highest of the levels of instruction, he so far cut himself loose from the others of his rabboni rank that he ate with unclean hands, publicans and lepers, and permitted the living dead, the unclean, and the harlots to address him and to touch him.

"He seemed to take little notice of the political affairs of our nation... paying your taxes owed to them. It is only Caesar's money that you pay, which is unlawful for you to have anyway, because of its images.

"He said that we could not conquer Rome, so honor them instead, and then they no longer would be enemies. Indeed the conduct of Jesus was so strange and incompatible with the interests of the Jews that it seemed to me that he was a subject employed by Rome to keep our nation submissive.

"As the people became more confused and divided, the authorities of Caesar became increasingly hostile, fearing sedition. So to preserve our nation, I ordered that Jesus be brought to me for interrogation. But understand I did not act rashly or illegally. I passed sentence only after intense interrogation in which Jesus refused to cooperate, by remaining silent or spoke few words of little worth. Thus I was forced to pass judgment. It was not a voluntary act, but a legal one. So after much more interrogation and questioning by myself, the Court of Elders and Priests, and this most honored Master of Israel Directorate, in which no one spoke on his behalf, only those spoke to his detriment, I was forced to pass a sentence worthy of death, for if he was to continue to promulgate his pernicious heresies and refuse to deny that he was that Theophus the Herodians claim him to be, of which the honored Valleus Paterculus has choice of but to believe, the Jews, as a nation, would perish at the hands of Rome. I thus sent him to Pilate for interrogation with my written conviction. Although the preservation of our nation was true reason for my conviction, the following is the purpose of his conviction that I sent with him to Pilate:

"Caiaphas, High Priest of the Most High, to his most honorable and worthy Pontius Pilate, Procurator of Judaea:

'Jesus from Nazareth of the Galilee is thus charged by the Court of Elders and Priests:

- Teaching a doctrine that there are more gods than one, which indeed he feels is himself, and by his silence refuses to desist from proclaiming, even to this high court.

- Through silence he acknowledges that he is The Theophus so sought by Tiberius Caesar Augustus.

- He teaches baptism is the seal of God, instead of circumcision, which is contrary to our law.

- He teaches asceticism as the means of salvation, contrary to our law.

- He has abrogated the priesthood and the laws and rituals of our law and our fathers, and has set the Temple at naught.

- He has proclaimed himself to be a king, while his followers have said that he is the king of the nation of the Jews. His silence has confirmed that such is the case of both.

- He says that he will destroy our Temple, God's gift to His children. Others have testified that he will not deny that he will destroy the Temple and will rebuild it in three days.

- He says that his kingdom will sweep away all other kingdoms and empires, present and future, and will last forever. Such seditious blasphemies against Rome must not be tolerated.

"For this cause is Jesus charged, convicted, and sentenced to death. We plead this resolve to our most honored governor Pontius Pilate.

"With these reasons for my actions, I submit my case favorably to The Theophus Commission of Ambassadors, most honored Valleus Paterculus, domain regulator governor Tiberius Julius Caesar Augustus, and most esteemed Masters of Israel.

In God's will and service. Joseph Caiaphas, High Priest of One God:"

PONTIUS PILATE'S DEFENSE TO THE THEOPHUS COMMISSION

Here is Pachomius's transcription of Pontius Pilate's letter (again, edited for brevity):

"To my most noble Sovereign Tiberius Julius Caesar Augustus and the honorable The Theophus Commission of Ambassadors and Valleus Paterculus. Greetings.

"The events that coincided with the trial and death of one Jesus, a Galilean Jew a year and some months ago have been such that I will give details in full as they occurred. Concerning these events, I should not be surprised if, eventually, they may change the destiny of our nation, for it seems of late that all the gods have ceased to be propitious. Cursed be the day that I succeeded Vallerius Flaceus; my life with these Judaeans has been one of continual uneasiness and distress.

"On my arrival in Jerusalem I took possession of the Praetorium, and ordered a splendid feast to be prepared, to which I invited the tetrarch of the Galilee, with the High Priest and his officers. At the appointed hour no guests appeared. This I considered an insult offered to my dignity, and to the whole of Rome. A few days after, the High Priest deigned to pay me a visit. His deportment was grave and deceitful. He pretended that his religion forbade him and his attendants to sit at the table with authorities from Rome. Although I thought it expedient to accept his excuse, from that moment, I was convince that the conquered had declared themselves the enemy of the conquerors. It seems that of all conquered regions, Judaea, and especially the state of Judea, is the most difficult to govern. So turbulent are the people that I live in momentary dread of an insurrection.

"Among the rumors that came to my ears, there was one in particular that attracted my attention. A young stonemason, having been educated as a rabboni of the Jew's religious authority, who was said to be a legal ward by adoption and right of our state's Minister of Mines appeared from no one knows, although his boyhood home was in the refuse garden of Nazareth. He was a preacher of a new religious law in the name of the God of the Jews, who said he was sent by Him. At first I was apprehensive that his design was to stir up the people against our authority, but my dread was soon dispelled. This man, Jesus, spoke as a son and as a friend of Rome, rather than as one of the Jews. To further focus my attention upon him, the Herodians from the court of Herod, whom your most excellent Tiberius has appointed to investigate for the honored Commission of Ambassadors, sent to my seat in Caesarea, a court messenger informing me that they had petitioned the Commission in the name of Tiberius Caesar for representation to come as quickly as can be possible to the Galilee of Syria to perform a Theophus interrogation of this Jesus. My own attention proved that this man had no malice intended for your Sovereign's authority; his words seemed to be more wisdom and philosophy in the tradition of our own Cato, Suetonius, or Posidonius of the Grecians.

"It was on this account that I granted him much liberty; for it was in my power to have him arrested. I must conclude that he was neither seditious nor rebellious, except perhaps to the brothers of his own religious consanguinity. This liberty provoked the Jewish leaders of their religion. It is true that Jesus was severe on these leaders, and this was a political reason for not restraining the liberty of him while his leave was Judaea. At times of celebrations of the Jews in Judea and in Jerusalem, complaints were many against his insolence.

"In December before the record reflected in this report, soon after the return of our most honorable Valleus Paterculus to Capri, the enemies of Jesus addressed themselves to Herod, to wreak their vengeance upon him. Herod, unsure of The Theophus investigation concerning Jesus, and not willing to offend neither our most excellent Tiberius nor this Commission made no judgment concerning his fate, nor of his actions or message. Instead he requested my audience. Whereupon he asked my opinion concerning the matter of Jesus. I told him that I could not judge on the matter on behalf of the commission but that Jesus appeared to me to be a great philosopher and that his message was neither seditious nor did I consider him a threat to the authority of Rome. I further stated that the intentions of Rome were to leave him to his freedom of his proclamations and actions, unless such actions threatened the peace of Judea.

"In February before the events of this report, I arrived in Jerusalem to insure the peace of the masses during Passover. I was instructed by informants that, during the celebration, misfortune would likely befall Jesus and an insurrection would follow. Not having enough force in Jerusalem to suppress a state insurrection, I resolved upon adopting a measure that promised to assure tranquility of the city.

"The permitted extended Passover, a 17-day celebration, was approaching and my emissaries had warned that because of Jesus' attribution to that Theophus, the religious leaders of the Jews, especially the Sadducees, whom say that Jesus disrupted the traditions of their Temple ordinances and practice, were intent to raise a sedition on Jesus' account and force his execution either with or without our approbation, to prevent your Sovereign from selecting their State as

your ward. My emissaries had further informed me that the treasury
of their temple had been employed in bribing certain vile characters
to swear witness against him and to incite calls for his execution. I
sent a messenger demanding reinforcements of the governor of Syria.
The governor sent back word that reinforcements could not be sent
until 20 days thence. Alone against incited rabble of rebels, who
knew nothing of Jesus, but rather were being inflamed by gold given
them by contemptuous religious Jews, I determined that if this Jesus
had to be sacrificed for the advantage of peace and to secure the
authority of Rome, then that expiration had to be heavily weighed.

"Very late on the first night of their 7-day Passover portion of
the 17-day celebration, the preliminary court of the Jews, on instruction from the High Priest, asked permission to proceed with a trial.
Knowing that for spite they had brought his arrest, I felt that before
a court Jesus would be released for lack of condemning testimony. I
gave my approval. My wife bid me leave the decision to the Jews and
give no judgment. Three days later, Jesus was presented to me for
condemnation. I interrogated him and found in him nothing worthy
of death. So not qualifying for execution, I sent him to the lower civil
court of Herod, who was in Jerusalem for the celebration, so that
judgment for a less minor offense would be passed.

"Herod, whose intent was more to prove whether Jesus was that
Theophus, demanded of Jesus miracles to prove his Theophus character. Jesus refused all opportunity. Herod, convinced that if Jesus
would remain silent in the very midst of a possible exaltation, then
he could not be that Theophus; so Herod mocked his silence and his
position as a false Theophus, although he had no reason to do so.
Herod then in disgust released Jesus as deserving nothing more than
minor punishment for the crime of insolence for remaining silent
before his authority. He sent Jesus back to me.

"Again I interrogated Jesus and found in him nothing worthy
of death, yet I knew that if he were released without a punishment,
rebellion would likely encompass the city and spread to the regions.
The Jewish religious leaders, and the rabble that they had paid to
solicit his death, demanded his crucifixion and proclaimed that I,
your most loyal of servants, would no longer be a worthy governor for my Sovereign and that they would register a complaint to
our Senate that my actions incited a riot and that my lack of action
expanded the riot to rebellion.

"After fruitless attempts to release him or to send him back to the Jews for a lesser crime, I adopted a measure that appeared to me to be the only action that would both save his life and satisfy the Jews for his blood. I proposed to them, as was their custom, that Jesus be proclaimed as their scapegoat and let him to be released into the desert and to dwell among the rocks, never being allowed into the region again. They chose instead another criminal, one Barabbas, a murderer, and appealed to me to offer this man for a scapegoat. I could not withdraw my offer, so the criminal was set free. I then had Jesus mercilessly scourged to satisfy their demand for his life. But they wanted him dead.

"My Sovereign, to avoid rebellion and regional revolt, I condemned Jesus to death, washing my hands and Rome's involvement forever of the blame and responsibility of his death. As you see, I had no choice. Yet, I fear that I have condemned to death the one man who in all of the world could have qualified for the distinction as The Theophus of my most excellent Augustus, Tiberius Julius Caesar.

"Before the dawn of the second day of the 4th month after the month of winter solstice celebrations, in the 18th year of the sovereignty of my most excellent Tiberius, Jesus was led with 46 others condemned for crimes against your Sovereign and our state to the scoria hollow of death, Gehenna.

"By the time the sun had risen over the hills, the condemned were being raised to their post of death. To my astonishment, by mid-afternoon of that same day, amid blackened clouds and terrible natural circumstances, I received word that Jesus had died. An earthquake that was later said to have been felt as far as Egypt and Parthania followed this announcement. Our most honored Minister of Mines and Senator of our holding in Britannia, Joseph Marmore claimed the body of Jesus as his own son by adoptive guardianship, demanding his immediate release into his care. Whereupon I hastily released his body. At the request of the Jews, I placed a guard of six to guard the tomb, but at the insistent demand of our Minister of Mines I raised the number by 60 to secure the tomb from robbers for seven days.

"Benius Ishamius, my Commander of the Guard, later reported, three days after the guard was set, an incredible story about how this man Jesus had likely risen from his death. I do not doubt my Commander, but I cannot believe in myths and stories. If it is true that he has raised from death and his tomb failed to hold himself, then Jesus is that Theophus.

"Now, noble Sovereign, honored statesman, and most respected Commission, this is as near as I recall the facts concerning the trial and condemnation of this man, Jesus. With the promise of faithfulness and hopes for good to my noble Sovereign, I am your most obedient servant. Pontius Pilate."

As this chapter draws to a close, here is Pachomius's transcription of the letter written by Herod Antipas:

HEROD ANTIPAS'S DEFENSE TO THE THEOPHUS COMMISSION

"To Tiberius Julius Caesar Augustus and to The Theophus Commission of Ambassadors.

My Noble Lords, Greetings.

"As my most gracious and honorable Valleus Paterculus, Chief Ambassador of The Theophus Commission, has demanded in the name of my most excellent Sovereign, Tiberius Caesar Augustus, the following is, to my best recall, the matter of the events concerning the trial and death of the builder of stone, whose work has been witness to even residents of Capernaum, whom his followers call Jesus the Christ of the Galilee, of the dross disposal city of Nazareth.

"About two years before his trial by the Jews, a prince of my house reported to my chamberlain that his son had been raised from the bed of sickness unto death by Jesus, a rabboni of the Jews, whose father by adoption was our most honorable Senator representing the frontiers of Britain, whom we had heard nothing of fact, but only myth and rumor. The report of Caprinaius, the prince whose son was raised, claimed that Jesus was a distance of one day from the palace when the son was healed from his death. I called for Caprinaius to interrogate him on the possible Theophus connection between the said and Jesus. After much debate, in which he felt strongly that Jesus was qualified I demanded of Caprinaius that he appoint 25 aids and gather for six months all information as could be found concerning this Galilean stonemason turned rabboni of the Jews.

"There were other records of his defiance of the natural laws: of walking on water, of reprimand of storms, of taking water and it becoming wine, of miracles of restoration and of reversals of death. He also has been a friend to Rome and has many among the citizenship likened to himself and among our state's authority who look upon him in high regard. With so much that had been observed, I felt it justified sending for him to interrogate him and prove by some miracle that he is that one whom we seek. I too sent my finding to the Commission of Ambassadors, requesting representation for an investigation. Jesus never honored my demand for his presence, and, two years and four months past the time of my request, two ambassadors representative of the commission arrived at my seat, demanding to investigate.

"I arrived in Jerusalem for the 17-day distended celebration of the Passover observance, one day removed from its first feast. To my astonishment, it came to me that Jesus, who we were investigating on behalf of the Commission of Ambassadors, was arrested. I assigned five servants the task of collecting the happenings of his arrest and to report to me anything that would characterize a justification for a pronouncement of The Theophus.

"On the day following the general Sabbath, Pilate sent Jesus to me for judgment of a lesser crime than one worthy of death. At last I was to meet this man face to face. But for me to rule and to declare that he was to be released on fear that we had detained The Theophus, he must show cause for his release by executing a miracle of proof. Yet, he did nothing and said nothing. He retained contemptuous silence. After many attempts to break his silence, I turned him aside to my guard for insulting treatment, knowing that if he was that Theophus that he would speak it plainly and would be proud to be proved correct and right within the eye of approval of our great and Sovereign Tiberius Caesar. But having found nothing worthy of death and having found no cause to judge on a lesser act of offense, I returned him to Pilate.

"As to the rumors of his raising from the tomb, if he is that Theophus, it cannot be beyond his powers. If he is not, then how easy can a lie become truth, if the lie is more to be believed than truth.

"These facts and causes I submit to my most excellent Caesar and our most honored Theophus Commission of Ambassadors for your consideration, praying for clemency if, by chance, justification has not come forth from my actions concerning this matter.

"Antipas of the House of Herod, most humble Tetrarch of my most excellent Sovereign."

Now, it's impossible to confirm the validity of these three letters, as we don't have the original documents, only Pachomius's purported transcription of them. Because the letters confirm undisputed historical facts regarding Jesus' crucifixion, I am inclined to accept their authenticity.

These letters reveal that Jesus' death was not just a local interest story, which would be easily justified and quickly forgotten. This event sent shock waves through the highest levels of the Roman government.

Dicrecitmus, a court historian for Caligula, documented the finality of the issue of The Theophus when he recorded that in Valleus Paterculus's final interview with the Senate (in April AD 40), he proudly declared, "My work is now complete. My retribution on his behalf is finished. Those who were responsible for the murder of my lord Tiberius's Theophus have now been abolished. The small flicker of light and hope that once was, is no longer. Such a one as He will never again rise among us. Now those who are responsible for His light being extinguished are no more."

Of course, Paterculus's closure on The Theophus issue was not, and is not, the end of the story. When word spread that Jesus had risen from the dead, a series of events was set in motion. These events resulted in the crumbling of the mighty Roman Empire, the destruction of the proud Jewish state, and the creation of a new religion founded upon the life, teachings, death, and resurrection of Jesus.

The valley of Gehenna as it looks today. It was in Gehenna that Jesus was crucified. It was the garbage dump of Jerusalem during the time of Jesus—Israel.

The hill traditionally identified as Mount Calvary by Protestants—Israel.

The Via Dolorosa in Jerusalem. The route that tradition says Jesus took to the place of crucifixion—Israel.

CHAPTER 27

꙳ ꙳

A New Beginning

PART 1

*"Nero fabricated scapegoats...and punished with every refinement the noto-
riously depraved Christians (as they were popularly called). Their originator,
Christus, from whom they derive their name, had been condemned to death in
the reign of Tiberius by the Procurator Pontius Pilate."*
*From The Annals of Imperial Rome, written by Roman Senator
and historian Cornelius Tacitus (56-117 AD).*

JEWISH HISTORIAN RECORDS

"It was at that time a man appeared, if it be lawful to call
him a man, who had all the attributes of a man but seemed to be
something greater. His actions, certainly, were other than human,
for he worked such wonderful and amazing miracles that I cannot
regard him as a man; yet, in view of his likeness to ourselves I
cannot regard him as an angel either. Everything that some hidden
power enabled him to do, he did by authoritative word. [He] was
a teacher of such men as receive the truth with pleasure. Some
people (the Jews) said that their first Lawgiver had risen from
the dead and had effected many marvelous cures; others thought

he was a messenger from heaven. However, in many ways he broke the Law. For instance, he did not observe the Sabbath in the traditional manner. At the same time, his conduct was above reproach. He did not need to use his hands, his word sufficed to fulfill his every purpose. He was the Messiah.

He earned by his actions an incomparable reputation. The exponents of the Law were mad with jealousy, and gave Pilate 30 talents to have him executed. Accepting the bribe, he gave them permission to carry out their wishes themselves. So they seized him and crucified him in defiance of all Jewish tradition. **He appeared to them alive again the third day, as the divine Prophets had foretold.*** Ten thousand other wonderful things concerning him, and the race of Christians, so named from him, are not extinct even now."

From *The Jewish War* by Joseph ben Matthias, who took the Latin name Flavius Josephus

(Author's note: The two boldface sentences above might have been added to Josephus's work, after his death, by Christians.)

(Footnote: Flavius Josephus lived from AD 63 to 100. His four principle works are *The Jewish War, Antiquities of the Jews, Life,* and *Against Apion.* G.A. Williamson was the translator who brought Josephus's work into modern light. Williamson discovered that most of Josephus's writings had been back-edited during the reign of Domitian (eleventh Emperor of the Roman Empire), to remove all statements pertaining to Jesus. However, Williamson uncovered an early Greek variation of Josephus's *The Jewish War.* This version included discussions about Jesus, John the Baptist, James (the brother of Jesus), and the original apostles.

Although common tradition holds that Jesus was crucified on a Friday and rose from the dead on a Sunday, there is little evidence to authenticate this. Nonetheless, the Resurrection, whenever it happened, is a momentous event in human history.

THE RESURRECTION

I gained new insight into the Resurrection while visiting the library of the Bordeaux Abbey in Orléans, France.

Portions of the Bordeaux Abbey date to the thirteenth century. During the Hundred Years War, it was badly damaged, and then it suffered neglect for almost 200 years. Repair efforts were attempted, but they were inconsistent.

The library attached to the abbey was originally built in the seventeenth century. It houses a beautiful collection of artwork and sculptures, but only a few books and documents. When I first saw the building, I wondered why they called it a library, rather than a museum.

As I was wandering through this small library, the head librarian asked me in French, English, and German, respectively, if he could help me.

I introduced myself and told him I was seeking information about the life of Jesus. He confessed, "We don't have many documents or manuscripts here. Most of them were destroyed in a revolutionary riot in 1789, when the library was set on fire. When the rioters ransacked the abbey and library, they left the works of art virtually untouched, but they destroyed every book, document, or manuscript that had not been hidden.

"Of course, you are welcome to review the documents we *do* have and to view the artwork for as long as you like."

I walked around for a while, examining books and documents, but I found nothing relevant to my search. Then I started reviewing the impressive collection of Renaissance art.

One painting caught my eye. It was large compared to the others, and it was divided into four squares. Each square depicted a scene from what appeared to be Christ's resurrection. I became so intrigued by this painting that I went to ask the librarian about it.

He told me that the painting did depict Jesus' resurrection and that there was background information available on microfiche.

"The microfiche won't tell you everything about the painting," he informed me, smiling. "If you want to know that, you will have to ask me."

He introduced himself as Mr. LeSaul. Then he led me into one of the microfiche research rooms so that we would not be disturbed.

After a few minutes of viewing the microfiche film, LeSaul began to speak. I paraphrase his words:

This artwork was produced by Ambrogio Lorenzetti, the Italian story painter. It was presented to Pope Boniface XII on Christmas Day, 1342, on the dedication of the Pope's new palace in Avignon.

Boniface XII admired the painting and placed it near his private altar in the palace. However, within two weeks, Clement VI succeeded him.

Because of the subject matter and the controversy associated with the four differing renderings of Jesus' resurrection, Clement VI claimed that the painting offended him. So he had it removed and placed in storage.

It remained in storage for many years. In January of 1377, Gregory XI abandoned Avignon and re-established papal residency in Rome. Gregory had never seen the painting. Nonetheless, he wanted it destroyed.

However, purely by accident, this painting ended up being sold to finance Gregory's move to Rome.

Henry, Duke of Orléans, purchased, sight unseen, 25 works of art and entrusted his steward Andrea of Tours to select them.

Once Henry realized that one of the paintings was something Gregory wanted destroyed, he brought the painting to this abbey for safe keeping. It remained hidden until 1859, when the abbot placed it on display in *this* library. It was hidden again when the Nazis invaded, and then brought out of hiding and put back on display in 1950.

With this, we returned to the microfiche. All the text was written in French, so I asked LeSaul to translate for me.

He said that before explaining the painting itself, he wanted to describe the religious atmosphere of the painter Lorenzetti's world.

At this time, he began, the big theological controversy in the Church was whether Mary Magdalene went to the tomb to see Jesus one last time to prepare his body, or to worship him and pray for him to be released from Paradise, so that he could ascend back to his Father.

Also, the Church was beset with controversies rooted in "new revelations" that had come to light from the study of non-Christian commentaries on previously unknown Talmuds. These commentaries told a different story from the Bible's, regarding the women who came to Jesus' tomb. These commentaries, which were said to be based on eyewitness accounts, reflected several *different* records of Jesus' resurrection.

LeSaul paused a moment before continuing: "It seems obvious that these commentaries were intended to create confusion and polarization within the church.

"These differing stories could have destroyed the foundation of Catholic theology. This is why I believe that these reports were circulated chiefly for political reasons. Yet, some of the information may have been grounded in truth.

"I feel that the events of Jesus' resurrection have been extremely confusing, ever since the first century.

"On one hand, we have the modern tradition or the last four hundred years, of the resurrection. On the other, we have the eight centuries' worth of earlier tradition. Both of these traditions have chosen to omit very important Scriptures. Meanwhile, a third tradition arose in the ninth century. Its most popular period of acceptance was the 300 years from the ninth century to the twelfth century. In reality, this tradition used more scriptural justification than the other two. The thirteenth through the sixteenth centuries brought a multitude of other traditions, some logical, and some so controversial and mystical that they bordered on the ridiculous. During this era, Lorenzetti completed this painting, which addresses some of the Resurrection controversies.

"According to tradition, each of the painting's four scenes illustrates a different version of the women's post-Sabbath visit to Jesus' tomb.

"In our Bible, this event is recorded in John 20:1-18, Luke 24:1-11, Mark 16:1-8, and Matthew 28:1-10."

My librarian friend then told me that he would highlight obvious areas of controversy. He would explain the painting's four different scenes and then explain the three traditions that the four scenes represented, drawing from information that he discovered in commentaries on first and second century Christian Greek texts.

"The painting's most obvious differences," he explained, "are the day (and *time* of day), the number and identities of the women, and the location of the tomb's sealing stone.

"I must note that the tomb's sealing stone plays a very important role in this story. Typically, a sealing stone did not close the tomb opening for at least four days, and in some cases, five days. In some cases, the stone was rolled in front of the tomb opening after four days but not sealed until all the tomb's burial spaces had been filled. Of course, this could take months or even years. However, in Jesus' case, the stone was rolled into the mouth of the tomb on the day he died, and the tomb was sealed. This is very unusual, unless Joseph of Arimathea's influence was far greater than the church has traditionally given him credit for.

"Now, let's return to the subject of day and time: John's account, represented in the painting's first scene, reports that the women came to the tomb on Wednesday morning, the 22nd of Nisan, while it was still dark. Luke's account, represented in scene two, also indicates Wednesday morning, the 22nd of Nisan. But it shows the time to be early dawn.

"The Mark version, represented in the bottom-left scene, also depicts the day as Wednesday morning, the 22nd, but the time is later dawn. The sun has already risen. The Matthew version, represented in scene number four, indicates the day as Thursday evening, the 30th of Nisan, after sundown."

LeSaul then gave his explanation concerning the number of women who came to the tomb In the John setting (the top left picture), there is only one woman, Mary E. Magdalene. In Luke, the second picture, at least five women are present: Mary E. Magdalene, Joanna, Mary E. James, and others. In the Mark version, there are three women: Mary E. Magdalene, Mary E. James, and Salome. The Matthew version depicts two women: Mary E. Magdalene and another Mary.

Now, let's return to the subject of the sealing stone. In John, the stone has been rolled away *before* the women arrive. In Luke and Mark, the stone has also been rolled away. However, in the Matthew scene, the stone is still in the mouth of the tomb when the women arrive. They witness the angel rolling the stone away.

What, then, is the probable sequence of events?

John's version:

- Mary E. Magdalene comes to the open tomb, but she does not enter.

- She reports what she has seen to Peter and John. They go to the tomb.

- Mary E. Magdalene returns to the tomb. After Peter and John depart, she enters the tomb.

- When she emerges from the tomb, Jesus meets her. She thinks he is the gardener. He then reveals himself to her.

- Jesus warns her not to touch him, because he is yet to be resurrected to the Father.

- She again reports to the disciples.

Luke's version:

- Five women enter the open tomb, and then emerge

- They see two men in shining clothing, who tell them the Resurrection has occurred.

- They report their experience to the 11 disciples who don't believe them.

Mark's version:

- Three women enter the open tomb and find a young man sitting inside.

- The man, or angel, speaks, telling them to report to the disciples.

- The women are terrified and do not report anything to anyone.

- (This version indicates that, after the women's visit, soldiers sent by Pilate replace the stone in the mouth of the tomb, and then seal it.)

Matthew's version:

- The two women don't enter the tomb, because the sealing stone is in place and soldiers are standing guard.

- The women witness the stone being rolled away.

- They see a messenger of the Lord outside of the tomb. He tells them the Resurrection has taken place.

- The two women run from the tomb to report to the disciples. Jesus meets them en route. They touch him, embracing his feet. He tells them to inform his disciples that he will meet them in the Galilee.

- The women report all these things to the disciples.

After LeSaul provided this overview, he moved on to a discourse of the most common traditions associated with Jesus' resurrection, including the women's visit to the tomb. In the following paragraphs, I will paraphrase LeSaul:

RESURRECTION TRADITION ONE

Tradition number one, the tradition of the last four centuries, holds that Jesus was crucified on Friday morning. He died on Friday afternoon and was entombed Friday evening. He descended into Hades and ministered to those in captivity there and set free any who believed in him. This tradition holds that the righteous went to Paradise upon death. Paradise being a place of peace and rest, connected to Heaven. There they remained until they were judged. After the crucifixion, Jesus released these righteous ones from Paradise and allowed them into Heaven.

Jesus remained in Hades for two nights, Friday and Saturday. Before Sunday's sunrise, there was a great earthquake, and an angel rolled away the tomb's sealing stone. Jesus rose from the dead and exited the tomb. The guards fell as dead men (Matthew 28:2-4). Saints (the ones released from Hades) rose from their graves and went into the city (Matthew 27:53). Then they ascended into heaven with Jesus. A short time later, while it was still dark, Mary E. Magdalene left her house alone to go to the tomb (John 20:1). Then, just as day began to break, Mary E. James, the mother of James; Joanna, the wife of Chuza; Salome, the wife of Zebedee; and some other women met Mary E. Magdalene at the tomb (See Mark 16:1-2, Matthew 28:1, and Luke 24:1.) As they approached the tomb, they discovered that the tombstone had been rolled away (Luke 24:2, Mark 16:3-4).

Mary E. Magdalene turned and ran back to Peter and John, informing them that Jesus' body had been stolen (John 20:2). Peter and John ran to the tomb to investigate (John 20:3-7). Meanwhile, after Mary's departure, some of the remaining women entered the tomb. Inside, two angels met them. One spoke and told them Jesus had risen and they should tell the disciples the news. (Luke 24:3-8, Mark 16:5-7). The women fled the tomb, terrified (Mark 16:8). By the time Peter and John arrived at the tomb, the women were gone. Peter and John saw the empty tomb and the abandoned graves clothes (John 20:7-9). They then believed Mary's story that someone had stolen Jesus' body. They returned to where they were staying (John 20:10). Mary E. Magdalene followed them back to the tomb, but she did not return with them. She was left alone. She lingered outside the tomb, weeping.

Eventually, she entered the tomb. There, she also saw the two angels. One of them talked to her (John 20:11-12). As she was talking with the angels (perhaps believing they were gardeners), Jesus approached her and spoke, revealing his identity (John 20:15-17). Mary dashed away to tell the disciples that Jesus had risen.

Meanwhile, the other women were fleeing to their homes. As they fled, Jesus appeared to them and confirmed what the angel told them (Matthew 28:8-10). They then reported to the disciples. As they were informing the disciples, Mary E. Magdalene arrived with *her* story. At this, Peter again ran back to the tomb. Again, he found nothing (Luke 24:12). Later that day, Jesus appeared to two disciples in the country (Mark 16:12). They returned to the other disciples and told them what they had seen. These disciples did not believe them (Mark 16:13). That night, Jesus appeared to ten disciples (John 20:19-20). Eight days later, he appeared to two disciples going to Emmaus (Luke 24:13-32).

Then Jesus appeared to all of them. (See John 20:24-29, Luke 24:33-35, and Mark 16:14.) After this, the disciples went into the Galilee, as Jesus instructed (Matthew 28:16) and waited. After waiting a while, they went fishing (John 21:1-23). Jesus eventually arrived on the seashore and taught them. Forty days after his resurrection, he gave his final instructions before ascending into heaven.

RESURRECTION TRADITION TWO

Tradition number two is the one accepted for the first eight centuries after Jesus' resurrection. This tradition is quite similar to the first one, apart from some time-based differences. This tradition holds that

Jesus was crucified Friday morning. He died Friday afternoon, and he was entombed Friday evening. Immediately after death, Jesus descended into Hades, which was divided into two compartments: The Abyss and Paradise. The Abyss, also known as Hell at the time, was where the souls of the non-righteous dead were held in torment until the Day of Judgment. Paradise was where the souls of the righteous dead—from the time of Adam until Christ—were held in peace. This tradition says that Jesus descended into the Abyss and preached to the damned. He then entered Paradise, where he released the souls of the righteous dead. He later took these souls to heaven with him when he ascended. During this era, the church taught that the Abyss was occupied by the souls of the non-righteous, whose number were increasing daily. Conversely, Paradise was emptied by Jesus. It was empty and would remain so forever. Adherents to this tradition believed that once Jesus had emptied Paradise, the righteous could go immediately to heaven upon their deaths.

Also, this tradition held that Jesus was in Hades for three full days before rising from the dead. The remaining events, including those involving the women, follow the same sequence as tradition number one.

Resurrection Tradition Three

Tradition number three enjoyed wide acceptance from the ninth through the twelfth centuries. This tradition was more radical than the other two. However, it seems more scripturally based and more logical in its sequence of events. Tradition number three holds that Jesus was crucified on Monday morning, died Monday afternoon, and was entombed Monday evening, the 20th of Nisan. The stone was probably rolled in front of the tomb by Joseph of Arimathea. This tradition strongly emphasized the physical death of Jesus and his perfect sacrificial death. Upon death, he descended into the Abyss portion of Hades. He stayed there Monday evening and all day Tuesday. On Wednesday morning, the 22nd of Nisan, Jesus' physical body rose from the dead. This was the *first* resurrection.

Shortly thereafter, while it was still dark, Mary E. Magdalene came to the tomb. She saw that the sealing stone had been rolled away. She did not enter the tomb. She left and reported to Peter and John that someone had stolen Jesus' body. Peter and John ran to the tomb and found it empty. Then they returned to where they were staying. Mary, however, lingered outside the tomb and wept. She then entered the tomb and saw two angels. One of them talked to her. She exited the tomb and met the physical Jesus, whom she mistook for the gardener. He revealed himself to her, ordering her to avoid touching him, because he had not yet ascended to his Father. She left him and again reported to the disciples.

Soon thereafter, seven other women came to the tomb. They saw that the stone had been rolled away. They went inside, then came right back out. Then, as they were departing, they were met by two men in shining clothing. These men told them that the physical Jesus had risen from the dead. They hurried to the 11 disciples and reported their experience. The 11 did not believe them (Luke 24:1-11).

Later that morning, three *more* women arrived at the tomb. When this trio arrived, they entered the tomb and found a young man sitting inside. He spoke to them, instructing them to report what they had seen to the disciples. The three became terrified and ran off. They did not go to the disciples, nor did they say anything to anybody (Mark 16:1-8).

At mid morning on the 22nd of Nisan, Pilate's guards arrived at the tomb. Finding the stone removed, they replaced it and sealed it (Matthew 27:62-66; 28:11-15). (Because a deceased person's body was placed deep within a tomb, the soldiers may have seen no reason to enter the tomb. There was no sign that Jesus' body was missing. Also, since it was known that Jesus' body had only been temporarily prepared, and would be permanently prepared after the Sabbath, there was no reason for the soldiers to be suspicious of the sealing stone not being in place.)

Later that day, the physical Jesus appeared to two disciples in the country (Mark 16:12). That evening, the physical Jesus appeared to 10 disciples. Thomas was not with the group at this time (John 20:19-25). After this, the physical Jesus appeared to no one for almost a week. The disciples began to doubt. Perhaps they had merely seen a vision. Perhaps Jesus was dead after all.

At this point, tradition number three gets a bit mystical: Six days later, on the morning of the 28th of Nisan, Christ died *spiritually* to sin (See Romans 5:8 and 2 Corinthians 5:21). This was the *second* death.

Jesus became The Christ when he died to sin. Christ descended into the Paradise section of Hades. There he remained for two days and one night. This makes a total of three days and three nights that he stayed in Hades. (See Luke 24:45-47, Mark 9:31, and Matthew 12:40.) He stayed two nights and one day in the Abyss and two days and one night in Paradise. At the 12th hour, eight days after the resurrection of the physical Jesus, the second resurrection took place: The Resurrection of Christ and the Resurrection of Justification.

Upon this resurrection, Christ set free those who had been in Paradise. As the day ended and a new day began (6:00 p.m.), Mary E. Magdalene and the other Mary went to the tomb, probably as they had done every day. By this time, they, like the disciples, were probably convinced that their encounter with Jesus was a vision or dream. The stone was in the mouth of the tomb, which had been under Roman guard for more than a week.

Suddenly, there was a huge earthquake and an angel rolled the sealed stone away from the mouth of the tomb and sat upon it. The women and the soldiers saw it all happen. The guards became terrified and fell, as dead men. The angel told the women that Christ had risen. They were to tell his disciples to meet him in the Galilee. The women ran from the tomb to report to the disciples. Christ met them en route and confirmed the angel's instructions. The women embraced Jesus' feet and worshipped him. Then they ran to tell the disciples the news (Matthew 28:1-10). The next morning, before 6:00, Christ appeared to the two who were going to Emmaus. He spent all day with them. They then went to Jerusalem to tell the disciples about their experience (Luke 24:13-35). The disciples did not go to the Galilee as Christ had instructed. They still didn't believe the news. So Christ appeared to them while the two Emmaus travelers were telling their story. This time, Thomas was present (Luke 24:36-37, John 20:26-29).

After this, the disciples did go into the Galilee and waited for Christ to join them. However, his arrival time didn't meet their expectations. They decided to go fishing (John 21:1-23). Ultimately, Jesus joined them and spent 40 more days (after his second resurrection) with them, teaching and fellowshipping. Afterwards, he ascended into heaven to take his place as advocate and mediator.

LeSaul told me, "Each of these three resurrection traditions has taken its turn as *THE ACCEPTED LAW AND DOCTRINE OF THE CHURCH* during the past twenty centuries. Each has taken its turn as *God-inspired and revealed* doctrine. Meanwhile, many, many other traditions have been rejected as heresy and, each of the three traditions we have discussed has taken its turn as heresy as well.

"Clearly, all three cannot be correct. So we are left with a decision. Which of these three traditions is true or, is there another version?

"I will conclude by saying that what really matters is not which tradition is right, but that each confirms the fact that Jesus rose from the dead. One resurrection or two? It matters little. What matters is that Jesus is living, even to this day. As for me, I accept none of the three as absolute fact. Yet I accept all three as conditional fact. All three have strong points, and all three have gaping theological and doctrinal holes. Tradition number three seems to have a more consistent flow and a more logical sequence of events."

With this comment, LeSaul had to leave. I took the opportunity to sit there in silence, marveling at how much could be conveyed by one painting. No wonder the Pope wanted it destroyed. It would have been far too controversial for that era. It's probably too controversial for *our* era.

So, we are left with many questions. How long did Jesus stay in the tomb before he rose from the dead? If we take Jesus' words literally, then he was in the tomb for three days and three nights. Thus, if he was entombed on Monday evening and he stayed in the tomb for three days and three nights, he rose from the dead on Thursday evening, before dawn on Friday. What about the two resurrections, one physical and one spiritual—separated by six days? In my research, I have not discovered enough information to affirm this. Yet, it seems to be the only explanation that reconciles the inconsistency between Matthew's Resurrection account and that of the other three Gospels. So, I will continue to search for the truth regarding this matter. Until I discover enough truth to warrant a re-evaluation, I choose to stand by the words of Jesus. He said he would remain in the tomb for three days and three nights (three FULL days and three FULL nights) and then rise from the dead.

The Garden Tomb or Gordon's Tomb. Many Protestants believe that this could be the tomb of Jesus—Israel.

CHAPTER 28

✦

A New Beginning

PART 2

AFTER JESUS ROSE from the dead, he remained on earth for 40 more days. Many eyewitnesses testified to his appearance. Jesus spent much of this time with his disciples and followers, preparing them to carry on after his departure. He instructed them and gave them power to minister with Christ-like authority. He commissioned them to spread his teachings, his doctrines, and the truths exemplified by his life to the far corners of the earth to every culture, and to every people group.

At the end of the 40 days, Jesus led the 11 disciples to Bethany. There, he gave them two final commands (Acts 1:4-11):

- *Tarry in Jerusalem until you receive the gift of the Holy Ghost and power from on high (this was realized 10 days later on the Day of Pentecost).*

- *Be witnesses in Jerusalem, Judea, Samaria, and to the utter-most parts of the earth.*

Then Jesus ascended to heaven and took his rightful place seated on the right hand of the Father. As the disciples gazed at the sky, two men dressed in white (perhaps angels) stood by them and told them that Jesus would return (the Second Coming) in the same manner he departed.

After the ascension, the disciples did as Jesus commanded. They returned to Jerusalem and tarried in the upper room, waiting for the Holy Spirit.

Although Jesus ascended, his work did not stop. Over the next two centuries his message was taken to the far corners of the known world. To cover the spread of Christianity would take another book, perhaps even a series of books.

While researching at the Toledo Public Library in Toledo, Ohio, I found an essay titled *Boyd's Paul,* written in 1953 by Dr. Clive Emerson, a professor of Roman History at Dallas Theological Seminary. The essay was a commentary on a treatise written in 1795 by a Scottish history professor named Richard F. Boyd. (Boyd's work was titled *Paul Unveiled.*)

Dr. Emerson's essay was divided into two parts, titled *Boyd's opinion* and *Boyd's flummox.*

Part 1 was typical of many theological commentaries I have read. Nothing stuck out enough to inspire me to start taking notes.

Then I got to Part 2, in which Emerson explores Boyd's vast knowledge of Jesus and the apostles Peter and Paul.

Discussing Jesus, Emerson quotes Boyd directly:

> "Because Jesus was a ward and son by adoption of Joseph of Arimathea, he probably traveled with Joseph all over the Roman Empire, from Britain to Arabia and from the North Sea to Egypt. He could have even traveled by caravan as far east as the Himalayan Mountains. Joseph of Arimathea was one of the richest men in all of Syria and probably the richest Jew in Judaea. He owned and/ or controlled virtually all the metal and mineral trade between Syria and Europe and exclusively controlled all metal and mineral trade between Syria and Britain. Because Joseph was the Imperial Minister of Mines and Mining for the Roman Empire, as well as a Roman Senator representing Britain, a great deal of time was spent in Britain. Hence Jesus, if he traveled with Joseph, could travel anywhere mines were being worked to sell ore and minerals to or buy for the Roman Empire."

Boyd adds that, according to the traditions of Glastonbury, Jesus and his mother, Mary, built a home on the south end of Lake Glastonbury and lived there on two different occasions. Glastonbury is located near the headwaters of the Thames River, within the region of the Silurian Kingdom, a center of Druidic worship.

PETER IMPRISONED

Next, Emerson moves on to Boyd's writing about Peter and Paul. According to Boyd, following Peter's imprisonment (Acts 12:2-4), Joseph of Arimathea, along with a handful of Jesus' followers, including Mary his mother, were cast adrift off the coast of Caesarea by the Jewish Sanhedrin, in January of AD 37. Boyd adds,

> "Without sails or oars, they drifted with the currents until they arrived at Cyrene on the coast of Africa. After obtaining sails and oars in Cyrene, they sailed to Rome. Emperor Caligula was infuriated with the Jewish Sanhedrin who had dared treat Joseph of Arimathea with such disdain. To keep the actions of the Sanhedrin under extreme examination, Caligula ordered the death of 112 members of the Jewish Sanhedrin and the death of 33 Jewish priests who had supported Joseph's dismissal. Joseph was immediately returned to his position in the Sanhedrin in Jerusalem by the High Priest. Some three years after his reinstatement (in AD 40), Joseph, Mary, Mary Magdalene, and a small band of followers set sail from Caesarea with a Roman military escort of 50 soldiers. They sailed as far west as Massilla in Gaul, and what is now called the coast of France."

Boyd continues,

> "Cardinal Caesar Barinius served as head librarian to the Vatican from 1538 to 1609, and he recorded events in his Ecclesiastical Annals, a *History of the Christian church from the resurrection of Christ up to AD 1198*. He wrote that Joseph, travelling to Massilla (Marseilles) had in his company 67 souls, including the 50-guard Roman escort. They included the sisters Mary and Martha of Bethany, their brother Lazarus, Eutropius, Salome, Cleon, Saturninus, Mary Magdalene, Mercella the maid of Mary of Bethany, Maximin, Martial, Mary the mother of Jesus, and Trophimus or Restitutus.

> "Joseph of Arimathea, and his party plus the Roman escort, travelled the length of Gaul, following the Rhone and then the Liger

(Loire) Rivers and then on to what is known as Brittany, to what became the city of Brest. From there they traveled by military transport to Britain. In Britain they traveled to Glastonbury, where Jesus had established a home for himself and his mother some years before in that Celtic-Druid region. Joseph built the first physical Christian church in Glastonbury. Hence, although Christianity was eventually confessed throughout the Empire, the region that proclaimed it as their religion first was Roman Britain.

"Among the first converts in Britain were the royal house of Siluria, including the king of Siluria, Caradoc. Also converted was his daughter Gladys, his father Bran, and his brother (or brother-in-law) Aviragus, who became king. In 1086 King William the Conqueror had all the previous historic records accumulated into several volumes called the Doomsday Book. King Aviragus is recorded as having granted to Roman Senator Joseph of Arimathea and his followers 12 hides of land or approximately 1900 acres, tax free, in Yniswitrin, afterwards called the Isle of Avalon. This notable act of the King gave the recipients many British concessions, including the right of citizenship with its privileges of freedom to pass unmolested from one district to another in time of war, and both Joseph of Arimathea and Mary the mother of Jesus (according to local tradition) are buried in the church courtyard of Glastonbury. King Arthur has traced his lineage directly to the daughter of Joseph of Arimathea, Anna, the cousin of Mary the mother of Jesus."

Additionally, Boyd says:

"Lazarus became the first bishop of Marsilla (or Marseilles). Lazarus and his sisters, along with Mary Magdalene, remained in France until their deaths."

PAUL

According to Boyd,

"The famed Paul was not converted into Christianity until about AD 37 or 38, shortly before the first Christian church in Britain was founded by Senator Joseph in Glastonbury. It is the letters that Paul wrote between AD 55 and 69 that establish the fundamentals of today's Christian doctrine. The remarkable letter that Paul wrote to the church in Rome contains the full essence of Christianity, (but to whom was Paul writing when he wrote this letter around AD 59, and what was the occasion)?

"Most historians agree that the letter to the Romans was written either from Paul's prison cell in Corinth or from his residence in Corinth just before he was imprisoned. The recipients of the letter were the 2,300 Christians living in Rome. For the most part, these were Roman Christians, not Jews or Jewish converts. Claudius had expelled all the Jews from Rome almost a decade before the time the letter was written (Acts 18:2), so most of the Christians in Rome were Romans or other non Jews.

"Because of his imprisonment, Paul was unable to come to Rome in person to set things right doctrinally with the Roman Christians, so he sent this letter of compassion and discipline to Rome by way of Phebe, the sister of Zephyrinus, the Roman proconsul.

"Paul did not expect to stay in prison long because he felt the need to go to Spain. The letter also served as his pronouncement that he would come to Rome on his way to Spain."

Boyd notes:

"In the sixth year of Nero's reign (AD 59) something inside Nero snapped. This man, who had for five years ruled so admirably, now made an abrupt about-face. By his seventh year, Nero had bankrupted the Roman central bank with his lavish lifestyle and building projects. In a six-month period, he raised taxes throughout the Empire 16 times, and for the first time ever Roman citizens were taxed. By the end of Nero's seventh year as emperor, Rome's citizens, except the nobility, the military hierarchy, and members of the Senate, were paying 60 percent of their earnings in taxes. Non-Roman residents were paying upwards of 75 percent in taxes. During that seventh year, inflation grew in Rome from just under two percent to well over 300 percent.

"Apolodius, the leader of the 2,300 Roman Christians, began to stir up discontent over the forced payment of taxes to Nero (Romans 13:6-8). Procluius, a Jew who had converted to Christianity, rebelled against Apolodius's authority and demanded submission to Nero's order. A major rift developed between the two leaders. A split developed in the Roman Christian community also.

"Hearing of this unrest, Nero arrested Christian leaders throughout Italy, Macedonia, and Greece. Among those affected by this order was Paul, who was imprisoned in Corinth.

"About a year and a half later, Nero ordered the middle portion of Rome to be burned and he blamed the Christians for the fire. Ruthless persecution of Jesus' followers followed.

"At first the persecution was restricted to Christians who were slaves. Within two years the persecution had expanded to include all non-Roman Christians. One year later, it had expanded to include Roman citizen Christians. It is estimated that 1,700 Christians in the city of Rome and another 3,000 throughout Italy were victimized.

"Shortly after this, Paul wrote his letter to the Romans.

"About a year after Procluius and Apolodius were arrested, Zephyrinus, the Roman proconsul, arranged for the release from prison of Procluius, who served as a tutor to his children. However, Apolodius remained in prison. Therefore, with Apolodius still in prison, Procluius became the sole, unchallenged leader of the Christians in Rome.

"Nero's persecution had far-reaching impact. Procluius, the Christian leader who had rebelled against Apolodius's authority, began to teach that the blood of Jesus was mandatory for salvation from hell and damnation but obeying the Law of Moses was necessary for securing resurrection and a place in heaven. If people accepted Jesus as Savior they would not go to hell when they died, he taught. However, if they had failed to keep the Law of Moses, they would forever remain asleep in the grave. They would never be resurrected and enter heaven."

Boyd adds:

"Procluius taught that God always responded to prayers that were prayed in the Hebrew language, since Hebrew was the language of God. He responded to non-Hebrew prayers only after Hebrew prayers had been answered, which could take months or even years. He also taught adherence to the old law of Augustus, which said that if a woman's husband died, she could never marry again or she would be considered an adulteress. Procluius claimed that God had also adopted this position concerning marriage. He also taught that both men and women had to submit to circumcision, along with keeping the Law of Moses, to be assured of a resurrection."

"His primary emphasis was that it is better to commit suicide than to submit to the persecution of Nero.

"At this point, it is important to note that Nero's atrocities against Christians, which were contrary to the Law of Moses, included forcing them into homosexuality, bestiality, eating the flesh of boiled babies, drinking blood, and all kinds of sexual perversions.

"Nero's persecution, combined with Procluius's doctrine," says Boyd, "caused an eruption of suicides within the Christian community and a great rift among the Roman Christians. The Christians were so busy fighting each other that they had no strength to fight off the spiritual attacks of evil.

"When Paul heard about what was happening, he became furious and wrote a stinging letter of rebuke (Romans 2:1) to Procluius and within the same letter comforted the embattled Roman church.

"In the letter, Paul said that even in the midst of evil, suffering, and persecution, good will overcome evil. Christ is the common denominator that holds all Christians together. Look to him and only him for hope and assurance. Even as the forces of evil are waging an all-out war, Christ will have the ultimate victory.

"Those familiar with the book of Romans know that Paul ends his correspondence with some greetings. He writes, "Greet Andronicus and Junias, my relatives, and my fellow captives, who are well known among the apostles, and were in Christ prior to me" (Romans 16:7).

"Paul had relatives living in Rome who had become Christians before he did. Most historians place Paul's conversion at about AD 37 or 38. This means that these relatives were among Christianity's earliest converts.

"Paul writes, 'Greet Rufus, the chosen one in the Lord, and his mother and mine' (Romans 16:13). In the Greek, the phrase kai ten metera aytoy kai emoy means 'and the mother of him and of me.' In other words, Paul's mother and Rufus, his brother or half-brother, were living in Rome at the time of his writing. Paul calls Rufus the chosen one, indicating that this brother was a man of significance in the church's early years."

ROYAL HOUSE OF CARADOC

Boyd says,

"As for Joseph of Arimathea, some of his early converts were the royal household of Caradoc and Aviragus. Caradoc and Aviragus were kings of Siluria, and their father, Bran, was the son of King Lear [of Shakespearean fame]. Another convert was Caradoc's daughter Gladys.

"Caradoc was the grandson of the Silurian King Lear. He was an absolute terror to the Roman forces that invaded Britain from AD

40 to 43. In 40 battles the Romans never defeated Caradoc. He was betrayed and was brought to Rome.

"According to the Roman historian Tacitus, Caradoc's wife and family were eventually taken prisoner by the Romans. Caradoc himself was turned over to Emperor Claudius by Queen Catimandua, with whom he sought refuge after escaping during a battle.

"In a speech before the Senate, Caradoc was so impressive that the Senate pleaded with Claudius to spare his life. Claudius reprieved Caradoc and his family. Claudius, the Empire's fourth emperor, treated Caradoc and his family well. They were required to remain in Rome for seven years on what might today be called parole. Overseeing this parole was Aristobulus, a personal friend of Claudius.

"Caradoc and his family stayed in Aristobulus's palace as houseguests for seven years. When Paul wrote his letter to the Roman Christians, the parole period was nearing its end. Paul made sure that the letter arrived in Rome before Caradoc was freed and allowed to return home."

Boyd notes,

"Aristobulus's name means 'best counselor.' He was the younger brother of Herod Agrippa, the same Herod who was appointed King over the area that became known as Palestine, by Caligula in AD 41. Aristobulus (or Eubulus in Greek) is mentioned in II Timothy 4:21 and Romans 16:10. He was the father of the apostle Simon Peter's wife. It was (this) wife's mother that Jesus healed of the plague, as recorded in Luke 4:38-39. Aristobulus was one of the 70 sent out by Jesus, and he was in Jerusalem on Pentecost, when the church was founded and when Peter preached his first sermon.

"The household of Aristobulus was the household in which Christianity had its first foothold in Rome. The members of Aristobulus' family were all Christian converts, and were well-known by both Caligula and his successor Claudius. Aristobulus was both a good friend and a wise advisor to both Caesars.

"By way of background, Joseph of Arimathea had converted Caradoc's family to Christianity some years earlier. "Caradoc's daughter, Gladys," Boyd writes, "was among the first British converts. She soon became engaged to a young Roman Praetor named Rufus Pudens. She was responsible for the conversion of Rufus Pudens. They were married in Rome. Rufus was the younger brother or half-brother of the apostle Paul.

"In Rome, because of Claudius Caesar's close relationship with Caradoc's family, Gladys was adopted by Claudius. He changed her name to Claudia. Second Timothy 4:21 records Paul's forwarding of greetings sent by her.

"Caradoc had sons: Selinus succeeded his father on the Silurian throne. Simon, called Lane or Linus, was consecrated the first Bishop of Rome by Paul, around the time of Paul's writing of the second letter to Timothy.

"From the marriage of Rufus and Claudia came children: Timithus, Novacus, Podenciana, and Proxcedus. They were all later sainted by the Roman Catholic Church. Bran, Caradoc's father, was responsible for taking some of the first copies of the early Christian writings back to Britain."

THE MISSING "ACTS?"

Near the end of his essay, Dr. Emerson again pauses to make some personal notes regarding Boyd's belief that some of the New Testament Book of Acts has been lost or deliberately eliminated. Emerson writes:

"Some years ago I was privileged to read a portion of C.S. Sonnini's 'Sonnini's Travels in Turkey and Greece.' After reading it, I (like Boyd) was amazed at the possibility that a portion of the Acts of the Apostles had perhaps been purposely altered to dislodge from history Paul's trip to Britain. Sonnini's document seems to me to be an accurate record, as he has reported to have discovered it during his investigation in the ancient city of Constantinople.

"Allow me to quote the presumed missing Acts 29th chapter, the final chapter of the Acts of the Apostles, by beginning my quote with the familiar Acts 28:28 and then going directly into the 29th chapter. Acts 28:29-31, as Sonnini speculated, was probably added by Emperor Phocas of Rome in AD 610, after he had the 29th chapter stricken from the permanent record of the Acts.

ACTS 28:28 and on
[28] Be it known therefore unto you, that the salvation of God is sent unto the Gentiles, and that they will hear it.

And Paul, full of the blessings of Christ, and abounding in the spirit, departed out of Rome, determining to go into Spain, for he had a long time proposed to journey thitherward, and was minded also to go from thence to Britain.

For he had heard in Phoenicia that certain of the Jews, about the time of the Assyrian captivity, had escaped by sea to the Isles afar as spoken of by the prophet Ezra and called by the Romans, Britain.

And the Lord commanded the Gospel far hence to all of the Gentiles and to the lost sheep of Israel.

And no man hindered Paul; for he testified boldly of Jesus before the tribunes and among the people; and took with him certain brethren which abode with him in Rome, and they took ship at the harbor of Ostrium and having winds fair, were brought safely to Spain.

And much people were gathered together from the towns and villages and the hills country, for they had heard of the conversion of the apostle, and the many miracles that were wrought at the hands of the apostles.

And Paul preached mightily in Spain, and great multitudes believed and were converted, for they perceived he was an apostle of Jesus sent from God.

And they departed out of Spain, and Paul and his company, finding a ship sailing into Britain, they were therein, and passed along the south coast, they reached a port called Raphinus. (Raphinus was the Roman name for Sandwich-in-Kent, north of Dover and east of London.)

Now when it was voiced abroad that the Apostle had landed on their coast, great multitudes met him, and they treated him with honor, and he preached Christ unto them.

And Paul abode in his lodging three months in Raphinus, confirming in the faith and preaching Christ continually.

And after these things Paul and his brethren departed Raphinus and sailed to Atium.

And they went forth and came to Illyricum and strengthened Titus and the church in Dyrrhachium and grace was found in all the churches, and they prospered and had peace. Amen!

I concluded reading the essay and sat in total amazement. I had discovered what was, possibly, missing Scripture. Also, I had learned that both Peter and Paul had direct connections to Rome's royal court. A close friend of Roman Emperor Claudius was *also* Peter's father-in-law. Paul's sister-in-law was adopted by the emperor himself!

PLINY THE YOUNGER

It would take a lifetime to write the history of Christianity's spread and influence. People like Paul, his brother Rufus, Peter, and Joseph of Arimathea helped carry the torch handed to them by Jesus.

The Roman author and lawyer Pliny the Younger, who zealously persecuted Christians, provides an apt (if unlikely) summation of early Christianity, in his *Epistles* (Number 10:96), written circa AD 115. He was writing, while Govenor of Bithynia and Pontus, to Emperor Trajan to seek advice on how he should deal with the Christians in his province.

He writes:

"In the meantime, respecting those who were referred to me as Christians, I have followed this course. I have asked them whether they are Christian: if they confessed it a second and third time I asked them, threatening torture; if they persevered I ordered them to be led away to the penalty. For I had no question, whatever that might be which they professed, that this fixed determination and inflexible obstinacy ought to be punished. Others there were of like unreasonableness, which, because they were Roman citizens, I made a note of to be remanded to the city. Straightway, when this policy had been inaugurated, the crime extended itself, as is often the case and several varieties arose. A list containing the names of many was published.

"They affirmed also that the sum of their guilt, or error, was to assemble on a fixed day before daybreak and sing in responses a song to Christ as to a god, and to bind themselves with an oath not to enter into wickedness, or commit thefts, robberies, or adulteries, or falsify their word, or repudiate trusts committed to them: when these things were ended, it was their custom to depart, and, on coming together again, to take food, men, and women together, and yet innocently."

"Wherefore the more necessary I deemed it to seek, even by torture, from two maidens, who were called deaconesses, what was true. I found nothing else than an immoderate, vicious superstition. And so, the investigation concluded, I have hastened to consult you."

This letter, as much as any other documentation from that period, shows that Christianity was here to stay, despite all the persecution. Moreover, its numbers and influence were growing so rapidly in the Roman Empire that it was safe to say that Rome's traditional and historical religions' days were numbered. The political power of the once mighty empire was rapidly losing ground to the followers of Christ.

A Roman amphitheater in ancient
Dyrrhachium (Duress, Albania).
The amphitheater was constructed
by Christian slave labor. Tradition
says that Titus was martyred
here along the 5,000 other
Christians—Albania.

A burial stella
identifying the burial
place of Titus,
indicating that he
had died because of
his refusal to deny
Christ in the circus
(amphitheater) of
Dyrrhachium—Albania.

Byzantine mosaics in the amphitheater of Dyrrhachium
dedicated to those who had lost their lives for the
cause of Christ. Titus is depicted at the foot of
Gabriel, the angel in the middle—Albania.

EPILOGUE

My Search Continues

FOR MORE THAN 43 YEARS, I have been searching for fragments of information and documentation that confirm the authenticity of the Gospel accounts of Jesus' life. For 15 of those years, while continuing to research, I assembled my notes and documentation into manuscript form in anticipation of publishing my findings. Then one day, four 4-drawer file cabinets and four floor-to-ceiling bookshelves full of notes and compiled information later, I knew it was time to stop researching and write the book.

Even as I conclude this account, I realize that my work has just begun. Even as comprehensive as this book has become, it is obvious that I have not even scratched the surface of Jesus' life. In fact, I look upon this book as somewhat of an outline. There are so many items that need to be investigated, and it would take five lifetimes to cover them all. So, once the final period has been placed in this book, my research efforts will resume.

I know those efforts will be a blessing. You see, until I began my research, Jesus was distant to me. Too holy to comprehend, and too far away to care about my daily life. I knew he was mandatory for eternal life, but he seemed to hold little value for *this* life, on earth.

I had been taught that Jesus is personal, that he loves me and cares about what happens to me but it did not soak in. It was feel-good Sunday-sermon stuff. To me, Jesus was untouchable. Encased in plastic.

But as I researched and studied, I realized that this man/Son of God was truly one who could relate to us humans. He knows how we all feel. He is our perfect example for how to act and react in any number of situations.

Yes, his sacrifice gives us life after death, but there is so much more! Jesus came *alive*. He is the most remarkable man who ever existed, but he can sympathize with and relate to my every situation, decision, emotion, temptation, failure, success, thought, or question.

Jesus is so much more than my free pass to eternal life. He is my friend for this present life!

May you find him to be your friend as well.

APPENDIX A

A Chronology of the life of Jesus

THE FOLLOWING is a slightly condensed version of the chronology I developed and have used throughout my years of research and writing. I hope that you will find it to be a useful reference. The chronology below is not exhaustive, but it lists most of the important events connected with Jesus' life.

THE LIFE OF JESUS

8 BC

1. The angel Gabriel appears to Zacharias, telling him that his wife, Elizabeth, will bear a son in her old age. (Luke 1:5-23)

2. In Elizabeth's sixth month of pregnancy, Gabriel visits Mary, a virgin living in the Galilee. He tells Mary that she will have a son. (Luke 1:26-28)

3. Mary goes to live with Elizabeth, until the birth of Elizabeth's son. (Luke 1:39-56)

4. Elizabeth's son is born. (Luke 1:57)

5. Elizabeth's son is circumcised and named *John* (Luke 1:59-66)

6. Zacharias prophesies about John and about the coming Messiah. (Luke 1:67-79)

7 BC

7. Mary returns home to Nazareth. Mary's fiancé, Joseph, discovers that she is going to have a baby. (Matthew 1:18-19)

8. An angel appears to Joseph in a dream and tells him to take Mary as his wife. (Matthew 1:20-23)

9. Joseph marries Mary. (Matthew 1:24)

10. The Roman Syrian district of Judea is due to pay taxes, by order of a proclamation by Augustus. (Luke 2:1-3)

11. Joseph and Mary travel from their home in Nazareth to Bethlehem, Joseph's birthplace, to register and pay their tax. (See Matthew 2:5 and Luke 2:4-6.). During the Passover celebration (sometime between April 12 and April 18), Jesus is born. (Matthew 1:25; Luke 2:7)

AUTHOR'S NOTE: *The traditionally accepted date of Jesus' birth and the method of reckoning the Christian Era (BC and AD), were introduced in the sixth century by Dionysius Exiguus, a Scythian monk. He made a mistake in his calculations, missing the actual birthdate by at least six years, perhaps as many as 11. Many historians have proposed the year of Jesus' birth to be anywhere from 17 BC to 14 AD, but I have chosen the year 7 BC, because this seems most logical when I compare the Bible to Roman, Greek, Syrian, and Persian historical records.*

12. Consecrated shepherds, caring for the Passover sacrifice sheep, visit Jesus at his birthplace. (Luke 2:8-20)

13. Eight days after his birth, Jesus is circumcised and named. (Luke 2:21)

14. Forty days after his birth, Jesus is taken to the Temple in Jerusalem by his parents, to be presented at the Temple Redemption Ceremony (Luke 2:22-24. Also, see Leviticus 12:2-8.)

15. Simeon recognizes Jesus as Messias, God's anointed prophet of sacrifice and the religious reformer he had been waiting to see.

16. Anna recognized Jesus as the Messiah, a king greater than David who would bring social and political reform.

17. Joseph and Mary, with the infant Jesus, return to Nazareth in the Galilee. (Luke 2:39)

18. PEACE AND PROSPERITY IN THE LAND

5 BC

19. Wisemen (magi) come to Jerusalem in search of the baby king. (Matthew 2:8-10. Note: Daniel 7:13-14 records the prophecy that drove the magi to search for the baby king.)

20. Herod the Great sends the magi to Bethlehem to find the baby. Instead, they travel north to Nazareth, following a guiding star. (Matthew 2:8-10)

21. The magi find the toddler Jesus, worship him, and give him the *Gifts of Ramses*. (Matthew 2:11)

22. In a dream, God warns the magi not to return to Herod. They are instructed to return to their own countries. (Matthew 2:12)

23. An angel appears to Joseph in a dream, instructing him and his family to flee to Egypt. They depart immediately. (Matthew 2:13-15)

24. Herod orders the slaughter of infants within a 15-mile radius of Bethlehem, including Jerusalem. (Matthew 2:16-18)

4 BC TO AD 6 (10 YEARS)

25. Herod the Great dies (in 4 BC), and his kingdom is divided between Herod Archelaus, Herod Phillip, and Herod Antipas.

26. An angel appears to Joseph, telling him to take his family from Egypt and return home. They obey, circa 2 BC. (Matthew 2:19-20)

27. They return to Nazareth sometime between 2 BC and 6 AD. Jesus could have been as young as 5 years old or as old as 12 years old.

28. In AD 6, just before his 13th birthday, Jesus and his parents go to Jerusalem for Passover so that Jesus could participate in his bar mitzvah ceremony. (Luke 2:42)

29. After the *Son of the Law* ceremony, Jesus' parents join a caravan returning to the Galilee. However, Jesus stays behind. (Luke 2:43-45)

30. Realizing that Jesus is missing from the caravan, his parents return to Jerusalem, where they find him in the Temple. (Luke 2:44-49)

31. Jesus returns to Nazareth with his parents and remains under their authority. (Luke 2:51)

AD 6 TO AD 23

These are years of silence in Jesus' life, commonly called the "unknown years." However, important events took place in the Roman Empire.

32. In AD 6, the Roman province of Judaea is formed. The province is placed under the control of a Roman Procurator and includes the states of Judea and Idumaea and the district of Samaria.

33. In AD 7, Judaea's people revolt against the new Roman Procurator. The revolt is mercilessly crushed.

34. AD 10-13 M.Ambivius Roman Procurator of Province of Judaea

35. In AD 14 Augustus dies. Tiberius succeeds him. Tiberius rules until AD 37. Annius Rufus appointed Procurator of Judaea. The beginning of mandatory emperor worship.

36. In AD 15, Valerius Gratus is Procurator of Judaea until AD 26, when Pontius Pilate replaces him. (Jesus would have been about 33 years old in AD 26.)

37. In AD 17, Tiberius dreams of The Theophus. Tiberius stated that on his death he should neither be deified, exalted or worshiped.

38. In AD 18 the city of Tiberias is founded. Jews do much of its construction.

AD 23

39. Jesus, age 30, travels from Nazareth to the Jordan River to be baptized by John, the son of Zacharias and Elizabeth. (See Matthew 3:13-16, Mark 1:9-11, and Luke 3:21-23.)

40. After his baptism, Jesus goes into the wilderness to be tempted. (See Matthew 4:1-11, Mark 1:12-13, and Luke 4:1-13.)

41. AD 23 to AD 26 For the 3 years between the time of his wilderness temptations until the beginning of his ministry at age 33, nothing is known of Jesus' life.

42. Jesus increases in wisdom, and in favor with God and man. (Luke 2:52; 4:14)

AD 26

43. Pontius Pilate is appointed Procurator of Judaea.

44. John, called "The Baptist," continues his preaching and baptizing, drawing thousands of people. (See Matthew 3:1-12, Mark 1:3-8, and Luke 3:2-18.)

45. On three different days Jesus appears at Bethabara, where John is baptizing. John proclaims loudly, "Behold the Lamb of God." (the Messias (John 1:29-40). Two of John's disciples, Andrew and John, follow Jesus.

46. Jesus travels to the Galilee, where he finds Philip, who becomes his first "called" disciple. (John 1:43)

47. Jesus confronts Bartholomew, a Nathanael, who becomes another disciple. (John 1:45-51)

48. Jesus goes to the synagogue, where the people reject him. They attempt to kill him, but he escapes. (Luke 4:29-30)

49. In late summer of AD 26, Jesus attends a wedding and turns water into wine. (John 2:1-11)

50. In the winter of AD 26, Jesus (along with his two disciples and some of his family) moves to Capernaum. (John 2:12)

AD 27

51. In the spring of AD 27, Jesus goes to the Temple in Jerusalem and throws out the money-changers for the first time. (John 2:14-22)

52. Tiberius retires to Capri.

53. Later in the spring, Jesus has a confrontation with Nicodemus. (John 3:1-12)

54. John's testimonial of Jesus. (John 3:13-21)

55. Controversy develops between the disciples of John and the Jewish religious leaders. (John 3:25-36)

56. In early summer of AD 27, Herod Antipas arrests and imprisons John the Baptist. (See Matthew 4:12 and Mark 1:14.)

57. Jesus confronts a woman at Jacob's well in Sychar, a town just south of city of Samaria A revival follows. (John 4:5-43)

58. Jesus and his disciples arrive in the Galilee, where they are welcomed warmly. (John 4:45) They go back to Cana. (John 4:46)

59. A Herodian approaches Jesus and asks him to heal his son. (John 4:46-53) Jesus heals the Herodian's son. (John 4:50-53)

60. In August of AD 27, Jesus and his disciples go to the Sea of Galilee, where Jesus teaches from Simon's boat. (Luke 5:1-3), and Simon and his partners catch a haul of fish. (Luke 5:4-6)

61. Simon, Andrew, James, and John are called to be disciples. (See Matthew 4:18-22, Mark 1:16-20, and Luke 5:8-11.)

62. Jesus and his disciples enter a synagogue in Capernaum, where he teaches and heals a demoniac. (See Mark 1:21-28 and Luke 4:33-37.)

63. Sometime between September and October of AD 27, Jesus heals Simon's mother-in-law of Bubonic Plague. (See Matthew 8:14-15, Mark 1:30-31, and Luke 4:38-39.)

64. By the fall of AD 27, Jesus' fame has spread throughout the Roman province of Syria. (Matthew 4:24-25)

65. Out of sheer exhaustion, Jesus sought a place to pray. (Mark 1:35) The following morning, people began to search for him. (Luke 4:42) His disciples find him. (Mark 1: 36-37)

66. Jesus takes his six disciples into a mountain (perhaps a cave) and teaches them "The Sermon on the Mount." (Matthew 5:1-7:29)

67. Coming down off of the mountain, Jesus heals a leper Matthew 8:2-4; Mark 1:40-45; Luke 5:12-15

68. Sometime during the winter of AD 27, Jesus calms a storm while sailing to Gaulanitis with his disciples. (Matthew 8:23-26). Before he left, a scribe met him. This was followed by his confrontation with one of his disciples. (Matthew 8:18-22; Luke 9:57-62)

AD 28

69. In the spring of AD 28, Jesus is invited to participate in the great religious conference held in Capernaum. There, he heals a paralyzed man. (See Matthew 9:1-8, Mark 2:1-12, and Luke 5:17-26.)

70. Jesus calls Matthew (Levi) to be his disciple. (See Matthew 9:9, Mark 2:14, and Luke 5:27-28.)

71. Jesus travels throughout the Galilee, teaching, preaching, and healing. (Matthew 9:35)

72. In mid-spring of AD 28, Jesus and his disciples leave the Galilee and travel to Jerusalem to attend Passover. (John 5:1)

73. At Jerusalem's Pool of Bethesda, Jesus heals a man who had been diseased for 38 years. (John 5:2-47)

74. Early in the summer of AD 28, Jesus' disciples are reprimanded for picking corn on the Sabbath. Jesus responds with his "Lord of the Sabbath" teaching. (See Matthew 12:1-8, Mark 2:23-28, and Luke 6:1-5.)

75. Jesus heals a man with a withered hand. (See Matthew 12:9-14, Mark 3:1-6, and Luke 6:7-11.)

76. In mid-summer of AD 28, Jesus chooses 12 disciples to be apostles. He commissions them to minister to Jews in Judaea *only*. (See Matthew 10:1-15, Mark 3:14-19, and Luke 6:13-16). Sermon on the Plain given to the commissioned and ordained apostles. (Luke 6:12-49)

77. Jesus is accused of casting out demons by the authority of Beelzebub. (See Matthew 12:24-30 and 12:43-45, Mark 3:22-27, and Luke 11:16-20 and 11:24-26.)

78. On August 29 of AD 28, Jesus travels to the Roman military town of Nain. There, he raises a Roman soldier from the dead. (Luke 7:11-17)

79. In December of AD 28, Jesus attends the Feast of Dedication celebration in Capernaum, at the home of Simon the Pharisee. At the feast, a woman anoints Jesus' feet. (See Luke 7:36-50 and 11:45-53.)

AD 29

80. On January 3 of AD 29 (during his birthday celebration), Herod Antipas has John the Baptist beheaded. (See Matthew 14:1-2 and Mark 6:14-28.)

81. In the spring of AD 29, Jesus leads his disciples to a fish-drying area near Tiberias. There, he feeds the 5,000. (See Matthew 14:13-21, Mark 6: 33-44, Luke 9:10-17, and John 6:1-14.)

82. After feeding the 5,000, Jesus walks on water and enables Peter to do so as well. (See Matthew 14:24-33 and Mark 6:47-51.)

83. In early summer of AD 29, Joseph (Jesus' earthly father) dies. Jesus' mother and brothers visit him. (Matthew 12:46-50 and Mark 3:31-35)

84. Late in AD 29, Jesus instructs the 12 apostles to minister to people everywhere. (See Matthew 10:16-47 and Mark 6:1-13.)

85. In early November of AD 29, Jesus and the 12 travel to Caesarea Philippi. There, Peter confesses that Jesus is the Christ, the Son of the Living God. (See Matthew 16:13-25, Mark 8:27-28, and Luke 9:18-27.)

86. Peter pays a special Temple tax with a coin found in a fish's mouth. Who is greatest controversy. (Matthew 17:24-18:8))

87. In December of AD 29 (possibly January of AD 30), Jesus calms another storm at sea. (See Matthew 8:26-27, Mark 4:35-41, and Luke 8:23-25.)

AD 30

88. In the early spring of AD 30, Jesus is confronted by scribes and Pharisees accusing his disciples of not following the tradition of washing their hands. (See Matthew 15:1-20 and Mark 7:1-23.)

89. In April of AD 30, Jesus and his disciples travel to the Phoenician cities of Tyre and Sidon. There, he confronts a woman whose daughter is demon-possessed. (See Matthew 15:21-29 and Mark 7:24-31.)

90. In September of AD 30, at the Feast of Tabernacles in Jerusalem, Jesus makes his "rivers of living water" proclamation. (John 7:11-44)

91. In late September or early October of AD 30, Jesus heals a blind man by rubbing mud on his eyes and instructing him to wash in the Pool of Siloam. (John 9:1-37)

92. In late October of AD 30, Jesus and his disciples leave the Galilee and travel to Peraea and Judea Beyond Jordan. (Matthew 19:1-2; Mark 10:1)

93. Jesus heals a woman who has been stooped over for 18 years. (Luke 13:10-21)

94. In December of AD 30, Jesus and his disciples travel to Jerusalem, where they celebrate the Feast of Dedication at the home of the Chief Pharisee. Jesus delivers the parable of the wedding feast. (Luke 14:1-24)

AD 31

95. Near the beginning of the year, Jesus teaches lessons on the lost sheep, the prodigal son, and the unjust steward. (Luke 15:1-17)

96. In late January of AD 31, Jesus raises Lazarus from the dead. (John 11:1-46)

97. Jesus travels through Jericho and heals Bar-Timaeus. (Luke 18:35)

98. March 13 of AD 31 marks the first of Jesus' two triumphant entries into Jerusalem. (Matthew 21:1-11, Mark 11:1-10, and Luke 19:29-44.)

99. Jesus goes to the Temple and for the second of three times casts out the moneychangers. (Matthew 21:12-13; Luke 19:45-46)

100. Days later, Jesus goes to the Temple and, for the third time, casts out the moneychangers. (Mark 11:15-17)

101. On March 22 of AD 31 Mary anoints Jesus' feet. Judas complains about this act. (John 12:1-8)

102. March 23 marks the second of Jesus' two triumphant entries into Jerusalem. (John 12:12-19)

103. Jesus explains "the greatest commandment." (See Matthew 22:23-46, Mark 12:18-37, and Luke 20:27-44.)

104. On March 27 of AD 31, Jesus and his disciples dine at Simon the leper's house. Judas sneaks away to make a deal to betray Jesus. (Matthew 26:6-16 and Mark 14:3-11) Jesus experiences his third anointing.

105. On March 28 of AD 31, Jesus prays in the garden and is later arrested. (See Matthew 26:36-56, Mark 14:32-52, Luke 22:39-54, and John 18:1-12.)

106. The period from March 29 to April 3 of AD 31, brings the trial and flogging of Jesus. (See Mark 14:53 to 15:25, Luke 22:54 to 23:31, and John 18:13 to 19:18.)

107. On April 2 of AD 31, Jesus is crucified. (See Matthew 27:38-56, Mark 15:25-47, Luke 23:32-49, and John 19:16-30.)

108. Later on April 2, Jesus is buried. (See Matthew 27:57-66, Mark 15:42-47, Luke 23:50-56, and John 19:31-42.)

109. Jesus' Resurrection and post-resurrection. (Matthew 28, Mark 16, Luke 24, and John 20-21.)

110. Ascension (Acts 1:4-11), the Day of Pentecost (Acts 2), and the spread of Christianity.

APPENDIX B

※ ❧ ※

Identifications and Definitions

ABODAH ZARAH—One of the tractates of the fourth division of the Jewish Mishnah and Talmud.

ABOTH or PIRKE ABOTH—A collection of ethical maxims. One of the tractates of the fourth division of the Jewish Mishnah.

ACELDAMA—The name of the Potter's Field purchased by the "blood money" returned to the priests by Judas.

ACTS OF THE APOSTLES—A New Testament book, traditionally believed to have been written by Luke. Its focus is the founding of the Christian church and the ministry of the Apostle Paul.

AGRICOLA—Roman governor of Roman Britain who died in AD 93. He was the father-in-law of the Latin historian Tacitus. He entered into Rome's official records the establishment of Glastonbury and the establishment of the first Christian church in Britain (by Joseph of Arimathea).

ALLELUIA—From the Hebrew *hallelujah* meaning, "Praise the Lord."

ANDREW—A fisherman from Bethsaida. He introduced his brother, Simon Peter, to Jesus. Andrew was originally a disciple of John the Baptist, but later became an apostle of Jesus.

ANNA—An aged prophetess, who was widowed for 84 years after only 7 years of marriage. When Jesus was presented at the Temple, she spread the word throughout Jerusalem that she had seen the Messiah.

ANNAS—The former Jewish High Priest to whom Jesus was brought for questioning, before the Crucifixion.

APOCALYPSE—From the Greek word meaning *revelation*. It is a prophetic description of the end of the world.

APOCRYPHA (of the New Testament)—From the Greek word meaning *hidden away*. Early Christian and quasi-Christian works that resemble New Testament writings, but are not recognized as New Testament Canon.

APOSTLES—The 12 men Jesus selected from the ranks of his many disciples to be his chief disciples and whom he anointed and sent out to minister on his behalf.

APPEARANCES OF THE RISEN JESUS—This includes all of Jesus' appearances after he was resurrected. He appeared to the women at the tomb, to two in the country, two on the road to Emmaus, to the 11 disciples on many occasions, to 500 on two occasions, and to James, his brother.

ARAMAIC—A Semitic language. In Jesus' time, Aramaic was the common speech of Judea's Jewish residents.

ARISTOTLE—Greek philosopher (384-322 BC) and tutor to Alexander the Great.

ASCENSION—The doctrine that after Jesus' resurrection from the dead, he was taken up into heaven *bodily*.

ASSUMPTION OF THE VIRGIN MARY—The dogma stating that at the end of Mary's life, she was taken up to heaven *bodily*. This became a doctrine of the Catholic Church in 1950, by papal mandate of Pope Pius XII.

ATONEMENT—The doctrine that Jesus died to atone for the sins of all humankind.

AUGUSTUS—Augustus Gaius Octavius (36 BC-AD 14). He was emperor of the Roman Empire when Jesus was born. He has been acknowledged by many historians as the best and wisest of all Roman Emperors.

BARA MEZIA—One of the tractates of the fourth division of the Jewish Mishnah and Talmud.

BARABBAS—A Jewish revolutionary who was in prison while Jesus was tried and convicted. The people chose to release Barabbas instead of Jesus.

BARTHOLOMEW—One of the 12 whom Jesus chose out of the ranks of his disciples to be an apostle. He was likely a Nathanael. (See also NATHANAEL.)

BAR-TIMAEUS—The son of Timaeus. He was healed of blindness during the last year of Jesus' ministry.

BATH-SHEBA—Uriah's wife, with whom King David committed adultery. After Uriah's death, she became David's wife and birthed Solomon.

BEATITUDES—The nine blessings of Jesus, recorded in Matthew's Gospel and presented in the Sermon on the Mount.

BEEL-ZEBUB—"The Lord of the flies." The god of the Philistine city of Ekron. The Pharisees wrongly claimed that Beel-zebub was the "prince of devils."

BERAKOTH—The first tractate of the first division of the Jewish Mishnah and Talmud.

BETHANY—A village located on the east side of the Mount of Olives. It was a Greco-Roman village inhabited by Jews of Egyptian lineage. Bethany was the home of Lazarus, Mary, and Martha.

BETHESDA—A twin pool in Jerusalem near the sheep market. Here, Jesus healed a crippled man on the Sabbath.

BETHLEHEM—A small town about five miles south of Jerusalem. David was probably born in Bethlehem, as was Joseph, Jesus' earthly father. It was also the birthplace of Jesus.

BETHSAIDA—A fishing village located near the north shore of the Lake of Gennesaret (Sea of Galilee). It was the probable the home of Peter, Andrew, and Philip.

CAESAR—A title of the Emperors of Rome, derived from Gaius Julius Caesar, who died in 44 BC.

CAIAPHAS—Joseph Caiaphas was Jewish High Priest from AD 18 to 37. Caiaphas resided over the Sanhedrin when Jesus was brought to trial. After Jesus' resurrection, Caiaphas continued to persecute the church until he was relieved of his position in AD 37, by order of Tiberius.

CALVARY—Called the place of death, the place of bones, and the place of the skull. In Hebrew the term is Golgotha. Calvary identified the part of Gehenna where offenders whose crime was against Rome were put to death. (See also, GEHENNA.)

CALVINIST—A person who accepts the theological viewpoints and dogmas of John Calvin (1509-1564). The focal point of Calvin's teaching is predestination. Some are predestined to everlasting life, Calvin taught, while others are predestined for damnation.

CANA—A village in the Galilee, northeast of Nazareth. At a wedding celebration held here, Jesus turned water into wine. This was his first recorded miracle.

CANAAN—Originally the designation for Phoenicia but subsequently used to describe all the area of what became called Palestine.

CHARLEMAGNE—King of the Franks (742-814). He was the first Emperor of the Holy Roman Empire. He is acknowledged to be the first of the royal saints.

CIRCUMCISION OF JESUS—Following the Law of Moses, Jesus was circumcised at the end of the eighth day after his birth (Luke 2:21).

COCK—A male peacock. Called the fowl of conscience. It crowed twice while Peter was denying Jesus.

CONSTANTINE the GREAT—Roman Emperor who died in 337. He issued the *Edict of Milan*, which provided religious tolerance of Christianity. He rebuilt the city of Byzantium and renamed it Constantinople. He and his mother, Helena, did much to further the acceptance and spread of Christianity. He was baptized a Christian shortly before his death.

COUNCIL OF TRENT—The general council of the Roman Catholic Church, held at Trent (1545-1563). At this council, many doctrines of the Catholic Church were established. Among these was the insistence on the Seven Sacraments.

DANIEL—A sixth century BC Jew who was a Chaldean magus. He rose to prominence in the courts of Babylon and Persia. He was *the* most respected magus of the ancient world. After his death, he was deified by many ancient societies. He prophesied the coming of the Messianic world leader. His prophecy persuaded the magi to venture to Judea in search of the King of the Jews. An Old Testament book (written circa 166 BC) portrays some of his experiences and prophecies.

DAVID—Second king of the united nation of Israel (1085-1015 BC). He ruled for 40 years. He was an ancestor of Jesus. He is considered the greatest of Israel's kings.

DECAPOLIS—A league of 10 Greek cities in Syria. Although far removed from the region, Damascus served as Decapolis's capital. A major portion of the Decapolis was under Roman military control.

DEMON—An evil spirit designation. Many theologians believe evil spirits are either the disembodied human souls of those who joined Lucifer's original rebellion, those who died during Noah's flood, or fallen angels who joined Lucifer's rebellion.

DEUTERONOMY—The fifth (and final) book of the Old Testament Pentateuch. Jesus quoted from Deuteronomy to combat the tempter during his wilderness experience.

DEVIL—A level of the evil spirit world. They serve as observers, and they direct demonic activities. (Also, see DEMON, above.)

DIASPORA—Jewish communities living outside of the area that became known as Palestine.

DIONYSIUS EXIGUUS—A sixth century Scythian monk who miscalculated the date of Jesus' birth.

'H—A Tishbite of Gilead, a ninth century BC Hebrew prophet who ͡ot die of natural causes. He was taken to heaven before dying.

͡ successor to Elijah's prophetic ministry. He is considered reat Hebrew prophets.

ͻ   ulers of the Roman Empire. Augustus was the first ͡er whose rule Jesus was born. The second Emperor was opted son, Tiberius. Under Tiberius's reign, Jesus was

ERUBIN—One of the tractates of the second division of the Jewish Mishnah and Talmud.

EUSEBIUS—(AD 260-340). He was Bishop of Caesarea Maritima. He wrote a *History of the Church*.

EXORCISM—An injunction addressed to evil spirits to force them to abandon a possessed person.

EZRA—A Babylonian Jew who (circa the fourth century BC) led a group of Jews back to Jerusalem. There, they re-established the Jewish religion. He is featured in an Old Testament book that bears his name.

FRANCIS OF ASSISI—Founder of the Order of Friars Minor. He was born in Assisi in 1181. He ministered to the poor and to lepers.

FRANKINCENSE—A sweet-smelling resin of the balsam tree. It was one of the gifts given to the child Jesus by the magi.

GABRIEL—An archangel who carries out special assignments for God. He announced the births of John the Baptist (to Zacharias) and Jesus (to Mary). He is also revered in Islam because he is said to have dictated the Koran to Mohammed.

GALILEE—The northern region of Syria. Galilee lies north of Judaea and east of the Sea of Galilee and the Jordan River. Jesus and all but one of his apostles (Judas) were from the Galilee.

GEHENNA—A valley south of Jerusalem's walls. In Jesus' time, it served as the city garbage dump. Gehenna was used by Jesus as a representation of hell.

GETHSEMENE—A garden on the eastern slopes of the Mount of Olives, and site of an olive press. Here Jesus prayed before he was arrested.

GENTILES—From the Latin *gentes*, meaning races or nationalities. The Hebrew term is *goyim*. Non-Jews were classified by Jews as Gentiles.

GLASTONBURY—Called Avalon during the Middle Ages. On this plot of land, Joseph of Arimathea built the first Christian church in Britain.

GNOSTIC—A doctrine that taught that salvation is obtained through "knowledge" of the secrets of the universe. Gnostics authored many of the apocryphal writings.

GOSPEL—The "good news" of Jesus' life, ministry, and redemptive work. A Gospel is also a record of his work as written by the authors of the first four books of the New Testament, called The Gospels.

GREGORY THE GREAT—He was pope from 590 to 604. He, more than any other pope, was responsible for the spread, through force of arms, of the "Mary, mother of God" dogma. Because he insisted that one must accept Mary as the mother of God *before* accepting Jesus as the Son of God, Mary came to be viewed as a pagan goddess by Arabs. Gregory is considered one of the most influential popes in Catholic Church history.

HASMONAEANS or HASMONEANS (MACCABEES)—The name of the Jewish family who descended from Haesmon. They led a successful Jewish revolt against the Seleucids in the second century BC and established a dynasty that lasted until the rule of Herod the Great.

HERMIT—One who chose to live alone in a hermitage, devoting himself to prayer, fasting, meditation, and spiritual consciousness.

HEROD—The family name of many rulers in the region that became known as Palestine. Herod the Great was king when Jesus was born. Herod Antipas was Tetrarch of the Galilee when Jesus was crucified.

HERODIANS—Members and political supporters of the House of Herod. Their ultimate loyalty was to Caesar. They were selected to represent Tiberius's Theophus Commission in Syria. Some Herodians respected Jesus. Others were hostile to him.

HERODIAS—The daughter of Herod Aristobulus. She was married to Herod Philip and then to Herod Antipas. She instructed her daughter, Salome, to demand from Antipas the head of John the Baptist as a reward for dancing for him.

HERODOTUS—A fifth century BC Greek historian. Herodotus is called "The father of history."

HOLY GHOST (SPIRIT)—God the Holy Ghost (Spirit); the third person of the Trinity, along with God the Father and God the Son—coequal and coeternal but distinct. Also called the Holy Paraclete or Comforter.

HOSANNA—From the Hebrew *hoshi'a na*, meaning, save us or save me, please. It is a lament and plea to the Messiah.

IGNATIUS OF ANTIOCH—Second or third bishop of Antioch, said to be a disciple of John the Evangelist, Peter, or Paul. He was martyred in the Coliseum of Rome in 107.

INQUISITION—An ecclesiastical tribunal set up in 1229 by Pope Gregory IX. Its purpose was to investigate cases of heresy and to prevent its spread. In 1252, Pope Innocent IV sanctioned torture to procure evidence. The notorious Spanish Inquisition began in 1479. It lasted until 1808, when Joseph Bonaparte suppressed it. It was briefly revived under Ferdinand VII from 1808-1814.

INRI—The initial letters of *Ieusus Nazarenus Rex Judaeorum, Jesus of Nazareth, King of the Jews*. This Latin phrase, together with a translation in Hebrew and Greek, was inscribed by Pilate on a titulus and secured on the cross of Christ (John 19:19).

IRENAEUS—Lived circa 130 to 200. He was the Bishop of Lugdunum (modern Lyon, France). He was the first to accept Matthew, Mark, and Luke as the only true Gospels. He rejected all other records of Jesus' life. In 380, John Chrysostom claimed Irenaeus's spirit appeared to him in a dream, saying that John's Gospel should be added as a true Gospel and that each Gospel was authored by its namesake. Thus, it became accepted as fact that Matthew the tax collector wrote the Gospel of Matthew, John Mark (a companion of Paul) wrote the Gospel of Mark, the physician Luke wrote the Gospel of Luke, and John the evangelist (a disciple of Jesus,) wrote the Gospel of John. The 1215 Council of Bishops held in Toledo, Spain, confirmed and upheld John Chrysostom's declaration as truth.

ISAIAH—One of the greatest of the Hebrew Old Testament prophets. He lived in Judah in the latter part of the eighth century BC. He prophesied of the virgin birth of Jesus.

ISHMAEL—The son of Abraham and Hagar. His wife was an Egyptian. He is the ancestor of the Arabic tribes.

JACOB'S LADDER—Jacob, the son of Isaac, had a dream at a place called Luz. In the dream, he saw a ladder (or stairway) reaching from heaven to earth. He saw angels ascending and descending the ladder. Jacob named the place Bethel. In Jesus' day, it was taught that if a Nathanael (one studying to be a priest), slept under a fig tree in Bethel and dreamed of Jacob's ladder, that Nathanael would become the High Priest who would identify and introduce the Messiah to the Jews.

JAMES THE APOSTLE—A disciple of Jesus who was selected by Jesus to be an apostle. He was the brother of John. They were Jesus' cousins. James was killed in 44 AD, by order of Herod Agrippa I.

JAMES, THE BROTHER OF THE LORD—He has been called James the less, James the younger, and James the twin. A brother of Jesus, James might have followed his brother during his ministry. (This cannot be confirmed.) However, after Jesus' death and resurrection, James became the leader of the Christian sect. He was considered, until the Council of Bishops, to be the greatest of the early church leaders. He was martyred in 62 AD. He is the undisputed author of the Epistle of James. Some theologians claim that he also authored the Gospel of Mark, the Epistle to the Hebrews, and the last three-quarters of The Revelation.

JEREMIAH—Old Testament Jewish prophet (650-585 BC). He warned Judah about its destruction at the hands of Nebuchadnezzar. He was spared by the Babylonian king and was allowed to stay in Jerusalem. He was later forced to flee to Egypt, where he died. Jeremiah's tomb is located in the Coptic region of the city of Cairo.

JERICHO—An ancient Canaanite city. It is one of the world's oldest cities. In Roman times it was a very wealthy city.

JERUSALEM—The ancient and holy city sacred to three religions: Judaism, Christianity, and Islam. Its original name was Salem. David conquered this city and made it his capital. It has been destroyed and rebuilt many times. Jesus was crucified outside Jerusalem's city walls, in Gehenna. Mohammed is said to have been taken to heaven from Jerusalem.

JOHN THE APOSTLE—A disciple of Jesus, chosen to be one of his 12 apostles. Jesus called John and his brother, James "the sons of thunder." John and James were also Jesus' cousins. At the 1215 Council of Bishops, it was declared that John had lived to be almost 100 years old and that he was exiled to a Roman penal colony on the island of Patmos. There, he wrote the Gospel of John, the Epistles of John, and the Revelation, before dying of natural causes.

JOHN CHRYSOSTOM—Born at Antioch in 347, he became one of the Four Greek Doctors of the Church. He became Bishop of Constantinople in 397. Throughout his life, his passion was ministering to the poor. He is, perhaps, the most influential bishop of Christianity's first 500 years.

JOHN THE BAPTIST—He was the last of the Old Testament-style prophets, and the forerunner of Christ. He baptized Jesus and proclaimed him to be the Lamb of God. He was imprisoned by order of Herod Antipas and later beheaded.

JOSEPH THE CARPENTER—Joseph was a descendant of the House of David. He was the husband of Mary, Jesus' mother. Early church tradition says that he was a master stonemason. (Later church tradition holds that he specialized in wood carpentry.) Early church tradition says that he died during Jesus' ministry, while later tradition contends that he died when Jesus was a child.

JOSEPH OF ARIMATHEA—A respected (and Rome-appointed) member of the Jewish Sanhedrin. He was also Provincial Senator representing Britain and the Imperial Minister of Mines. He was the younger brother of Mary's father (Mary, the mother of Jesus). Tradition says that he adopted Mary and her unborn child after the death of Mary's father and before her marriage to Joseph. Tradition says that he built the first Christian church in Britain.

JOSEPHUS—A Jewish historian (AD 37-95). He fought in the first Jewish revolt and was captured by the Romans. He was released and then commissioned by the Romans to write a history of the Jewish people. He authored the *Jewish War, Jewish Antiquities, Against Apion,* and *Life.*

JUDAEA—The Latin name for the central part of what became known as Palestine, annexed by the Romans as a province. By the third century, this area had become known as Syria Palaestina. The Roman province of Judaea was formed in AD 6. (See below.)

JUDEA (ROMAN STATE)—Under Roman occupation, the province of Judaea was divided into states. The state that included Jerusalem and its environs was called Judea. Most of the Jewish residents of Judaea lived in the state of Judea.

JUDAEO-CHRISTIAN—Christians of Jewish origin. After the death and resurrection of Jesus, James (Jesus' brother) led these people.

JUDAS ISCARIOT—An archetypal traitor. He betrayed Jesus for money and identified him with a kiss. He was the only one of Jesus' apostles who was not from the Galilee. Tradition says that he was a member of the Zealot revolutionaries. After betraying Jesus, Judas hanged himself.

JULIAN THE APOSTATE—Roman Emperor from AD 361-363. Under his rule, the empire, which had converted to Christianity under Constantine the Great, reverted (temporarily) to paganism.

JUSTIN MARTYR—One of the greatest of the early Christian apologists.

LAMB OF GOD—John the Baptist identified Jesus as the *Lamb of God*, traditionally because he was the first to recognize Jesus as the suffering servant.

LAST SUPPER—The final meal Jesus shared with his disciples before his crucifixion. During this meal, Jesus instituted the Lord's Supper (or Eucharist).

LAW (THE TORAH)—In the Jewish religion, the Torah signifies the Pentateuch. The term can also denote the entire Hebrew Scriptures, including oral interpretations.

LAZARUS—A beggar who is the central focus of one of Jesus' parables. This parable is commonly called *The Rich Man and Lazarus*.

LAZARUS OF BETHANY—One of Jesus' best friends. He was the brother of Mary and Martha. Jesus raised him from the dead.

LIVY—(59 BC-AD 17). A Latin historian who wrote a 142-volume history of Rome. Only 35 of these books survived.

MAGI—The plural of the Latin *magus*, meaning magician. Magi were ambassadors of eastern empires who came to Judaea in search of the new-born King of the Jews. When they found Jesus, they gave him gifts of gold, frankincense and myrrh.

MARY—The virgin mother of Jesus. She and her unborn son, Jesus, were adopted by her uncle, Joseph of Arimathea, before Jesus was born. Her husband was Joseph the carpenter. It is not known whether she believed Jesus was the Messiah, although the Scriptures imply that she supported his ministry and believed that he was able to perform miracles. She was present at the cross when Jesus was crucified, and she was in the upper room on the day of Pentecost.

MARY MAGDALENE—A woman from Magdala, whom Jesus exorcized of seven demons. She supported Jesus' ministry financially and followed him throughout the Galilee and Judea. She was at the cross when Jesus was crucified and was the first person to whom Jesus revealed himself after his resurrection.

MESSIAH—The anointed king and leader. The Jews were expecting a descendant of king David to be a king greater than David. A social and political leader, a deliverer, bringing in a new dispensation. The Christ. Jesus was recognized by the Prophetess Anna as Messiah at his Redemption Ceremony. One of two anointed personalities the Jews were expecting at the time of Jesus' birth. (See below.)

MESSIAS—The anointed prophet of sacrifice. The Jews were expecting a religious leader and reformer, like Moses but greater. He was to be the sacrifice for sin. Savior. Redeemer. The Son of God. One of two anointed personalities the Jews were expecting when Jesus was born. They were not expecting Jesus to be both Messiah and Messias. They were expecting two people: a Messiah and a Messias. Simeon recognized Jesus as Messias at his Redemption Ceremony.

MIDRASH—A term applied to methods of biblical exposition and to Jewish writings using these methods.

MISHNAH—A collection of Jewish precepts that forms one of the two main parts of the Talmud.

MOSES—Perhaps the greatest figure of the Old Testament. He received the Law from God and then presented it to the Jews. He led the Israelites out of Egyptian slavery and to the borders of the Promised Land.

MOTHER OF GOD—A designation and title given to Mary, the mother of Jesus, by papal proclamation.

NABATAEANS—People of Arabic descent who occupied the region east of the Jordan River.

NATHANAEL—One studying to become a Jewish priest. The most prominent Nathanael in Scripture was the one introduced to Jesus by Philip. This Nathanael could have been the disciple Bartholomew.

NEBUCHADNEZZAR—King of Babylon (605-562 BC). He destroyed Jerusalem and carried off most of its people to Babylon. Daniel, one of these displaced Jews, became the most prominent magi in Nebuchadnezzar's court.

NERO—The Roman Emperor (AD 54-68) responsible for the first of many persecutions of Christians.

NICODEMUS—A Pharisee and member of the Sanhedrin. He came to Jesus at night to question him. Jesus told him that he must be born again. He defended Jesus before the Sanhedrin after Jesus' arrest.

NIDDAH—One of the tractates of the sixth division of the Jewish Mishnah and Babylonian Talmud.

ORIGEN—(AD 185-254). He was one of the most outspoken defenders of Christianity to the Greeks, especially in Alexandria.

PACHOMIUS—(AD 292-346) A disciple of Antony of Egypt, he founded the Nile community of monks at Tabennisi.

PASSOVER—A Jewish feast celebrating the most momentous event in Jewish history: the Exodus. Passover commemorates the night when Jewish homes in Egypt were spared by the death angel.

PAUL THE APOSTLE—A Pharisee from Tarsus and an enemy of the Christian sect. Paul was later converted to Christianity. He became a tireless missionary, and his writings are integral to current Christian doctrine.

PETER—A fisherman from the Galilee who was in business with James and John and their father, Zebedee. He became a disciple of Jesus after the miracle of the multitude of fish. He was the first to recognize Jesus as *"The Christ, the Son of the Living God."* He once denied Jesus, but later repented and became one of the pillars of the early church.

PHARISEE—A Jewish religious sect that originated in the second century BC. The Pharisees were largely responsible for establishing synagogues. They also helped introduce oral interpretations of the Law, the Talmud. Jesus' rabboni training was likely completed with the Pharisees.

PHILIP THE APOSTLE—A Greek fisherman from the Galilee. He was the first disciple to be called by Jesus.

PHILO—(30 BC-AD 40). The outstanding Jewish philosopher/historian of the Dispersion. He was largely responsible for insisting that the Jewish religion be more Hellenized.

PONTIUS PILATE—He was the extremely ruthless Roman procurator of Judaea during the time of Jesus' ministry. (He was appointed in AD 26.) He condemned Jesus to be crucified, even though his wife, Claudia Procula, (a granddaughter of Emperor Augustus), warned him not to have anything to do with Jesus.

POLYCARP—A Bishop of Smyrna who was martyred in AD 155. He was said to have been converted by the Apostle John. He became one of John's disciples.

PRESTER JOHN (JOHN PRESBYTER)—A legendary priest and king said to rule over a fabulously wealthy Christian kingdom somewhere in the east. Tales of his existence began to circulate about the third century and continued up until the seventeenth century. It is not known if these tales are true.

Q (standing for the German word, *Quelle*, meaning source)—The designation given to a possible common source for the Gospels of Matthew and Luke—a source not shared with the Gospel of Mark.

QUMRAN—A community of semi-monastic Jewish hermits residing in the area of the Dead Sea. These hermits are thought to be the authors of the Dead Sea Scrolls. They existed from circa 140 BC until the beginning of the first Jewish revolt against Rome in AD 66.

RABBI, RABBONI, RABBAN—Level designations of Jewish teachers, based on years of educational experience and training. These three designations were established circa AD 2 and continued until just after the first Jewish rebellion in AD 70.

REBELLION (The Jewish revolt against Rome) The first rebellion started in AD 66, under Nero, and ended in AD 70, under Vespasian, with the destruction of the Temple and the fall of Masada in AD 73. The second rebellion took place in AD 132-135, under Hadrian. Hadrian suppressed the rebellion and destroyed Jerusalem.

SADDUCEES—A conservative Jewish religious sect who were pro-Roman. By the time of Jesus' ministry, the Roman authorities looked upon them as a religious cult, whose political loyalties lay with Rome, but whose emotional loyalties lay with the physical Jewish Temple. They did not accept the Talmud as authoritative. They also did not believe in a resurrection, demons, or angels. Most of the Jewish Sanhedrin was made up of Sadducees. Most chief priests and High Priests were also Sadducees. They were extremely powerful because of their working relationship with Roman authorities. They ceased to exist after the AD 70 destruction of the Temple.

SALOME—The daughter of Herodias, the wife of Herod Antipas. Her dance at Herod's birthday so pleased him that he offered her up to half of his kingdom as a reward. At her mother's prompting, Salome demanded the head of John the Baptist. Herod reluctantly honored her demand.

SANHEDRIN—from the Greek *synedrion,* meaning council. It was the highest Jewish court at the time of Jesus' life. It existed until the AD 70 destruction of the Temple. Most Sanhedrin members were pro-Roman Sadducees; although there was also representation by the Pharisees and at least one Roman-appointed representative. During Jesus' life, Joseph of Arimathea was this Roman-appointed representative. The Sanhedrin's authority was recognized by Rome in the state of Judea only, and their actions were limited to Judea.

SCRIBES—Doctors of the Law (lawyers). Scribes were Jewish experts on the Law. Although most scribes were Pharisees, some were Sadducees.

SELEUCIDS—A dynasty of Greek monarchs founded by Seleucus, one of Alexander the Great's generals. Their empire included the region that became called Palestine.

SEPTUAGINT—The earliest Greek translation of the Old Testament, created during the third and second centuries BC. The "Holy Scriptures" of Jesus' day.

SHABBAT—One of the tractates of the second division of the Jewish Mishnah and Talmud.

SIMON OF CYRENE—A man from Cyrene who was in Jerusalem during the Passover that preceded the Crucifixion. When Jesus could no longer carry his cross member, Simon was forced to carry it to the place of crucifixion.

SIMON THE LEPER—At a dinner at Simon the leper's house (in Bethany), Jesus was anointed—during the week preceding his crucifixion.

SOTAH—One of the tractates of the third division of the Jewish Mishnah and Talmud.

SUETONIUS OF HIPPO REGIUS—(AD 69-132) The Latin biographer of the *Twelve Caesars.*

SYNAGOGUE—A meeting place for the Jewish community to pray, read the scriptures, and worship. After the destruction of the Temple in AD 70, the synagogue became the central site of Jewish worship.

TACITUS—(AD 55-117?) Cornelius Tacitus the multi-volume historian, was the son of Cornelius Tacitus the Elder, a Senatorial Latin historian (4 BC-AD 55) whose writings reference Jesus' life and ministry. The writing of Tacitus the Elder were often repeated by his son.

TALMUD—The written (and oral) interpretations of Jewish law and ethics. Revered by Jews as sacred.

THEOPHUS, THE—A world leader dreamed about by Emperor Tiberius. At the time of his death, Jesus was being investigated by Tiberius's Theophus Commission, as a possible "Theophus."

THOMAS (GOSPEL OF)—An apocryphal Gospel found in 1945 near Nag Hammadi in Egypt. Its authorship is attributed to Thomas, the apostle of Jesus.

VALLEUS PATERCULUS was a prominent Roman citizen, close friend of Augustus Caesar and well-respected Roman historian. Tiberius made him chief ambassador of the 130-strong "Theophus Commission of Ambassadors" with unprecedented power and vast financial resources to locate the Theophus.

VIRGINITY (PERPETUAL) OF MARY—A doctrine originally proposed by John Chrysostom and later adopted by the Catholic Church. The doctrine states that Mary was, is, and always will be a virgin. This teaching claims that Mary remained a virgin her entire life.

VULGATE—The Latin version of the Bible. It was mainly the work of Jerome, at the request of Pope Damasus I (366-384).

ZACCHAEUS—A rich tax assessor who lived in Jericho. After his confrontation with Jesus, he gave of his wealth to the poor.

ZACHARIAS—The father of John the Baptist (and Elizabeth's husband). He was a priest from the line of Aaron.

ZADOK—High Priest of the Jews in the time of King David (tenth century BC).

ZION—The eastern-most of two hills of ancient Jerusalem. The term is often used poetically, referring to earthly Jerusalem and the new, heavenly Jerusalem.

Dr. Ron Charles with close friend + colleague Dr. Al Pleysier at the Great Sphinx.

DR. RON CHARLES worked as a structural engineer for 12 years and served as a senior pastor for 14 years.

He is passionate about history and archaeology, particularly New Testament and Roman-era history. He fed this passion by earning an M.A. in Theology, a Ph.D. in Ancient History and a Th.D. in Historical Theology.

Dr. Charles's quest for the historical Jesus has spanned over 43 years, with travels to more than 50 countries. He has taken part in archaeological investigations in five countries in search of information about the life of Jesus.

Dr. Charles is co-founder of the Albania-American Archaeological Society, and he has served on the board of directors for Pacific International University and Final Frontiers International. Until recently he also served on the Board of Governors for The International Biographical Centre of Cambridge. Cambridge has awarded him its One Thousand Great Americans designation.

Today, Dr. Charles serves as a missionary to the people of the Middle East. He also conducts historical/education tours to Europe and the Middle East. For more information on these tours and for information about the author, visit the website www.cubitfoundation.org.

Dr. Ron Charles may be contacted as follows:
CUBIT Foundation
PO Box 1316 :: Monroe, Georgia 30655 :: USA

email: rpalban@cubitfoundation.org
www.cubitfoundation.org